FOSSILS
OF THE WORLD

FOSSILS
OF THE WORLD

A comprehensive, practical guide to collecting and studying fossils.

V. TUREK, J. MAREK, J. BENES

EDITED BY JULIAN BROWN

Arch Cape Press
New York

The material in the illustrations comes from the palaeontology collections of the National Museum in Prague and of the Faculty of Science, Charles University, Prague.

The general chapters and the descriptions of Bryozoa, Brachiopoda, Cephalopoda, Arthropoda, Echinodermata, Hemichordata and Plantae are written by V. Turek, the text on other invertebrates by J. Marek and the descriptions of Vertebrata by J. Beneš.

Translated by Margot Schierlová
Photographs by Marek Kořínek, Monika Kořínková
and Karel Drábek
Line drawings by Miloš Váňa
Graphic design by M. Kořínek

First published by The Hamlyn Publishing Group Limited,
a Division of the Octopus Publishing Group,
Michelin House, 81 Fulham Road,
London SW3 6RB, England

This 1990 edition published by Arch Cape Press,
a division of dilithium Press, Ltd.
Distributed by Crown Publishers, Inc.,
225 Park Avenue South,
New York, New York 10003

Printed and bound in Czechoslovakia
3/19/02/51-03

ISBN 0-517-67904-3

hgfedcb

Contents

A word in introduction

Our Earth is over 4,700 million years old, but its geological history goes back 'only' 3,800 million years, to the time when its continental crust was consolidated. After that, it was not long before the first, simplest organisms appeared, to be followed, during further evolution, by their differentiation and by improvement of their anatomical organization. Evolutionarily unsuccessful groups died out and other, more successful groups took their place. The whole of their history is to be found, written more or less completely, in the Earth's rocks. The science which tries to give the fullest possible picture of life in the geological past is palaeontology and the main source of its information are the petrified remains of organisms and traces of their activities, known to us under the general term 'fossils'. People do not give palaeontology the attention it deserves. Its very name, which comes from Greek and means, literally, the 'science of the ancient', has something exotic, obscure — and hence unprofitable — about it. The biological basis of palaeontology has in recent years been underlined by adoption of the term 'palaeobiology' (divided into palaeozoology and palaeobotany). Palaeontology is the main source of knowledge of the historical development of animate nature and of the entire geological development of the Earth. The study of fossils is essential for determining the relative age of rocks and hence for geological mapping, which is the first prerequisite of systematic geological research, investigating possible deposits of important minerals, etc.

Care should be taken that the considerable interest of amateur fossil collectors is not confined to the mere collection, sorting or financial evaluation of their collections. The aim of this book is not only to bring home to all those interested in palaeontology the diversity and beauty of fossils, but to help them to place their finds in the group, genus or even species of organisms to which they belong and to emphasize their animate origin. Fossils were once creatures living in a close relationship to an environment and they can furnish unique information about that environment.

Apart from a very short historical survey, the general chapters of this book touch on palaeontological problems and explain basic concepts. The systematic survey contains only the palaeontologically most important groups (down to class level). In the case of phyla and subphyla, a concise biological characterization is given. In the illustrations, a survey of the most abundantly represented groups is supplemented by pictures acquainting the reader with the most essential morphological types and with the anatomy of the representatives of those groups. Owing to the extent and subject matter of the book, the identification key is confined to multicellular invertebrate animals and it is arranged so as to allow the classification of commonly found fossils in the proper phyla or classes. The illustrations cover over 800 species of the commonest — but also the most interesting — fossil animals and plants, traces of their activities and pathological manifestations, etc. Genera and species were chosen with special reference to central and western Europe, although the actual geographical range of most of the genera represented is far wider. The fossils are classified up to class or subclass level according to the biological system; within these groups they are further classified according to the age of the strata (from older to more recent) in which they occur.

This guide is not a palaeontology textbook. Basic data of systematic importance are often missing in the characterizations of the various groups, but that is usually either because they cannot be evaluated by an ordinary collector, or because their evaluation requires specially and expertly prepared material (orientated polished sections, etc). With the exception of large Foraminifera and Ostracoda, microfossils are not included in the illustrations; they must be collected and photographed by special methods and amateur collectors are generally not interested in them.

The book might possibly never have seen the light of day without the numerous experts who helped to look up and identify some of the material or contributed valuable comments on parts of the manuscript, in particular Dr. I. Chlupáč and Dr. M. Šnajdr (Arthropoda), Dr. O. Nekvasilová and Dr. V. Havlíček (Brachiopoda), Professor V. Pokorný (Foraminifera, Ostracoda), Dr. R. Prokop and Dr. J. Žítt (Echinodermata) and Dr. V. Zázvorka (Coleoidea). The authors are indebted to Dr. F. Holý for the choice and identification of the palaeobotanical material and for reading through the relevant parts of the manuscript. They likewise wish to thank Mr. A. Skalický for technical assistance. Special thanks are due to Dr. I. Chlupáč and Dr. R. Prokop for their untiring interest and willing help with the parts concerning invertebrates and with the general chapters.

A historical survey

Palaeontology is a relatively young branch of science which, as such, did not come into being until the end of the eighteenth century. Interest in fossils, for various reasons, has been known since prehistoric times, however. Fossils have been found more than once in prehistoric graves, where they were placed as ornaments or because of their 'magic' powers. The earliest written remarks on fossils were made by ancient philosophers. Some, like Xenophanon of Colophon (about 565–470 B.C.), interpreted them correctly, while others (e.g. Empedocles of Agrigentum, about 490–430 B.C.) actually pointed out that they were the remains of animals different from those that then inhabited the Earth. The greatest of these old philosophers, Aristotle (384–322 B.C.), regarded fossils as structures formed by some power acting inside the rocks. However incomprehensible this may appear to us today, it was the generally accepted view in the Middle Ages. Albertus Magnus, a famous thirteenth century scholar whose real name was Albert von Bolstaed, expressed the conviction that some fossils were the remains of genuine plants and animals, while the talented Leonardo da Vinci (1452–1519), who came across fossils during his engineering work, unequivocally described them in his diary as being of organic origin. He likewise mentioned that the sea must have swept over the dry land several times and that, when it receded, the ooze which had previously filled different kinds of shells solidified. Georgius Agricola, a Saxon physician whose true name was Georg Bauer (1494–1555), was extremely interested in geology and mining; he considered fossils to be forms of minerals, but correctly regarded fossil 'fishes, bones and wood' as the remains of animals and plants. Nevertheless, the view that fossils were a *lusus naturae* formed by the action of supernatural forces persisted until almost half way through the eighteenth century. In his *Histoire naturelle*, Georges-Louis Buffon (1707–88) meditated over the Earth's past history; he considered unequivocally that fossils had once been living organisms and noticed that they were different from present forms. The accumulation of a tremendous amount of natural history material made it urgently necessary to find a suitable classification system and nomenclature – a task which was brillantly resolved by the Swedish physician and naturalist Carl Linné (1707–78), better known under his Latinized name Linnaeus. Linnaeus classified all organisms known at that time in a hierarchy (i.e. a graded system) and introduced the consistent use of a binomial nomenclature, giving every species a generic and a specific name. He embodied this classification system in his famous *Systema naturae*, which was first published in 1735 and whose tenth edition, published in 1758, became a milestone in the history of the natural sciences. The names published in this work are regarded as the oldest valid names in zoology (botany dates from 1735) and since that year the 'law of priority' (i.e. where a given species has been described under several names, it is the first name to have been published that is valid) has applied in systematics.

The end of the eighteenth century is generally regarded as the beginning of scientific palaeontology. An Englishman, William Smith (1769–1839), laid the foundations of stratigraphy, which he summed up in two laws – the 'Law of Superposition' and the 'Law of the Faunal Succession'. The French scholar Georges Cuvier (1769–1832) is regarded as the founder of the comparative anatomy and palaeontology of vertebrates. His greatest contribution was the formulation and demonstration of the validity of the 'Law of Correlation', according to which the parts of an animal's body are all interconnected and changes in one part bring about changes in the other parts also. Cuvier showed how the appearance of a whole animal could be reconstructed from the morphology of a given isolated bone. He believed in the persistence of species, however, and attributed the pronounced differences between the fauna found in deposits of different ages to worldwide so-called catastrophes. Jean-Baptiste Lamarck (1744–1829), in his *Philosophie Zoologique* (1809), submitted a complete, but insufficiently substantiated theory of evolution, which was consequently not generally accepted, with the result that the author remained overshadowed by Cuvier for the rest of his life. The development of the geological sciences was greatly advanced by the work of the Englishman Charles Lyell (1797–1875), famous for his formulation of the 'Principle of Uniformity' in geology, according to which the changes through which the Earth passed in the course of its history were caused by the same forces as those which act on it today.

Among the nineteenth-century naturalists, the one who stands out the most in the history of the biological sciences is Charles Darwin (1809–82), who is regarded as the author of the scientific theory of evolution. In his *'Origin of Species*, first published in 1859, he not only elaborated his views on evolution theoretically, but substantiated them through many examples. The keystone of his theory is the principle of natural selection, which explains the tremendous diversity of the organic world and the basis of the adaptability of organisms to the environment in which they live. Darwin saw natural selection as the main cause of the splitting up of evolutionary lines and the origination of new species. The weak points of his theory stem simply from a contemporary lack of knowledge of how genetic information is coded and of how it is passed on from parents to offspring.

Nineteenth-century history of palaeontology is inseparably connected with the names of many outstanding personalities. We cannot continue without mentioning at least a few of the basic works associated with study of the fossils of central and western Europe, such as those of Ernst Friedrich von Schlotheim (*Petrefactenkunde,* 1820–23), Georg August Goldfuss (*Petrefacta Germaniae,* 1826), Heinrich Georg Bronn (*Lethaea geognostica,* 1835–38) and Friedrich August Quenstedt (*Petrefactenkunde Deutschlands,* 1846–84; *Der Jura,* 1858; *Handbuch der Petrefactenkunde,* 1852; *Die Ammoniten des Schwäbischen Jura,* 1885–88). Prominent among French palaeontologists are Alcide Dessalines d'Orbigny (*Paléontologie française,* 1840–55) and one of the founders of phytopalaeontology, Adolphe Théodore Brongniart (*Histoire des végétaux fossiles,* 1828–47). The most outstanding English research workers included James Sowerby and his son James de Carle (*Mineral Conchology of Great Britain,* 1812–14), while Swiss vertebrate palaeontology was made famous by Louis Jean Rodolphe Agassiz (*Recherches sur les poissons fossiles,* 1833–42). The study of invertebrate fossils in the Bohemian Palaeozoic basin is linked primarily to the name of the French palaeontologist Joachim Barrande, whose *Système silurien du Centre de la Bohême* (1852–81), with its 22 volumes, is the most extensive palaeontological work ever to have been compiled by a single author. Antonín Frič, a Czech zoologist, geologist and palaeontologist (*Fauna der Gaskohle* 1879–1901), paid attention mainly to the Permo-Carboniferous fauna of central Bohemia. Czech phytopalaeontology also has its classic author in the person of Count Kaspar Sternberg (*Flora der Vorwelt,* 1820–33).

The origin of fossils

By 'fossils' we generally mean the preserved remains of organisms, or traces of the activity of organisms, which inhabited the Earth in bygone geological ages. Since they kept a given shape and/or structure, they furnish definite, concrete information on the original animal or plant. The process by which dead organisms (or parts of organisms) are transformed to fossils is known as fossilization.

When animals or plants die, their fleshy parts quickly decompose and sooner or later the solid parts of their shells or skeletons likewise vanish without leaving a trace. The conditions for fossilization are determined by a series of special favourable circumstances, comprising quick burial of the organism under a layer of sediment, the physical and chemical properties of the environment (including the sediment), the nature of the organic residue itself and the conditions to which the fossil-containing sediments were secondarily exposed. Rapid formation of a layer of sediment over an organism protects the residue from mechanical destruction; it also shuts out the air and slows down or even stops processes of decomposition. This condition commonly occurred in the case of organisms which actually lived in sediment. Negative physical properties of the environment and sediment, such as turbulent water and a constantly shifting gravelly shore, will soon destroy even the strongest shells, however. The chemistry of the environment is no less important. For instance, peat-bogs form an acid medium in which all calcareous structures are soon dissolved. Similarly, in the oceans, at depths of over 5,000 metres the solubility of calcium carbonate ($CaCO_3$) increases to such an extent that all calcareous shells are soon destroyed. Special emphasis should be placed on the different chances of different groups of organisms of being preserved in the fossil state. For instance, fossilized terrestrial organisms are far rarer than fossilized aquatic organisms. Fossilization took place especially if the material was buried under volcanic ash or sand, or if it fell into a cave and was buried in the soil on its floor, etc. Many organisms were preserved in calcareous or siliceous sinter deposits precipitated from water. Hard shells and skeletons were preserved the most often. Residues buried in sediment became a part of that sediment and, together with it, they underwent the processes that led to its consolidation (diagenesis). When they were made porous by the decomposition of their organic matter, skeletons and shells absorbed mineral solutions circulating in the rocks. The skeletons became more compact and the original matter of the shells was often recrystallized and modified to a mineral more stable in the given environment (for example, aragonite was converted to calcite). In other cases the shell was completely dissolved, leaving only a stone core of its interior surface commonly known as Steinkern. As it dissolved, the shell was often replaced by new material which faithfully reproduced all the details of its outer and inner surface. Saturation with mineral solution sometimes left even the finest details of anatomical structure visible, as in the case of silicified tree trunks, for example. If the circumstances were exceptionally favourable (e.g. in mummification in a desert environment or in a draughty cave, or if the organism was embedded in a natural resin or preserved in ice), some soft parts of the body also remained intact.

The remains of organisms are most frequently fossilized by calcium carbonate ($CaCO_3$) or silica (SiO_2), but also by calcium phosphate ($Ca_3PO_4)_2$ (chiefly vertebrates), pyrite, limonite, haematite, asphalt and amber, etc. Plants and chitin carapaces were often carbonized during fossilization, since the cellulose, under anaerobic conditions, was broken down to carbon dioxide and methane, which escaped during further decomposition, leaving only carbon behind.

In the case of many animals, the only evidence that they ever existed are their trails, burrows and excreta, known collectively as trace fossils.

Not all fossilized organic remains have necessarily been preserved down to the present. Mountain-forming processes caused many rocks to shift to deeper levels of the Earth's crust, where they were partly remelted and recrystallized, so that all organic remains were utterly destroyed. Very often such remains were corroded away by solutions penetrating through porous rocks, or were destroyed by weathering processes. It is thus obvious that only a minute fraction of the total number of organisms ever to have inhabited the Earth has actually been preserved. Consequently, every fossil is a largely unique piece of evidence of what life was like in remote ages.

The classification of fossils

The oldest organisms appeared on the Earth about 3,500 million years ago. Since then, life has gone on developing, organisms have evolved and millions of generations have succeeded one another. It is more than difficult to estimate, even roughly, how many species have existed on our planet during all that time. The extant species which have been described number 1.5 million and their total number is estimated at 3 million. Obviously, if we are to find our way about among such quantities of organisms, or do any work on them, they have to be classified according to suitably chosen criteria, irrespective of whether they are extant or extinct. No doubt we could find

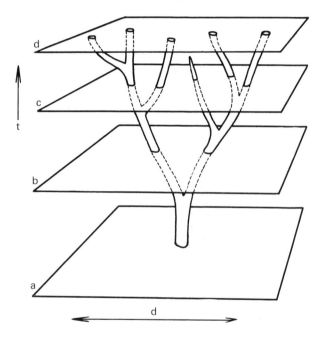

Fig. 1. Fragment of the 'phylogenetic tree' illustrating the vertical and horizontal boundaries between palaeontological populations. The vertical dimension illustrates the time (t), the horizontal dimension morphological differences (d). The various planes (a, b, c, d) stand for different stratigraphic horizons and the intersections of these planes, with the various branches, correspond to interrelated but distinctly different species. If the organisms lived for a long time in the same spot and if the palaeontological record were complete, it would be impossible to define unequivocally the characteristic features of the species. In that case, the definition of the species in the individual evolutionary branches would be purely conventional (arbitrary).

many ways of sorting out fossils, but palaeontologists try to classify them in such a way that the resultant system expresses their mutual familial relatedness (kinship). In this respect, palaeontologists have a far harder task than zoologists or botanists. They do not possess whole organisms to go by, but only parts of organisms (shells, skeletons, carbonized remains) and very often only fragments of those, so that they are unable to make a direct study of their anatomy, physiology and biochemical or serological relationships, etc. The possibilities are nevertheless not so limited as they might appear to be at first glance. A detailed study of morphology, a practical approach to the problems (i.e. utilization of knowledge of suitable, closely related extant organisms) and complex treatment of these questions in general will often furnish sufficient material on which to base the determination of relationships.

In evolutionary classifications or taxonomy, every unit (classification level) comprises more or less related organisms. To be able to express degrees of kinship, it was necessary to elaborate a hierarchic system. The principle of a hierarchic classification is that every higher level unit contains several lower level units. The highest (and broadest) category is the kingdom, followed, in descending sequence, by the

> phylum,
>> class,
>>> order,
>>>> family,
>>>>> genus,
>>>>>> species.

These seven levels are not sufficient for classification of the majority of organisms, however, and so further categories, e.g. subphylum, superclass, subclass, etc. are interpolated between them as required.

The basic category, the only category which can actually be seen and touched, is the species. This has been defined biologically as an ensemble of populations which actually or potentially interbreed and are reproductively isolated from other such ensembles under natural conditions. 'Potential interbreeding' means that if isolated populations living on different territories were to come

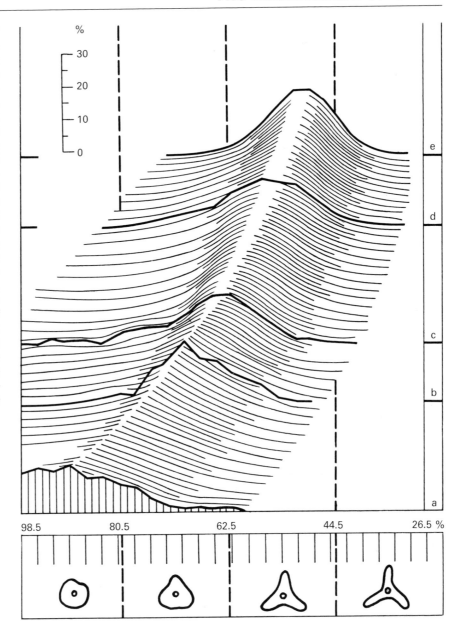

Fig. 2. Diagrammatic illustration of the phylogenetic transformation of the Cretaceous foraminiferan *Haphlophragmium subaequale* to the new foraminiferan genus *Triplasia gorgsdorfensis*, after H. Gerhardt. Samples were taken from five different stratigraphic horizons (a – e) and variation curves for the individual palaeopopulations were constructed. The criterion was the shortest distance between the axis and the wall of the shell, expressed as a percentage of the maximum distance between the wall and the axis of the shell (the abscissa). The change is illustrated by the corresponding main types of shells, depicted at the bottom of the diagram. The percentual frequency of the individual morphological groups (variation classes) can be read by a comparison with the scale in the top left corner. The spaces between the individual variation curves are shaded in the form of a block diagram.

into contact, they would interbreed. When considering species in palaeontology, the time factor must also be taken into account. The commonest graphic illustration of evolution is the evolutionary tree, from whose trunk (common ancestor) branches (evolutionary lines) break away at different levels corresponding to a chronological sequence and continue to branch themselves. Evolutionary differences are thus illustrated on the horizontal plane, while time is shown on the vertical axis. In palaeontology, every species corresponds to a given segment of an evolutionary line. Since evolution is continuous (although it may proceed at different rates), in palaeontology the time limits for the existence of a given species have to be determined artificially.

Principles of nomenclature

Like living organisms, fossil remains are described by two Latin or latinized names; the first is the generic name, the second the name of the species. The specific name is followed by the name of the author who named the species. If this appears without brackets, it means that the same author placed the species in the given genus; if it appears in brackets, it means that the species in question was originally assigned to another genus. The generic name under which the species is now given, however, is regarded as the correct one. In botanical nomenclature, in such cases the name of the author who reclassified the species is also given, after the name in brackets. The name of the author is usually followed by the year in which the description of the species was published for the first time (in palaeobotany the year of reclassification is also given). To be scientifically exact, the name of a fossil animal and plant should thus be written as follows:

Ellipsocephalus hoffi (Schlotheim, 1823)
Glyptostrobus europaeus (Brongniart, 1833) Unger 1850

The year when a species is described for the first time is especially important in palaeontology, since it is not uncommon for the same species to be described under several names. This made it necessary to decide what should be done in such a case and which name should be given precedence. According to the rules of nomenclature, the name first published is the valid name, although even for this it was necessary to set an earliest time limit. The year chosen for this limit was 1758, when the tenth edition of Linnaeus's *Systema naturae* was published. The whole problem is much more complicated, however, since before a species can be recognized as nomenclatively valid, other exactly specified requirements must be fulfilled. Many fossils have only a generic name and their specific name is represented by the abbreviation sp. (Latin *species*). The author does this if he cannot decide which species the specimen actually belongs to. Doubts as to whether the generic classification is correct are expressed by a question mark after the generic name. The abbreviation cf. (*confer,* i.e. compare) after the generic name means that the author has certain doubts over the identification of the species.

Although palaeontologists now establish species on the basis of the largest possible amount of material, the study of populations and the like, every species is based on an actual individual (holotype), or − if the individual was chosen secondarily from an original series − on a lectotype. Similarly, every genus is defined on the basis of a single concrete species, which is known as the type species.

From the above outline of the problems it can be seen that the exact determination of fossils is often fraught with difficulties. None of the biological systems is as yet completely unified and universally accepted, so that the classification of fossils is still exceedingly unstable. Not infrequently, the same species has been placed by contemporary authors in different genera, or the same genus in different families, etc. The scientific revision of individual groups of organisms is based, inter alia, on re-evaluation of the systematic significance of various morphological characters. More detailed study and the use of new methods and techniques bring new findings and upset deep-rooted views on systematics. In evolutionary classification, the individual authors' conceptions of the taxons (species, genera, etc.) are also of considerable consequence.

Ontogenesis, variability, phylogenesis

Ontogenesis is the development of the individual from its origination to its death. The study of ontogenesis in palaeontology is just as important as in biology. A collector or an amateur in palaeontology not acquainted with ontogenetic changes would certainly make many mistakes when identifying fossil remains. Outwardly, ontogenesis is often manifested in gradual or sudden changes in morphology, as well as in mere growth. In some groups of animals, such as molluscs and brachiopods, the shell grows primarily along its free margin and ontogenetic development is manifested in more or less continuous growth, sometimes accompanied by given changes in the sculpture and/or the convexity of the valves, etc. In echinoderms, new skeletal elements are added during growth. Still more striking are the changes in the exoskeleton of arthropods. Winged insects undergo significant morphological changes (metamorphosis) during ontogenesis in a very short space of time, and the larval stage has a very different appearance from the adult insect (imago). Arthropods are characterized by a chitin covering, which, as they grow, is shed several times and replaced by a larger one. In their earliest stages, trilobites have very different carapaces from those of their later stages of growth. In many animals (e.g. vertebrates), the skeleton is fundamentally reconstructed during growth, with a change in both the shape and the internal structure of the bones. It would therefore be best to present the descriptions of species or genera as descriptions of the various stages of growth, but that is possible only if we have a thorough knowledge of the material. The usual method is therefore to describe the adult individuals (or their shells or skeletons), at the same time giving some of the most fundamental ontogenetic changes (the course of sutures, a cross section or description of the shape of the shell, etc.).

Whatever the population, the individuals composing it are never absolutely identical. Their diversity is known as variability and is the result of recombination of genes from parents to offspring.

Differences in genetic constitution (genotype) are more or less reflected in outward traits (phenotype). The degree of variability in a population is also influenced by environmental factors. The reorganization and measure of variability of species often requires a large number of specimens. It is certainly not easy for the layman – and often not even for the expert – to resolve this question, but a solution is essential for correct identification of the relevant fossil.

One of the basic tasks of palaeontology is to present a comprehensive picture of the evolution of the organic world. Questions of mutual evolutional relationships are in turn projected into the evolutional classification. Development occurs in all living matter, whatever form it may be – acellular, cellular, tissue or organ – and it is the result of the interaction of both internal and external factors. The evolution of organisms is based on a genetic code incorporated in a carrier – deoxyribonucleic acid (DNA) – in the nuclei of their cells and on changes in the transmission of the code (mutations). Mutations are manifested in variability, i.e. in differences between the individuals comprising a population. In a given environment and at a given time they can be an advantage (progressive) or a disadvantage (regressive). The process by which individuals with progressive characters are given precedence over individuals with regressive characters is known as natural selection and its outcome is a steady shift of the genetic basis of the population in a given direction. Progressive changes in time, when one species is transformed to the next (successive) species, are known as phylogenesis. Isolation (particularly geographical isolation) is a very important external factor influencing evolution. The influence of geographical isolation on the origination of new species can be demonstrated in a whole series of examples. The development of populations in an isolated environment can greatly hasten the evolutionary process. Charles Darwin described a splendid example of such speciation (origination of new species), when he described how Galapagos finches, in a new, ecologically free environment, became adapted to different diets and rapidly diversified.

One of the basic features of evolution – inequalities in its rate – is clearly visible in the palaeontological record, in which stages of virtually explosive development alternate with stages of stagnation or of mass extinction. What is the explanation of these differences? The diversification of organisms is also reflected in their environmental requirements. Access to a previously unoccupied or little occupied environment (new adaptive zones) meant that some species were presented with new possibilities of asserting themselves and the result was rapid and practically simultaneous evolution of whole series of new species. In palaeontology this process is known as adaptive radiation; it is wonderfully illustrated, for example, by the sudden development of the Lower Cambrian fauna which has been shown to follow an increase in the oxygen concentration in the atmosphere; by the diversification and worldwide spread of vascular spore-bearing plants in the Devonian period in association with adaptation to life on dry land; by the radiation of echinoids in the Lower Jurassic, determined by adaptation to living within the sediment; by the onset of angiosperm plants towards the end of the Mesozoic era; and by the radiation of placental mammals at the beginning of the Cainozoic era,

reflections of a successful form of reproduction. Individual groups of organisms can evolve in different directions. On the one hand, differences between two groups of organisms may be intensified, in which case we speak of mutual divergence. Differences may also become stabilized at a given level and in that case we speak of parallel development. Very often, two originally evolutionally remote groups come to resemble each other morphologically, owing to similarity of their mode of life (e.g. the outer similarity of fish, Mesozoic ichthyosaurians and cetacean mammals), and then we speak of convergence. The differentiation of convergence from kinship is one of the most complex, but basic, problems of palaeontology.

Mass extinction is just as striking a feature as adaptive radiation of different groups of organisms. Its causes often remain unresolved, but are considered to include marked physical changes (palaeogeographical changes, folding, volcanism, the climate, changes in the Earth's magnetic pole, the salt concentration in the oceans, etc.), cosmological factors (changes in the intensity of solar or cosmic radiation, the explosion of supernovae, collisions of the Earth with other bodies, etc.) and changes in the organisms themselves (overspecialization, loss of evolutional plasticity, etc.).

Palaeoecology

No organism lives (or has ever lived) in isolation, but always in a close relationship with its environment. By environment, we mean not only the physical and chemical properties of the surroundings, but also relationships to other organisms. Palaeoecology deals with these problems in connection with fossils.

Just as we need basic terms for describing animals and plants, when discussing palaeoecological questions we need to be acquainted with at least a few standard concepts. Since the majority of organisms depicted in this book come from marine sedimentary rocks, which have the most complete palaeontological records,

attention has been paid primarily to marine animals and the marine environment.

Animals can be divided into several groups, according to their mode of life and their habits. Animals living on the sea floor are known as benthos. Those which are sessile are termed sessile benthos and those which move about on or in the sediment are vagile benthos. Benthic animals are today often divided into infauna, i.e. organisms living in the sediment, and epifauna (animals living on its surface). Nectonic organisms are active swimmers, while plankton comprises organisms floating on or in water; as a rule, the latter are capable of active movement, but in relation to the motion of the water it is negligible. Epiplanktonic animals live attached to swimming or floating organisms or objects. Necroplankton is the term applied to organisms, or rather parts of organisms, which continue to float long after the animal's death (e.g. the gas-filled shells of many cephalopods).

As far as nutrition is concerned, we can distinguish between suspension feeders, which take up and digest the organic component suspended in the water, deposit feeders, which swallow the sediment and digest the organic substances it contains, or pick out organic particles, and herbivorous, carnivorous and omnivorous organisms.

The commonest classification of the marine environment is based on depth and on the relationship to the continent. The zone between the high and low tide limit is known as the littoral zone. Then comes the gently sloping continental shelf, down to a depth of about 200 metres, which forms the sublittoral zone, while the sea above it is known as the neritic zone or shelf sea. In an idealized cross section the sea becomes suddenly deeper (the continental slope) and descends to bathyal (down to 3,000 metres), abyssal (to 6,000 metres) and hadal depths (to 11,000 metres). The part of the sea leading from the continental slope out to the ocean is known as the oceanic zone.

The way palaeoecological questions are approached is based on a number of principles. The most important is the uniformitarian approach, i.e. the use of discoveries in recent ecology. Palaeoecological studies concentrate on individuals, populations, species and whole assemblages and sometimes attempt syntheses.

Every species has its specific environmental requirements. In some cases these are broad, while in others the species can live only under strictly defined conditions. Benthic organisms have completely different requirements from planktonic or nectonic organisms. With benthic animals, whose environment is usually the best substantiated, the main factors influencing their distribution are the character of the substratum and the salinity of the water. Other, more general ecological factors include the temperature of the water, pressure, turbulence, currents, the oxygen concentration in the water and the food supply. These questions are all common to both ecology and palaeoecology. Where does the palaeo-

ecologist obtain his information on the life and habits of a given species? If similar, closely related extant organisms are available, he will no doubt first of all refer to these. The way in which the animals have been preserved is another source of information. Discoveries of animals such as bivalves and crustaceans inside their burrows furnish conclusive evidence that they lived in the sediment. Sessile animals which lived attached to the shells, carapaces or skeletons of other animals provide a wealth of information. For instance, if an animal lived partly buried in the sediment, only its exposed part would be occupied. Of course, it is not always easy to tell whether the 'guest' settled on its host while it was still alive, or only after it was dead. The nature of the substratum also contributes to an interpretation of habits. A hard (rocky) substrate mostly precludes the presence of burrowing animals. Similarly, if the lamination of the deposit — caused by seasonal changes during sedimentation (e.g. in diatomites) — or the alternation of petrographically or mineralogically different layers is intact, it shows that no burrowing animals lived there, since they would soon have disturbed the top layers and obliterated every trace of lamination. Another indirect method is functional morphology, which attempts to explain the purpose and function of the various structures of an exoskeleton. Traces of the animals, activities (trails, bore-holes, excreta and their composition, etc.) are also a rich source of information.

The analysis of plant and animal communities (biocoenoses) is approached in much the same way as reconstruction of the life of the individual or the species. Only part of a community which lived in a particular place is found preserved in the fossil state. The quantitative and qualitative relationship between the original biocoenosis and the assemblage found in the sediment (thanatocoenosis) depends on many factors, e.g. on the proportion of soft-bodied organisms, on the physical and chemical properties of the sediment, on the motion of the water and on the presence of scavengers, etc. Thanatocoenoses, however, generally include organisms which actually lived in the place where they were found (autochthonous organisms) and elements from other thanatocoenoses (foreign, allochthonous organisms), and one of the palaeoecologist's main tasks is to differentiate the one from the other. In the reconstruction of the environment, important information is furnished primarily by autochthonous components, while allochthonous components supply valuable information on hydrodynamic conditions on the sea bed, etc. A collector needs experience to be able to distinguish between the two components and in many cases it is a very complicated matter even for the expert. Our conclusions must be based not only on a knowledge of the ecology of a given group of organisms, but also on the sedimentological findings (sedimentology is the science dealing with the way in which sedimentary rocks are formed). Autochthonous organisms are chiefly those which were sessile, i.e. which lived attached to a substrate. During their lifetime they may have been very firmly attached, but the organic matter in their stem (brachiopods) or byssal threads (bivalves), etc., could have decomposed soon after their death. Brachiopods cemented to a firm substratum, burrowing bivalves in fossil burrows and reef-forming corals or stromatoporoids are definitely autochthonous. Conversely, the shells of planktonic, epiplanktonic, necroplanktonic and nectonic organisms are definitely allochthonous. If we can separate the autochthonous from the allochthonous components, we can go on to resolve further palaeoecological questions, such as interrelationships between the organisms, depth and temperature conditions and hydrodynamics. Sessile benthic bryozoans, brachiopods and crinoids living in very fine-grained sediments were often simply attached to the hard shells or skeletons of other animals and an analysis of this epifauna (as such sessile organisms are collectively called) and of finds of the bore-holes or tunnels inside skeletons and other structures will often lead us to a verdict of symbiosis (a bilaterally profitable relationship) or parasitism (a unilaterally profitable relationship).

Much basic data can be learned from the character of the sediment itself. Its grain size reflects the energy of the environment in which it was formed. Turbid sedimentation in a shallow-water environment is characterized by a series of phenomena, some of which are plain even to a layman — quick changes in the petrographic character of the rocks (facies change) and in the thickness of the layers; the presence of rippling, oblique intrastratal stratification, etc. Many organisms allow the hydrodynamic conditions to be reconstructed. The straight shells of cephalopods and tentaculitids and the skeletons of graptolites are often found lying parallel, or facing in two directions, according to the currents or the effect of the waves. Conclusive evidence of the cause of this arrangement is also furnished by certain crinoids and asteroids, e.g. in Bundenbach shales (p. 390) and by graptolites attached to cephalopod shells (p. 423). The degree of orientation of the shells and separation of the material also informs us about the relative rates of the currents.

Thanatocoenoses can also tell us a great deal about the temperature and salinity of the environment. Corals, brachiopods, cephalopods and echinoderms are all exclusively marine animals and there is no reason to suppose that they were any different in the geological past. They are also characterized by low salinity tolerance (stenohaline) and occur chiefly in water of normal salinity. Reef living corals occur in tropical and subtropical seas at depths of down to about 100 metres. Their optimum depth is not more than 20 metres, however, because the symbiotic unicellular algae which live inside their bodies need light. Although we do not know whether Palaeozoic corals also contained such algae, they certainly had similar temperature, depth and salinity requirements. Brachiopods, certain crustaceans and other animals are also good indicators of the original see depths.

Biostratigraphy and palaeobiogeography

Sediment layers form a more or less complete geological record. There are two basic ways in which geologists can determine their age. One is the expression of their radiometric age, in thousands or millions of years, and the other is to determine their relative age, i.e. on the basis of the

Biostratigraphy and palaeobiogeography

superposition of the rocks and the fossils they contain. The two methods are complementary. When determining radiometric age, geologists utilize the radioactive isotopes present in newly formed minerals which contribute to the composition of the rock, whose relative age can be determined from the ratio of the amount of undecayed isotope to the resultant products. This is a somewhat exacting method for laboratory use, however; it cannot be employed in every case and the further back one goes into geological history, the less accurate it becomes. Biostratigraphy, a method of determining relative geological age based on the study of fossils, is far more satisfactory, simpler and in many respects more accurate in actual practice. The main principles on which it is based are the 'law of superimposition' and the 'law of the same fossils', defined at the end of the eighteenth century by the English geologist W. Smith, the founder of stratigraphy (the science of stratal sequence). Rock layers are formed in succession and normally (i.e. if they are not overturned) the lower layers are older than those lying above them. Strata of the same age contain the same fossils, but we must also compare deposits formed in the same type of environment, because we should hardly find the same species in marine and fresh-water sediments, for instance. Biostratigraphy is concerned with the classification of stratal sequence (i.e. with the order in which the layers were formed) according to their fossils.

The Earth's geological past is divided chronologically into eras (e.g. Palaeozoic), periods (e.g. Silurian), epochs (e.g. Lower Silurian) and ages (e.g. Llandoverian), which stand for internationally valid chronostratigraphic units. These are geological units which are defined according to a chronological sequence and are termed erathem, system, series and stage. Both classification systems use the same terminology, however. Erathems (eras) correspond to fundamental changes in the development of the Earth's crust which were also accompanied by important changes in the composition of the organic world. They are divided into systems (periods) which are generally named after the place where they were first determined, or after the characteristic type of sediment formed during that period, e.g. Carboniferous after *carbon* (coal), Cretaceous after *creta* (chalk). Stages (corresponding in time to ages), which are the smallest international

chronostratigraphic units, likewise have local names. In practice, in Phanerozoic times (i.e. after the Precambrian), the boundaries between the various systems, series and stages are based on biostratigraphic principles. That means that they are characterized by the incidence of a given type of organism or group of organisms and by the absence of other organisms. Just as in systematics every plant and animal species is based on an actual individual (holotype, lectotype) and sometimes on further auxiliary individuals too, in modern stratigraphy it is the principle to base the dividing line between two chronostratigraphic units on an actual geological section or stratotype. For instance, the first international standard stratotype of the Silurian/Devonian boundary — Klonk near Suchomasty (Czechoslovakia) — was determined according to this principle in 1972, and the Lower Devonian/Middle Devonian stratotype — Wetteldorf (West Germany) — in 1981.

The definition of the boundaries between systems, series and stages and other, more detailed subdivision of stages into zones characterized by the vertical span of a given species in a section is based on chosen (index) fossils. Species which developed quickly (which have a small stratigraphic span), occur in abundance over large geographical areas (e.g. many planktonic organisms), are found in different types of sediments and are easy to identify, are chosen as index fossils. In the Cambrian they include many trilobites, in the Ordovician and Silurian graptolites, in the Devonian and Carboniferous conodonts, from the Devonian to the Cretaceous ammonites, in the Mesozoic era foraminifera and ostracods and in the Cainozoic era mammals. Zones are named after the relevant zonal fossil, e.g. the *Spirograptus turriculatus* zone (after the given graptolite species).

Comprehensive palaeontological study also accumulates data for palaeogeographical conclusions (the distribution of the continents, seas and oceans in geological history) and palaeoclimatology (the science of climate and climatic changes in the geological past). Today it is evident, and almost generally accepted, that the position of the continents is not stable and that they float on the Earth's mantle like ice floes. They do not shift at random and their movements are associated with expansion of the ocean floor at the sites of mid-oceanic ridges, as a result of complex movements of the matter in the interior of the Earth. Palaeontology in particular has supplied a great deal of the basic evidence supporting the theory of continental drift. The best known examples are fossil animal and fossil plant evidence of the existence of the southern continent of Gondwanaland, which, in the Palaeozoic and early Mesozoic era, comprised Africa (except the north), Madagascar, part of southern Asia, Australia, South America and the Antarctic. These territories all have certain characteristic types of organisms in common – a phenomenon which could scarcely be explained unless it was accepted that they were once all joined together. That is not the only evidence, however; other branches of natural science have also furnished convincing evidence of the existence of Gondwanaland.

When studying such questions, we need a palaeobiogeographical picture, i.e. a survey of the spatial distribution of fossils. Some species occur over a small area only, in which case they are termed endemic. Most organisms are more widely distributed, however, and many occur over practically the whole of the globe (cosmopolitan species). The geographical distribution of some species or higher categories of organisms is wide, but at the same time sharply defined, i.e. it does not go beyond certain limits. Such areas are known as palaeozoogeographical or palaeophytogeographical provinces. While it must have been easy for the given animals or plants to spread within the province, there were interprovincial barriers which prevented them from spreading any further. As an example we can cite the Lower-Cambrian Olenellus province, which is characterized by an incidence of the trilobite genus *Olenellus* (confined to the eastern coast of the USA and to north-western Europe) or the Late-Palaeozoic Euro-American palaeophytogeographical (palaeofloristic) province comprising the tropical zone of the Carboniferous (a large part of Europe together with northern Africa, the Near East and North America), which is characterized primarily by a high proportion of giant club mosses. The extent of these palaeoprovinces is related to the position of the various climatic belts at that time, so that the significance of palaeobiogeography for their reconstruction is more than obvious.

A systematic survey of fossil organisms

The systematic survey chiefly contains the palaeontologically significant phyla and classes presented to the reader in the illustrations.

PROKARYOTIC ORGANISMS
Organisms with a very small body and lacking a true cell nucleus and nuclear membrane. They comprise viruses, bacteria and blue-green algae.

EUKARYOTIC ORGANISMS
Larger organisms whose cell or cells have a well developed nucleus with a nuclear membrane.

1. KINGDOM: PLANTAE
The characteristics of the various groups are given in the text to the illustrations.
Subkingdom: Thallobionta (Algae)

Unicellular or multicellular autotrophic organisms differing primarily as regards their pigments.
Division: Rhodophyta (Cambrian to Recent)
Division: Chromophyta (Precambrian to Recent)
Division: Chlorophyta (Precambrian to Recent)
Subkingdom: Cormobionta
Higher plants with a highly differentiated structure formed of true tissues.
Division: Rhyniophyta (Silurian to Devonian)
Division: Bryophyta (Devonian to Recent)
Division: Lycopodiophyta (Devonian to Recent)
Division: Equisetophyta (Devonian to Recent)
Division: Polypodiophyta (Devonian to Recent)
Division: Noeggeratiophyta
(Carboniferous to Permian)
Division: Lyginodendrophyta
(Devonian to Cretaceous)

Fig. 3. Rhizopoda − Foraminifera. A − foraminiferan of the genus *Miliona;* the pseudopodia, with microorganisms attached, are extruded only through the aperture. B − morphology of a foraminiferan shell; 1 − initial chamber (proloculum), 2 − chambers, 3 − sutures, 4 − aperture. C − different types of foraminiferan shells showing presumed evolutionary trends.

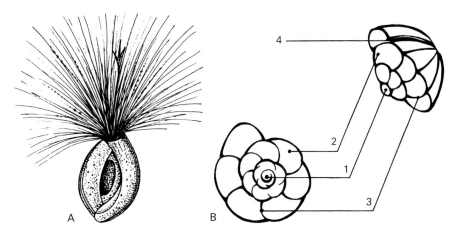

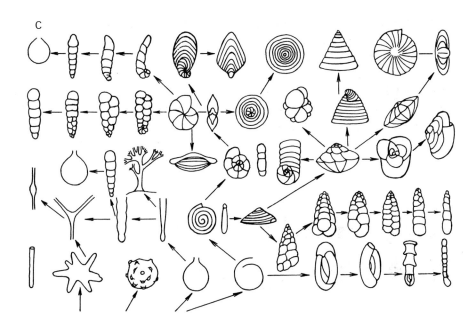

Division: Dicranophyllophyta
(Carboniferous to Permian)
Division: Cordaitophyta
(Carboniferous to Permian)
Division: Ginkgophyta (Permian to Recent)
Division: Cycadophyta (Carboniferous to Recent)
Class: Cycadopsida (Carboniferous to Recent)
Class: Cycadeoideopsida (Triassic to Cretaceous)
Division: Pinophyta (Carboniferous to Recent)
Division: Magnoliophyta (Cretaceous to Recent)
N.B.: The divisions Lycopodiophyta to Polypodiophyta (Pteridophyta) comprise vascular spore-bearing plants and Lyginodendrophyta to Pinophyta gymnospermous plants (Gymnospermae − seed-bearing plants with unprotected seeds).

2. KINGDOM: PROTISTA

Heterotrophic unicellular organisms.
Protozoa:
Phylum: Rhizopoda (Precambrian to Recent)
Protozoans characterized by the short-term presence of cytoplasm processes (pseudopodia). The pseudopodia have both locomotor and nutritional function, i.e. they catch and digest food or withdraw it into the cell, where it is digested. Their cytoplasm contains one or several nuclei.
Class: Foraminifera (Precambrian to Recent)
Class: Actinopoda (Precambrian to Recent)

3. KINGDOM: ANIMALIA

Heterotrophic multicellular organisms.
N.B.: The animals in the following phyla have

A systematic survey of fossil organisms

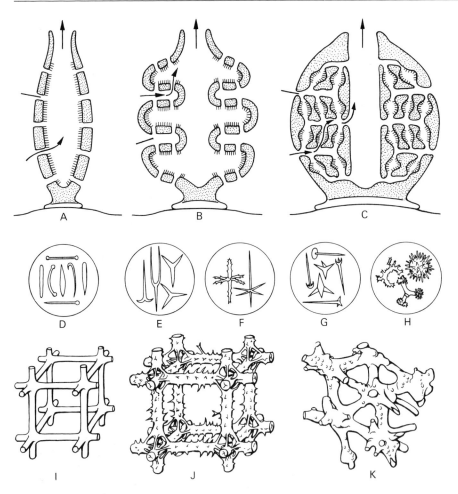

Fig. 4. Diagrams of basic structural types of sponges (Porifera) and types of spicules (sclerites). A – ascon, B – sycon, C – leucon, D – sclerites with one axis (mono-axons), E – sclerites with three rays (triactins), F – sclerites with three axes (triaxons), G – sclerites with four axes (tetraxons), H – irregular, multiaxial and spherical sclerites (polyaxons, desmones and spheres). I and J – fused triaxial sclerites, K – fused desmones.

a primitive body cavity (blastocoele) formed when the egg is at the blastula stage.

Phylum: Porifera   (Cambrian to Recent)
Sponges are aquatic (mainly marine) multicellular animals whose body organization is still at the cellular stage (i.e. it is formed of more or less independent and little specialized cells). Sponges possess neither organs nor nervous tissue. Their body is asymmetrical or radially symmetrical. They have no mouth and water enters a digestive cavity (or cavities) lined with collar-like cells (choanocytes) through pores and canals in the body wall and leaves it via a larger opening known as an osculum. The body is reinforced by an endoskeleton formed of siliceous or calcareous spicules or organic fibres. Sponges are sessile and reproduce both sexually and asexually (in the latter case by budding or by the formation of proliferative buds known as gemmules). The free-living larvae are able to swim.

Class: Demospongea   (Cambrian to Recent)
Class: Hyalospongea   (Cambrian to Recent)
Class: Calcispongea   (Cambrian to Recent)
Class: Sclerospongea   (Triassic to Recent)

Phylum: Archaeocyatha   (Cambrian)
Archaeocyathids are extinct marine animals with a goblet-shaped calcareous skeleton formed, as a rule, of two concentric walls (outer and inner) separated by an interval divided into compartments by radial septa. Almost the entire skeleton is riddled with pores, through which – as in sponges – water probably entered the body cavity. Archaeocyathids were sessile animals. It is assumed that they reproduced both sexually and asexually and that they had free-living, swimming larvae.

Group of phyla: Coelenterata
          (Precambrian to Recent)
Coelenterates are primitively organized, aquatic

Fig. 5. Coelenterata – Anthozoa. A – longitudinal section of a scleractinian coral of the genus *Flabellum*, showing the relationship between the polyp and the skeleton, and a detail of a cross section. B – longitudinal section of the skeleton (corallite) of a rugose coral. 1 – tentacles, 2 – pharynx, 3 – outer wall of corallite (epitheca), 4 – mesentery (a partition formed of soft epithelium), 5 – septum, 6 – calyx, 7 – dissepimenta (vacuolated tissue), 8 – tabulae, 9 – root-like outgrowth.

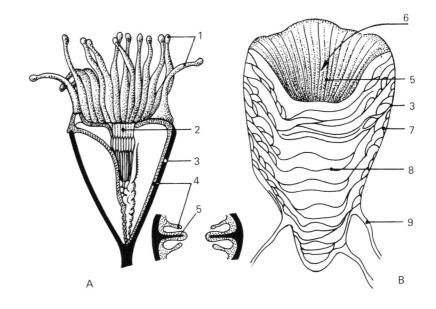

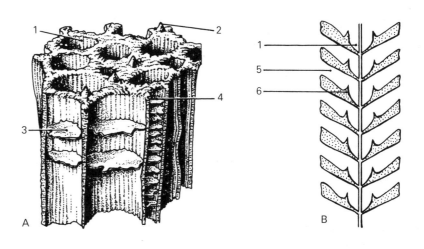

Fig. 6. Bryozoa. A – structure of the zoarium of a trepostomatous bryozoan. B – longitudinal section of a branch of a cryptostomatous bryozoan. C – diagram of part of the zoarium of a cheilostomatous bryozoan. 1 – zooecium, 2 – acanthopore, 3 – diaphragm, 4 – mesopore with numerous diaphragms, 5 – vestibule, 6 – hemiseptum, 7 – operculum, 8 – ovicoele, 9 – avicularium, 10 – anal orifice, 11 – tentacles, 12 – oral orifice, 13 – an extruded zooid, 14 – septulae, 15 – muscles, 16 – compensatory sac, 17 – a withdrawn zooid.

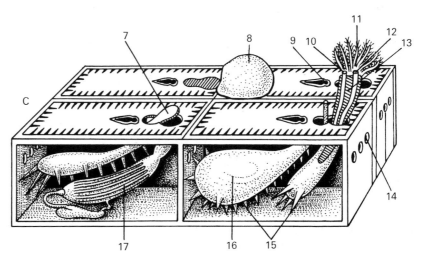

A systematic survey of fossil organisms

(mainly marine), hollow-bodied animals with differentiated tissues. Their body wall is formed of two basic epithelia — an outer ectoderm and an inner endoderm — with mesoglea (an amorphous gelatinous substance) interposed between them. There is no central nervous system. The body is radially symmetrical. The mouth, which is also the anus, opens into a wide gut cavity — the coelenteron — which is usually divided by incomplete septa. Coelenterates do not possess a special respiratory, vascular and excretory system. The majority build a strong calcareous skeleton.

Phylum: Cnidaria   (Precambrian to Recent)
Cnidarians have stinging cells round their mouths and on their tentacles. They are either sessile (in the polyp stage), or free-living (in the medusa stage). In some groups, sexual and asexual generations (medusae and polyps) regularly alternate. Sexual reproduction produces ciliated larvae (planulae), which settle on the bottom and turn into polyps.

Class: Hydrozoa   (Cambrian to Recent)
Class: Scyphozoa   (Precambrian to Recent)
Class: Anthozoa   (Cambrian to Recent)
N.B.: The animals in all the following phyla have a secondary, true body cavity (coelom) formed of mesoderm and superseding the primary body cavity.

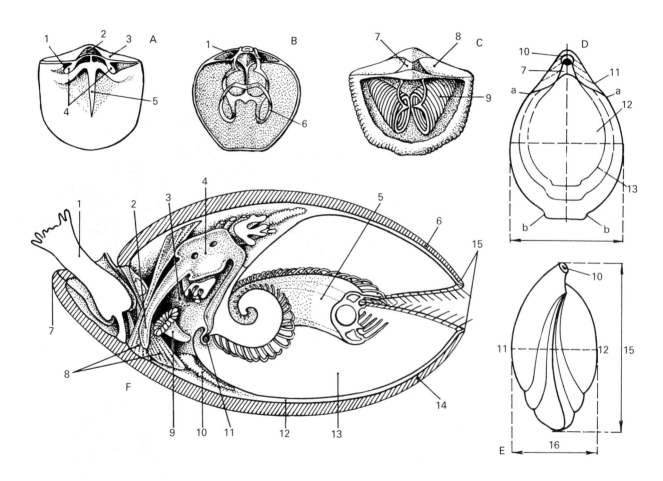

Fig. 7. Brachiopoda — Articulata. A to C — different types of brachial supports in orthid, terebratulid and spiriferid brachiopods. D and E — morphology of the shell of a member of the genus *Megallania,* seen from the dorsal (D) and the lateral (E) aspect. 1 — tooth sockets, 2 — closed middle field on dorsal valve (chilidium), 3 — interarea of dorsal valve, 4 — brachiophores (rod-like brachial supports), 5 — median septum, 6 — loop-like brachial supports, 7 — median cavity closed by two deltidial plates, 8 — interarea of ventral valve, 9 — spirally coiled brachial supports, 10 — pedicle foramen, 11 — ventral valve, 12 — dorsal valve, 13 — growth lines, 14 — width of shell, 15 — length of shell, 16 — thickness of shell, a — a: posterior segment of commissure, a — b: lateral segment of commissure, b — b: anterior segment of commissure, F — diagram of the anatomy of a member of the genus *Terebratulina;* longitudinal section. 1 — pedicle, 2 — blind-ended gut, 3 — visceral cavity, 4 — stomach, 5 — lophophore, 6 — dorsal valve, 7 — posterior margin of the shell, 8 — muscles for opening and closing the shell, 9 — nephridium, 10 — gonads, 11 — mouth, 12 — mantle, 13 — mantle (brachial) cavity, 14 — ventral valve, 15 — anterior margin of the shell.

Fig. 8. Mollusca — Gastropoda. A — shell morphology. 1 — suture, 2 — spiral rib, 3 — columella, 4 — parietal lip, 5 — columellar lip, 6 — columellar folds, 7 — umbilicus, 8 — siphonal canal, 9 — apex, 10 — spira, 11 — anal sinus, 12 — aperture, 13 — outer lip of aperture, 14 — body whorl.
B — shell, with the body, of a member of the genus *Buccinum*. 1 — mantle fold, 2 — shell, 3 — inhalant siphon, 4 — operculum, 5 — eye, 6 — tentacle, 7 — foot, 8 — head, 9 — proboscis with mouth.

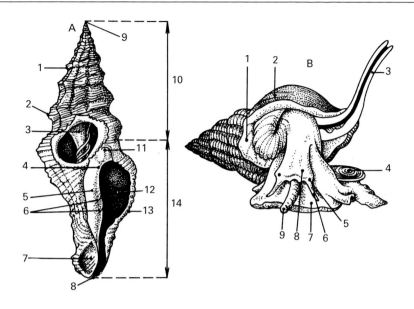

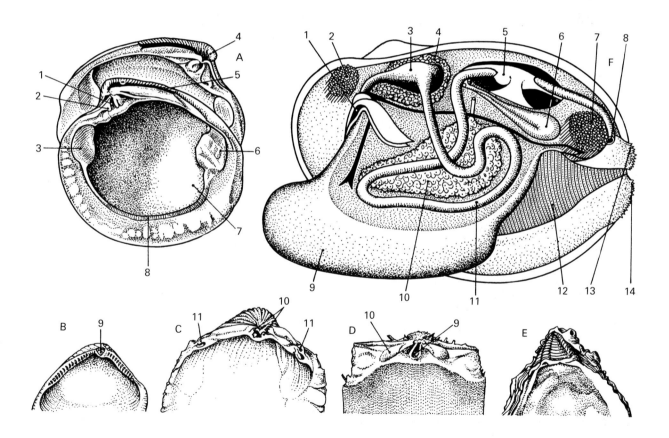

Fig. 9. Mollusca — Bivalvia. A — internal structure of the shell of the genus *Cyprina*. B to E — various types of hinge; B — taxodont, C — heterodont, D — isodont, E — dysodont. 1 — hinge socket, 2 — hinge tooth, 3 — anterior muscle scar, 4 — apex of shell, 5 — ligament, 6 — posterior muscle scar, 7 — internal surface of valve, 8 — pallial line, 9 — resiliary groove, 10 — main (cardinal) hinge tooth, 11 — side (alate) tooth of hinge.
F — diagram of a bivalve's anatomy. 1 — mouth, 2 — insertion of anterior muscle, 3 — stomach, 4 — liver, 5 — heart, 6 — organs of excretion, 7 — insertion of posterior muscle, 8 — anal orifice, 9 — foot, 10 — ovaries, 11 — gut, 12 — gills, 13 — exhalant siphon, 14 — inhalant siphon.

A systematic survey of fossil organisms

Phylum: Bryozoa (Ectoprocta)

(Ordovician to Recent)

Bryozoans (moss animals) are chiefly marine animals forming sessile colonies of microscopic individuals (zooids). The mouth is surrounded by a circular or horseshoe ridge surmounted by tentacles (the lophophore). The U-shaped alimentary tube opens outside the lophophore. There is no respiratory, vascular or excretory system. The walls of the body cases (zooecia) are calcified, chitinous or gelatinous. Bryozoans reproduce asexually – by budding, or sexually – via a free-swimming larval stage.

Class: Stenolaemata (Ordovician to Recent)
Class: Gymnolaemata (Ordovician to Recent)

Phylum: Brachiopoda (Cambrian to Recent)

Brachiopods are sessile marine animals with a non-segmented body enclosed in a bilaterally symmetrical bivalve shell. Their body is wrapped in a mantle and the intervening space is divided by a septum into a small posterior cavity containing the viscera and a larger anterior cavity containing the whirling lophophore. The coelom penetrates the mantle by way of the mantle canals, which have respiratory function. Two main ganglia form the nerve centres, there is an open vascular system and excretion is effected by metanephridia. The highly developed muscular system is primarily responsible for opening and closing the valves and may also help to keep the animal anchored to its base. The shells are calcareous or chitino-phosphatic in composition; the plane of symmetry cuts across the valves. The sexes are usually separate; hermaphroditism is rare. During ontogeny brachiopods pass through a trochophore larva stage.

Class: Inarticulata (Cambrian to Recent)
Class: Articulata (Cambrian to Recent)

Phylum: Mollusca (Cambrian to Recent)

Molluscs are non-segmented aquatic and terrestrial animals with (except for gastropods) a bilaterally symmetrical body divided into a head, a foot and a visceral sac. The visceral sac is covered with a mantle – soft tissue which generally secretes a calcareous shell containing a certain amount of organic matter. The folds of the mantle partly seal off the mantle cavity, which lies posteriorly to the viscera. In many aquatic molluscs there are gills inside the mantle cavity, into which the excretory, secretory and genital sys-

tems open. The complete alimentary tract is usually equipped with jaws and a rasp-like tongue (radula). The respiratory, vascular, excretory and genital systems are highly developed. Molluscs are generally of different sexes, but some are also hermaphroditic. As a rule, their ontogeny includes a trochophore larva and veliger larva stage, but these are sometimes missing.

Class: Polyplacophora (Cambrian to Recent)
Class: Monoplacophora (Cambrian to Recent)
Class: Rostroconchia (Cambrian to Permian)
Class: Scaphopoda (Ordovician to Recent)
Class: Hyolitha (Cambrian to Permian)
Class: Tentaculita (Silurian to Devonian)
Class: Gastropoda (Cambrian to Recent)
Class: Bivalvia (Cambrian to Recent)

Phylum: Annelida (Precambrian to Recent)

Annelids are aquatic and terrestrial animals with a worm-like segmented body with a single preoral segment. The segments usually each carry a pair of non-segmented limbs (parapodia), but sometimes only tufts of bristles. Inside the body they are separated by cross septa. The body wall consists of two layers of muscle – a circular outer layer and a longitudinal inner layer. The nervous system is composed of a central ganglion and a pair of ganglia in each of the segments. The digestive system begins with a mouth and terminates with an anus at the other end of the body. The anterior end of the alimentary tube is equipped with jaws (finds of fossil jaws are known as scolecodonts). The excretory system is composed of protonephridia and there are also vascular and respiratory systems. Marine species go through a trochophore larva stage.

Class: Polychaeta (Precambrian to Recent)

Phylum: Arthropoda (Cambrian to Recent)

Arthropods are highly organized, bilaterally symmetrical animals living in water, on land and in the air. They have a segmented body and on each of the segments (at least in embryogenesis) they have a pair of jointed limbs. The surface of their body is covered with a chitinous cuticle, which is shed several times during growth and is replaced by a larger cuticle, a process known as ecdysis. The nervous system is constructed like a ladder, there is a well developed brain, and in general there is considerable similarity to the nervous system of annelids. The vascular system is open. Arthropods breathe by means of gills or tracheae,

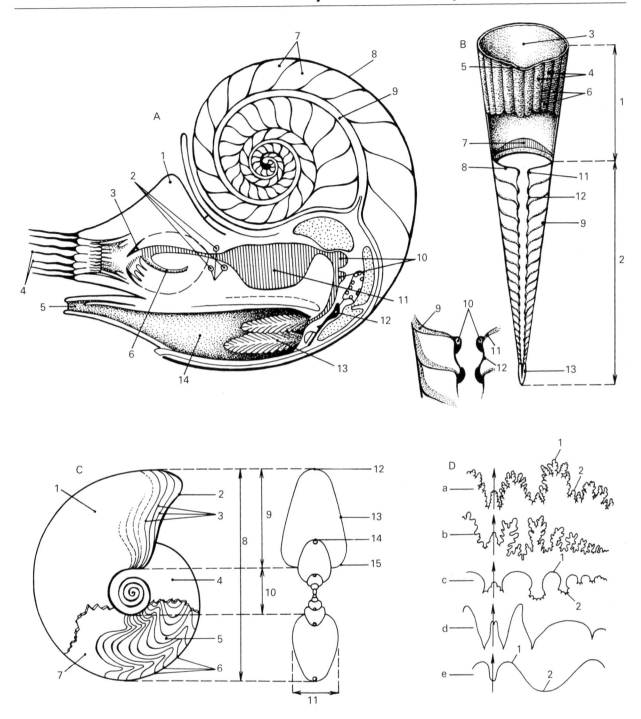

Fig. 10. Mollusca – Cephalopoda. A – a schematized longitudinal section of a recent chambered *Nautilus*. 1 – hood, 2 – ganglia, 3 – jaw, 4 – tentacles, 5 – locomotor organ (hyponome), 6 – radula, 7 – gas chambers (camerae), 8 – outer wall of the shell, 9 – siphon, 10 – alimentary tube (gut), 11 – stomach, 12 – heart, 13 – gills, 14 – mantle cavity.
B – morphology of the shell of a nautiloid cephalopod. 1 – body chamber, 2 – phragmocone, 3 – shell aperture, 4 – longitudinal ribs, 5 – hyponomic sinus, 6 – growth lines, 7 – muscle scar, 8 – septum, 9 – calcareous cameral deposits, 10 – annular deposits inside the siphuncle, 11 – septal neck, 12 – connecting ring, 13 – initial chamber (protoconch).
C – diagram of an ammonoid shell (side view and cross section). 1 – shell wall over the living chamber, 2 – aperture, 3 – growth lines, 4 – shell wall over the phragmocone, 5 – gas chamber, 6 – sutures, 7 – core (a stone mould of the shell), 8 – diameter of the shell, 9 – height of whorl, 10 – diameter of umbilicus, 11 – width of whorl, 12 – outer (ventral) side of whorl, 13 – side of the shell, 14 – siphuncle, 15 – umbilical wall.
D – basic types of ammonoid sutures. a – ammonitic suture, b – phyloceratitic suture, c – ceratitic suture, d – goniatitic suture, e – agoniatitic suture. 1 – saddle, 2 – lobe. (Arrows pointing to the aperture indicate the centre of the ventral side of the shell.)

A systematic survey of fossil organisms

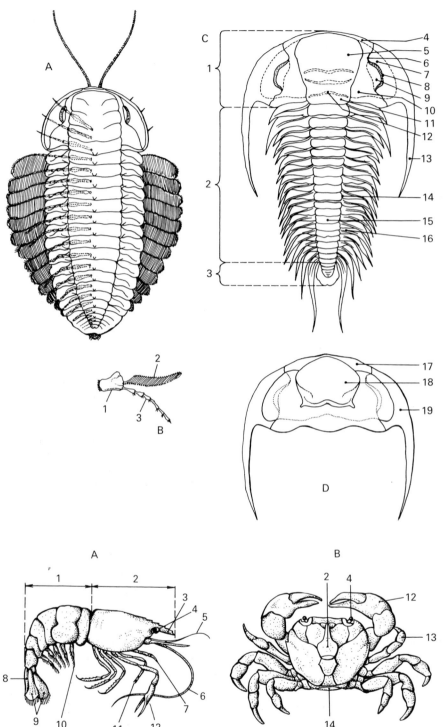

Fig. 11. Arthropoda – Trilobita. A – reconstruction of a Cambrian trilobite of the species *Triarthrus eatoni*.
B – structure of a biramous appendage. 1 – coxa, 2 – exopodite, 3 – telopodite.
C, D – morphology of *Paradoxides gracilis;* C – the carapace seen from the dorsal surface; D – the cephalon seen from the ventral surface. 1 – cephalon, 2 – thorax, 3 – pygidium, 4 – border of cephalon, 5 – glabella, 6 – genal (facial) suture, 7 – free cheek, 8 – eye, 9 – palpebral lobe, 10 – fixed cheek, 11 – occipital ring, 12 – glabellar groove, 13 – genal spine, 14 – axial groove, 15 – axial ring, 16 – pleura, 17 – rostrum, 18 – hypostome, 19 – doublure.

Fig. 12. Arthropoda – Crustacea. Basic morphological terminology of decapods (Decapoda). A – lobster or crayfish, B – crab. 1 – abdomen, 2 – carapace, 3 – rostrum, 4 – eye, 5 – antennula, 6 – antenna, 7 – maxillipeds, 8 – telson, 9 – flattened appendages of the sixth abdominal segment (uropodia), 10 – first pair of abdominal appendages (pleopodia), 11 – first pair of thoracic appendages (pereipodia), 12 – claw (chela), 13 – first pair of walking legs, 14 – proximal part of the inturned abdomen.

or over the whole surface of their bodies. The sexes are generally separate. Ontogenetic development passes through larval stages, or is secondarily shortened.

Subphylum: Trilobitomorpha
(Cambrian to Permian)
Trilobitomorpha are Palaeozoic aquatic arthropods with preorally situated uniramous feelers and biramous limbs.

Class: Trilobita   (Cambrian to Permian)

Subphylum: Chelicerata   (Cambrian to Recent)
Chelicerata are aquatic or terrestrial arthropods whose first pair of appendages has been transformed to claws (chelicerae). Their body consists

26

of a cephalothorax (prosoma) with six segments and of an opisthosoma with twelve segments.
Class: Merostomata (Cambrian to Recent)
Class: Arachnida (Silurian to Recent)

Subphylum: Crustacea (Cambrian to Recent)
Aquatic and terrestrial arthropods with two pairs of feelers and a body differentiated to a head, a thorax and an abdomen.
Class: Branchiopoda (Cambrian to Recent)
Class: Cirripedia (Carboniferous to Recent)
Class: Ostracoda (Cambrian to Recent)
Class: Malacostraca (Cambrian to Recent)

Subphylum: Myriapoda
(Carboniferous to Recent)
Myriapods are terrestrial arthropods with a vermiform body differentiated to a head with one pair of feelers and a trunk. They breathe by means of tracheae.
Class: Diplopoda (Carboniferous to Recent)
Class: Cheilopoda (Carboniferous to Recent)

Subphylum: Hexapoda (Devonian to Recent)
Hexapoda are terrestrial or secondarily aquatic arthropods, and the most highly organized, with a body differentiated to a head, a thorax and an abdomen. They have one pair of feelers, three pairs of legs and usually two pairs of wings. They breathe by means of tracheae.
N.B. The subphyla Myriapoda and Hexapoda are usually grouped together as a single subphylum, Tracheata.
Class: Insecta (Devonian to Recent)
N.B.: All the above phyla of animals with a secondary body cavity (coelom) belong to Protostomia — animals whose mouth is formed during embryogenesis from the primary opening in the gastrula (the blastopore). In Deuterostomia (all the following animal phyla), the anus develops at the site of the original primitive mouth and the mouth is formed secondarily at the opposite end of the embryo.

Phylum: Echinodermata (Cambrian to Recent)
Echinoderms are completely marine animals characterized, as a rule, by pentamerous symmetry, a water vascular system (ambulacral system), an undifferentiated head and a mesodermal endoskeleton. The alimentary tract is simple, but complete. The nervous system is very primitive and there is no brain. The sexes are generally

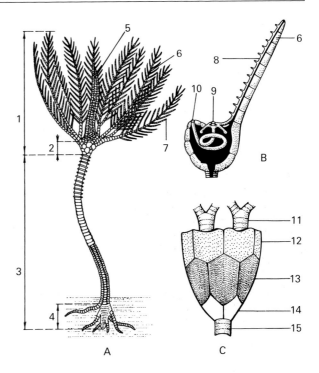

Fig. 13. Echinodermata — Crinoidea. A — diagram of the structure of a crinoid. B — schematized section of a calyx and one arm. C — dicyclic calyx with the base of the arms and with three stem ossicles (columnals). 1 — crown, 2 — calyx, 3 — stem, 4 — radicular part, 5 — anal part of the alimentary tube produced to an anal pyramid, 6 — arms, 7 — pinnules, 8 — ambulacral groove, 9 — oral orifice, 10 — periproct, 11 — brachial plate, 12 — radial plate, 13 — basal plate, 14 — infrabasal plate, 15 — stem ossicle (columnal).

separate, but some echinoderms are hermaphrodites. During ontogenesis they pass through a bilaterally symmetrical, free-swimming larval stage. In adulthood they may be sessile or free-living.

Subphylum: Homalozoa (Cambrian to Devonian)
Homalozoa have an asymmetrical theca, but with varyingly expressed bilateral symmetry.
Class: Homostelea (Cambrian)
Class: Homoiostelea (Cambrian to Devonian)
Class: Stylophora ('Calcichordata')
(Cambrian to Devonian)

Subphylum: Crinozoa (Cambrian to Recent)
Crinozoa are (at least in their young stages) sessile, radially symmetrical echinoderms, which are usually anchored by a stalk growing from the under side of the theca. The ambulacra are produced to arms or to arm-like appendages (brachioles).

A systematic survey of fossil organisms

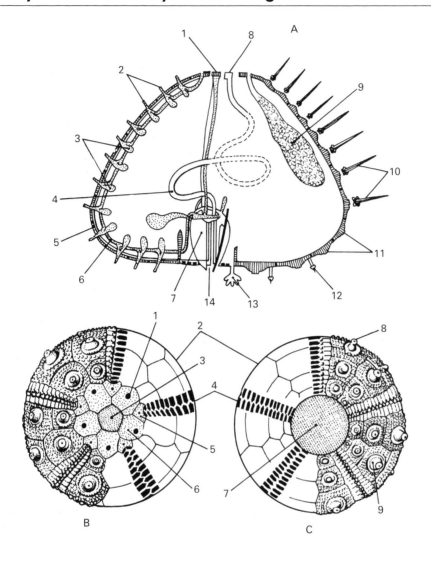

Fig. 14. Echinodermata — Echinoidea. A — a schematized section of a sea urchin. 1 — madreporal plate, 2 — tube-feet, 3 — ampullae, 4 — gut, 5 — test (skeleton), 6 — ambulacral (water) vessels, 7 — Aristotle's lantern (jaw apparatus), 8 — anus, 9 — genital organs, 10 — spines, 11 — tubercles, 12 — pedicellaria, 13 — gills, 14 — mouth.
Main morphological elements of the test: B — aboral (dorsal), C — oral (ventral) view. 1 — madreporal plate, 2 — interambulacrum, 3 — periproct, 4 — ambulacrum, 5 — ocular plate, 6 — genital plate, 7 — peristome, 8 — first order tubercle for carrying spine, 9 — areola of tubercle.

Class: Eocrinoidea   (Cambrian to Ordovician)
Class: Diploporita   (Ordovician to Devonian)
Class: Rhombifera   (Ordovician to Devonian)
N.B.: The classes Diploporita and Rhombifera are usually grouped together in a single class — Cystoidea.
Class: Blastoidea   (Silurian to Permian)
Class: Crinoidea   (Cambrian to Recent)

Subphylum: Asterozoa   (Ordovician to Recent)
Asterozoa are free-living, radially symmetrical echinoderms with a stellate body, on which the mouth lies on the under side.
Class: Stelleroidea   (Ordovician to Recent)

Subphylum: Echinozoa   (Cambrian to Recent)
Echinozoa are echinoderms with a radially symmetrical and almost spherical to discoidal skeleton, without arms or brachioles.

Class: Edrioasteroidea
    (Cambrian to Carboniferous)
Class: Echinoidea   (Ordovician to Recent)

Phylum: Hemichordata   (Cambrian to Recent)
Hemichordata are animals whose body is divided into a prosoma, a mesosoma and a metasoma, the last of which may, or may not, terminate in a stalk-like stolon. The mouth lies on the ventral surface, between the prosoma and the metasoma. The pharynx protrudes in the form of a loop-like evagination — the hemichord. External gill slits open into a peribranchial sac. There is also a tubular nervous system.
Class: Graptolithina (Cambrian to Carboniferous)

Phylum: Conodonta   (Cambrian to Triassic)
Conodonts are an extinct group of small marine — and evidently segmented — animals, whose

Fig. 15. Hemichordata – Graptolitha. A – detail of skeleton (rhabdosome) of a dendroid of the genus *Dictyonema*. B – reconstruction of part of a colony of the genus *Climacograptus*. C – proximal part of a graptolite rhabdosome. 1 – autothecae, 2 – bithecae, 3 – dissepimenta, 4 – virgula, 5 – theca, 6 – zooid, 7 – aperture of theca tapering off into spines, 8 – sicula.

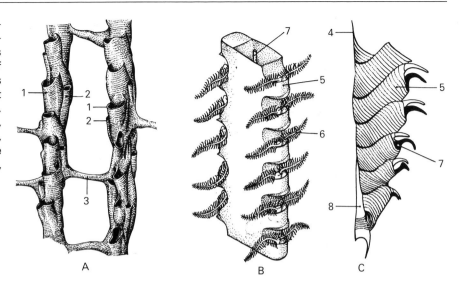

vermiform, laterally flattened body terminates in a widened, fin-like border reinforced with rays. The rostral part of the body is equipped with tooth- or plate-like structures which seem to have acted as jaws; they are formed of calcium phosphate and have a laminar structure.

Phylum: Chordata   (Cambrian to Recent)

Chordates are the evolutionally most advanced animal phylum. They are characterized (at least during embryogenesis) by the presence of a chorda dorsalis (notochord), as the primordium of an axial endoskeleton, and by lateral gill clefts in the wall of the pharynx. The tubular nervous system lies dorsally to the notochord and the digestive tube (gut) ventrally to it, towards the end of the body. The heart also lies ventrally to the notochord.

Subphylum: Vertebrata   (Cambrian to Recent)

Vertebrates are highly specialized chordate animals living in the most diverse environments. Their solid body axis consists of a segmented spinal column formed from the sheaths of the notochord. The spine may be cartilaginous or bony and the same applies to the skull, which protects the brain and the sensory organs. The central nervous system is divided into a brain and a spinal cord. The sensory organs are fully developed. Locomotion is effected by limbs (usually two pairs) and the endoskeleton. There is a closed circulatory system and a well developed heart. Paired kidneys act as excretory organs. The multi-layer epidermis may be covered by various keratinized structures, or it may be bare.

Class: Agnatha   (Cambrian to Permian)
Class: Placodermi   (Devonian to Carboniferous)
Class: Acanthodii   (Silurian to Permian)
Class: Chondrichthyes   (Devonian to Recent)
Class: Osteichthyes   (Devonian to Recent)
Class: Amphibia   (Devonian to Recent)
Class: Reptilia   (Carboniferous to Recent)
Class: Aves   (Jurassic to Recent)
Class: Mammalia   (Triassic to Recent)

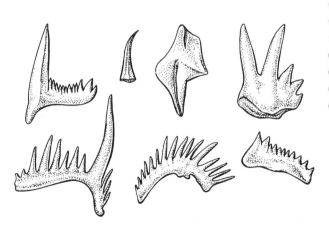

Fig. 16. Conodonta. Different types of conodonts.

Key to the systematic classification of fossil multicellular invertebrate animals

1
a. A shell (skeleton) formed of two valves   .   2
b. A shell (skeleton) of a different type 6, 14, 22

2 (1a)
a. Valves with concentric growth lines on their surface   3
b. Valves without growth lines, small (usually 1– 3 mm) and often elongate . . . .   **Arthropoda, Ostracoda**

3 (2a)
a. Valves usually larger (over 5 mm), calcareous or chitin-phosphate . .   4
b. Small valves (under 5 mm), chitinous, often 'squashed' in the fossil state . . . .   **Arthropoda, Phyllopoda**

4 (3a)
a. The plane of symmetry cuts across the valves .   5
b. The plane of symmetry passes between the valves. The shells may occasionally be asymmetrical. The valves are often joined together by a locking device, with teeth and sockets on both valves . . . .   **Mollusca, Bivalvia**

5 (4a)
a. A calcareous shell; the valves are joined together by a locking device with the teeth on one valve and the sockets on the other. The valves are often found joined together . . . .   **Brachiopoda, Articulata**
b. A generally chitin-phosphate shell, less often calcareous, with no tooth-and-socket device. The valves are found separate . . . .   **Brachiopoda, Inarticulata**

6 (1b)
a. A complete skeleton formed of three parts – cephalic, thoracic and pygidial   7
b. A different type of skeleton (shell)   8

7 (6a)
a. A skeleton with striking segmentation, divided longitudinally and transversely into three parts . . . .   **Arthropoda, Trilobita**
b. A longitudinally undivided skeleton, a thorax with three segments, with wings on the second and third . .   **Arthropoda, Insecta**

8 (6b)
a. A cephalothoracic carapace formed in one piece or in two halves. A thorax with eight segments and an abdomen with six or seven seg-

ments terminating in a telson . . . . **Arthropoda, Malacostraca**

b. A different type of skeleton (shell)   9

9 (8b)

a. A conical or almost cylindrical, straight, slightly curved or variously spirally twisted shell with internal septa   10

b. A different type of shell, without septa   11

10 (9a)

a. A shell, usually large, divided by septa into chambers interconnected by a tube. The septate part may be embedded in the cavity of a very massive cylindrical, fusiform or digitiform structure (rostrum) . . . . **Mollusca, Cephalopoda**

b. Small shells with unconnected chambers . . . **Mollusca, Tentaculita**

11 (9b)

a. A taperingly conical, straight-sided or slightly curved shell   12

b. A spirally coiled (occasionally vermiform) shell   13

12 (11a)

a. A slightly curved shell open at both ends . . . **Mollusca, Scaphopoda**

b. A straight shell with a round-cornered triangular or lenticular cross section, whose wider end was closed by an operculum . . . . . . **Mollusca, Hyolitha**

13 (11b)

a. A shell usually coiled in a three-dimensional spiral, less often two-dimensional, and sometimes conical or vermiform in shape. In the microstructure of the shell wall, the outer calcareous layer is usually composed of crystals oriented perpendicularly to the surface of the shell proper . . . . **Mollusca, Gastropoda**

b. A vermiform or spiral shell coiled in one plane: in the microstructure of the shell wall the calcite crystals curve towards its outer surface in an arch . . . . **Annelida**

14 (1b)

a. A goblet-shaped, conical, cylindrical, pouch-like spherical, discoid, pyramidal skeleton with a spongy appearance, irregular and both separate and forming tuft-like colonies   15

b. A different type of skeleton   18

15 (14a)

a. An outer wall with numerous pores   16

b. An outer wall without any pores   17

16 (15a)

a. Outer appearance goblet-shaped, cylindrical, pouch-like, spongy or irregular. A skeleton formed of microscopic spicules . . . . **Porifera**

b. A calcareous conical or goblet-shaped skeleton, formed as a rule of two walls interconnected by

Key to the systematic classification

radially organized septa

. . . . **Archaeocyatha**

17 (15b)

a. A chitin skeleton, most often shaped like a four-sided pyramid, frequently with a rib or a groove running down the centre of the walls and usually with transverse sculpturing on the surface . . **Coelenterata, Scyphozoa, Conulata**

b. A calcareous goblet-shaped, cylindrical, conical, pyramidal or discoidal skeleton, with vertical, radially oriented septa on the cup . . **Coelenterata, Anthozoa**

18 (14b)

a. A massive calcareous, bulbous, conical, plaque-like, tuberiform or densely lamellar skeleton in which the lamellae are joined together by columellae . **Coelenterata, Hydrozoa, Stromatoporida**

b. A different type of skeleton 18b

19 (18b)

a. A colony with a calcareous, discoid, plaque-like, hemispherical or tuberiform skeleton. The skeletons of the single individuals composing the colony are cylindrical or prismoidal 20

b. A different type of skeleton 21

20 (19a)

a. A polymorphous colony with tubes (left by zooids) with different diameters (up to 0.5 mm), without a system of vertical septa and spines . . . . **Bryozoa**

b. A colony with cavities of the same size, or dimorphous, with cavities (corallites) over 0.8 mm in diameter. The corallites are contiguous or are separated by a calcareous matrix. Septa or spiny outgrowths are present or reduced . . . **Coelenterata, Anthozoa**

21 (19b)

a. The calcareous skeleton of the colony is net-like and is fan-shaped, spiral, funnel-shaped or branched, or it may be encrusting, discoid or saucer-like, with tiny orifices; the outer contours of the orifices are specific for the various types . . . . **Bryozoa**

b. A colony with a skeleton originally of chitin (carbonized by fossilization processes), shaped like a bush or like branched or plain, straight or twisted rods, one or both of whose edges are toothed . . . . **Hemichordata, Graptolithina**

22 (1b)

a. A calcareous skeleton formed of large numbers of usually polygonal plates with incompletely expressed pentameral symmetry 23

b. A skeleton of the same type, but with striking pentameral symmetry – in some species secondarily modified to bilateral symmetry . . .   24

23 (22a)

a. A skeleton whose main part — the theca — is spherical or pear-shaped. Pairs of pores on the thecal plates are connected by simple canals . . . .   **Echinodermata, Diploporita**

b. A theca with distinctly expressed pentameral symmetry. The pores are arranged in rhomboid fields . . . . . .   **Echinodermata, Rhombifera**

24 (22b)

a. A skeleton differentiated to a stalk, a calyx and arms. A calyx with two or three rings of plates .   25

b. A stalk-less skeleton . .   26

25 (24a)

a. A calyx without deep grooves, i.e. in which the position of the ambulacral fields is indistinct . .   **Echinodermata, Crinoidea**

b. A calyx with deep grooves holding the ambulacral fields . . . . .   **Echinodermata, Blastoidea**

26 (24b)

a. A stellate skeleton . . .   **Echinodermata, Stelleroidea**

b. An almost spherical, bulbous or discoid skeleton formed of firmly connected plates with a warty surface. Arms are missing. The tubercles were surmounted by diversely formed spines . . . .   **Echinodermata, Echinozoa**

Pictorial part

Key to symbols used:
Symbols of zoological and botanical phyla or groups of phyla

 Algae and Bryophyta

 Rhyniophyta and Pteridophyta

 Gymnospermae

 Angiospermae

 Rhizopoda

 Porifera

 Archaeocyatha

 Coelenterata

 Bryozoa

 Brachiopoda

 Mollusca

 Annelida

 Arthropoda

 Echinodermata

 Hemichordata

 Chordata

 Palaeobiology

 Typical species

Symbols of living environments

 salt water

 brackish water

 fresh water

 dry land

Stratigraphic data

 Q Quaternary

 Ng Neogene

 Pg Palaeogene

 Cr Cretaceous

 J Jurassic

 T Triassic

 P Permian

 C Carboniferous

 D Devonian

 S Silurian

 O Ordovician

Cm Cambrian

Note:
The stratigraphic data and symbols representing the living environment refer to the species illustrated and described and may not conform to the stratigraphic range of the whole genus.

The marginal line drawings are intended to complete the concept of morphology or ecology of the representatives of the given or closely related genus and need not thus relate to the species illustrated in colour.

35

Palaeoporella variabilis STOLLEY

Order: Siphonales
Family: Codiaceae

Algae, which comprise a series of lower plant groups are, together with bacteria and blue-green algae, the oldest organisms on the Earth. We have evidence of their existence in sediments almost 2,000 million years old. Many of them, such as unicellular golden yellow algae (Coccolithophorida, Silicoflagellata) or diatoms, form siliceous or calcareous tests which are the main constituents of certain types of sediments. Other algae, which precipitate inorganic material inside the cell walls or on their surface, contribute to the formation of coral reefs. Débris caught and cemented together on the surface of algae gives rise to stromatolites. One of the basic systematic criteria for the classification of algae is the type of their assimilation pigment.

Among green algae (Chlorophyta) we most frequently find tubular, internally non-septate, originally multinuclear encrusted cells forming the thalli of siphonal algae. Codiaceae are exclusively marine algae which today still live largely in warm water. The thalli are formed of tubular branched fibres, often interwoven in an untidy tangle, whose widened ends are usually oriented perpendicularly to the surface of the thallus.

Teutloporella herculea STOPPANI

Order: Siphonales
Family: Dasycladaceae

The thallus of dasycladate algae is an irregularly or whorl-wise branching tube whose side branches may put forth further branches. Inside the thallus there are incomplete septa. As a rule, these algae are able to precipitate calcium carbonate on the surface of their thalli. Many of their over 150 fossil species contributed, in the tropical and subtropical belt, to the formation of reefs, especially in the late Palaeozoic and the Mesozoic era. All that is left of them today is a tiny group of nine genera.

Teutloporella is a European Permian to Triassic genus.

Acanthochonia barrandei HINDE

Order: Receptaculitales
Family: Receptaculitaceae

For a long time nobody knew to which kingdom receptaculitids belonged — to the algae or to relatives of the sponges. Today it is clear that these Palaeozoic marine organisms are calcareous algae. They have a spherical thallus and form a solid 'skeleton' from characteristically organized elements (meromes) of the same shape, but of different sizes, according to their distance from the growth pole (fig. 4 — the thallus from the side). Unlike dasycladate algae, calcium carbonate was not precipitated on the surface of the thalli, but the cell walls underwent calcification.

The members of the genus *Acanthochonia* — a typical representative of the order — occur in European Silurian deposits. Like other receptaculitids, they grew in shallow water, often in the vicinity of coral reefs.

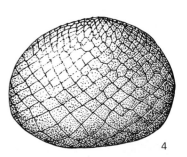

4

1,4. *Acanthochonia barrandei*, Lower Silurian (Wenlock), Bubovice, Czechoslovakia. Diameter of the larger thallus about 25 mm. The majority of finds come from shallow-water tuffite limestones which also contain an abundance of benthic fauna. 4 — a reconstruction.

2. *Palaeoporella variabilis*,* Upper Ordovician, Frognö, Ringerike, Norway. Rock from which parts of thalli are weathering out; length 55 mm.

3. *Teutloporella herculea*, Lower Triassic (Anisian-Ladinian), Dobšiná, Czechoslovakia. A rock with parts of thalli; length 65 mm.

Riccia cf. *fluitans* LINNAEUS

Order: Marchantiales
Family: Ricciaceae

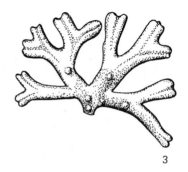

3

Reliable palaeontological evidence of the existence of mosses and liverworts (Bryophyta) is available from the Devonian onwards. Like all higher plants, they already have tissues differentiated according to their functions. The cell membranes are composed of cellulose or hemicellulose. Unlike other higher plants, bryophytes have a generation cycle in which the sexual generation (gametophyte) preponderates over the asexual generation (sporophyte) and forms a viable plant. The sporophyte is reduced, lives in dependence on the gametophyte and dies after maturation of the spores. The plants are always small and seem to be primitively constructed, but only because their bodies have been reduced. Bryophytes probably evolved from green algae, from which they are outwardly very different, but to which they display striking biochemical similarity. Evolutionally they are very conservative and have hardly changed over a period of more than 300 million years. Their present-day representatives are know in all kinds of environments and in various geographical zones, but primarily in damp surroundings. As today, in the geological past bryophytes played a significant role in the accumulation of organic matter in peat-bogs and in the precipitation of calcium carbonate from aqueous solutions, but since they have very fine bodies it is somewhat exceptional for them to be found as fossils.

The genus *Riccia* dates back to the Cainozoic era. It is one of the liverworts (Hepaticae), which have a thallate or a foliate gametophyte and no central vein in their leaves (fig. 3).

Moss travertine

Mosses (Musci) are geologically more important than liverworts. They always have a leafy gametophyte and centrally veined leaves. Their oldest known fossil representatives date from the Devonian. In the Carboniferous period, especially in a mild climate, such as prevailed in those days in Siberia, for example, they participated in important measure in the formation of coal seams and (as today) played an important role in the development of peat-bogs. When mosses grow in water with a high calcium content, the assimilating plants take up carbon dioxide from the water. This converts the soluble bicarbonate to insoluble calcium carbonate, which is precipitated on the surface of the plants. When the organic matter of the plants decomposes, it leaves a cavity which is an exact replica of their form. In water rich in calcium, this activity of mosses, liverworts and other plants leads to the accumulation of a more or less hardened freshwater calcium carbonate known as travertine.

1. *Riccia* cf. *fluitans*, Neogene (Miocene), Sokolov, Czechoslovakia. Parts of thalli preserved in claystone, length 110 mm.

2. Moss travertine, Subrecent, Srbsko, Czechoslovakia. A rock sample 90 mm long. Travertine is characterized by high porosity and inadequate consolidation. The decisive role of mosses in its formation is clearly manifested in its structure.

3. A reconstruction of a member of the genus *Riccia*.

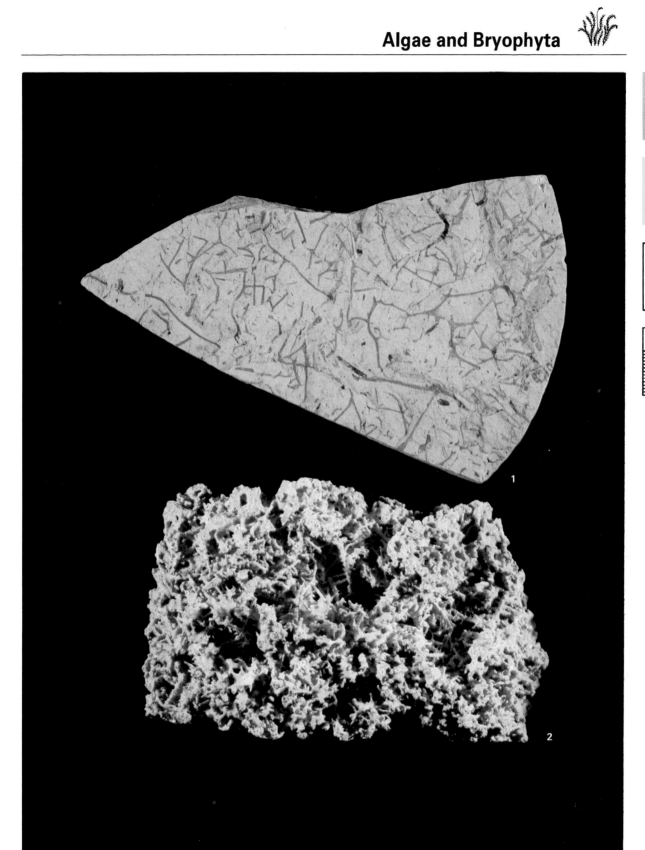

Cooksonia hemisphaerica LANG
Order: Rhyniales
Family: Rhyniaceae

Progressive colonization of the land probably began at the end of the Proterozoic and the beginning of the Palaeozoic era, when bacteria, blue-green algae, algae, fungi (decomposing vegetable matter) and lichens (organisms in which green or blue-green algae and fungi live in a symbiotic relationship) vegetated the Earth. The oldest vascular terrestrial plants used to be ranked among the psilophytes (Psilophyta), but are now named rhyniophytes (Rhyniophyta). They date back from the Upper Silurian to Upper Devonian and they heralded in the era of vascular spore-bearing plants (cryptogams) — the Palaeophytic, which ended at the transition from the Lower to the Upper Permian. These plants did not yet have either true roots or leaves and they assimilated through their stem or its lateral outshoots. Their tissues were already differentiated to dermal, vascular and ground tissue. The vascular bundles were simple and were arranged concentrically, with the wood in the centre (the protostelic type), or else, in cross sections of the stem, the wood rayed out (the actinostelic type). The stems usually forked (branched dichotomically) and at their ends they bore spore-cases (sporangia) with spores of equal size; the spores themselves bore a trilete mark. In rhyniophytes — as in all higher plants — the generations regularly alternated. The sexual generation (the gametophyte) closely resembled the non-sexual generation (the sporophyte). Rhyniophytes lived in damp, marshy surroundings and often round thermal springs. Some of them actually liked salty water.

Cooksonia is the oldest known genus of vascular plants. It occurs in Upper Silurian and Lower Devonian sediments in Europe, Asia, North America, Australia and Africa. It was a tiny plant only a few centimetres high, with a dichotomically branching stem. Spherical sporangia about 1 mm in diameter are occasionally found at the ends of the branches.

Thursophyton elberfeldense
(KRÄUSEL AND WEYLAND) HOEG
Order: Asteroxylales
Family: Asteroxylaceae

The Devonian flora includes many types of plants whose classification gives systematicians a problem. Until quite recently the members of the genus *Thursophyton* (fig. 3), which occur in Lower and Upper Devonian strata in Europe, Asia, North America and Australia, were classified as psilophytes. Today we incline to the view that they belong to the evolutionally oldest lycophytes — a view backed up by their appearance. Growing out from their main stem, which was about one metre tall, were thin side branches which continued to branch themselves. The thicker parts of the plants were covered with small, narrow leaves and with stomata, while in some species the thinner terminal branches were almost bare. The vascular bundles reached only to the base of the linear leaves.

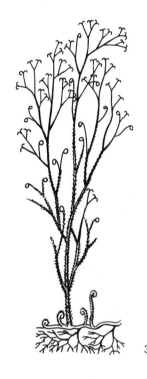

3

1. *Cooksonia hemisphaerica,* Upper Silurian (Pridoli), Kosov near Beroun, Czechoslovakia. A stem with terminal sporangia, length about 70 mm. Found in shallow-water marine sediments, to which it had been washed down from the adjoining land.

2, 3. *Thursophyton elberfeldense,* Middle Devonian, Kirberg near Elberfeld, West Germany. Parts of a stem, length of specimen 100 mm. The stems of this shrub-like lycophyte are not more than 5 mm in diameter. 3 — a reconstruction.

Barrandeina dusliana (Krejčí) Stur

Order: Barrandeiales
Family: Barrandeiaceae

The Devonian was a key period in the evolution of plants. Vascular plants had colonized the dry land and the coastal marshes and were spreading at a tremendous rate. The most luxuriant vegetation was to be found in the tropical and subtropical belts, to which a large portion of present-day Europe belonged. Plants also began to carpet the colder climatic belts, however. In close association with its explosive spread, the flora underwent diversification, with resulting increasing complexity of the plant bodies. Consequently, alongside rhyniophytes, in Devonian strata we also know bryophytes, pteridophytes, progymnosperms (precursors of gymnosperms), pteridosperms (seed-bearing ferns) and other gymnospermous plants. One of the main features of the Devonian flora is a progressive increase in the size of individual plants and although *Cooksonia* was only a few centimetres tall, by the end of the Devonian there were groups in which tree-like forms appeared.

One of the Middle Devonian plants whose systematic identity has not been definitely settled is *Barrandeina,* which grew in Europe, North America and Asia. Its appearance and anatomical structure are so unusual that it has been taken for a lycophyte, a psilophyte and even a marine alga. It was a shrub-like plant with regularly branching stems covered with oval bolsters where leaves had been. The leaves had long petioles and a large number of veins; they either had a cuneiform blade divided at the tip into narrow segments, or they were linear, again with a dissected tip. Sporophylls with sporangia clustered together in cones were seated on the ends of the side stems (fig. 3).

3

Drepanophycus spinosus
(Krejčí) Kräusel and Weyland

Order: Baragwanathiales
Family: Drepanophycaceae

Typical lycophytes are usually characterized by a forking stem with spirally organized linear or scaly (and generally single-veined) leaves. The sporophylls are similar to or identical with the assimilating leaves; sporangia are present in their axils or above their base. In most species the sporophylls form cones. This description fits the plants known under the generic name *Drepanophycus* very well. These plants occur in Devonian sediments in most parts of the world. Thorny leaves, each supplied by a thin vascular bundle, wound in a spiral round their forking stem, which grew to a height of about 50 cm. The sporophylls, which closely resembled assimilating leaves, did not form cones, but were scattered about among the sterile leaves (fig. 4).

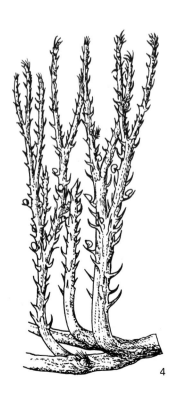

4

1, 4. *Drepanophycus spinosus,* Middle Devonian (Givetian), Srbsko, Czechoslovakia. The carbonized apical part of a small branch in sandy shale; size of rock sample 80 × 80 mm. 4 – a reconstruction.

2, 3. *Barrandeina dusliana,** Middle Devonian (Givetian), Srbsko, Czechoslovakia. Part of a small branch (2), length 110 mm. The isolated spores have a Y-shaped scar and resemble lycophyte spores. The dichotomous lobation of the leaves (3) differentiates *Barrandeina* from modern lycophytes.

Rhyniophyta and Pteridophyta

Lepidodendron simile KIDSTONE

Order: Lepidodendrales
Family: Lepidodendraceae

The damp, tropical climate prevailing during the Carboniferous period in what is now Europe, North America, northern Africa and even Spitzbergen and Greenland enormously encouraged the development of many vascular plants. Pteridophytes (club mosses, horsetails and ferns), many of which grew to tree-like proportions, were in those days largely responsible for the structure of the forests. Pteridosperms grew there in abundance and, bit by bit, other gymnosperms likewise gained a foothold.

Lepidodendron (fig. 2) is the best known Carboniferous lycophyte genus in the above Euro-American geobotanical province; it was particularly abundant at the beginning of the Upper Carboniferous. Its sturdy trees, which had a huge crown with forking branches, grew to a height of up to 40 metres, while the trunk measured up to 2 metres across. It was held in place in the soft ground by dichotomically branching 'roots' known as stigmariae, with 'rootlets' (appendices) growing from them. Both trunk and branches were covered with rhomboid leaf bolsters, which stayed behind after the leaves had been shed. In different species the linear leaves were different lengths, varying from a few millimetres to several dozen centimetres. The organs of reproduction were clustered together in cones, which grew either at the ends of the branches or directly on the trunk, where they left rounded scars behind them.

Our knowledge of the anatomy of lepidodendrons is fairly complete. In the centre of the trunk there was a wooden column surrounded by bast (the protostele). In evolutionally more advanced types there was a cylinder of wood enclosing medulla (pith) in the centre, surrounded by a layer of bast (the siphonostele). The bast was enclosed in a tremendously thick cortex accounting for up to 90 % of the bulk of the trunk. The cortex consisted of an inner layer, from which ventilating canals led to the surface of the trunk, and an outer layer with stabilizing function. The cortex surface, with the leaf bolsters, is one of the most characteristic features of lepidodendrons. The cylindrical or ovoid cones were made up of sporophylls with sporangia on the upper surface of their base. The spores were differentiated to small male spores (microspores) and larger female spores (megaspores), both with a Y-shaped scar.

As a rule, lepidodendrons have been preserved as isolated parts — stigmariae, branches and foliage, cones (strobili) and spores. Since there are not many cases (and those based, as a rule, on isolated finds) in which it can reliably be claimed that the various parts of different organs all belong to the same species, a separate terminology has been invented for the individual organs, since that is the only possible means of orientation among the multitude of finds. For instance, *Lepidodendron* 'roots' have been given the generic name *Stigmaria* and the cones *Lepidostrobus,* etc. Similar difficulties arise over the cortex, which on old parts of the trunk and branches has peeled away to varying depths. The surfaces of such decorticated trunks are characterized by different features and were erroneously given different generic names.

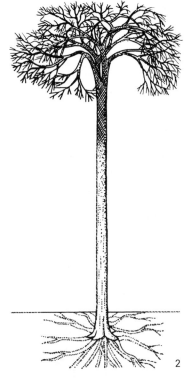

1, 2. *Lepidodendron simile,* Upper Carboniferous (Westphalian), Nýřany, Czechoslovakia. 1 — the foliate part of a branch, about 350 mm long, with S-shaped leaves. This was a widespread species in Upper Carboniferous Europe and North America. 2 — a reconstruction.

Rhyniophyta and Pteridophyta

Lepidodendron aculeatum STERNBERG

Order: Lepidodendrales
Family: Lepidodendraceae

The most characteristic *Lepidodendron* finds are parts of the surface of the cortex, with elongate-rhomboid leaf bolsters, each with a leaf scar roughly in the centre. The scar is also rhomboid and in it there are three minute depressions. The central depression corresponds to the vascular bundles that supplied the leaf and those on either side of it to interstitial tissue. Below the leaf scar the bolster is generally divided by a longitudinal ridge, which has two further traces of interstitial tissue on its sides.

Lepidophloios laricinus STERNBERG

Order: Lepidodendrales
Family: Lepidodendraceae

The genus *Lepidophloios* is closely related to *Lepidodendron* and the two genera often occur together. *Lepidophloios* species survived into the Lower Permian, however. They had long leaves like blades of grass and their unisexual cones grew on short branches leading directly from the trunk. When the leaves were shed, they left zones of spirally arranged scars on the trunk. The leaf bolsters bulged, curved downwards and overlapped each other like scales.

1. *Lepidodendron aculeatum,** Upper Carboniferous (Westphalian), Plzeň, Czechoslovakia. An impression of the surface of a trunk with leaf bolsters some 40 mm in diameter. Spiral organization of the leaves is manifested on parts of the branches and trunks in arrangement of the leaf bolsters in oblique rows.

2. *Lepidophloios laricinus,** Upper Carboniferous (Westphalian), Nýřany, Czechoslovakia. Impression of the surface of a trunk showing the elongate form of the uncovered parts of leaf bolsters about 6 mm long.

C

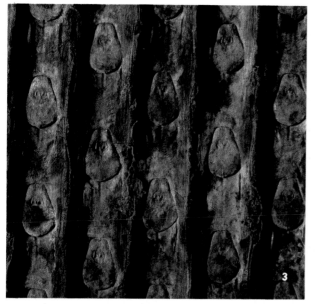

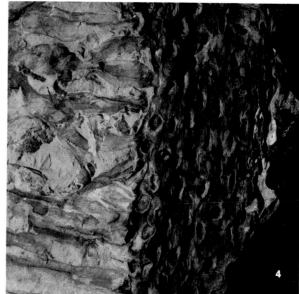

3. *Sigillaria scutellata,** Upper Carboniferous (Westphalian), Břasy, Czechoslovakia. Impression of the surface of a trunk with leaf bolsters arranged in vertical rows about 12 mm wide.

4. *Stigmaria ficoides,** Upper Carboniferous (Westphalian), Otovice near Kralupy, Czechoslovakia. Fragment of a root 35 mm in diameter, with undeformed rootlets preserved in a tuffaceous bed.

5. A reconstruction of a member of the genus *Sigillaria*.

5

Sigillaria scutellata BRONGNIART

Order: Lepidodendrales
Family: Lepidodendraceae

Sigillarias (fig. 5) were likewise an important element of the Carboniferous and Lower Permian Euro-American plant province. These arboraceous lycophytes grew to a height of up to 20 metres and had an unbranched or only slightly branched trunk. Two vascular bundles ran down the middle of their long, linear leaves. On both the trunk and the branches the leaves were arranged in spirals, and at the same time in longitudinal rows (orthostichi); they left characteristic scars on the surface of the cortex. The loose, catkin-like strobili grew from the top of the trunk or from the thickest branches; they either contained sporophylls of both sexes (heterosporous strobili), or grew as separate male and female strobili.

Stigmaria ficoides (STERNBERG) BRONGNIART

Order: Lepidodendrales
Family: Lepidodendraceae

The trunk of arboreal lycophytes generally split up at its base into four thick, dichotomically branching 'roots' from which runner-like, up to one metre long, 'rootlets' (appendices) projected. Separation of these 'rootlets' left characteristic crateriform scars on the surface of the 'root'. Stigmariae are often found in their original position and they are important evidential material for resolving the origin of coal seams.

47

Rhyniophyta and Pteridophyta

Sphenophyllum myriophyllum CRÉPIN

Order: Sphenophyllales
Family: Sphenophyllaceae

The typical plants of the late Palaeozoic era also include horsetails (Equisetophyta), known from the Devonian onwards. In the Mesozoic era they retreated into the background and only one genus – *Equisetum* – has survived down to the Recent. The most salient feature of equisetophytes is their segmented axis with its whorls of branches on which the leaves are also arranged in whorls. The sporophylls are generally grouped together in whorls forming structures like spikes or cones. As today, fossil equisophytes were fond of moisture.

The members of the genus *Sphenophyllum* are known from Upper Devonian to Lower Triassic strata in both the northern and the southern hemisphere. They comprise clinging, climbing plants with long, thin stems with few branches and with ribs running all the way along them. The roots grew in nodes; it was evidently also normal for adventitious roots to be formed on the stems. The leaves were arranged in whorls formed either of three leaves or of further leaves in multiples of three. *Sphenophyllum* species were characterized by triangular vascular

1. *Sphenophyllum myriophyllum*, Upper Carboniferous (Westphalian), Rakovník, Czechoslovakia. Size of rock sample 70 × 40 mm. An important species in European Carboniferous formations, it has deeply dissected leaves.

2. *Sphenophyllum majus*, Upper Carboniferous (Westphalian), Radnice, Czechoslovakia. A leafy branch about 60 mm preserved in tuffite. A species distributed over Europe, Asia Minor and North America.

3

3, 4. *Sphenophyllum cuneifolium,** Upper Carboniferous (Westphalian), Kladno, Czechoslovakia. Isolated whorls preserved in a sample of calcareous claystone measuring 90 × 40 mm. One of the commonest *Sphenophyllum species.* 4 – a reconstruction.

4

bundles (seen in cross sections of the stem) and leaflets with cuneiform contours, which are preserved even when the leaflets are dissected. In some species there were two types of leaflets on individual plants (heterophylly), so that whorls of dissected leaflets alternated with whorls with undivided leaflets. Some sphenophylls are also characterized by plagiotropic organization making more effective use of solar energy, the higher whorls being shorter than the ones below them, so as not to deprive them of sunlight. The fertile branches of sphenophylls are sometimes almost indistinguishable from the sterile branches, while at other times they carry cones. Apart from a few exceptions the spores are all of one type.

Order: Sphenophyllales
Sphenophyllum majus BRONN   Family: Sphenophyllaceae

The classification of sphenophylls is largely artificial and is based on differences in the shape of the leaflets. The cones, which would otherwise provide better classification material, are usually isolated and the number of cases in which the two organs can be brought together is very restricted. In the case of the leaflets there is a clearly expressed evolutionary trend from more dissected leaflets in geologically older forms to undivided blades in more recent forms (e. g. *S. majus*).

Order: Sphenophyllales
Sphenophyllum cuneifolium STERNBERG   Family: Sphenophyllaceae

Heterophylly is very pronounced in this species, which occurs in Europe and in North and South America. Its massive cone-shaped sporangia grow to a length of about 60 mm (fig. 4).

49

Rhyniophyta and Pteridophyta

Calamites suckowi BRONGNIART

Order: Equisetales
Family: Calamitaceae

Calamites are the best known equisetophytes of the late Palaeozoic era, when they grew almost everywhere. They attained their prime in the Upper Carboniferous and the Lower Permian. In constrast to the liana-like sphenophylls, calamites looked like sturdy trees and grew to a height of 20 to 30 metres. Branched segmented rhizosomes kept them anchored in the ground. Their trunks were thickly or loosely branched and their general form (habitus) was conical (fig. 4). The leaves grew in alternating whorls; in evolutionally older types they were forked, in more progressive types they were linear. The sporangia were organized in cones. Down the centre of the trunk ran a huge column of pith, but this was soon broken down, leaving behind it a cavity which was partly constricted at the nodes. The stele and the cortex were also strongly developed.

The commonest calamite remains to be found include impressions of parts of trunks and branches preserved either as petrified pith casts of the inner surface of the cavity, or as imprints of its outer surface. Characteristic ribs and grooves are present on the surface of such casts. The grooves are the imprints of vascular bundles, which fork and unite, at the end of the segments, with the arms of adjacent grooves, thereby giving the surface of pith casts a riffled appearance. The nodal

1. *Calamites suckowi,* Upper Carboniferous (Westphalian), Saarbrücken, West Germany. A compressed cast of a pith cavity, length 150 mm.

2. *Calamites undulatus,* Upper Carboniferous (Westphalian), Radnice, Czechoslovakia. A severely deformed pith cast, length 150 mm.

3. *Calamodendron* sp., Upper Carboniferous (Stephanian), Hilbersdorf, East Germany. A cross section of a silicified trunk with a small pith cavity and with clearly discernible secondary xylem wedges. Diameter not more than 80 mm.

4. A reconstruction of a member of the genus *Calamites*.

3

4

constrictions correspond to incomplete septation of the medullary (pith) cavity. Imprints of the outer surface of calamite trunks or branches are generally smooth or irregularly cracked. The nodal line is almost straight and alternating rounded scars left by fallen leaves can also be seen.

Calamites undulatus STERNBERG	Order: Equisetales Family: Calamitaceae

This species is known from Upper Carboniferous and Lower Permian strata in Europe and North America. Characteristically undulating grooves are to be seen on the surface of pith casts. This species, like the preceding one, is included in the subgenus *Stylocalamites,* which is characterized by an unbranched trunk.

Calamodendron sp.	Order: Equisetales Family: Calamitaceae

The internal structure of calamites trunks can best be seen in silicified and dolomitized material. Cross sections clearly show the characteristic features of calamites — a pith cavity of varying sizes in the centre, surrounded by a thick wood cylinder (the stele), segmented to systems of independent wedges, and the secondary cortex. The wood cylinder and the cortex are approximately the same thickness. As in arboraceous lycophytes, the cortex evidently had an important function in calamites as a stabilizer. The classification of different types of calamite trunks in 'genera' is based on the structure of their medullary (pith) rays. *Calamodendron* is a common type in European Upper Carboniferous and Permian deposits.

Asterophyllites equisetiformis
(SCHLOTHEIM) BRONGNIART

Order: Equisetales
Family: Calamitaceae

Calamite leaves are of two types. Those on the trunk and the thicker branches are long and linear; they often adhere to the axis, or are partly fused together to form a sheath, as in present-day horsetails. The main assimilating leaves were those on the thin branches, which diverged from the axis and adhered together only at their base. These leaves are simply linear, single-veined and fairly thick, and roughly rhomboid in cross section. As a rule, calamite branches with leaves are found separately; they are therefore given independent generic and specific names and their nomenclature does not depend on that of the trunks or the spore cones.

The genus *Asterophyllites* is known from Upper Carboniferous to Permian strata in Europe, Asia and North America. Fusion of their leaves at the base is almost indiscernible and the leaves project obliquely upwards, in all directions. In individual species there is a varyingly expressed tendency to the formation of plagiotropically oriented branches (i.e. in a single plane). The asterophyllite type is the geologically oldest form of foliage, although it also appears in Lower Permian representatives. The majority of species are known from the Westphalian age.

1

C

2

Annularia stellata (SCHLOTHEIM) WOOD

Order: Equisetales
Family: Calamitaceae

Equisetophytes belonging to the genus *Annularia* are found in Carboniferous and Permian sediments practically everywhere in the world. The commonest are those in Upper Carboniferous and Permian strata. They represent the most advanced type of foliage, in which not only the branches growing out from the nodes, but also the leaves in the whorls, are all oriented in the same plane. Some of the leaves in the whorl are often shorter, so as not to overshadow the others. The leaves are usually flatter and wider than in members of the genus *Asterophyllites,* although narrow-leaved types are also known. The leaves are fused together at their base.

Cones which grew either directly from the trunk or from side branches are often found together with branches classified as *Asterophyllites* and *Annularia,* although generally they are found separately. Whorls of sterile leaves alternate on them with whorls of sporangiophores. As a rule, the sporangiophores each contain four sporangia and their free ends often terminate in a shield. A whole series of types of cones, such as *Calamostachys* and *Palaeostachys,* etc, are differentiated, according to the detailed organization of the sporangiophores, the sterile leaves and other anatomical characters.

1. *Asterophyllites equisetiformis,* Upper Carboniferous (Westphalian), Kladno, Czechoslovakia. Part of a small branch with leaves, preserved in a coal bed. Length 140 mm. An evolutionarily more advanced type of the genus *Asterophyllites,* with long leaves.

2. *Annularia stellata,* Upper Carboniferous (Westphalian), Stradonice near Beroun, Czechoslovakia. Part of a leafed branch, length about 110 mm. One of the most widespread species, with long, narrow lanceolate leaves.

53

Rhyniophyta and Pteridophyta

Schizoneura paradoxa SCHIMPER

Order: Equisetales
Family: Schizoneuraceae

The tremendous abundance of equisetophytes during the Carboniferous and Lower Permian was gradually succeeded by a decline, which was particularly marked at the beginning of the Mesozoic era. Owing to the increasing dryness of the climate, arboraceous types of equisetophytes died out and their place was gradually taken by herbaceous types. The oldest finds of the herbaceous equisetophytes of the genus *Schizoneura* came from the temperate belt of Gondwanaland (the southern primary supercontinent comprising South America, Africa — except the northern parts — India, Australia, New Zealand and the Antarctic). These equisetophytes grew in inner Asia during the Lower Triassic and evidently invaded Europe in the Middle Triassic. Their thin stems grew to a height of roughly two metres and were usually richly branched. Their long leaves, which grew in whorls, were fused for their entire length, forming long sheaths which then split up into two or more parts along the course of the veins. The sporangia formed long cones at the end of small side branches (fig. 4).

4

Equisetites münsteri STERNBERG

Order: Equisetales
Family: Equisetaceae

The species of the genus *Equisetites* are characteristic equisetophytes of the Mesozoic Era, although they may also, perhaps, have grown in the late Palaeozoic. They attained maximum abundance and distribution in the Upper Triassic and Lower Jurassic periods and they included both herbaceous and arboraceous types with a height of up to 10 metres. The members of this genus grew mainly on sandy soil. Cross sections of the trunk show a large pith cavity and poorly developed secondary wood. The trunks had a smooth surface, but on the thin branches there were longitudinal ribs corresponding to bulging vascular bundles. Tuberiform structures considered to be storage organs (as in present-day horsetails) were present on the underground rhizomes, which did not have a pith cavity. The pointed, linear leaves were fused together in whorls and appressed very closely to the stems. Although severely reduced, they participated in assimilation, together with the stem. In this respect they differ from the last remaining genus, *Equisetum,* in which the assimilatory function has been taken over entirely by the stem, while the leaves, fused to form a sheath, protect the ends of the growing branches. The spore-bearing cones of equisetites were situated at the ends of the stems or on the side branches. The still extant genus *Equisetum* is evidently derived from *Equisetites,* but there is no reliably substantiated palaeontological evidence of its existence until the Tertiary.

1, 3. *Equisetites münsteri,** Upper Triassic (Rhaetian), Franken (Bavaria), West Germany. A sheath, 45 mm long, with fused leaves (3) and a pith cast measuring 225 mm (1).

2, 4. *Schizoneura paradoxa,** Upper Triassic (Rhaetian), France. The commonest and most thoroughly studied European species, whose spore cones have also been found. Length of rock sample (2) 135 mm. 4 — a reconstruction.

Noeggerathia foliosa STERNBERG

Order: Noeggerathiales
Family: Noeggerathiaceae

Noeggerathiophytes are a peculiar group of Permo-Carboniferous spore-bearing plants combining characteristics of lycophytes, equisetophytes and pteridophytes, whose origin is still obscure. The genus *Noeggerathia* is a typical representative of the whole group and its members occur in Carboniferous and Permian sediment in central and western Europe. They grew in the form of bushes or possibly of short trees. The branches grew round the thick trunk in a spiral and the leaves, which likewise grew round the branches in a spiral, stood out on either side in the same plane, so that the branches look like fern fronds (fig. 4). The leaves are ovally cuneiform to ovally lanceolate, with incised tips and dense, regularly forking veins. The leaves, which are microphyllous, i.e. from a single telome, are of the same origin as in equisetophytes. The reproductive organs (the cones) are reminiscent of lycophytes. The sporophylls are arranged in a spiral pattern, with the sporangia on the upper surface, and not on the under suface as in ferns. On the surface of the thick stems there are elongate transverse scars left by side axes which have dropped off.

1, 4. *Noeggerathia foliosa,** Upper Carboniferous (Westphalian), Lužná near Rakovník, Czechoslovakia. A side axis with leaves; length of leaves about 25 mm (1). The leaves are ovally cuneiform. Cones described separately under the name *Noeggerathiostrobus bohemicus* belong to this species. 4 – a reconstruction of a branch.

2. *Noeggerathiostrobus bohemicus,** Upper Carboniferous (Westphalian), Rakovník, Czechoslovakia. An incomplete cone, length 75 mm.

3. *Rhacopteris bipinnata,* Upper Carboniferous (Westphalian), Lubná near Rakovník, Czechoslovakia. A foliate branch, length about 80 mm, resembling the fronds of ferns in appearance.

3

Noeggerathiostrobus bohemicus
FEISTMANTEL

Order: Noeggerathiales
Family: Noeggerathiaceae

Noeggerathiophyte cones were about 15 cm long and cylindrical and are described under the name *Noeggerathiostrobus.* Sporangia with female or male spores grew in large numbers on veins on the upper surface of the sporophylls. The female sporophylls (megasporophylls), carrying megaspores, were concentrated at the base of the cones, while the male microsporophylls grew at their apex. Both types of spores are almost indistinguishable from calamite spores.

Rhacopteris bipinnata NĚMEJC

The artificial group
Sphenopterides

Leaves or leafy branches ('fronds') of the late Palaeozoic cosmopolitan genus *Rhacopteris* are usually classified among Neoggerathiophyta. In Europe they are particularly common in Upper Carboniferous strata of Westphalian age. The 'fronds' are uni- or bi-imparipinnate, with distinctly asymmetrical cuneiform leaflets, whose tips are split up into narrow points. The venation is dense and fan-like, with forking veins. Since it is not known for certain what the reproductive organs of these plants looked like, they have been placed in an artificial system of leaves with a fern-like appearance. However, there are finds indicating that they had cones similar to those of noeggerathiophytes.

4

Pseudosporochnus verticillatus
(Krejčí) Obrhel

Order: Pseudosporochnales
Family: Pseudosporochnaceae

In addition to the above plants, ferns (Polypodiophyta) abounded in the Devonian period. Ferns have non-segmented and often severely reduced stems without secondary wood, and as a rule with large uni- or multi-pinnate leaves, which in young plants are coiled with the dorsal surface facing outwards. In some species, the sporangia, which are generally distributed over the under side, contain spores of the same size and in other species spores of different shapes and sizes. Ferns are evidently descended from rhyniophytes. They are an evolutionally very plastic group, with many ups and downs in their geological history, and are still very well represented today.

The climate of Devonian Europe was strongly influenced by various branches of the equatorial current. In the Lower and Middle Devonian the flora evidently formed a continuous cover mainly in the coastal zones and that is why we often find the fossilized remains of terrestrial plants in shallow-water marine sediments and also in continental deposits of marshy origin in present-day Europe, Asia and North America. Species of the genus *Pseudosporochnus* (which probably belongs to the ferns) (fig. 4) grew beside the sea in the Middle and at the beginning of the late Devonian. They were not very much like ferns in appearance, however, and so some palaeobotanists ranked them among the rhyniophytes. These odd-looking plants had a stem a few dozen centimetres tall, from which the successively branching branches of the crown rose steeply into the air. The leaves did not develop and assimilation took place through the surface of the branches. Classification of these plants among the ferns is based on the distribution of the branches and the type of ramification.

Protopteridium hostinense Krejčí

Order: Protopteridiales
Family: Protopteridiaceae

Protopteridium species, which are very widespread in Middle Devonian sediments, look much more like ferns, but even so, palaeobotanists do not agree over their classification. Some consider that they belong to the very similar genus *Rellimia,* whose stele, in an anatomical study, was found to contain secondary wood, and rank them among the precursors of the gymnosperms ('Progymnospermopsida'). Protopterids were bushes or small trees. The side branches, which arose from the main branches in the same plane, continued to branch dichotomically or dichopodially (unequally). Very occasionally, small terminal branches with spirally coiled leaflets or a few fusiform sporangia are found. Coiling of the tips of the branches is one of the pieces of evidence indicating that protopterids belong to the oldest pteridophytes.

4

1, 2. *Protopteridium hostinense,** Middle Devonian (Givetian), Srbsko, Czechoslovakia. Impression of branches in sandy shale; lengths 90 mm (1) and 180 mm (2). Sterile forking branches described under this name are very abundant in places and evidently belong to more than one type of plant.

3, 4. *Pseudosporochnus verticillatus,** Middle Devonian (Givetian), Srbsko, Czechoslovakia. A carbonized part of a plant, length 310 mm (3). 4 — a reconstruction.

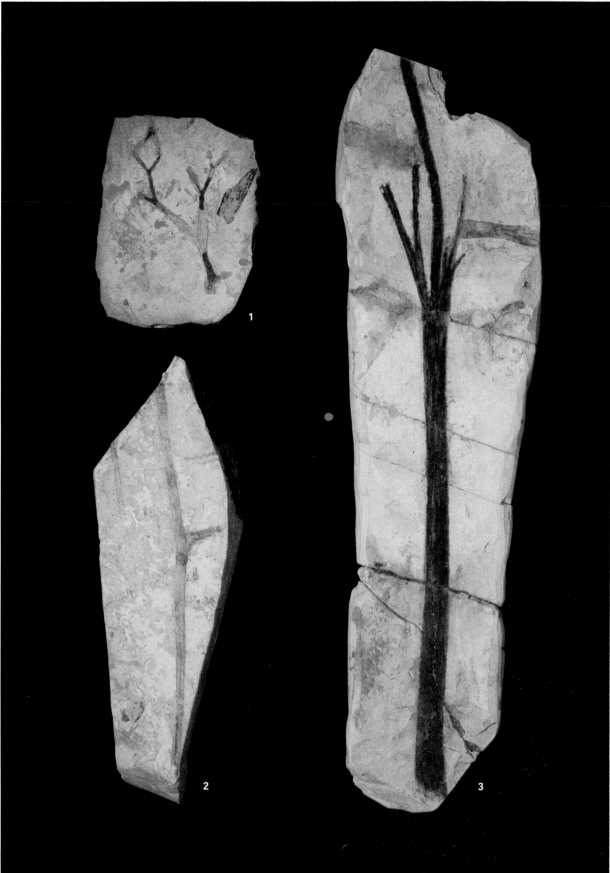

Corynepteris angustissima
(STERNBERG) NĚMEJC

Order: Zygopteridales
Family: Zygopteridaceae

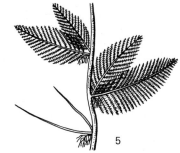

5

Ferns are an important component of the late Palaeozoic flora, although they are not so abundant as would appear at first glance. Seed-bearing ferns (pteridosperms), which attained their peak in the late Palaeozoic era, were very much like them in appearance and have often been mistaken for them. During the Carboniferous ferns achieved tremendous variety and included herbaceous, arboraceous, prostrate, climbing and liana types.

Zygopterid ferns have 'phyllophores', intermediate structures between a stem and a petiole. *Corynepteris* is one of the characteristic representatives of the order and is abundant in Upper Carboniferous sediments of the Euro-American province. It evidently had prostrate stems and very long phyllophores. Alternating pairs of fronds, oriented in the same plane, grew from the sides of the undulating main axis (fig. 5). Small, asymmetrical leaflets, fused on the under side, were attached to their side branches.

Desmopteris longifolia
(PRESL IN STERNBERG) STUR

Order: Zygopteridales
Family: Zygopteridaceae

The genus *Desmopteris* comprises a small number of species known from European Upper Carboniferous deposits. The petioles carry wide, band-like leaflets projecting obliquely or almost at right angles sideways; the leaflets are attached to the rachis by the full width of their base.

Kidstonia heracleensis ZEILLER

Order: Osmundales
Family: Kidstoniaceae

Representatives of modern ferns, whose descendants are still widely distributed everywhere, are known from the Carboniferous. They did not

1, 6. *Desmopteris longifolia*, Upper Carboniferous (Westphalian), Nýřany, Czechoslovakia. Part of a frond with long, ribbon-like leaves measuring about 80 mm (1). 6 – a part of a leaflet.

2. *Kidstonia heracleensis*, Upper Carboniferous (Westphalian), Žebrák, Czechoslovakia. Part of a frond preserved in tuffite sandstone measuring 45 × 45 mm.

3. *Corynepteris angustissima*, Upper Carboniferous (Westphalian), Radnice, Czechoslovakia. Fragment of a frond with strikingly incised leaves. Size of rock specimen 70 × 70 mm.

4. *Zeilleria haidingeri*, Upper Carboniferous (Westphalian), Stradonice, Czechoslovakia. Fragment of a sterile frond 90 mm wide.

5. 'Phyllophores' of zygopterid ferns.

1

C

form phyllophores and they have a more complex anatomy. The construction of their vascular bundles shows a clear tendency to move away from protostely (a wood cylinder surrounded by bast) towards polystely (a system of apparently independent vascular bundles). The Upper Carboniferous genus *Kidstonia*, a representative of aphyllophorate ferns, is known from Europe and Asia Minor. It has multi-imparipinnate fronds; the small leaflets are divided into segments.

6

Order: Polypodiales
Family: undetermined

Zeilleria haidingeri Ettingshausen

The genus *Zeilleria*, a widespread genus in Carboniferous strata in Europe, comprises ferns whose sterile leaves have variously incised leaflets and are attached to the axes by a narrow base (the sphenopterid type) or a wide base (the pecopterid type). Spherical synangia (fused sporangia) lie on the fertile leaves in a continuation of the veins at the end of the leaf segments.

Rhyniophyta and Pteridophyta

Psaronius sp.
Psaronius bibractensis RENAULT

Order: Marattiales
Family: Psaroniaceae

Like equisetophytes and lycophytes, ferns were also represented by arboraceous types in the late Palaeozoic era, but in Europe they flourished somewhat later than the other two groups, i. e. with incipient aridity of the climate in the Uppermost Carboniferous and Lower Permian. The best known arboraceous types of Palaeozoic ferns, *Psaronius* species, belong to the order Marattiales, which today is still represented, in the tropical and subtropical belts, by several genera. These plants are characterized by a number of special anatomical features. On the one hand, their vascular bundles evolved progressively away from a protostelic structure towards a polystelic structure, but on the other hand we evaluate as conservative the formation of sporangia from a group of cells and not from a single cell, as in evolutionally progressive types of ferns.

Psaronius species grew during the late Palaeozoic era over the whole of the northern hemisphere and were particularly abundant in western and central Europe. Their geologically most recent representatives are known from the Lower Triassic. They grew to a height of about 10 metres and their long trunk was surmounted by a crown composed of large multi-pinnate leaves. The internal structure of the trunk is very characteristic. The ground parenchymatous tissue contained vascular bundles, which in cross sections of the trunk had a horseshoe or variously curved appearance and fitted into one another cornet-wise. The trunk was enveloped in a huge mantle of aerial roots many times thicker than the trunk itself. The inner part of this mantle lay in the

1, 3. *Psaronius* sp., Upper Carboniferous (Westphalian), Radnice, Czechoslovakia. 1 — a carbonized part of a trunk, diameter 110 mm. Psaronius trunks are often found in the original biological position. 3 — a reconstruction.

C

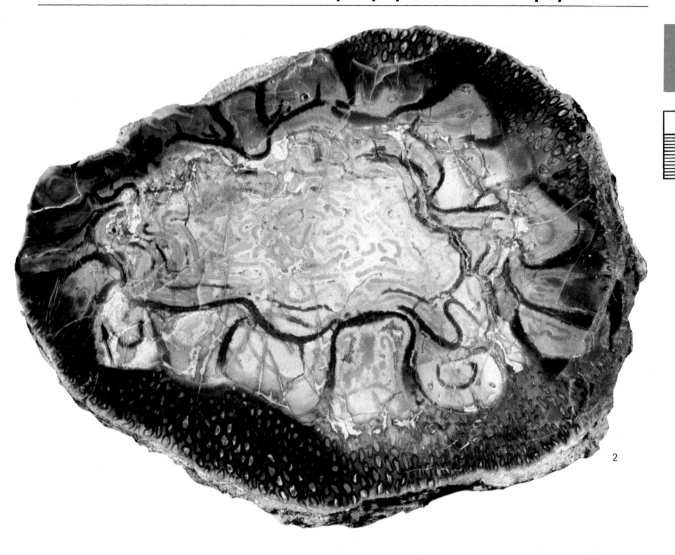

2

2. *Psaronius bibractensis,* Upper Carboniferous (Stephanian), Nová Paka, Czechoslovakia. A polished cross section of a trunk, diameter 150 mm.

parenchyma, while the outer part consisted of free aerial roots forming a dense covering. Since the main root was weak, the aerial root envelope helped both to increase the general stability and strength of the trunk and to keep the plant supplied with nourishment.

Psaronius trunks are often found in a silicified or dolomitized state. Under favourable fossilization conditions the various tissues, one by one, were saturated and replaced by silica or calcium carbonate, with the result that details of anatomical structure are generally preserved. Particularly clearly discernible in polished sections are the bands corresponding to the vascular bundles and the circular and elliptical cross sections of the inner part of the aerial root envelope. The free roots have generally been secondarily snapped off. If the trunk has been stripped of the aerial roots, oval scars left by lost fronds can be seen on its surface. As with other plants of tree-like proportions, trunks are found separately from the other organs. A knowledge of the internal structure of the trunks is not an adequate basis for the elaboration of a natural system. Consequently, the name *Psaronius* is largely a cumulative term for all ferns with the above anatomical structure and it no doubt actually covers a whole series of genera. The same applies to the sterile fronds, to which we shall pay special attention.

Pecopteris arborescens
(SCHLOTHEIM) BRONGNIART

Order: Marattiales
Family: Psaroniaceae

Sterile leaves like fern leaves are very common fossil plant finds. Given types of leaves have a limited stratigraphic range, but before they could be used in geological practice appropriate criteria for their classification had to be found. The first artificial system for leaves with a pteridiform (fern-like) appearance was elaborated by the French palaeontologist Brongniart in 1822. This, later improved, classification is based on the contours of the leaflets (pinnules), the character of their venation and the way in which they are attached to the rachis (stem). Such taxons are far from forming a natural biological system, since they group together, under a single generic name, species which are hardly related to one another. Unfortunately, there is no other possible way of working with this material.

Psaroniaceae comprise large, multi-imparipinnate fronds. The pinnules are either free, or are partly fused along the sides, and have a straight or undulating margin and a rounded tip. They are attached to the rachis by a wide base. Their main vein is imparipinnate. Among pteridiform plants, pinnules of this type are known as pecopterid (fig. 5). The fronds of sterile leaves go under the generic name *Pecopteris.*

Asterotheca aspidioides
PRESL IN STERNBERG

Order: Marattiales
Family: Psaroniaceae

In addition to sterile leaves, in a number of pecopterid ferns we also know leaves with sporangia and are able to compare these finds. Such finds are classified in separate natural genera. Fronds with different types of sporangia are included in the family Psaroniaceae. Ferns belonging to the genus *Asterotheca* are known from the late Palaeozoic and the Triassic. They have rounded sori with free sporangia. Some of the members of this genus are stratigraphically important.

Acitheca polymorpha BRONGNIART

Order: Marattiales
Family: Psaroniaceae

Fronds described under the name *Acitheca* likewise belong to Psaroniaceae. They are known from late Palaeozoic sediments in Europe and the Caucasus. Pecopterid pinnules have divided lateral veins. The elongate sporangia are fused at the base.

Dactylotheca plumosa ARTIS

Order: Polypodiales
Family: uncertain

Some of the representatives of the extremely plastic order Polypodiales had pecopterid pinnules and tree-like proportions. The members of the genus *Dactylotheca,* which was very widespread in Carboniferous and Permian Europe, has multi-imparipinnate fronds with large paired leaf-like structures (aphlebiae) at their base, whose function it was to protect the young fronds. The large sporangia are attached singly to secondary veins.

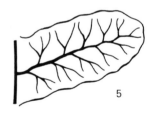

1. *Asterotheca aspidioides,* Upper Carboniferous (Westphalian), Rakovník, Czechoslovakia. A carbonized part of a frond, size of sample about 110 × 75 mm.

2. *Dactylotheca plumosa,** Upper Carboniferous (Westphalian), Rakovník, Czechoslovakia. Part of a frond, length 80 mm.

3. *Acitheca polymorpha,** Upper Carboniferous (Stephanian), Slaný, Czechoslovakia. Part of a frond in pellocarbonate, size of sample 120 × 60 mm.

4. *Pecopteris arborescens,* Upper Carboniferous (Stephanian), Slaný, Czechoslovakia. End of a frond, length 80 mm.

5. A pecopterid pinnule.

Gymnospermae

Alethopteris decurrens ARTIS

In the artificial fern leaf system there is a whole series of groups comprising 'genera' with a characteristic type of frond and foliage. As new fossil flora finds come to light, their true systematic position is gradually being elucidated. For instance, today it is clear that the leaves known under the generic name *Alethopteris* all belong to seed ferns. They are found particularly frequently in Upper Carboniferous and Lower Permian strata in Europe and North America. Their fronds are multi-pinnate, while the leaflets are attached by a broad base at which they are usually joined together by a wide border. The venation is pinnate, with alternating simple and forking lateral veins leading from the conspicuous main vein.

3

Neuropteris heterophylla BRONGNIART

Neuropteris type leaves occur in Lower Carboniferous to Lower Permian deposits, chiefly in the northern hemisphere. They belong to seed ferns with large, forking fronds with aphlebiae at the base of their common rachis. The leaflets are relatively large, rounded to lingulate, rounded at their lower end and attached by a greatly narrowed base or a short petiole; they are pinnately veined (fig. 5).

1. *Neuropteris heterophylla,** Upper Carboniferous (Westphalian). Radnice, Czechoslovakia. End of a frond 90 mm long, with striking progressive differentiation of the leaves. Seeds found on the fronds of this species were one of the first tangible proofs warranting the separation of seed ferns from true ferns.

2. *Alethopteris decurrens,* Upper Carboniferous (Westphalian), Eschweiler near Aachen, West Germany. Part of a frond, length 80 mm.

3. *Callipteridium trigonum,* Upper Carboniferous (Stephanian), Ledce near Plzeň, Czechoslovakia. Part of a frond, length 90 mm. The venation of the leaves is clearly discernible.

4. *Callipteris conferta,** Lower Permian (Autunian), France. Part of a frond, length about 150 mm. An index species with pecopterid leaves, occurring over the whole of the northern hemisphere. Stratigraphically important, characteristic of the Autunian age.

Callipteridium trigonum FRANKE

The artificial group
Callipterides

The seed ferns included in the genus *Callipteridium* are characteristic of the uppermost Upper Carboniferous (Stephanian) in the northern hemisphere. They have a strikingly zigzag rachis, with alternating bi-imparipinnate side fronds leading from the angles. The frequent presence of small side fronds on the main rachis is an interesting character. The leaflets are of the pecopterid type and are pinnately veined.

Callipteris conferta STERNBERG

The artificial group
Callipterides

Seed ferns classified as *Callipteris* are also known from Upper Carboniferous and Permian deposits in the southern hemisphere. They had large pinnate and dichotomically branching fronds and pinnately veined pecopterid leaflets. Foliage of the rachis — on which small leaflets sometimes also developed — is a striking feature.

 # Gymnospermae

Dicranophyllum sp.

Order: Dicranophyllales
Family: Dicranophyllaceae

Remarkable seed-bearing plant remains known as dicranophyllous, after *Dicranophyllum,* the most widespread genus with the largest number of species, in the group Dicranophyllophyta, come from Upper Carboniferous and Lower Permian strata (i.e. at the end of the Palaeophytic) in Europe, North America and Asia. Dicranophylls proper were bushes — and possibly trees — with widely spaced branches which had leaves either along their entire length or only at their tips. The leaves are long and narrow; they may fork several times, may be split into just two segments or may be undivided. The shape of the leaflets varies with their age, as well as with the species. In the typical species of the genus, *Dicranophyllum gallicum,* it was demonstrated that young leaflets were undivided, while older ones branched twice in succession. Their venation, which is simple and takes the form of parallel veins, is generally indistinct. During phylogenesis dicranophyll leaves underwent simplification to a narrow linear type. The arrangement of the leaves on the branches in a spiral gave dicranophylls the appearance of conifers. The leaves grew on leaf bolsters. The reproductive organs of some dicranophyll species are also known. The simple ovoid male cones grew in the leaf axils, while the female organs looked like branched shoots, or else the ovules were concentrated on the under side of the leaves, at their base. Dicranophylls evidently evolved from seed ferns. Some experts consider them to be the initial group from which conifers were derived.

Dicranophyllum domini NĚMEJC

Order: Dicranophyllales
Family: Dicranophyllaceae

Nothing is known about the internal structure of dicranophylls. All that is certain is that they were woody plants (relatively thick branches have been found) and branch imprints indicate that the pith was strongly developed. The elongate-rhomboid leaf bolsters on the surface of small branches, which are reminiscent of the leaf bolsters of some lycophytes, e. g. lepidodendra, are a remarkable feature. When a leaf dropped off, it left a tiny trace in the upper part of the leaf bolster, with an imprint of the vascular bundle.

1. *Dicranophyllum* sp., Upper Carboniferous (Westphalian), Lubná near Rakovník, Czechoslovakia. Very long, double-forked leaves preserved in tuffaceous sandstone; length of specimen about 240 mm.

2. *Dicranophyllum* sp., Upper Carboniferous (Westphalian), Kladno, Czechoslovakia. An imprint of a small leafy branch 80 mm long.

3. *Dicranophyllum domini,* Upper Carboniferous (Westphalian), Lubná near Rakovník, Czechoslovakia. A carbonized part of a small branch 130 mm long, clearly showing the leaf bolsters.

Gymnospermae

Cordaites borassifolius
(STERNBERG) UNGER

Order: Cordaitales
Family: Cordaitaceae

Cordaites (Cordaitophyta) were late Palaeozoic seed-bearing plants of tree-like proportions with a fairly uniform appearance. They flourished mainly in regions with a temperate climate like the one then prevailing in what is now Siberia and on the southern supercontinent (Gondwanaland), but they were also fairly common in the tropical belt, in which most of Europe and North America lay. Cordaites are named after A. Corda, a prominent nineteenth-century Czech naturalist. Their straight trunk was 10 metres tall or even taller and they had a spreading crown. A strongly developed system of roots which grew sideways rather than downwards kept them firmly anchored in the soft ground. Cordaite leaves were simple and needle-like, band-like, elongate-lanceolate or elliptical, with parallel venation (i.e. they had no central vein), and at a superficial glance they look like the leaves of monocotyledonous plants. The unisexual cones grew in the leaf axils.

The members of the genus *Cordaites* — the typical representatives of the group — were characterized by cosmopolitan distribution during the Carboniferous and the Permian. The leaves, which were deciduous in the temperate belt, were firm and the probabilities of their being preserved were good. They are very varied and since many types are stratigraphically important the experts created a provisional artificial system of cordaite leaves. One of the ways in which true kinship can be determined is to study the cuticle of the leaves (the thin elastic cutin membrane on their surface), which shows the shape of the surface cells and the distribution of the stomata, etc.

1. *Cordaites borassifolius,** Upper Carboniferous (Westphalian), Stradonice, Czechoslovakia. Leaf fragments in coal shale; length of sample 290 mm. The fern leaflet near the margin of the rock belongs to the species *Eurhacopteris elegans*.

2. *Cordaianthus sp.*, Upper Carboniferous (Westphalian), Kotíkov, Czechoslovakia. Top of a cone 80 mm long and the base of a cordaite leaf.

3. *Cordaicarpus sp.*, Upper Carboniferous (Westphalian), Stradonice, Czechoslovakia. A carbonized seed like a round nut; length about 15 mm.

4. *Artisia* sp., Upper Carboniferous (Westphalian), Stradonice, Czechoslovakia. Core of a septate pith cavity, length 90 mm.

5. A reconstruction of a member of the genus *Cordaites*.

C

Cordaianthus sp.

Order: Cordaitales
Family: Cordaitaceae

The generic name *Cordaianthus* is the term applied to cordaite cones which have a straight main rachis with supporting scales in two rows or in a spiral. Small strobili carrying sporophylls with either ovules or anthers grew in the axils.

Cordaicarpus sp.

Order: Cordaitales
Family: Cordaitaceae

Cordaicarpus is one of the many names given to cordaite seeds, which are circular or heart-shaped and are markedly flattened in cross section. The embryos probably did not develop until the seeds had fallen from the mother plant.

Artisia sp.

Order: Cordaitales
Family: Cordaitaceae

The secondary wood of cordaite trunks was strongly developed and the cortex was suppressed. Such trunks are often indistinguishable from conifer trunks and the two together are known as araucarites. Cordaites are characterized by septation of the pith, which is clearly discernible in the pith cavity cores known as *Artisia*.

 **Gymnospermae**

Ginkgo adiantoides (UNGER) HEER

Order: Ginkgoales
Family: Ginkgoaceae

Ginkgopsida finds date back to the early Permian. These plants abounded during the Mesozoic era in the temperate belt of the northern hemisphere, but today there is only one species still extant, which grows in south-eastern China. Ginkgopsida are ligneous plants with secondary xylem; they grow to tree-like proportions and have a richly branching crown. In evolutionarily older types the leaves were sessile, deeply dissected, and had parallel veins, while in later types they were petiolate and flat, with fan-like venation. Little is known about the reproductive organs of fossil species. In the genus *Ginkgo*, the male sporophylls are clustered together in catkins, while the ovules generally grow in pairs on modified petiolate leaves. In general, we can say that the members of this evolutionarily conservative group formed resting embryos, which did not begin to develop until the seeds had left the mother plant.

Plants allied to the genus *Ginkgo* can already be found in Upper Triassic sediments all over the world. It is remarkable that they also appeared in very high latitudes, such as Franz Josef Land, Greenland and Patagonia. During the roughly 150 million years of their existence, ginkgos have not undergone any fundamental changes and their last remaining representative, *G. biloba,* is a popular example of a 'living fossil'. The commonest ginkgo finds are the leaves, which are extremely variable, but in their typical form are broadly cuneiform, with a lobate tip and a long petiole. Stratigraphically they are of little value.

1. *Sphenobaiera digitata,* Upper Permian, Mansfeld, West Germany. An impression of a leaf; size of the sample 160 × 70 mm. The oldest ginkgoopsids had deeply dissected leaves.

2. *Ginkgo adiantoides* (on the left a leaf of the beech *Fagus pliocenica*), Neogene, (Middle Pliocene), Spišské Podhradie, Czechoslovakia. Length of leaf 80 mm. Without a detailed study the leaves of this unusually wide-spread Mesozoic species are indistinguishable from the leaves of the recent *G. biloba* (3). It occurs in Pliocene travertins in Slovakia and is one of the latest fossil ginkgo finds in Europe.

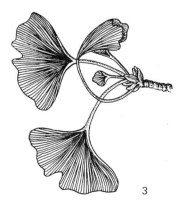

Order: Ginkgoales
Sphenobaiera digitata (Brongniart) Florin   Famil : Sphenobaieraceae

The genus *Sphenobaiera* is a cosmopolitan representative of the evolutionally oldest ginkgoopsids, with a stratigraphic range from the Lower Permian to the Upper Cretaceous. The leaves, which grew on short side branches (brachyblasts), are split up into linear leaf segments with parallel venation, arranged in a fan-like formation. During the evolution of ginkgoopsids the leaf blades display a marked tendency towards union to the form encountered in the genus *Ginkgo*.

75

Gymnospermae

Cycadeoidea sp.

Order: Cycadeoideales
Family: Cycadeoideaceae

In the Mesozoic era, as in the late Palaeozoic, a large portion of Europe lay in the tropical belt. Increasing rainfall transformed the arid climate of the beginning of the Triassic to a humid one. The European flora has many features in common with the flora of southern and south-eastern Asia and together they form a basis for delineation of the Indo-European palaeophytogeographical province. Among the gymnosperms, cycadophytes (Cycadophyta) grew in abundance alongside conifers and ginkgopsids. They already appeared in the Upper Carboniferous and later they split up into two independent evolutionary branches – cycads proper (Cycadopsida) and bennettites (Cycadeoideopsida). True cycads still survive in the tropical and subtropical belts, but the palaeontologically more important and more specialized bennettites, known with certainty from the Triassic, died out at the end of the Cretaceous.

Bennettites are ligneous plants up to 3 metres tall. The trunks are often stumpy, cylindrical, barrel-shaped or spherical, with few or no branches, and they terminate in a tuft of large leaves resembling fern or palm fronds. Internally, the trunks are monostelic, with a large amount of pith, and the secondary wood forms several concentric tubes. The thin cortex has several persisting petioles on its surface. The reproductive organs bear a strong resemblance to the flowers of angiosperms; this caused some palaeobotanists to speculate whether evolutionary associations existed between the two groups of plants. The uni- or bisexual cones, which are distributed evenly over the whole of the stem, have very short

1. *Pterophyllum jaegeri,* Upper Triassic, Lunz am See (Austria). Part of a leaf with leaflets not more than 60 mm long.

2. *Zamites suprajurensis,* Upper Jurassic (Tithonian), Salzhemmendorf, Hanover, West Germany. Part of a leaf with leaflets about 50 mm long.

3, 4. *Cycadeoidea* sp., Upper Cretaceous (Cenomanian), Slaný, Czechoslovakia. 3 — a fragment of a silicified stem, 90 mm long, with clearly discernible 'flower' receptacles. 4 — a reconstruction.

receptacles surrounded by bracts. The male sporophylls lie round the base of the receptacle, the female sporophylls closer to the centre of the 'flower'. The free ovoid seeds protected by interseminal scales are up to 10 mm long.

The members of the genus *Cycadeoidea* (= *Bennettites*) are typical representatives of this group. In the Upper Jurassic and the Cretaceous they abounded in the northern hemisphere. They have thick stems like pineapples in appearance. The large, tough leaves are simply imparipinnate (fig. 4).

Pterophyllum jaegeri BRONGNIART

Order: Cycadeoidales
Family: uncertain

Bennettite leaves, which are found more often than other parts, are classified in an artificial system. The leaves known under the generic name *Pterophyllum* occur in sediments of Triassic to Cretaceous age; they are particularly common in Upper Triassic sediments in Europe and North America. They are simply imparipinnate and the short, linear leaflets, which have parallel veins, are sessile over their entire width.

Zamites suprajurensis RÖMER

Order: Cycadeoidales
Family: uncertain

The distribution and stratigraphic range of *Zamites* leaves are similar to those of *Pterophyllum,* but the leaves themselves are long and oval (tapering towards the petiole and the apex).

Gymnospermae

Lebachia hypnoides (Brongniart) Florin

Order: Lebachiales
Family: Lebachiaceae

Conifers (Pinophyta) are the most diverse and evolutionally the most advanced group of gymnosperms. Representatives of these plants, whose anatomical structure is hardly any different from that of Recent forms, are known from the Upper Carboniferous. In progressive aridity of the climate during the Permian and the Lower Triassic, conifers (together with other groups of gymnosperms) were better able to cope with the altered situation than pteridophytes, whose reproductive cycle was far more dependent on a wet environment. In consequence, conifers expanded tremendously during the Mesozoic era and it was not until the Upper Cretaceous, when angiosperms suddenly began to colonize the dry land, that they receded into the background.

Conifers are richly branching ligneous plants (mostly trees), as a rule with single-veined sessile or shortly petiolate leaves which, in the majority of cases, are not shed. The cones are differentiated to male and female. The pollen grains usually have characteristic air sacs, which make it easier for the wind to spread them.

The genus *Lebachia* comprises some of the evolutionally earliest types of conifers characteristic of the Upper Carboniferous and Lower Permian in Europe and North America. They were tall trees with strongly developed secondary wood; their branches were arranged in whorls, in each of which they spread out in the same plane (fig. 3). The branches were thickly overgrown with needle-like leaves, which often had forked and upturned tips. The small male cones were composed of male sporophylls growing round the rachis in a spiral; the rachis of female cones (megastrobili) was overgrown with supporting scales arranged in a spiral, with fertile twigs bearing sterile scales and female sporophylls growing in their axils.

Dadoxylon sp.

Among the commonest conifer finds are foliaged branches, cones and parts of trunks, which are often silicified. Identification of the trunk parts is frequently impossible. The nature of the tracheids is important for taxonomy, but in many cases not even this trait allows an unequivocal conclusion as to whether the given fragment belongs to a conifer or a cordaite. Many Carboniferous and Permian trunks undoubtedly belong to *Lebachia* species, which are characterized by strong development of the pith. The general structure of these trees corresponds to the character of the wood of recent araucarias and in common practice finds of this type are therefore usually referred to as araucarites. *Dadoxylon* is the name given to the wood of representatives of both groups of gymnosperms, i.e. conifers and cordaites.

3

1, 3. *Lebachia hypnoides,* Lower Permian, Lodève, France. A carbonized twig 90 mm long (1). *Lebachia* is better known under the name of *Walchia,* but this is today generally applied only to sterile twigs. 3 – a reconstruction.

2. *Dadoxylon* sp., Lower Permian (Autunian), Studenec near Nová Paka, Czechoslovakia. A cross section of a silicified trunk, diameter 140 mm.

HAMDEN PUBLIC LIBRARY
Miller Memorial Library
10/21/11 01:06PM
CURRENT CHECKOUTS

Patron name: Wolf, Frank

Prehistoric life /
31200007312761 Due: 11/18/11

Fossils of the world : a comprehensive p
31200003309696 Due: 11/18/11

TOTAL: 2

www.libraryelf.org

Gymnospermae

Cunninghamites elegans
(CORDA) ENDLICHER

Order: Cupressales
Family: Taxodiaceae

One of the most abundant groups of conifers in the Cretaceous period were Taxodiaceae, which still have representatives in south-eastern Asia and North America. They are bushes or trees and they also include the tallest trees in existence, sequoias, which in California attain a height of up to 100 metres.

The conifers of the European Cretaceous genus *Cunninghamites* were about 20 metres tall. In appearance they resembled the members of the present-day genus *Cunninghamia,* which grows in China and on Taiwan. The leaves were long and linear and the scales on the cylindrical cones terminated in a square shield with a spiny outgrowth in the centre.

Geinitzia cretacea UNGER

Order: Cupressales
Family: Taxodiaceae

The genus *Geinitzia* occurs in Cretaceous deposits in Europe and North America. It has been described from the female cones, which are ovoid or short and cylindrical and whose scales terminate in four- to six-sided shields. The leaves are short and needle-like.

Glyptostrobus europaeus
(BRONGNIART) UNGER

Order: Cupressales
Family: Taxodiaceae

In the Cainozoic era the greater part of Europe (excluding the north) lay in the warm temperate to subtropical belt. The climate was not stable; the

1. *Cunninghamites elegans,* Upper Cretaceous (Cenomanian), Peruc, Czechoslovakia. Part of a twig about 90 mm long. A species characteristic of the Upper Cretaceous.

2. *Geinitzia cretacea,* Upper Cretaceous (Senonian), Březno near Louny, Czechoslovakia. Claystone with an impression of a twig some 65 mm long. Geinitzias were formerly mistaken for sequoias, because of the shape of the cones.

3

4

3. *Pinus oviformis,* Neogene (Lower Miocene), Břešťany near Bílina, Czechoslovakia. An almost undeformed cone 80 mm long preserved in a ferrous concretion.

4. *Glyptostrobus europaeus,* Neogene (Lower Miocene), Břešťany near Bílina, Czechoslovakia. A twig with cones, length about 150 mm.

temperature fluctuated and displayed a general tendency to become cooler, with the result that elements of both the subtropical and the temperate zones are represented in the vegetation. Coal-forming swamps are typical of this era. The coal seams were formed not only from the local vegetation, but also — and very often on a decisive scale — from plant debris washed in by flood water.

Glyptostrobus, known from the Upper Cretaceous, was one of the most important coal-forming genera. During the Miocene it was distributed over most of the northern hemisphere; today it has a single surviving species in south-eastern China. Fossil species grew in swamps in assemblages comprising tupelos, alders, willows and maples, etc.

Order: Pinales
Family: Pinaceae

Pinus oviformis ENDLICHER

Pines (*Pinus*) are likewise known from Miocene sediments and their evolution can be followed from the Upper Cretaceous over the whole of the northern hemisphere and partly in the tropical belt as well. In Oligocene and Miocene Europe they were represented by a wealth of species. Pleistocene cooling, which spelt doom for the majority of European exotics, evidently led in the case of pines to a marked decrease in the number of species.

81

'Magnolia' amplifolia HEER

Order: Magnoliales
Family: Magnoliaceae

The oldest angiosperms are known from Lower Cretaceous strata. These plants evolved at an extraordinary rate and within 25 to 30 million years they underwent unheard-of differentiation and conquered the entire Earth. The change in the structure of plant assemblages is so pronounced that the division between the Lower and Upper Cretaceous is also the division between the Mesophytic (the era of the gymnosperms) and the Cainophytic (the era of the angiosperms). The main feature of angiosperms is that the ovules are enclosed in a carpel (the fused female sporophylls). Maturation causes the ovules to develop into seeds enclosed in a fruit formed from the transformed walls of the carpel. The origin of angiosperms still remains to be elucidated.

Magnolias are one of the oldest angiosperm genera, with fossil finds from the end of the Cretaceous in both hemispheres. Recent magnolias grow chiefly in the tropical and subtropical parts of North and South America, in the Indo-Malaysian region, on the Philippines and in Oceania.

Aralia kowalewskiana SAPORTA AND MARION

Order: Araliales
Family: Araliaceae

Fossil aralias (*Aralia*) were distributed over the northern hemisphere from the Lower Cretaceous onwards. Today they grow in the tropical and subtropical parts of North America and Asia. They are closely related to ivy (*Hedera*). They comprise trees, bushes and herbaceous plants; many of them are climbers and some of them are thorny. The alternate leaves are entire, palmate, lobate or compound (imparipinnate).

Platanophyllum laeve
(VELENOVSKÝ) NĚMEJC

Order: Hamamelidales
Family: Platanaceae

Leaves from trees related to *Platanus* are known in the northern hemisphere from the Lower Cretaceous onwards. As a rule they are palmate-lobate, with large-toothed lobes and with a cuneiform blade at the junction with the petiole. Their venation is of the palmate type (fig. 6).

Credneria bohemica VELENOVSKÝ

Order: Hamamelidales
Family: Platanaceae

As a rule, the members of the genus *Credneria* are considered to be closely related to the plane-trees. They abound in Cretaceous sediments in the northern hemisphere. The leaves are characterized by a widened base (fig. 7).

Dewalquea coriacea VELENOVSKÝ

Order: Ranunculales
Family: Ranunculaceae (?)

Although very diversely represented in the Cretaceous flora, herbaceous plants had fewer chances of fossilization, as a rule, than woody plants. The genus *Dewalquaea* comprises primitive buttercup-like plants whose imprints are found in deposits in various parts of Europe and Asia; they

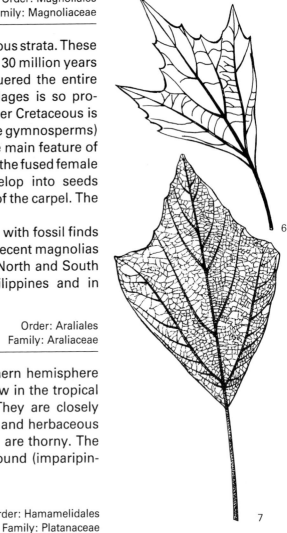

6

7

1. *Dewalquea coriacea*, Upper Cretaceous (Cenomanian), Vyšehořovice, Czechoslovakia. Claystone with the imprint of a leaf about 20 mm long.

2. *Aralia kowalewskiana*, Upper Cretaceous (Cenomanian), Vyšehořovice, Czechoslovakia. A palmate leaf with seven segments, total length about 120 mm.

3. *Platanophyllum laeve*, Upper Cretaceous (Cenomanian), Vyšehořovice, Czechoslovakia. An imprint of an incomplete leaf, length about 110 mm.

4. *'Magnolia' amplifolia*, Upper Cretaceous (Cenomanian), Vyšehořovice, Czechoslovakia. Imprint of a leaf, length 120 mm. In the Cainozoic era magnolias also grew in Europe.

82

5. *Credneria bohemica,* Upper Cretaceous, Vyšehořovice, Czechoslovakia. Impression of a leaf, length about 230 mm.

6, 7. Comparison of leaves of the genera *Platanophyllum* (6) and *Credneria* (7).

died out at the beginning of the Palaeogene. They are sometimes compared to the recent genus *Helleborus.* The compound leaf is composed of three to five lanceolate leaflets, which are imparipinnate with widely spaced teeth or entire and grow at the end of a long common petiole.

Cr

Angiospermae

Dryophyllum furcinerve
(ROSSMÄSSLER) SCHMALHAUSEN

Order: Fagales
Family: Fagaceae

Cainozoic angiosperms resemble present-day forms, but their species structure reflects the generally warmer climatic conditions in Europe in those days. The most objective picture is provided by palynological analyses, i.e. by the study of sporomorphs preserved thanks to their resistance.

Representatives of the genus *Dryophyllum,* which is closely related to the oak, grew in large numbers in the northern hemisphere at the end of the Cretaceous and during the Cainozoic.

Cercidiphyllum crenatum (UNGER) BROWN

Order: Cercidiphyllales
Family: Cercidiphyllaceae

Cercidiphyll finds date back to the Upper Cretaceous. In the Cainozoic era these trees grew chiefly in the temperate belt of the northern hemisphere; today they survive in Japan and China. They have ovate or heart-shaped leaves with palmate venation, with the main veins curving towards the tip. Beautifully preserved leaves are found in diatomites — sediments composed mainly of the siliceous shells of small unicellular algae (diatoms) which found especially favourable conditions in small lakes with an adequate silicic acid concentration (e.g. from volcanic products).

Platanus neptuni
(ETTINGSHAUSEN) BŮŽEK, HOLÝ AND KVAČEK

Order: Hamamelidales
Family: Platanaceae

Plane-trees (*Platanus*), which occur mainly in the northern hemisphere, are known from the Upper Cretaceous onwards. These handsome trees, noted for their flaking bark, generally have palmately lobed leaves. *Platanus neptuni* is an exception, since it has elliptical to lanceolate leaves with characteristic pinnate venation.

Acer tricuspidatum BRONN

Order: Sapidales
Family: Aceraceae

Maple (*Acer*) leaves are very common finds among Cainozoic plant fossils. Many of the European finds are closely related to North American, eastern Asian and Mediterranean types.

Comptonia acutiloba BRONGNIART

Order: Myricales
Family: Myricaceae

Comptonia species, which are very closely related to candleberry myrtles (*Myrica*), were common shrubs in Europe in the late Cainozoic era. Today they survive in the temperate belt of North America.

1. *Comptonia acutiloba,* Neogene (Lower Miocene), Břešťany near Bílina, Czechoslovakia. Claystone with the imprint of a leaf 80 mm long.

2. *Dryophyllum furcinerve,* Palaeogene (Upper Eocene), Žitenice near Litoměřice, Czechoslovakia. Length of leaf 60 mm. A characteristic subtropical plant with entire-margined, mainly leathery leaves ('dryophyllous flora').

3. *Acer tricuspidatum,* Neogene (Lower Miocene), Břešťany near Bílina, Czechoslovakia. Claystone with a leaf imprint 40 mm long.

4. *Cercidiphyllum crenatum,* Palaeogene (Upper Oligocene), Bechlejovice near Děčín, Czechoslovakia. Diatomite with a leaf 50 mm long. The diatomite is characteristically banded from the side. The light bands consist almost entirely of diatom shells, whereas the dark bands contain more organic matter and débris.

5. *Platanus neptuni,* Palaeogene (Middle Oligocene), Suletice near Ústí nad Labem, Czechoslovakia. Diatomite with a leaf imprint 70 mm long. A species indistinguishable from the recent *P. kerri,* discovered in Laos as late as the 1930s.

Angiospermae

Myrica hakeifolia UNGER

Order: Myricales
Family: Myricaceae

Candleberries (*Myrica*) were common plants in the damp-floored forests of Miocene Europe. The oldest finds of *Myrica* type leaves come from Lower Cretaceous sediments. In the Cainozoic era these aromatic bushes and trees grew in both the northern and the southern hemisphere and their recent representatives are to be found in the warm temperate to subtropical parts of Europe, North America, Africa and elsewhere; in the tropics they colonize mountainous regions. *Myrica* leaves are extremely diverse, both dentated and entire, with pinnate venation.

Nyssa haidingeri
(ETTINGSHAUSEN) KVAČEK AND BŮŽEK

Order: Cornales
Family: Nyssaceae

Nyssa species were an important element of Miocene coal-forming forests. The oldest indubitable fossil finds of these handsome trees are of Palaeogene age. Today they grow only in the eastern part of North America and in eastern and south-eastern Asia, on residual islands of what was once a coherent area. They grow to a height of 20 to 40 metres. The large, simple alternate leaves are often concentrated at the ends of the branches; they are either entire or have a few coarse teeth.

Alnus julianiformis
(STERNBERG) KVAČEK AND HOLÝ

Order: Betulales
Family: Betulaceae

Alder finds date back to the Palaeogene. Then, as now, alders were common trees growing mainly in the northern hemisphere. The leaves are ovate, ovate-lanceolate, or obovate with a serrate margin and pinnate venation.

Daphnogene polymorpha
(A. BRAUN) ETTINGSHAUSEN

Order: Laurales
Family: Lauraceae

Daphnogene is an extinct European Cainozoic genus similar to the cinnamon tree (*Cinnamomum*). The leaves were entire, wide or narrow, with strikingly lengthened side veins on their under side, stretching almost to the tip of the leaf. The other pinnate veins were short and leaves with this type of venation are therefore described as three-veined.

Laurophyllum pseudoprinceps
WEYLAND AND KILPPER

Order: Laurales
Family: Lauraceae

The earliest leaves known definitely to belong to types closely related to the bay-tree (*Laurus*) come from Palaeogene strata and in the Oligocene and Miocene these plants were richly represented. Their two still extant survivors grow in the Mediterranean countries and on the Canary Islands. The leaves are entire and widely lanceolate, with pinnate venation. Fossil leaves whose generic identity with recent bay-trees cannot be demonstrated exactly are termed *Laurophyllum*.

1. *Daphnogene polymorpha*, Neogene (Lower Miocene), Břešťany near Bílina, Czechoslovakia. Length of leaf about 50 mm. A wide-leafed type.

2. *Alnus julianiformis*, Neogene (Lower Miocene), Břešťany near Bílina, Czechoslovakia. Claystone with a leaf imprint 50 mm long.

3. *Myrica hakeifolia*, Neogene (Lower Miocene), Břešťany near Bílina, Czechoslovakia. Imprint of a leaf 70 mm long.

4. *Nyssa haidingeri*, Neogene (Lower Miocene), Břešťany near Bílina, Czechoslovakia. Length of leaf 130 mm.

5. *Laurophyllum pseudoprinceps*, Neogene (Lower Miocene), Břešťany near Bílina, Czechoslovakia. Impression of a leaf 90 mm long.

6. A branch of a present-day member of the genus *Nyssa*.

Angiospermae

Parrotia fagifolia (GOEPPERT) HEER

Order: Hamamelidales
Family: Hamamelidaceae

At the end of the Cainozoic era, during the Pliocene, further cooling occurred in Europe. The climatic changes are characterized well by the altering vegetation of central Europe. Thermophilic elements rapidly diminished and wooded steppes and steppes spread. Valuable information on the flora of this period is supplied by travertines formed round thermal springs and springs with a high calcium concentration. In addition to animal remains (chiefly gastropod shells), these highly porous rocks contain imprints of various parts of plants. Very often we find in them the imprints of plants from hilly country in the heart of mountains, where, as a rule, the conditions for fossilization are poor, with the result that little is known about these assemblages.

For instance, one of the plant genera known from Pliocene highlands in central Europe is *Parrotia.* These short woody plants appeared in Europe during the Oligocene. The leaves are obovate (i.e. wider at the tip than at the base), with shallow lobes in the upper part of the blade and with pinnate venation. The only species still extant grows in the north of Iran and in the region of the Caucasus.

1. *Parrotia fagifolia,* Neogene (Middle Pliocene), Spišské Podhradie (Dreveník), Czechoslovakia. A leaf imprint in travertin; length of leaf 55 mm.

2. *Fagus pliocenica,* Neogene (Middle Pliocene), Spišské Podhradie (Dreveník), Czechoslovakia. An impression of a leaf measuring 75 mm. This species is almost indistinguishable from the recent *F. orientalis.*

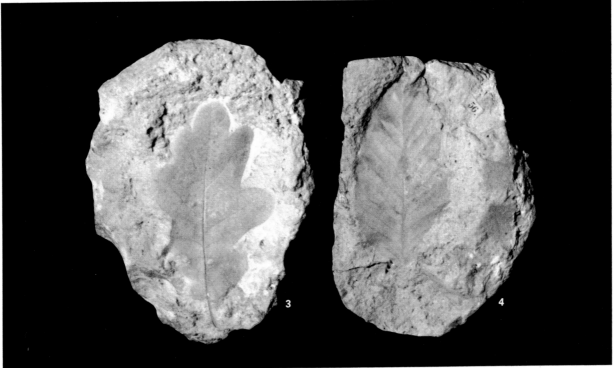

3. *Quercus roburoides,* Neogene (Middle Pliocene), Spišské Pod-hradie (Dreveník), Czechoslovakia. An impression of a leaf 90 mm long. Although oaks tolerate a harsh climate well, they were originally thermophilic.

4. *Carpinus grandis,* Neogene (Middle Pliocene), Spišské Pod-hradie (Dreveník), Czechoslovakia. An impression of a leaf 75 mm long.

Order: Fagales
Family: Fagaceae

Fagus pliocenica SAPORTA

The beech (*Fagus*) is a characteristic element of the Arctotertiary flora and is widespread in the cold and temperate belt of the northern hemisphere. It is already known in Upper Cretaceous sediments. In mixed deciduous woods it was evidently the most abundantly represented tree. The ovate leaves have an undulating or dentate margin and pinnate venation.

Order: Fagales
Family: Fagaceae

Quercus roburoides RÉROLLE

Oaks (*Quercus*) already grew in the Lower Cretaceous, chiefly in the northern hemisphere. It is a genus unwontedly rich in species, over 500 of which are known to be still extant. Oak leaves are morphologically likewise very diverse and alongside the characteristic blunt-lobed types we also find sharp-toothed to thorny and often fairly narrow types, whose identification generally requires a study of the cuticle.

Order: Betulales
Family: Betulaceae

Carpinus grandis UNGER

The hornbeam (*Carpinus*) has grown in Europe since the Palaeocene. It is widespread over the whole of the northern hemisphere, but its main region is eastern and south-eastern Asia. The reason for the present discontinuity of its incidence was severe cooling of the climate during the Quaternary glacials. The leaves are ovate to broadly lanceolate and often have a tapering tip; they have serrate margins and pinnate venation.

Rhizopoda

Nummulites cf. *irregularis* DESHAYES
Nummulites lucasanus DEFRANCE

Order: Nummulitida
Family: Nummulitidae

5

6

Foraminiferids are marine animals, the majority being benthic and only a few planktonic. Their locomotor organs − pseudopodia − are also used for catching diatoms (Bacillariophytes) and other micro-organisms. Foraminiferida are characterized by alternation of sexually and asexually reproducing generations. That means that one species forms two types of tests (dimorphism) or even three types (trimorphism). The tests generally differ only as regards their size and the size of the initial chamber (proloculus) and seldom as regards their shape. The sexual form (macrospherical, from its large proloculus) has a small test, while the form which reproduces asexually, by fission (microspherical, with a small proloculus), generally has a larger test.

The genus *Nummulites* inhabited warm Eurasian and Central American seas from the Palaeocene to the Oligocene. Their usually large (up to 120 mm in diameter) and lenticular or discoid tests are markedly involute, with a large number of whorls. In cross section, the numerous chambers are shaped like an inverted 'V'; they communicate by a system of canals. The porous walls of the whorls are secondarily reinforced and are further strengthened by transverse buttresses which protrude from the outer surface of the test as nipple-like protuberances. As a rule there is no aperture.

Assilina spira (DE ROISSY)

Order: Nummulitida
Family: Nummulitidae

Assilina species have the same geographical distribution as nummulites, but occurred only from the Middle Palaeocene to the Eocene. The

1. *Assilina spira*, Palaeogene (Eocene), Nice, France. Test diameter 8 mm. The test, sectioned in the equatorial plane, is hard to distinguish from *Nummulites* tests; it can be differentiated by its cross section and by the morphology of its inner surface.

2. *Nummulites* cf. *irregularis*, Palaeogene (Middle Eocene), Gebedye, Bulgaria. Diameter of the largest test 25 mm. Microspherical forms sectioned in the equatorial plane. *Nummulites* tests look like coins − hence their name (in Latin, *nummulus* means small coin).

3. *Nummulites lucasanus,* Palaeogene (Middle Eocene), Zakopane, Poland. Test diameter about 6 mm. Macrospherical forms, the majority in cross section. The Egyptian pyramids were built of similar nummulitic limestones.

4. *Actinocyclina furcata,* Palaeogene (Upper Eocene), La Vanade, France. Diameter of the largest test 12 mm.

5. Cross and longitudinal section through a *Nummulites* shell.

6. An *Actinocyclina* shell in cross section.

test is partly evolute, with fewer whorls, radial septa and a central depression on its surface.

Actinocyclina furcata Sella

Order: Orbitoidida
Family: Discocyclinidae

All orbitoid foraminiferids have a discoid test composed of a layer of large equatorial chambers, with many layers of small chambers on either side (fig. 6). A few strikingly large chambers — the embryonal apparatus — form the initial stage of the test in the middle of the equatorial layer.

The cosmopolitan Eocene genus *Actinocyclina* has a thinly lenticular test with a warty surface and a raised centre. Radial ribs arising from extra chambers in the lateral layers run from the centre to the margin of the test. The larger of the two spherical initial chambers completely encompasses the smaller one.

93

 **Porifera**

Astylospongia praemorsa (GOLDFUSS)

Order: Lithistida
Family: Astylospongiidae

Sponges (phylum Porifera) are the simplest sessile aquatic multicellular animals whose body is composed of only two germ layers — ectoderm and endoderm — separated by jelly-like mesoglea secreting the spicules supporting the skeleton. The body is pouch-shaped and has porous walls. Canals lead from the pores (ostia, prosopores) to the digestive cavity (spongiocoele), which opens on to the surface via an excretory orifice (osculum). The spongiocoele is lined with digestive epithelium composed of collar-like ciliated cells known as choanocytes. The whirling cilia suck water into the sponge through the ostia and, after the microscopic food has been taken up, force it out again through the osculum. Curvature of the body walls gives rise to three structural types: the ascon, with a pouch-like body, the sycon, whose walls are puckered into folds, and the leucon, in which the folds themselves are folded, so that the choanocytes between the folds are enclosed in chambers. Afferent canals lead from the ostia to the choanocytes, and from these to the spongiocoele, forming an outlet, lead efferent canals.

According to the type of spicule material, outer form, skeletal structure and other characters, the phylum Porifera is divided into the classes Demospongea, Hyalospongea, Calcispongea and Sclerospongea. The members of the first three of these classes are to be found in greater or smaller numbers from the Cambrian to the Recent, their maximum incidence occurring in the Lower Palaeozoic and in the Mesozoic. The last — and smallest — group is somewhat problematic and made its first appearance in the Ordovician. Most sponges belong to the Demospongea. Their skeleton is composed of opaline (siliceous) spicules or horny fibres and sometimes of both. The majority are thick-walled and belong to the leucon type. One of the most important fossil groups are lithistid sponges, which have a reticulate (lattice-like) skeleton formed of long, fused spicules with irregular processes known as desmones (fig. 5).

1. *Hydnoceras bahtense,* Upper Devonian (Frasnian), New York, USA. Height 155 mm. The thin-walled, funnel-shaped skeleton was anchored to the sediment by a bundle of long spicules at its lower end. Tufts of spicules were also present on the tips of the hollow processes.

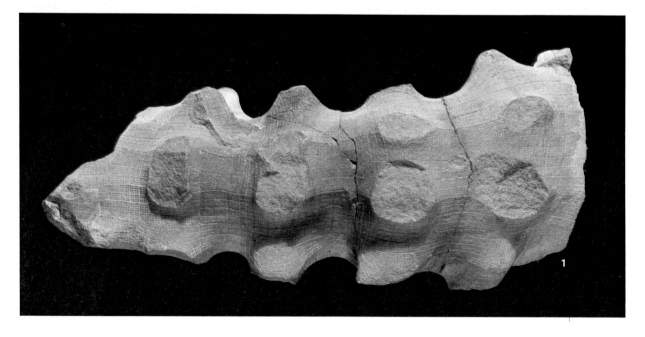

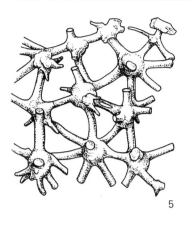

2. *Runia runica,** Silurian (Ludlow), Lejškov near Zdice, Czechoslovakia. Height of the cephalopod shell fragment 25 mm. The individual rows of bore marks probably represent several successive attacks on the shell by boring sponges.

3, 4. *Astylospongia praemorsa,** Ordovician, Gotland, Sweden. View from above (3) and from the side (4). Diameter 32 and 34 mm. Their spherical form and siliceous skeleton make these sponges very resistant to destruction. Consequently they are often found in glacial deposits in northern Germany and Poland.

5. A reticulate skeleton of lithistid sponges.

The members of the Euroamerican genus *Astylospongia* lived during the Ordovician period. Their outer surface is covered with small oscula and is furrowed by vertical grooves.

Runia runica MAREK	Order: Hadromerida Family: Clionidae

All that has been preserved of fossil boring sponges are their passages and chambers, whose shape often depends on the substrate. One of the oldest known traces of a boring sponge, the Silurian genus *Runia* in Czechoslovakia, consists of tunnels which are first of all linear and then branch by forking.

Hydnoceras bahtense HALL AND CLARKE	Order: Lyssakia Family: Dictyospongiidae

This sponge, which belongs to the Hyalospongea class, occurs in North American and French Devonian and Carboniferous strata. In cross section it is octagonal and on the edges there are several rows of blunt-tipped processes. The fused triaxial siliceous spicules have dissolved, leaving a dense rectangular network of grooves on the surface.

Cnemidiastrum rimulosum (GOLDFUSS)

Order: Lithistida
Family: Cnemidiastridae

In sponges, the body is supported by an internal skeleton composed either of interwoven fibres of a horny material (spongin), or of inorganic calcareous or siliceous spicules (sclerites). The sclerites sometimes lie loose in the mesoglea, but sometimes they are fused or joined together by spongin to form a strong lattice-work skeleton. They are secreted by special cells (scleroblasts) round an axial organic fibre, which leaves a central canal in them.

The sclerites are divided, according to their size, into macrosclerites (usually 0.1–3 mm, but also up to 3 metres, long), which form the skeleton proper, and microsclerites (0.01–0.1 mm long), which stiffen the gelatinous mesoglea. They exist in a multitude of forms, with dozens of types, but basically they can be classified as monoaxial (with one axis), triactinial (with three rays), triaxial (with three axes), tetraxonal (with a tetrahedral axis), polyaxial (with many axes) and non-axial (irregularly shaped or spherical).

Monoaxons are the commonest type among calcareous sponges, but also among sponges with a siliceous skeleton; tetraxons also occur in both groups. Triactins are typical only of calcareous sponges (Calcispongea) and triaxons only of siliceous sponges. These sclerites usually fuse to form latticed skeletons. Polyaxons and spheres are particularly abundant among Palaeozoic sponges, where they are often formed by the fusion of simpler types.

Sponges of the European genus *Cnemidiastrum* occurred from the Ordovician to the Jurassic. They have thick-walled, cylindrical, or wide cup-shaped skeletons. The sclerites are rhizoclones (root desmones) with blunt-tipped processes.

1. *Cnemidiastrum rimulosum,* Upper Jurassic, Roning, West Germany. Height 50 mm. The deep central cavity marked with vertical grooves into which the efferent canals open is a typical feature of this genus.

2. *Verruculina crassa,* Upper Cretaceous (Turonian), Nittlingen near Hanover, West Germany. Height 45 mm. Typical of the morphologically variable skeletons of this genus are the numerous apopores, with raised edges, on the inner surface.

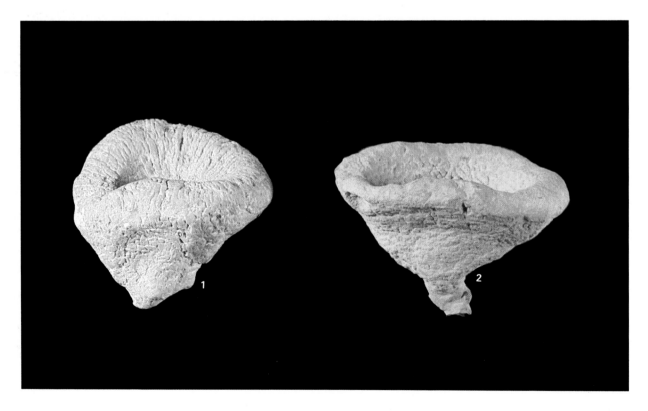

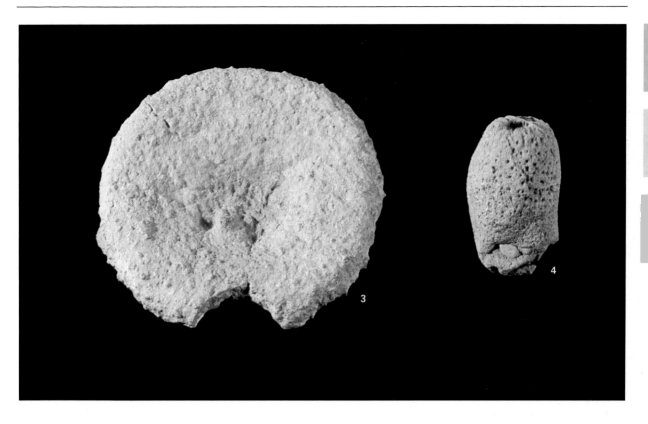

	Order: Lithistida
Verruculina crassa RÖMER	Family: Verruculinidae

The genus *Verruculina* flourished during the Cretaceous period, but was rarer in Tertiary Europe. The thick-walled skeletons are lobulate, cup-shaped or saucer-like and sometimes have a short stem. The spicules are small, branched rhizoclones.

	Order: Lithistida
Hyalotragos rugosum (MÜNSTER)	Family: Hyalotragosidae

The flat, saucer-like members of the genus *Hyalotragos* are European Upper Jurassic sponges and they are an important component of sponge reefs (Spongitenkalk). Their outer surface is finely porous, with a concentrically furrowed tegumental layer. Small apopores are present on the upper aspect. The rhizoclones are large and branched.

3. *Hyalotragos rugosum,* Upper Jurassic (Malm), Streitberg, West Germany. Diameter 73 mm.

4. *Cylindrophyma milleporata,** Upper Jurassic (Malm), Blaubeuren, West Germany. Height 42 mm. Often forms groups.

	Order: Lithistida
Cylindrophyma milleporata (GOLDFUSS)	Family: Cylindrophymatidae

The members of this Upper Jurassic European genus have thick-walled, cylindrical skeletons with a deep, tubular spongiocoele stretching right to their base. Their outer surface is densely covered with small ostia.

97

Porifera

Jereica multiformis BRONN
Order: Lithistida
Family: Jereicidae

Sponges are sessile (only the larvae are capable of free movement) and exclusively aquatic (mainly marine) animals; only a few species of the family Spongillidae have invaded fresh water. Recent sponges are to be found from the equator to the poles and from the littoral zone to depths of about 6,000 metres. Individual groups display a certain depth dependence, however. Calcispongea are most abundant at depths of down to 90 metres, Demospongea between 100 and 350 metres and Hyalospongea from 500 to 1,000 metres. Climatic factors play a smaller role, although most sponge orders are richer in species in tropical regions. Only horny sponges (belonging to the class Demospongea) are limited to warm shallow water. Many sponges require a solid rocky or sandy bottom and do not tolerate turbid water. The movement of the water has a strong effect on sponges and often influences their shape. In quiet water they tend to be cup-shaped, whereas in currents they merely form plaques. Consequently, as we descend to greater depths, we find more and more sponges with a stable form of skelet, but also with greater diversity of form. The ways in which they are anchored in the soft sea floor and maintain a given height above it, to enable them to suck in organic matter as well as water, are also more diverse, ranging from long, thin stems with root-like processes to large spicules reminiscent of stakes.

In a favourable environment, sponges may occur in large numbers and in a variety of species. The fossil sponge reefs in Upper Jurassic formations in Baden-Württemberg, West Germany, or in Upper Cretaceous strata in France are good examples. They were formed in tropical seas at depths of about 100 metres, when the development of the sponges was at its height; no such associations are known in present-day seas.

The German Upper Cretaceous genus *Jereica* (fig. 4) has a cylindrical or cup-shaped skeleton with a short stem attached to the bottom by a basal disc. Vertical efferent canals open into the shallow spongiocoele. The large, branched rhizoclones are curved.

Siphonia tulipa ZITTEL
Order: Lithistida
Family: Phymatellidae

The Cretaceous and Tertiary members of the genus *Siphonia,* which are known in Europe and Australia, have an ovoid or pear-shaped skeleton with a long, thin stalk anchored to the bottom by rhizoid processes. Curving efferent canals open into the deep, narrow spongiocoele.

Thecosiphonia sp.
Order: Lithistida
Family: Phymatellidae

This European Cretaceous and Tertiary sponge has an ovoid or pear-shaped skeleton with a slender stalk. The spongiocoele forms a shallow depression. This genus is also differentiated from *Siphonia* by its large spicules (desmones).

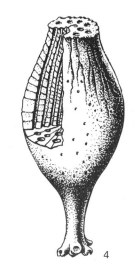

4

1. *Siphonia tulipa,* Cretaceous (Upper Albian), Blackdown, England. Height minus stalk 37 mm. A fragment of the long, thin stalk and the mouth of the narrow spongiocele can be seen. The whole sponge resembles a tulip – hence its specific name.

2. *Jereica multiformis,* Upper Cretaceous (Senonian), Misburg near Hanover, West Germany. Height 150 mm. The skeleton is typically goblet-shaped and has a short foot, the bottom of which has been snapped off.

3. *Thecosiphonia* sp., Upper Cretaceous (Senonian), Oberg near Halberstadt, East Germany. Height, together with stalk, 230 mm. These sponges lived in relatively deep, quiet water in the German Upper Cretaceous sea.

4. A reconstruction of a sponge showing the internal structure.

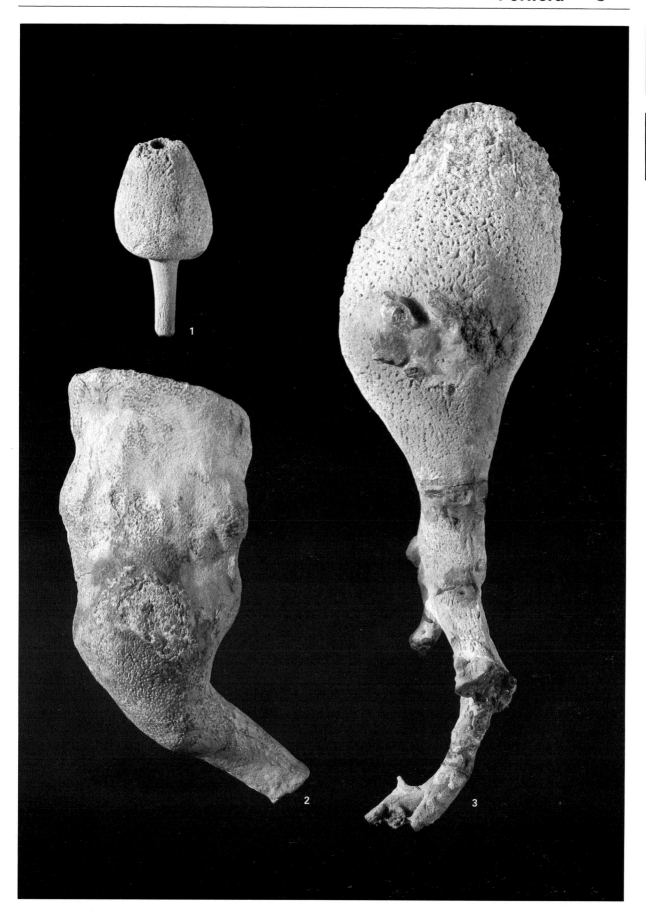

Porifera

Hallirhoa costata LAMOROUX	Order: Lithistida Family: Phymatellidae

Members of the genus *Hallirhoa* are to be found in Upper Cretaceous deposits in Europe. They are related to *Siphonia* sponges.

5

Ventriculites radiatus MANTELL	Order: Lychniskida Family: Ventriculitidae

The sponges belonging to the Hyalospongea class are mostly of the leucon type, with a large, wide spongiocoele and thin walls. The canal system is usually simple. The skeleton consists entirely of triaxial opaline spicules (hexactins), without any spongin. The spicules sometimes lie freely in the mesoglea, but their ends are generally joined together so that they form a three-dimensional network reminiscent of scaffolding. This type of skeleton is typical of the order Lychniskida, to which the majority of fossil Hyalospongea belong. The order takes its name from skeletal structures resembling old-fashioned lanterns (*lychnos* is Greek for lantern), whose short diagonals connect the individual spicule rays at places where they intersect. The order Lychniskida appeared in the Jurassic period, reached its maximum distribution in the Cretaceous period and then rapidly dwindled. Today it forms a very small group whose incidence is confined solely to Europe.

The most abundant lychniskid sponge is *Ventriculites,* a Middle and Upper Cretaceous genus. The skeleton is generally cornet-shaped (rarely shallow and saucer-shaped) and has thin walls. Branched rhizoid processes arise from its pointed base. One of the typical features of this

1. *Lopanella depressa,** Upper Cretaceous (Lower Turonian), Zbyslav, Czechoslovakia. Height of skeleton 55 mm. It abounds in Bohemian Lower Turonian shallow-water littoral sediments.

2. *Hallirhoa costata,** Upper Cretaceous (Turonian), Nogent-le-Rotrou, France. Diameter 70 mm. Viewed from above, showing the narrow, deep spongiocoele and the typical lobular form of the body.

3. *Ventriculites radiatus,** Upper Cretaceous (Senonian), Wiltshire, England. Maximum diameter of the whole specimen 115 mm. A view of the under side of the sponge, enclosed in a flint nodule. The concentric vertical grooving of the outer wall and the pointed base of the skeleton are clearly visible. The rhizoid processes have been broken off.

4. *Coeloptychium agaricoides,** Upper Cretaceous (Senonian), Germany. Diameter 78 mm. A view of the top of the skeleton, which is typically shaped like an umbrella. The radial ridges and small apopores in the furrows can be seen.

5. A reconstruction of a member of the genus *Coeloptychium.*

sponge is the winding transverse undulation of the calyx caused by the alternation of deep vertical grooves on its outer and inner aspect.

Coeloptychium agaricoides GOLDFUSS

Order: Lychniskida
Family: Coeloptychidae

The representatives of the European and North American Upper Cretaceous genus *Coeloptychium* have a mushroom- or umbrella-shaped skeleton and a short, thin stalk. Their under surface is divided by deep grooves into radial ridges in which we find large ostia (fig. 5). The furrows in the similarly, but less conspicuously, constructed upper surface contain small apopores.

Lopanella depressa POČTA

Order: Dictyida
Family: Pleurostomatidae

Sponges of the genus *Lopanella* occur in Upper Cretaceous shallow-water deposits in central Europe. They have a thick-walled cup- or saucer-shaped skeleton with a short, thick stalk. Both their outer and their inner surface are covered with fine pores. The hexactins are joined together by their tips to form a strong construction.

101

Porifera

Stellispongia glomerata (QUENSTEDT)

Order: Pharetronida
Family: Stellispongiidae

Calcispongea is a class of sponges with a skeleton of calcite spicules, which are generally unconnected and lie loose in the mesoglea, so that after the animal's death they often break up. The most frequent types of macroscierites are diactins, triactins (Y- or T-shaped) and tetractins; microsclerites are absent. Calcareous sponges have a wide variety of forms and they are also the only sponges to retain the simpler structural types (ascon and sycon) in adulthood. Already known from the Cambrian, they attained their maximum incidence between the Triassic and the Cretaceous; in the Cainozoic era their numbers dwindled again.

The members of the genus *Stellispongia* occur in Permian to Cretaceous deposits in Europe, northern Africa and South America. Their knobbly tufts are formed of hemispherical, claviform and sometimes cylindrical individuals. The shallow oscula, which have narrow apopores, are stellate or rayed.

Elasmostoma sp.

Order: Pharetronida
Family: Elasmostomatidae

These sponges are to be found in Jurassic – and in even greater abundance in Cretaceous – deposits in Europe. They are irregularly leaf-like, lobular or funnel-shaped. Their under side is finely porous and their upper aspect is covered with a smooth layer of tissue with large numbers of shallow oscula.

Raphidonema stellatum (GOLDFUSS)

Order: Pharetronida
Family: Lelapiidae

The skeletons of the European Triassic to Cretaceous genus *Raphidonema* look like funnels or vases. They have a rough, lumpy and porous outer surface and a smooth inner surface with numerous apopores.

Perodinella furcata (GOLDFUSS)

Order: Pharetronida
Family: Discocoeliidae

The sponges of the genus *Perodinella* inhabited shallow European seas from the Triassic to the Upper Cretaceous. Their thick-walled, cylindrical skeletons often form large and sometimes dendritic colonies by budding. The deep, narrow spongiocoele stretches to the base of the skeleton. The outer surface is finely porous.

Porosphaera globularis (PHILLIPS)

Order: Pharetronida
Family: Porosphaeridae

The European Cretaceous genus *Porosphaera* comprises sponges with a small, spherical or ovoid skeleton generally measuring not more than a few millimetres. The surface is finely spiny and porous. The osculum is deep and very narrow.

1. *Porosphaera globularis,** Upper Cretaceous (Santonian), Kent, England. Diameter 16 mm. Side view. Probably the largest *Porosphaera* species.

2. *Perodinella furcata,* Upper Cretaceous (Cenomanian), Essen, North Rhine-Westphalia, West Germany. A colony of over 10 individuals seen from above, height 30 mm. The colony was formed by lateral budding and growth. The osculum is often the only evidence of the individual.

3. *Raphidonema stellatum,* Upper Cretaceous (Cenomanian), Essen, North Rhine-Westphalia, West Germany. Height of fragment 22 mm. The tube of a polychaetous worm, *Glomerula gordialis,* is attached to the inner surface.

4. *Elasmostoma* sp., Lower Cretaceous (Neocomian), Achim, West Germany. Height 14 mm. A small specimen with a single osculum.

5. *Stellispongia glomerata,* Upper Jurassic, Nattheim, West Germany. Height of tuft 30 mm. A species abundant in shallow-water coral associations in the warm climatic belts of Jurassic Europe.

Coscinocyathus sp.

Order: Coscinocyatha
Family: Coscinocyathidae

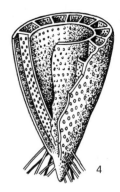

Archaeocyathids (phylum Archaeocyatha) are extinct animals with an internal calcareous skeleton in the form of two (rarely one) cones fitted one inside the other and joined together by perpendicular pseudosepta. In addition to the septa, the interval between the two walls was sometimes partitioned off by horizontal plates, rod-like synapticles or a bubbly mesh. The skeletal elements were all densely perforated. The skeleton was held fast by a basal disc or by lamellar processes at the base (fig. 4). Archaeocyathids appeared in the Lower Cambrian and died out in the Middle Cambrian. They inhabited warm, shallow seas in which they formed the first reefs in the Earth's history, up to 800 metres thick, which are known from Siberia, Mongolia, Australia, North America and north-west Africa; archaeocyathids also occur singly in south-western Europe and in southern and south-eastern Asia.

The cosmopolitan genus *Coscinocyathus* has conical or cylindrical double-walled porous cups, with dense septa and plates in the intervening space.

Pseudoconularia grandissima (Barrande)

Order: Conulariida
Family: Conulariidae

The phylum Coelenterata (hollow-bodied animals) comprises both sessile and vagile species (mostly marine) with a radially symmetrical body formed of two germ layers. The body cavity (the coelenteron), with longitudinal septa, has only one orifice, which combines both ingestive and excretory functions and is surrounded by tentacles carrying stinging cells. A simple diffuse nervous system and a muscular system are present.

Scyphozoa — the class to which medusae and conulariids belong — are characterized by tetragonal symmetry and by a free-swimming medusa stage as well as a sessile polypoid stage. Conulariids have a thin, tapering chitino-phosphatic skeleton which is square or octagonal in cross section and has triangular lobes at its wider (oral) end. Down the inside of each of the walls runs a longitudinal septum (sometimes with two others, one on either side); externally it forms a median line, groove or ridge. There are also grooves on the edges of the skeleton. Series of tubercles produced by the intersections of longitudinal and transversal ribs form a typical canvas-like texture. Most conulariids were attached to the sea bed by their narrower end, but some swam, apex upwards, by active contraction of their adoral lobes. Conulariids lived from the Cambrian to the Triassic period.

The skeleton of *Pseudoconularia*, an Ordovician and Silurian genus from Europe and America, is 300 mm long; it is square in cross section and widens at an angle of 20 to 25 degrees. The walls are slightly concave, with a median ridge and with grooves down the edges. Its sculpture consists of longitudinal rows of minute tubercles (fig. 5).

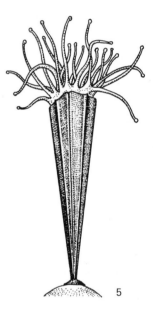

1, 5. *Pseudoconularia grandissima,** Middle Ordovician (Caradoc), Vráž near Beroun, Czechoslovakia. 1 — a crushed fragment of a shell; height 65 mm. 5 — a reconstruction.

2. *Anaconularia anomala,** Middle Ordovician (Llandeilo), Drabov near Beroun, Czechoslovakia. Height of shell core 65 mm.

3. *Coscinocyathus* sp., Lower Cambrian, Siberia, USSR. Archaeocyathid limestone showing weathered cross sections of cups. The round cross section of the cup at the bottom is 14 mm in diameter.

4. Structure of the skeleton of archaeocyaths.

O

Cm

Anaconularia anomala (BARRANDE)

Order: Conulariida
Family: Conulariidae

The European genus *Anaconularia* flourished during the Middle Ordovician. It is characterized by pyramidal, slightly spiral shells with sharp, non-grooved edges.

Coelenterata

Actinostroma vastum (PoČta)

Order: Stromatoporida
Family: Actinostromatidae

Stromatoporoids are extinct marine animals which lived in colonies and existed from the Cambrian to the Cretaceous. Traditionally they had been regarded as coelenterates (class Hydrozoa). Since 1970, however, following the discovery of several stromatoporoid-like species of sponges belonging to the class Sclerospongea, they are now classified with the Sclerospongea. The problem has not yet been resolved, because nobody has succeeded in identifying some of the structural elements of stromatoporoids with sponge skeletal structures. The diversely formed calcareous skeletons (cenostea) of stromatoporoids are composed of densely packed horizontal plates (laminae) joined together by large numbers of perpendicular rounded columns (pilae). The bottom of the skeleton is covered with a wrinkled crust, the epitheca. The surface of the skeleton is either smooth, with minute protuberances formed by the protruding ends of the pilae, or it may be tuberculate. On the tubercles we often find a stellate system of grooves with a vertical canal in the centre; this is known as an astrorhiza.

Stromatoporoids lived only in the sea — mostly in warm, shallow water. They usually occurred in large numbers. In the Palaeozoic era they contributed on an important scale to the formation of coral reefs. The shape of the colonies depended partly on the environment; on a hard floor they were hemispherical, on a soft bottom they formed thin plaques and sometimes they overgrew solid objects. In the littoral zone they were represented by thick, tabulate forms, whereas calm water was inhabited by dendritic species. Many are stratigraphically important.

The members of the cosmopolitan genus *Actinostroma* lived from the Cambrian to the Carboniferous. They have massive tabulate, tuberous or bulbous skeletons with an epitheca at the bottom and prominent coherent laminae. On the surface of the laminae there are columns connected by small ridges arranged in a retiform pattern. The surface of the skeleton is covered with small tubercles, with minute astrorhizae.

4

1, 4. *Densastroma* cf. *pexisum*, Lower Silurian (Wenlock), Körpklint, Gotland, Sweden. Transversal diameter of colony 47 mm. The spherical colony has overgrown a shell of the gastropod *Euomphalopterus alatus*, which provides it with a firm base and prevents it from sinking into the soft bed (1). 4 — a cross section of a colony.

2. *Actinostroma vastum,* Lower Devonian (Pragian), Koněprusy, Czechoslovakia. Height 105 mm. The outer surface of a colony fragment, showing the small tubercles. Tabulate *Actinostroma* skeletons often occur on top of Palaeozoic coral reefs, because they are highly resistant to the action of the breakers.

3. *Amphipora ramosa,** Middle Devonian (Givetian), Josefov near Blansko, Czechoslovakia. An *Amphipora* limestone thin section. Diameter of the recrystallized branches about 4 to 5 mm. *Amphipora* species are important European Middle Devonian fossils. They lived in large masses in the vicinity of coral reefs in lagoons and on inter-reef flats.

Densastroma cf. *pexisum* (YAVORSKY)

Order: Stromatoporida
Family: Actinostromatidae

This Silurian species from the Baltic region usually formed small tuberous colonies (fig. 4) overgrowing solid objects on the soft sea floor.

Amphipora ramosa (PHILLIPS)

Order: Stromatoporida
Family: Idiostromatidae

The members of the cosmopolitan genus *Amphipora* lived from the Silurian to the Permian, and possibly into the Jurassic. The ramified dendritic colonies are composed of thin cylindrical branches. The retiform skeleton has a pronounced axial canal and a layer of largish cavities just below the surface. Astrorhizae are absent.

Coelenterata

*Pachyfavosites polymorphus (*GOLDFUSS*)*

Order: Favositida
Family: Favositidae

Corals (class Anthozoa) are radially symmetrical solitary or colonial marine coelenterates. Their body cavity is divided radially by fleshy vertical septa known as mesenteries. Most of them secrete a calcareous external skeleton termed individually corallites, and for whole colonies corallum (coral). Fossil corals come under the subclasses Tabulata, Rugosa, Zoantharia and Octocorallia.

The completely colonial tabulate corals (Tabulata), which existed from the Cambrian to the Permian, formed various types of colonies – encrusting, tabulate, hemispherical and even branching – composed of thin-walled tubular or conical corallites, which were sometimes interconnected by pores. The under side is protected by a common calcareous layer known as a holotheca. Inside the corallites we find large numbers of well developed horizontal plates (tabulae). Vertical radial septa are absent or vestigial. The colonies grew by asexual budding.

Favositids were distributed all over the world from the Middle Ordovician to the Permian. Their colonies are tabulate, hemispherical or spherical and seldom dendritic; they are composed of tubular, irregularly polygonal thin-walled corallites interconnected by pores and partitioned off by large numbers of horizontal plates. Favositids are classified in some 30 closely related genera, according to the morphology of the corallites.

1, 2. *Squamofavosites kukuk,* Lower Devonian (Zlíchovian = Emsian), Prague-Klukovice and Prague-Zlíchov, Czechoslovakia. Diameter of the hemispherical colonies 22 and 38 mm. A concentrically furrowed holotheca with a cornute process from the oldest part of the coral can be seen on the under side of the smaller colony.

3. *Pachyfavosites polymorphus,* Middle Devonian (Eifelian), Gerolstein, West Germany. Height of the fragment of a tabulate colony 51 mm. Corallite walls, dense horizontal plates, fine septal spines and small mural pores can be seen on the fracture surface.

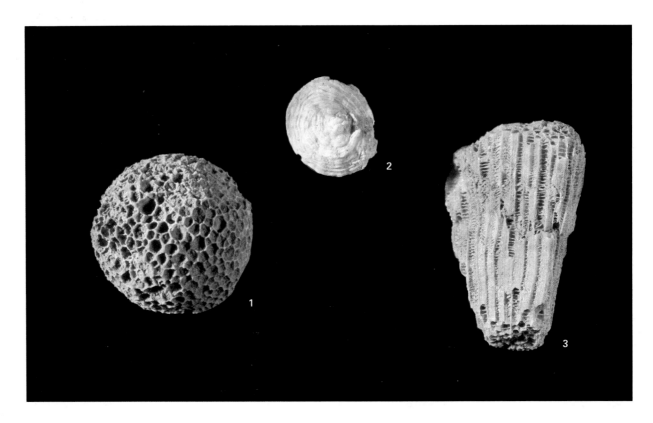

4. *Aulopora serpens,** Middle Devonian (Eifelian), Gerolstein, West Germany. Part of a colony encrusting the under side of a stromatoporoid. The vertical thickness of the colony is 60 mm.

5. *Pleurodictyum problematicum,** Lower Devonian (Emsian), Obserstadtfeld, West Germany. Diameter of core of the larger colony 27 mm. These corals abound in Lower Devonian sandy rock facies. All that remains of them in the fine grained quartzite is the sedimentary filling of the corallites and the pores. A tube of the worm *Hicetes innexus* is clearly discernible.

Squamofavosites kukuk GALLE	Order: Favositida Family: Favositidae

The corallites of this Upper Silurian to Lower Devonian genus are uneven and relatively thin-walled, with septal scales (squamulae) instead of spines and with large pores and very dense horizontal plates.

Pleurodictyum problematicum GOLDFUSS	Order: Favositida Family: Micheliniidae

This Upper Silurian to Middle Devonian coral, which has a worldwide distribution, forms small lenticular colonies, usually on the tubes of worms of the genus *Hicetes*. The large, prismatic corallites have thick and highly porous walls. The septa take the form of ridges or rows of spines; horizontal plates are generally absent.

Aulopora serpens GOLDFUSS	Order: Auloporida Family: Auloporidae

The cosmopolitan Ordovician to Permian genus *Aulopora* forms encrusting colonies formed of thick-walled cornet-shaped corallites. Horizontal plates (often incomplete) are present only in the basal parts of the corallites.

Coelenterata

Syringopora serpens Linnaeus

Order: Auloporida
Family: Syringoporidae

Tabulate corals achieved maximum distribution in shallow and warm Silurian and Devonian seas, where they formed reefs together with stromatoporoids and algae. Tabulate and plaque-forming types lived on the crests of the reefs, dendritic and encrusting forms in the crevices and lagoons and on the slopes of the reefs. Quiet water, often with a muddy bottom, was inhabited by spherical and hemispherical types and by coherent clumps of syringoporoids. With few exceptions, tabulate corals preferred shallow, moving water with slowly settling calcareous sediment. Occasional discovery of single colonies – usually overturned – in other environments can be attributed to posthumous transport, after the skeletons had been made buoyant by gases resulting from decay.

The corals of the cosmopolitan genus *Syringopora* lived from the Upper Ordovician to the Lower Permian. The clumps of narrow, cylindrical, thick-walled corallites, which were set far apart, were irregularly joined together by horizontal tubular connections. The tabulae are funnel-shaped, the septa have the form of rows of spines.

Catenipora escharoides (Lamarck)

Order: Heliolitida
Family: Halysitidae

The colonies of the cosmopolitan Ordovician and Silurian genus *Catenipora* are composed of elliptical tubular corallites, arranged like a pallisade in unequal, irregularly branching and reuniting rows. They have dense tabulae and spine-like septa.

1. *Syringopora serpens,* Upper Silurian (Wenlock), Dudley, England. Width of colony 105 mm. The spaces between the corallites are filled with sediment, but they might equally well have been overgrown by a stromatoporoid. In such cases they used to be regarded as stromatoporoids belonging to the genus *Caunopora.*

2. *Barrandeolites bowerbanki,** Upper Silurian (Wenlock), Amerika near Mořina, Czechoslovakia. Maximum width of colony 80 mm. Abundant in coral biostromes growing in Bohemian Wenlockian shallows near a volcanic island. The vivid colouring is due to the admixture of volcanic ash to the sediment.

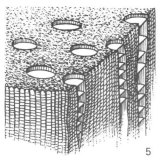

3. *Heliolites interstinctus,* Lower Silurian (Upper Llandovery), Visby, Gotland, Sweden. Larger diameter of colony 75 mm. Soft marls, unequally hardened, have weathered out unevenly from the wide corallites.

4. *Catenipora escharoides,** Lower Silurian (Upper Llandovery), Gotland, Sweden. A colony fragment 75 mm wide.

5. A section through a part of a heliolitid colony.

Heliolites interstinctus (LINNAEUS)

Order: Heliolitida
Family: Heliolitidae

The corals of the worldwide Middle Ordovician to Middle Devonian genus *Heliolites* have massive colonies composed of two types of tubes (fig. 5). The wide, cylindrical corallites have 12 strip-like septa and relatively sporadic tabulae. The connecting tissue between them secreted narrow, prismatic tubules with dense tabulae (coenenchyme).

Barrandeolites bowerbanki MILNE-EDWARDS AND HAIME

Order: Chaetetida
Family: Tivernidae

Owing to the simple structure of their colonies, which consist of narrow tubes without tabulae, septa or any other typical structures, the systematic position of chaetetids is somewhat obscure and their inclusion among the tabulate corals is only provisional.

The tabulate colonies of the European Silurian genus *Barrandeolites* are composed of narrow, laterally compressed polygonal corallites. Despite its abundance, this genus has not yet been described satisfactorily.

Coelenterata

Palaeocyclus porpita (LINNAEUS)

Order: Cystiphyllida
Family: Palaeocyclidae

The subclass Rugosa comprises mostly solitary corals with mainly conical corallites with a thick outer wall (epitheca). The animal lay in the upper, concave part (the calyx), while the lower part (the stem) was filled, along the walls, with a dissepimentarium (a collection of dissepimenta, i.e. of incomplete tabulae forming a bubble-like network), and in the centre with a tabularium composed of whole tabulae. At first there were six septa (protosepta), but the successive addition of further septa during growth considerably increased their number. In adulthood, long main septa and short secondary septa were developed. Owing to their sessile mode of life, the original bilateral symmetry of rugose corals was obliterated by radial symmetry. These corals originated in the Middle Ordovician and died out in the Upper Permian.

The European and American Silurian genus *Palaeocyclus* has small, button-like corallites (fig. 12) with septa visible throughout their entire length. The septa are bordered by minute spines and the epitheca is attached to a substrate by a central cone.

Goniophyllum pyramidale (HISINGER)

Order: Cystiphyllida
Family: Goniophyllidae

The species of the European and American Silurian genus *Goniophyllum* have squatly pyramidal, thick-walled corallites and ridge-like septa. The calyx is closed by four movable triangular opercula. Opercula are a very rare phenomenon in corals and occur only in the family Goniophyllidae.

Calceola sandalina (LINNAEUS)

Order: Cystiphyllida
Family: Goniophyllidae

The cosmopolitan Devonian genus *Calceola* has cornet-shaped and slightly curved thick-walled corallites with a semicircular cross section. The septa form fine ridges in the shallow calyx. The semicircular operculum is a typical character.

Microcyclus eifliensis KAYSER

Order: Stauriida
Family: Hadrophyllidae

The small, discoid corallites of the genus *Microcyclus* are to be found in Middle Devonian sediments in Europe, North America and Africa. They have long septa and a flat under side covered with an epitheca.

1–3, 12. *Palaeocyclus porpita,** Lower Silurian (Upper Llandovery), Gotland, Sweden. Diameter of the largest corallite (2), turned upside down, 14 mm. 12 – a lateral view.

4, 5. *Goniophyllum pyramidale,** Upper Silurian (Wenlock), Dudley, England. A corallite from above (4) and from the side (5); height 24 mm.

6–8. *Microcyclus eifliensis,* Middle Devonian (Eifelian), Prüm, West Germany. Diameter of the largest corallite, turned upside down (7), 15 mm. With *Palaeocyclus,* this is an example of morphological convergence of unrelated species produced by identical environmental conditions. The small size and flat shape of this species are due to its having settled on a soft, yielding bottom.

9. *Phaulactis cyathophylloides,** Upper Silurian (Wenlock), Irevik, Gotland, Sweden. A corallite, height 36 mm.

10, 11. *Calceola sandalina,** Middle Devonian (Eifelian), Eifel, West Germany. A shoe-shaped corallite (11), height 26 mm, with an operculum (10). An important index fossil.

Order: Stauriida
Family: Lykophyllidae

Phaulactis cyathophylloides RYDER

The species of this almost worldwide Silurian genus have conical corallites. The long, thin septa are hidden in the dissepimentarium and tabularium, so that in the shallow calyx they form only low, spiny ridges. The epitheca is vertically grooved and has irregular rhizoid processes.

113

Dohmophyllum cyathoides WEDEKIND

Order: Stauriida
Family: Ptenophyllidae

As a whole, the corals of the subclass Rugosa were ecologically fairly adaptable, and small solitary forms in particular were able to live in very deep, cold water. The occurrence of large numbers, however, was, in the photic zone, always confined to the warm, shallow part of the sea. Individual species often formed zonal 'carpets' on shallow platforms or on the sides of coral reefs and thus allow the depth and the distance from the crest of the reef to be estimated.

Because of the diversity of their species and their sessile mode of life, rugose corals are suitable for the demarcation of palaeobiogeographical provinces and for determination of the reciprocal position of the continents from the Middle Ordovician to the Carboniferous. Diminution of the diversity and the number of species towards the poles also helps in determination of the various climatic belts (except the polar belt). From the number of the daily growth lines on the epitheca of these corals it is even possible to study the progressive slowing down of the Earth's rotation; from the Ordovician to the Permian, the number of days interpreted from a single annual strip decreased from 412 to 390. This observation may be verified by the used molluscs, for example.

The members of the Devonian genus *Dohmophyllum,* known from Eurasia and Australia, have large, squatly conical corallites with many long, thin septa coiled together in a depression in the shallow calyx to form a corrugated column. The interseptal spaces are filled with fine dissepimenta; the centre of the calyx is filled with tabulae.

1, 2, 6. *'Amplexus' hercynicus,* Upper Devonian (Frasnian), Adorf, West Germany. 1, 2 — corallite fragments, height 32 and 55 mm. The species of the genus *Amplexus* form 'amplex limestones' in European Devonian deposits. 6 — cross section of a corallite.

3. *Dohmophyllum cyathoides,* Middle Devonian (Eifelian), Eifel, West Germany. A corallite, diameter 56 mm. A view of the shallow, flat calyx, showing the small depression in the centre.

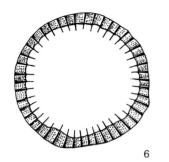

6

D

'Amplexus' hercynicus RÖMER

Order: Stauriida
Family: Amplexidae

This Devonian and Carboniferous genus is distributed over almost the entire globe. The curved, thin-walled corallites, which have numerous short septa, change over to dense tabulae like low radial ridges (fig. 6). Typical representatives of this genus occur only in the Carboniferous.

Cyathophyllum dianthus GOLDFUSS

Order: Stauriida
Family: Cyathophyllidae

The corals of the cosmopolitan Devonian genus *Cyathophyllum* have large, conical corallites with numerous thin septa, of which the main ones extend almost to the centre. They can be solitary or joined together in massive colonies. The wide dissepimentarium circumscribes the depression in the flat calyx.

Hexagonaria hexagona (GOLDFUSS)

Order: Stauriida
Family: Disphyllidae

The cosmopolitan Devonian genus *Hexagonaria* has tabulate colonies with large numbers of small, but massive corallites. The numerous thickened septa do not extend into the centre and are joined together by a wide dissepimentarium. In the calyx, above the tabularium, there is a deep, narrow depression.

4. *Cyathophyllum dianthus,** Middle Devonian (Givetian), Čelechovice na Hané, Czechoslovakia. Width of colony 61 mm. A relatively rare, morphologically striking coral of Middle Devonian coral reefs, whose colonies are generally composed of only a few individuals.

5. *Hexagonaria hexagona,** Upper Devonian (Frasnian), Senzeiles, Belgium. Length of colony 81 mm.

115

Coelenterata

Dimorphastrea concentrica (BECKER)

Order: Scleractinia
Family: Synastraeidae

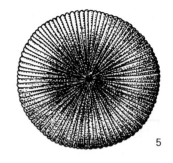

5

The members of the order Scleractinia are all marine and mostly colonial (less often solitary) corals with an external calcareous skeleton composed chiefly of septa organized in cycles of 6, 12 and 24, etc, so that first, second and further order septa can be distinguished, according to their size. The first order septa fuse (usually in the axis of the corallite) to form a columella. The epitheca is seldom strongly developed. The parts of the septa which protrude outside are called ribs. The corallites have a diversity of forms, from cylindrical to conical and from saucer-shaped to discoid. Similarly, the colonies, formed by budding, are tabulate, hemispherical, spherical and dendritic. The individual corallites in the colony are either separated by thin walls or merge into one another. All the parts of the skeleton are composed of microscopic bundles of calcium carbonate crystals, often organized in a loose porous structure; they may also be compact, however, and in some genera they are actually secondarily reinforced by calcareous deposits known as stereome. The order Scleractinia, which forms the greater part of the subclass Zoantharia, comprises practically all corals existing from the Middle Triassic to the Recent.

The representatives of the Upper Jurassic and Cretaceous genus *Dimorphastrea* come from Eurasia and northern Africa. The massive colonies of wall-less corallites have typical mutually merging septa reminiscent of the lines of force of a magnetic field.

Stylina delabechii
MILNE-EDWARDS AND HAIME

Order: Scleractinia
Family: Stylinidae

The cosmopolitan genus *Stylina* is known from the Upper Triassic to the Cretaceous. The massive, thick-branched colonies are composed of small, clearly separate, raised corallites with well developed septa and a small columella.

Montlivaltia lessneuri
MILNE-EDWARDS AND HAIME

Order: Scleractinia
Family: Montlivaltiidae

Montlivaltia is a worldwide coral genus dating from the Triassic to the Cretaceous. The corallites are usually large, solitary and hemispherical, conical or cylindrical. A columella is generally absent. If an epitheca is present (protecting the coral from being smothered by sediment), it is formed by fusion of the marginal dissepimenta.

Thecosmilia trichotoma (GOLDFUSS)

Order: Scleractinia
Family: Montlivaltiidae

The members of the cosmopolitan Triassic to Cretaceous genus *Thecosmilia* formed coherent colonies composed of a few large, separate montlivaltiid type corallites.

1. *Dimorphastrea concentrica,* Upper Jurassic, Blaubeuren, West Germany. A fragment of a colony, width 48 mm.

2. *Thecosmilia trichotoma,** Upper Jurassic, Sirchingen, West Germany. Length of colony 70 mm. These corals abounded in Upper Jurassic coral reefs; their colonies provide examples of every possible stage of budding.

3. *Stylina delabechii,* Upper Jurassic, Sirchingen, West Germany. A colony fragment, height about 110 mm. A common Upper Jurassic reef-forming species. *Stylina* is one of the oldest hexacoral genera.

4, 5. *Montlivaltia lessneuri,* Upper Jurassic, Le Havre, France. A corallite, height 70 mm. 5 – a view from above.

Coelenterata

Cyclolites ellipticus LAMARCK

Order: Scleractinia
Family: Cyclolitidae

Hexacorals (Hexacorallia) may have originated during the Middle Triassic, probably independently, from a few groups of the subclass Rugosa, i.e. polyphyletically. This explains the manifold developmental trends of their various lineages. In some, a compact or complex structure and the organization of the septa and columellae were modified, in others a simple epithecal wall was replaced by more complicated walls, while in others again the colonial habit developed, giving rise to colonies of different forms. It is to this diversity that the biological success of Scleractinia must be ascribed.

The members of the genus *Cyclolites* inhabited Eurasia, northern Africa and the Caribbean region from the Cretaceous to the Eocene. Their corallites are large, elliptical and dome-shaped, with a flat base. The very numerous thin, perforated septa (up to 1,200) are interconnected by synapticles. The pit in the cup is shaped like a furrow.

Aspidiscus cristatus (LAMARCK)

Order: Scleractinia
Family: Funginellidae

These representatives of the Upper Cretaceous genus *Aspidiscus* are known from Eurasia and Africa. They have rounded, dome-shaped colonies with a narrow border and a flat base. The rows of corallites, with compact septa, form low and generally radially organized ridges.

Rennensismilia complanata (GOLDFUSS)

Order: Scleractinia
Family: Placosmiliidae

The corals of this Upper Cretaceous European genus have conical corallites with markedly flattened sides. Their inner structure is similar to that of the genus *Montlivaltia.*

Actinastrea decaphylla (MICHELIN)

Order: Scleractinia
Family: Astrocoeniidae

The cosmopolitan genus *Actinastrea* has existed from the Upper Triassic down to the present day. Its polygonal corallites, which have compact main septa and laminar secondary septa, form small honeycomb-like or spherical colonies. The columella is well developed.

Dictuophyllia konincki (REUSS)

Order: Scleractinia
Family: Faviidae

The members of the Upper Cretaceous to Oligocene genus *Dictuophyllia,* known from Europe and North America, have massive colonies formed of meandering rows of corallites which join one another from the side. The individual rows are separated by raised septal walls. The septa are parallel and the columellae are fused, forming ridges.

1. *Cyclolites ellipticus,** Upper Cretaceous (Senonian), Gosau, Austria. Larger diameter of the corallite 54 mm. A characteristic and abundant species of Gosau Cretaceous formations and a typical species of the genus.

2. *Aspidiscus cristatus,* Upper Cretaceous (Cenomanian), Batna, Algeria. A colony: diameter 50 mm.

3. *Rennensismilia complanata,* Upper Cretaceous (Senonian), Gosau, Austria. Height of corallite 40 mm. Annual growth lines can be seen on the outer surface of the corallite.

4. *Actinastrea decaphylla,* Upper Cretaceous, Gosau, Austria. Larger diameter of the colony 38 mm.

5. *Dictuophyllia konincki,* Upper Cretaceous, Gosau, Austria. Fragment of a colony, width 71 mm.

6. *Thamnasteria* cf. *media,* Upper Cretaceous, Gosau, Austria. Fragment of a branching colony, height 60 mm.

Thamnasteria cf. *media* (KEFERSTEIN)

Order: Scleractinia
Family: Thamnasteriidae

The corals of the genus *Thamnasteria* occurred over practically the whole of the globe from the Triassic to the Cretaceous. The massive colonies are formed of indistinctly separated corallites with thin, granular septa which merge with one another. The columellae are rod-like.

Coelenterata

Oculina crassiramosa MICHELIN

Order: Scleractinia
Family: Oculinidae

7

Hexacorals were the ecological successors of the extinct coral subclasses Rugosa and Tabulata. Their oldest representatives were all reef-forming (hermatypic) and it was not until the Jurassic period that ahermatypic, mostly solitary, forms appeared. These belonged mainly to the family Caryophyllidae and they began to penetrate further and further into the cold (2−3 °C), deep (down to 6,000 metres) and dark parts of the sea. This led to marked expansion of Scleractinia, since reef-forming types can live only in warm, shallow, well-lit, clear salt water within the range of breakers, which bring them food and oxygen and wash sedimentary particles away.

Species of the genus *Oculina* are known in Europe, North America and Australia, from the Cretaceous down to the Recent. They form branching colonies whose corallites are rather loosely distributed in the compact cenosteum. The septa are few and thick and the columella is tuberculated.

Madrepora solanderi MICHELIN

Order: Scleractinia
Family: Oculinidae

The corals of the genus *Madrepora* form branching colonies. The small corallites, which have 6 to 12 septa, are distributed more or less regularly in the dense cenosteum and are filled internally with stereoma. The columella is spongy or absent.

Turbinolia sulcata LAMARCK

Order: Scleractinia
Family: Turbinoliidae

The members of the Eocene to Oligocene genus *Turbinolia* are known from Europe, Africa and both Americas. The small, conical corallites have 24 septa and a porous wall between the ribs. The rod-like columella is the outcome of the fusion of first order septa (fig. 7).

1. *Oculina crassiramosa,* Neogene (Pliocene), Sicily, Italy. A fragment of a branching colony, height 25 mm. The present-day representatives of these shallow-water corals live in the western Atlantic, in tropical waters.

2. *Turbinolia sulcata,** Palaeogene (Middle Eocene), Nesle, France. Height of the largest corallite 9 mm. These corals occurred at considerable depths (from about 150 to 500 m).

3. *Caryophyllia clava,* Neogene (Pliocene), Palermo, Italy. A corallite seated on a worm tube; height 17 mm.

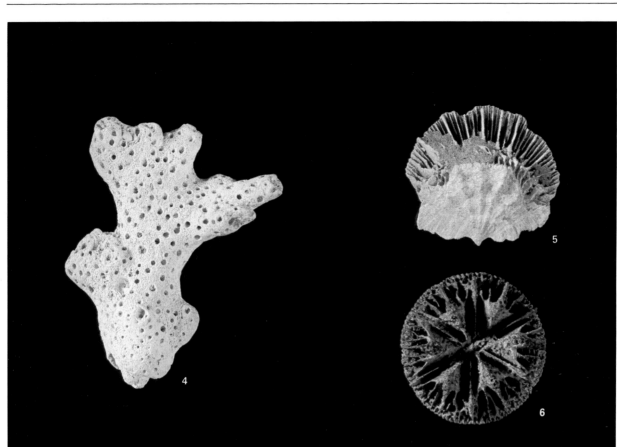

4. *Madrepora solanderi,* Palaeogene (Eocene), Antwerp, Belgium. A fragment of a branching colony, height 46 mm. Madrepores are common species in recent coral reefs; the earliest finds date back to the Eocene.

5. *Flabellum tuberculatum,* Neogene (Middle Miocene), Peelgebied near Beeringen, the Netherlands. Height of corallite 25 mm. An important reef-unforming genus, which spread rapidly into all the seas at the end of the Eocene and whose representatives have survived down to the present day.

6. *Stephanophyllia imperialis,* Neogene (Miocene), Antwerp, Belgium. Corallites, diameter 26 mm.

7. *Turbinolia* sp., a view from above.

Order: Scleractinia
Family: Caryophyllidae
Caryophyllia clava SACCHI

The genus *Caryophyllia* comprises the oldest ahermatypic hexacorals, whose adaptation to inclement conditions was the most successful. They even invaded the deep, cold parts of the sea. They appeared in the Upper Jurassic and are still extant. The corallites are conical and distinctly ribbed; the columella is tuberculated.

Order: Scleractinia
Family: Flabellidae
Flabellum tuberculatum KEFERSTEIN

The corals of the genus *Flabellum* have highly flattened V- or fan-shaped corallites with a raised posterior edge. The pronounced, radially undulating epitheca is thickened internally by stereoma. The septa are compact and numerous and the columella is often absent.

Order: Scleractinia
Family: Micrabaciidae
Stephanophyllia imperialis MICHELIN

The Eurasian genus *Stephanophyllia* has been known from the Eocene down to the Recent. The moderately large, domed, flat-bottomed corallites are composed of a network of porous septa and synapticles.

Monotrypa kettneri PRANTL

Order: Trepostomata
Family: Trematoporidae

Moss animals (Bryozoa or Ectoprocta) are sessile colonial animals living primarily in the sea and on a smaller scale in fresh water. Their oldest known remains stem from Lower Ordovician sediments. Every individual in the colony — the microscopic polypid or zooid — secretes a calcareous, chitinous or membranous case (the zooecium) round itself. The zooids are joined together in a colony (zoarium) formed from a maternal zooid by budding and constituting an intact functional unit. The individuals in the colony are usually polymorphous. The autozooids are responsible for nutrition and reproduction, the avicularia, with their beak-like jaws, protect the colony, the pouch-like ovicoeles protect the embryos, and the vibracula, with their chitin fibres, keep the colony at a given level above the substratum. The autozooids have a U-shaped alimentary tube. The mouth (stoma) is bordered by a ridge with a ring of tentacles (the lophophore); the anus opens outside the lophophore.

Two bryozoan classes — Stenolaemata and Gymnolaemata — are important for palaeontology. In Stenolaemata, which is particularly richly represented in the Palaeozoic, there is no operculum in the stoma of the zooecia. This class includes, among others, the order Trepostomata, which enjoyed its greatest prosperity in the Ordovician and whose youngest representatives occur in Lower Triassic sediments. The species of this order formed bulbous, hemispherical, tuberose, flat or branched zoaria. The zooecia are tubular or prismatic, with a small stoma at the end. In closely adjacent zooecia we find horizontal or diagonal septa. In many species there are further cavities between the zooecia, such as mesopores with numerous septa and thin acanthopores.

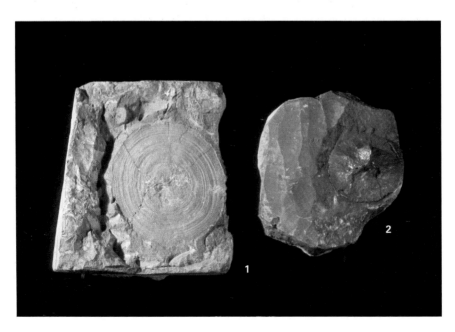

1, 2. *Polyteichus novaki** (2) and *Polyteichus* sp. (1), Middle Ordovician (Caradocian), Prague-Michle, Czechoslovakia. Diameter of the larger zoarium 31 mm. The species *P. novaki,* which formed dense colonies in shallow seas with sandy-argillaceous sediments, is characterized by organization of the lamellae in the shape of a three-pointed star.

O

3

3. *Monotrypa kettneri,* Middle Ordovician (Caradocian), Prague-Řeporyje, Czechoslovakia. A longitudinally bisected bulbous zoarium 67 mm wide, with radially diverging zooecia. The zooecia have undulating walls and a polygonal stoma.

The members of the genus *Monotrypa,* found in Ordovician to Permian sediments in the northern hemisphere, formed massive hemispherical, tuberose or discoid zoaria. The zoaria were either loose, or overgrew the shells of various invertebrates. Their growth on the shells of gastropods, for instance, could have been beneficial to both, since the massive bryozoan zoaria provided the gastropod with effective protection, while the domed shell and movements of the gastropod increased the water flow in the bryozoan colonies and thereby improved their food supply.

Polyteichus novaki PERNER
Polyteichus sp.

Order: Trepostomata
Family: Trematoporoidae

The bryozoans of the genus *Polyteichus,* which are distributed in European Ordovician sediments, have discoid zoaria. The zooecia and mesopores open on to the slightly bulging side, which has one or more prominent lamellae in the middle; the zooecia also open on to the lamellae. The discoid shape of the zoaria was evidently a manifestation of their adaptation to life on a soft substratum.

Bryozoa

Fenestella exsilis Počta

Order: Cryptostomata
Family: Fenestellidae

Stenolaematous bryozoans were represented in the Palaeozoic era chiefly by the order Cryptostomata. They died out in the Lower Triassic. The zoaria are reticulate, with interstices (fenestrulae) of different sizes, and have one or two layers. The branches of the zoaria are interconnected by dissepimenta, or curve over, unite and form anastomoses. The branches are usually surmounted by a sharp medial ridge and by various outgrowths. The zooecia are elongate, pear-shaped or tubular and in front of the orifice they are produced to a vestibule with an interior hemiseptum growing from its base. Mesopores and acanthopores are also present on the zoaria.

Fenestella s. l., a worldwide genus distributed in Ordovician to Permian sediments, is one of the commonest cryptostomatous bryozoans. The zoarium has a regular reticulate structure, in which the branches are joined together by short dissepimenta without zooecia. The zooecial chambers on the branches are arranged in two rows separated on the surface by a nodose ridge. The colonies were anchored to the substratum by a massive holdfast. *Fenestella* species occurred chiefly in shallow-water calcareous deposits; they inhabited both calm and turbulent water.

Hemitrypa tenella Počta

Order: Cryptostomata
Family: Fenestellidae

Like *Fenestella, Hemitrypa* is a cosmopolitan genus, with a similar stratigraphic range. The funnel-shaped zoarium has two layers. The

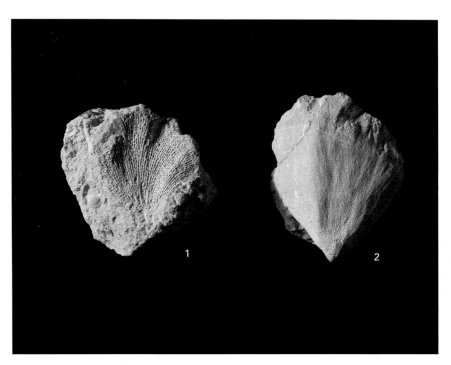

1. *Fenestella exsilis,* Lower Devonian, Prague-Zlíchov, Czechoslovakia. Part of a zoarium preserved in yellowish weathered limestone, length 45 mm. A species which frequented coral reefs.

2. *Hemitrypa tenella,* Lower Devonian, Prague-Zlíchov, Czechoslovakia. Part of a zoarium, length 30 mm.

3

3. *Isotrypa acris,* Lower Devonian (Praguian), Koněprusy, Czechoslovakia. A zoarium, width 70 mm. As with other bryozoans, the planktonic larvae, which gave rise to whole colonies, settled on a suitable solid base, in this case on a segment of a crinoid, which can be seen in the middle of the damaged part of the zoarium.

4. *Fenestella* s. l. – a reconstruction of a part of the colony with living individuals.

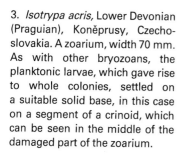

superstructure, seated on the lower layer, was undoubtedly of importance for protection. The interstices in the superstructure corresponded to the mouths of the zooecia in the lower layer.

Isotrypa acris POČTA

Order: Cryptostomata
Family: Fenestellidae

Owing to the mutual resemblance of the zoaria of the different fenestellid bryozoans, whose shape was strongly influenced by the movement of the water, they cannot be differentiated and accurately classified without a detailed knowledge of their internal structure based on exactly oriented sections. Fenestellid skeletons form an open network which allowed water (with food) to flow through. From the internal structure of the zoaria we conclude that the polyps were not functionally specialized. The Devonian members of the genus *Isotrypa,* which are found in Europe, North America and Asia, formed two-layered, funnel-shaped reticulate zoaria whose front and hinder aspects were practically the same. There were two rows of zooecial apertures on the outer surface of the branches. The ridges supporting the superstructure were present only on the branches and not on the dissepimenta.

Bryozoa

Semicoscinium sacculus (POČTA)

Order: Cryptostomata
Family: Fenestellidae

Particularly rich cryptostomatous bryozoan associations lived round and inside coral reefs. Bryozoans of the genus *Semicoscinium* occur normally in the facies of Silurian and Devonian reefs all over the world. They are characterized by funnel-shaped zoaria with a strikingly different outer and inner surface. The mouths of the zooecia open on to the outer surface of the branches, on which the zooecia are arranged in two rows separated by a high, sharp ridge. The branches are connected by dissepiments or anastomose. The inner surface of the zoarium is reticulate, with rhomboid fenestrulae.

4

Archimedes sp.

Order: Cryptostomata
Family: Fenestellidae

Spiral growth of shells or skeletons is encountered in a whole series of invertebrates, but among bryozoans it is uncommon. The best known example is *Archimedes,* a late Palaeozoic fenestellid bryozoan with highly calcareous, spiral, erect zoaria (fig. 6). The single-layered reticulate side branches, similar in construction to those of *Fenestella* species, grew out spirally from a massive central axis. In places, *Archimedes* formed dense populations in shallows protected against the action of the waves. The zooids in the individual 'storeys' filtered the water from a stream leading downwards along the spiral axis and caught microscopic food (e.g. unicellular algae) with a lophophore.

6

Polypora ehrenbergi (GEINITZ)

Order: Cryptostomata
Family: Fenestellidae

During the Permian, cryptostomatous bryozoans quickly died out. Among the fenestellids, *Polypora* – a cosmopolitan genus whose stratigraphic range stretches from the Ordovician to the Lower Triassic – was still abundant in places. The funnel-shaped zoaria are like

1, 2, 6. *Archimedes* sp., Lower Carboniferous, Fox Trap, Colbert, County, Alabama, USA. Slightly deformed zoaria, length of the largest individual 40 mm (1, 2). It is common for only the spiral central axis of these bryozoans to be preserved. 6 – spiral growth of the zoarium.

3. *Semicoscinium sacculus,* Lower Devonian (Praguian), Koněprusy, Czechoslovakia. A zoarium, length 40 mm. An imprint of the reticulate inner surface of the zoarium can be seen in the upper, damaged part.

4. *Polypora ehrenbergi,* Upper Permian, Pössneck, East Germany. Part of a zoarium, length 12 mm. Found in Zechstein reef limestones.

P

C

D

5

5. *Acanthocladia anceps,* * Upper Permian, Pössneck, East Germany. Part of a zoarium, maximum length 12 mm. This species also lived round or inside Upper Permian coral reefs.

those of *Fenestella,* but are more massive and have thick branches with over two rows of zooecia, which also open on to the dissepiments.

Acanthocladia anceps (SCHLOTHEIM)

Order: Cryptostomata
Family: Acanthocladiidae

The members of the genus *Acanthocladia* are known from Upper Carboniferous and Permian sediments all over the world. The zoaria are characteristically branched; side branches without dissepimenta grow out obliquely laterally at regular intervals from thick, straight or slightly curved main branches. The zooecia are organized in three or more rows.

Bryozoa

Berenicea sp.

Order: Cyclostomata
Family: Diastoporidae

Cyclostomata are the least specialized order of the phylum Bryozoa and they were already in existence in the late Ordovician. They reached their peak in the Cretaceous and since then they have declined, down to the present day. The zoaria are simple tubes terminating in an open aperture without an operculum. The walls between the zooids are porous. The zoaria are very diversely shaped.

Berenicea, known from the Triassic to the Recent, is one of the best known cyclostomatous bryozoans; very similar — and evidently closely related — species, often described under the same generic name, are already known from the Ordovician, however. Berenicea zoaria are encrusting, single-layered and circular, lobular or fan-shaped.

Ceriopora sp.

Order: Cyclostomata
Family: Heteroporidae

The stratigraphic range of Ceriopora species extends from the Triassic to the Miocene. They are known from Europe, North America and Asia. The zoaria are branched and the long, cylindrical or prismatic zooecia have transverse plates known as diaphragms (fig. 6).

Entalophora heros NOVÁK

Order: Cyclostomata
Family: Entalophoridae

The genus Entalophora has existed since the Jurassic and today its

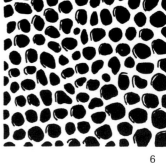

6

1. *Entalophora heros,* Upper Cretaceous (Cenomanian), Kutná Hora, Czechoslovakia. Parts of isolated zoaria, length up to 10 mm.

2. *Corymbopora,* sp., Upper Cretaceous, France. Parts of branched zoaria, maximum length 9 mm. The ends of the branches contained egg sacs.

3. *Osculipora plebeia,* Upper Cretaceous (Turonian), Kamajka near Čáslav, Czechoslovakia. Two fragments of zoaria; length of the larger branched zoarium 16 mm.

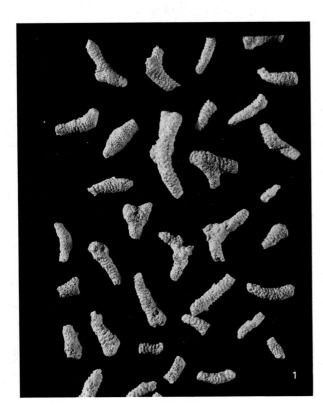

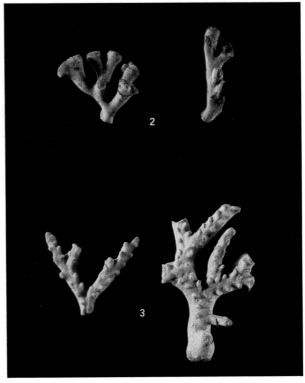

4. *Berenicea* sp., Jurassic (Bathonian), Bradford-on-Avon, England. A zoarium (maximum cross section 11 mm) has overgrown the calyx of a crinoid belonging to the genus *Apiocrinus*.

5, 6. *Ceriopora* sp., Upper Jurassic, France. 1 — part of a branched zoarium; maximum branch cross section 12 mm. 6 — detail of a colony.

7. *Entalophora* sp., detail of a colony.

7

species inhabit practically every sea except arctic waters. Fossil species are to be found in Europe and North America. The zoaria are erect, cylindrical and branched. The mouths of the zooecia lie all round the circumference of the branches (fig. 7).

Osculipora plebeia NOVÁK

Order: Cyclostomata
Family: Cytididae

The commonest types of Cretaceous cyclostomates are those with small, branched zoaria like the ones characteristic of the widespread European Upper Cretaceous genus *Osculipora*. The erect, long, tubular zooecia form bundles with the apertures at the ends of lateral branches and outgrowths.

Corymbopora sp.

Order: Cyclostomata
Family: Corymboporidae

The genus *Corymbopora* has survived from the Cretaceous down to the Recent. The zoaria are branched and distally widened; the ends of the branches are flat or rounded. Numerous pores left by previous zooecia can be seen round the periphery of the zoarium.

129

Bryozoa

Onychocella sp.

Order: Cheilostomata
Family: Onychocellidae

The zooecia of bryozoans belonging to the class Gymnolaemata have mouths that can be closed with an operculum. Cheilostomata are an important order of this class. They appeared in the Cretaceous and they are the most advanced of all the bryozoans. They underwent adaptive radiations very quickly and in present-day seas they are by far the most numerous. Polymorphism of the zooids is highly developed in this order. The zoaria are generally calcareous, but may occasionally be horny or membranous. They are either encrusting or free and are variously shaped. Short zooecia without cross connections are closely contiguous and are joined together by small openings. In many species of cheilostomates, only the edges of the zooecia are calcareous and all that remains of the membranous parts in the fossil state are large openings known as opesia. The polypids were pushed in and out of the zooecia by a hydrostatic system (a cavity between the cuticle and the anterior calcareous wall, or a 'compensatory sac'); when these organs were filled with water or emptied, the polypid either slipped out of the zooecium or was withdrawn again.

Onychocella still lives in tropical and subtropical seas, but has been known since the Cretaceous, in Europe, North America and northern Africa. Its encrusting zoaria have rounded to roughly hexagonal zooecia; the opesia are trilobular.

1. *Lunulites goldfussi,* Upper Cretaceous (Senonian), Rügen, West Germany. Diameter of the largest zoarium, shown from the under side, 4 mm.

2. *Discoporella umbellata,* * Neogene (Miocene), Beeringen, Haarlem, the Netherlands. Zoaria seen from above and below. Largest diameter 9 mm.

Ng

Cr

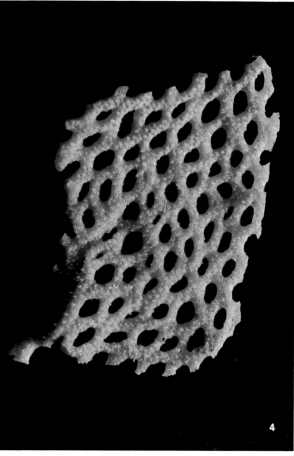

3

4

3. *Onychocella* sp., Upper Cretaceous, Meudon, France. A zoarium (largest diameter 16 mm) growing on an echino-dermid of the genus *Echino-corys*. The ventral valve of a brachiopod *(Ancistrocrania parisiensis)* is cemented to it alongside the zoarium.

4, 5. *Retepora* sp., Neogene (Mio-cene), Italy. 4 – fragment of a zoarium, length 10 mm. 5 – detail of a colony.

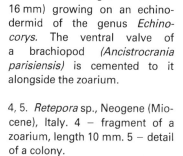

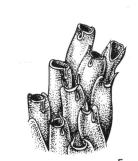

5

Lunulites goldfussi HAGENOW

Order: Cheilostomata
Family: Lunulitidae

Cheilostomatous bryozoans living freely on the substratum often have discoid or wide, cup-shaped zoaria. The latter are characteristic of the genus *Lunulites,* for example. These bryozoans occur in Cretaceous to Eocene sediments in Europe and North America. The zooecia are arranged in radial rows, which fork as they near the edge of the colony.

Discoporella umbellata (DEFRANCE)

Order: Cheilostomata
Family: Cupuladriidae

The zoaria of the bryozoan genus *Discoporella* are shaped similarly to those of the genus *Lunulites.* Their fossil representatives (the oldest date back to the Miocene) are known from various parts of Europe; present-day species occur in the Mediterranean and the Atlantic. They find optimum conditions in the tropical and subtropical belt. The zooecia have numerous pores and two rounded opesia.

Retepora sp.

Order: Cheilostomata
Family: Reteporidae

The genus *Retepora* is known from the Eocene to the present day. The branches of the reticulate zoarium do not anastomose and grow from a widened base. The zooecia have circular mouths, below which lies a small, slit-like opening (fig. 5) belonging to the compensation sac.

131

 **Brachiopoda**

Pompeckium kuthani (POMPECKIJ)

Order: Orthida
Family: Bohemiellidae

Brachiopods with a hinge (class Articulata) are a more advanced evolutionary line than Inarticulata, although they are also known from the very beginning of the Palaeozoic. They always have calcareous shells formed of two valves of unequal sizes. As a rule, the ventral (pedicle) valve is larger than the dorsal (brachial) valve and during the animal's lifetime a stalk (pedicle) anchoring it to the base led from its apical part; in fossil specimens the position of the stalk is denoted by an orifice (foramen). On the inside, in addition to various outgrowths, the dorsal valve carries calcareous supports of the lophophore (brachidia). On the posterior margin of the shell there is always a hinge controlled by the powerful muscles which open and close the valves, in which teeth in the ventral valve fit into sockets in the dorsal valve. The alimentary tube is blind-ended and any undigested food remains are expelled via the mouth. The Articulata attained their peak in the Devonian period; today they are only a secondary component of the marine fauna.

Orthida were evidently the phylogenetically oldest order of articulate brachiopods and they died out during the Lower Permian. Their only slightly domed shells have fine radial ribs and a wide locking margin. The members of the genus *Pompeckium* are known from Bohemian Middle Cambrian sediments from very shallow water. The valves bulge to almost the same degree and are transversely elliptical. The ribs are simple or sometimes branched; the concentric growth lines are indistinct.

Eodalmanella socialis (BARRANDE)

Order: Orthida
Family: Dalmanellidae

Species of *Eodalmanella* occur in Lower Ordovician sediments in central Europe. The dorsal valve of the tiny shell is flatter than the ventral valve. The hinge margin is produced to short, sharp-tipped 'wings'. The ribs are arranged in bundles. These brachiopods lived on an argillaceous substratum in gently moving water.

Drabovia redux (BARRANDE)

Order: Orthida
Family: Draboviidae

These brachiopods occur in Middle Ordovician deposits all over Europe and northern Africa. The shell is bilaterally convex, but the ventral valve bulges more than the dorsal valve. In outline, the shell is transversely elliptical; the ribs on its surface are arranged in bundles.

1, 2. *Eodalmanella socialis,** Lower Ordovician (Llanvirn), Osek near Rokycany, Czechoslovakia. Cores of dorsal and ventral valves preserved in an originally calcareous and secondarily silicified concretion. Length of the largest valve 7 mm.

3. *Drabovia redux,** Middle Ordovician (Caradoc), Beroun, Czechoslovakia. A core of a ventral valve preserved in quartzite together with numerous trilobite shell fragments. Length of valve 13 mm. This genus inhabited soft, sandy floor and sufficiently oxygenated water.

4. *Pompeckium kuthani,** Middle Cambrian, Skryje, Czechoslovakia. Sandstone 100 mm across full of limonitized shells. These brachiopods lived in very shallow water in the sublittoral — and also perhaps in the littoral — zone.

 **Brachiopoda**

Clitambonites squamata (Pahlen)

Order: Orthida
Family: Clitambonitidae

Clitambonites is an important European and Asian Lower to Middle Ordovician genus. The dorsal valve of its shells is only slightly convex and the back of the highly convex ventral valve is obliquely truncated. On the posterior aspect of the ventral valve, between the apex and the hinge line, there is a triangular field which is characteristic of many groups of brachiopods. The field is divided into two lateral sectors (interareas) and a middle sector (deltyrium). In *Clitambonites* species, the middle sector closed progressively from the hinge line towards the apex, leaving only a small foramen for the largely atrophied stalk. The surface sculpture of the shells gives the impression of overlapping tiles.

Euorthisina moesta (Barrande)

Order: Orthida
Family: Euorthisinidae

The genus *Euorthisina* abounds in Lower Ordovician sediments in Europe, northern Africa and South America. Both the valves are slightly convex, with interareas and an open middle sector. Their surface is ribbed.

Porambonites aequirostris (Schlotheim)

Order: Pentamerida
Family: Porambonitidae

After orthids, pentamerids are the phylogenetically second oldest order of articulate brachiopods. Their stratigraphic range extends from the

1–3. *Clitambonites squamata,* Middle Ordovician (Caradoc), Kohtla-Järve, Estonian Soviet Socialist Republic. The inner aspect of the dorsal (1) and ventral (2) valve. Dorsal view of a shell (3), width 27 mm. Teeth supported by dental ridges, fused to form a spoon-shaped cavity (spondylium) for insertion of the muscles, are clearly discernible inside the ventral valve.

4–6. *Porambonites aequirostris,* Middle Ordovician (Caradoc), Kohtla-Järve, Estonian Soviet Socialist Republic. View of a shell from the ventral (4) and the anterior (5) aspect and of a core from the side (6). Width of the largest shell 26 mm. *Porambonites* lived in the vertical position (tip downwards).

Middle Cambrian to the Upper Permian. The shells are usually highly convex, with a short hinge line, and are often smooth. In the apical part of the ventral valve there is a muscle platform raised off the floor – the spondylium. The brachial supports (brachidia) inside the dorsal valve are simple.

Porambonites occurs in Lower Ordovician to Lower Silurian sediments in most parts of the world. The shell is either biconvex, or the ventral valve is flattened. The sulcus formed during the growth of the shell in the ventral valve along the plane of symmetry is manifested in the anterior segment of the contact line of the valves (the commissure) as a medial sinus. The surface of the shell has very fine radial ribs, with minute dimples in the intercostal furrows.

7. *Rostricellula ambigena,* Middle Ordovician (Caradoc), Prague-Spořilov, Czechoslovakia. View of a dorsal and a ventral valve; width 8 and 9 mm. The large shells belong to the brachiopod *Rafinesquina pseudoloricata.*

8. *Euorthisina moesta,** Lower Ordovician (Llanvirn), Prague-Šárka, Czechoslovakia. Core of a ventral valve; width 33 mm. This species inhabited deep shelf water.

Rostricellula ambigena (BARRANDE)

Order: Rhynchonellida
Family: Trigonirhynchiidae

The representatives of this order have existed since the Ordovician. The shells are biconvex and posteriorly tapering, with a curved hinge line. The brachidia are in the form of simple processes. The tiny rhynchonellid brachiopods of the genus *Rostricellula* lived in the Middle and Upper Ordovician; today they are found in many parts of the northern hemisphere. The ventral valve of the coarsely ribbed shell has a well developed sulcus and the dorsal valve a conspicuous ridge.

Conchidium sp.

Order: Pentamerida
Family: Pentameridae

In the Silurian period, almost every type of marine environment was inhabited by brachiopods with the most diverse shapes and sizes. The cosmopolitan genus *Conchidium*, already known from Upper Ordovician sediments, had very large shells. Both valves are highly convex, but the apex of the ventral valve stretches far beyond the apex of the dorsal valve. The hinge line is very short and the contact line (commissure) between the valves is only slightly undulating. The surface of the valves is roughly ribbed. *Conchidium* lived in turbulent shallow water, attached to a base by a stalk for their entire life. They died out in the Lower Devonian.

Gypidula galeata (SOWERBY)

Order: Pentamerida
Family: Pentameridae

This genus lived from the Lower Silurian to the Upper Devonian practically everywhere in the world. The ventral valve is helmet-shaped and the dorsal valve is medially concave, so that anteriorly the commissure forms a shallow sinus. The surface of the valves is smooth or ribbed. These brachiopods lived mainly in shallow water. When young, they were attached to the substratum by a stalk, which atrophied during growth. The shell was stabilized in a suitable position, and protected from tilting or overturning by the thickened walls of the two apices, which also formed the centre of gravity of the shell.

1–3. *Gypidula galeata,* Lower Silurian (Wenlock), Gotland, Sweden. Width of the largest shell 25 mm. A dorsal valve (1), a side view of a shell (2) and a ventral valve (3). These pentamerids inhabited shallow water in the tropical belt.

4, 5, 7. *Meristina tumida,* Lower Silurian (Wenlock), Dudley, England. View of a ventral valve (4) carrying a sessile commensal organism (a cornulitid), corals and bryozoans, and a front view of a shell (5). Width of the larger shell 45 mm. 7 — a reconstruction of a living individual.

S

6

6. *Conchidium sp.,* Upper Silurian (Ludlow), Great Britain. A group of shells; width of the valves up to 50 mm.

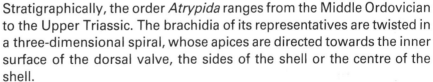

Meristina tumida (DALMAN)

Order: Atrypida
Family: Meristellidae

Stratigraphically, the order *Atrypida* ranges from the Middle Ordovician to the Upper Triassic. The brachidia of its representatives are twisted in a three-dimensional spiral, whose apices are directed towards the inner surface of the dorsal valve, the sides of the shell or the centre of the shell.

Meristina species are cosmopolitan Lower Silurian to Lower Devonian brachiopods. The large biconvex shell is not ribbed and in front it has a striking dorsally recurved commissure. The apical part of the ventral valve (the umbo) is conspicuously curved. A pedicle foramen is present in young stages only; later it closes over. Longitudinal sections of the shell clearly show pronounced thickening of the wall of the ventral valve in the region of the umbo; it was this that kept the shell of the adult animal, which was partly buried in the sediment, in an almost vertical position (fig. 7). These brachiopods preferred shallows in the vicinity of coral reefs or biostromes. Sometimes they occur in clusters.

7

139

 **Brachiopoda**

Atrypa sp.
Atrypa reticularis (LINNAEUS)

Order: Atrypida
Family: Atrypidae

The genus *Atrypa* is known from Lower Silurian to Upper Devonian sediments all over the world. The dorsal valve of the rounded shell is more convex than the ventral valve. The surface sculpture consists of dense radial ribs and of growth lamellae, which grow out at regular intervals and jut a long way from the curved surface of the shell, forming a 'train'. Adult specimens were free and often lived on a soft substratum, where the lamellae prevented them from sinking in.

Dayia bohemica BOUČEK

Order: Atrypida
Family: Dayidae

Dayia, an Upper Silurian and Lower Devonian genus found in Europe, Asia and northern Africa, is characterized by a small, smooth shell with a helmet-like convex ventral valve and an anteriorly slightly concave (sulcate) ventral valve.

Cyrtia exporrecta (WAHLENBERG)

Order: Spiriferida
Family: Cyrtiidae

Spiriferids appeared in the Lower Silurian and died out in the Lower Jurassic. Their biconvex shells, which have a long hinge line on the posterior edge, have three-dimensionally spiral brachidia inside. The tips of the spirals point laterally to ventrally.

1. *Dicaelosia biloba,** Lower Silurian (Wenlock), Djupvik, Gotland, Sweden. Whole shells and isolated valves. Width of the largest shell 5 mm. *Dicaelosia verneuiliana* (the two biggest shells), Lower Silurian (Wenlockian), Snäckgärsdbaden, Gotland, Sweden. Width 7 and 8 mm.

2–4. *Dayia bohemica* Upper Silurian (Pridoli), Prague-Řeporyje, Czechoslovakia. A shell from the ventral aspect (2), the dorsal aspect (3) and the side (4). Width of shells 10 mm. An important Upper Silurian species forming whole limestone banks in places.

5–7, 13. *Cyrtia exporrecta,** Lower Silurian (Wenlock), Dudley, England. View of a shell from behind, showing the clearly discernible pedicle foramen (5), from the ventral aspect (6) and from the front (7). Width of the largest shell 26 mm. 13 – a reconstruction of a living individual.

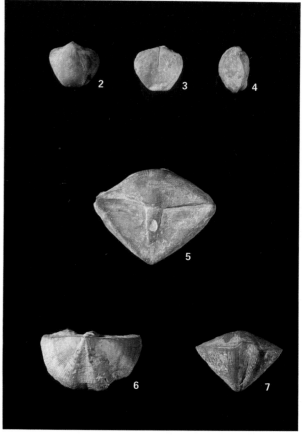

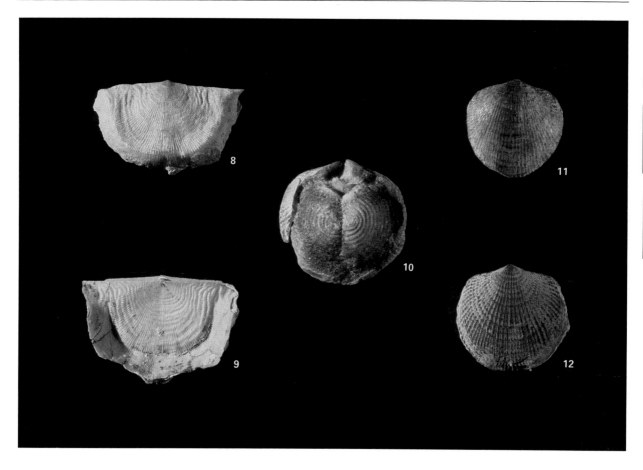

8, 9. *Leptagonia depressa,* Lower Silurian (Wenlock), Gotland, Sweden. A shell seen from the ventral (8) and the dorsal (9) aspect. Width of the larger individual 25 mm.

10. *Atrypa* sp., Middle Devonian, Sötenich, West Germany. A damaged dorsal valve, width 28 mm, showing the spirally twisted brachidia.

11, 12. *Atrypa reticularis,** Lower Silurian (Wenlock), Dudley, England. Shells seen from the dorsal (11) and the ventral (12) aspect, minus the 'trains'. Width of the larger shell 25 mm.

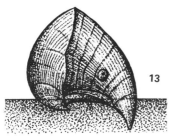

13

Cyrtia is a worldwide representative of Silurian and Devonian spiriferids. The shell has a high, pyramidal ventral valve and a slightly convex dorsal valve. The animal remained anchored by a stalk for the whole of its lifetime. The large, flat, triangular field between the ventral valve and the hinge line increased the stability of the shell (fig. 13).

Dicaelosia biloba (LINNAEUS)
Dicaelosia verneuiliana (BEECHER)

Order: Orthida
Family: Dicaelosiidae

The genus *Dicaelosia* comprises Upper Ordovician to Lower Devonian brachiopods with worldwide distribution. In front, the bilaterally sulcate shell forms two lobes separated by a deep notch. *Dicaelosia* species occur most frequently in very fine-grained sediments. They lived attached by a stalk to the shells of other invertebrates or to the thalli of algae.

Leptagonia depressa (SOWERBY)

Order: Strophomenida
Family: Leptaenidae

Leptagonia species are known from the Lower Silurian to the Lower Carboniferous. The shell, at first flat, curved dorsally like a knee in later stages of growth. The surface of the shell is radially ribbed, with undulating concentric ridges on the flat part of both valves.

Strophonella bohemica (BARRANDE)
Order: Strophomenida
Family: Strophonellidae

The peak period of the brachiopods was during the Devonian, when species living on the outskirts of coral reefs were particularly numerous. The representatives of the worldwide genus *Strophonella* are known from the Silurian and Lower Devonian. The dorsal valve of young individuals was concave, the ventral valve convex, but during further growth this was reversed and at the front and sides the shell began to grow in a ventral direction and formed a high 'train'.

Cymostrophia stephani (BARRANDE)
Order: Strophomenida
Family: Strophodontidae

Cymostrophia, which occurs in European Lower and Middle Devonian sediments, has large, wide shells with a high, dorsally oriented 'train'. On the surface there are fine radial ribs and in some species concentric ridges are present on the flat part of both valves.

Parachonetes verneuili (BARRANDE)
Order: Strophomenida
Family: Chonetidae

Chonetid shells have a convex ventral valve and a concave dorsal valve. One of their characteristic features are oblique laterally oriented, hollow spines on the posterior margin of the shell, which are thought to have had sensory function. Some chonetids may have been able to swim a little. *Parachonetes* is a worldwide genus found in Lower and Middle Devonian strata. The large shell is thickly covered with blunt ribs.

Merista herculea (BARRANDE)
Order: Atrypida
Family: Meristellidae

Merista species are known from Lower to Middle Devonian strata in Europe and North and South America. Both the valves are convex, longitudinally or transversely elongated and smooth, with a dorsal ridge and a ventral furrow.

Stenorhynchia nympha (BARRANDE)
Order: Rhynchonellida
Family: Rhynchotrematidae

Stenorhynchia, from Devonian formations in Europe and North America, has a typical rhynchonellid appearance. The young shells are flat, while adult shells are high with a striking saddle and lobe in front. Pronounced sharp-edged ribs are present on their surface.

Eoglossinotoechia sylphidea (BARRANDE)
Order: Rhynchonellida
Family: Uncinulidae

Uncinulid shells were at first flattened, but as the animal grew they became higher and, in some cases, roundedly cuboid. In front, the valves close with a tooth-like projection. Their sculpture consists of rounded ribs or bands separated by narrow grooves; in many species, long spines project from the grooves. *Eoglossinotoechia,* a European Silurian and Devonian genus, is a common representative of the family.

1, 2. *Merista herculea,** Lower Devonian (Pragian), Koněprusy, Czechoslovakia. Ventral (1) and dorsal (2) view of a shell. Width of the larger shell 35 mm.

3–5. *Stenorhynchia nympha,** Lower Devonian (Pragian), Koněprusy, Czechoslovakia. Ventral (3), anterior (4) and dorsal (5) view of a shell. Width of the largest shell 15 mm.

6–8. *Eoglossinotoechia sylphidea,* Lower Devonian (Pragian), Koněprusy, Czechoslovakia. A ventral valve (6) and a side (7) and anterior (8) view of a shell. Width of the largest specimen 19 mm.

9. *Cymostrophia stephani,* Lower Devonian (Pragian), Koněprusy, Czechoslovakia. Ventral valve; width 52 mm.

10. *Strophonella bohemica,* Lower Devonian (Pragian), Koněprusy, Czechoslovakia. Ventral valve; width 60 mm. The animals lived freely on the sea bed.

11. *Parachonetes verneuili,* Lower Devonian (Pragian), Koněprusy, Czechoslovakia. Ventral valve; width 43 mm. The spines are inconspicuous. The body cavity was much limited in space due to the marked concavity of the dorsal valve.

⬛ Brachiopoda

Stringocephalus burtini (DEFRANCE)

Order: Terebratulida
Family: Stringocephalidae

Terebratulida are the evolutionally most recent and today the most numerous order of brachiopods. Their history can be traced back to the Lower Devonian. The shells are similar to those of some atrypids, from which terebratulids probably split off during phylogenesis. Instead of being spirally twisted, however, the brachidia are loop-like with varying degrees of complexity.

Stringocephalus is an important Middle Devonian brachiopod genus distributed over almost the entire globe. The large, smooth shells have a striking, markedly curved apex, with large interareas and a pedicle foramen. They are to be found in coral reef, lagoon and even relatively deep sea sediments. In addition to the pedicle, the pronounced convexity of the shell helped to keep the animal stable in the biological position.

1, 2. *Stringocephalus burtini,* * Middle Devonian (Eifelian). Paffrath, West Germany. 1 — inner surface of the ventral valve, showing the median septum, which was also developed in the dorsal valve; 2 — a shell from the dorsal aspect. Width of the shell 65 mm.

3. *Cyrtospirifer* sp. Upper Devonian (Frasnian), Cerfonbaine, Belgium. A view of the dorsal surface of a shell; width 70 mm. The interareas of the ventral valve and the foramen for the stalk are clearly discernible.

4. *Xystostrophia umbraculum,* * Middle Devonian (Givetian?), Mühlemosald, Gerolstein, West Germany. A shell from the dorsal aspect; width 44 mm. A characteristic species of the Middle Devonian Rhenish zoogeographical province.

144

5

5, 6. *Acrospirifer primaevus,** Lower Devonian (Siegenian), Seifen, West Germany. 5 – a limonitized core of a dorsal valve, width 55 mm. A stratigraphically important species which inhabited shallow seas with a sandy bed. 6 – a reconstruction of a living individual.

Acrospirifer primaevus (STEININGER)

Order: Spiriferida
Family: Delthyrididae

The genus *Acrospirifer* is a cosmopolitan representative of Lower Devonian spiriferids. The shells are large, wide and biconvex. The umbonal cavity in the ventral valve is secondarily reinforced. During the animal's lifetime, this part of the shell kept the animal partly buried in the loose sediment (fig. 6).

Cyrtospirifer sp.

Order: Spiriferida
Family: Cyrtospiriferidae

A number of members of the worldwide genus *Cyrtospirifer* are characterized by strikingly wide shells. Stratigraphically, the genus ranges from the Upper Devonian to the Lower Carboniferous. The shell is biconvex, with a pronounced medial furrow on the ventral valve and a ridge on the dorsal valve.

Xystostrophia umbraculum (SCHLOTHEIM)

Order: Strophomenida
Family: Chilidiopsidae

The ventral valve of the large shells of the European Middle Devonian genus *Xystostrophia* is slightly convex near the apex and then becomes slightly concave; the dorsal valve is convex. Both valves have interareas between the apex and the locking margin. The pedicle foramen is closed. Narrow radial ribs are the dominant sculptural element. *Xystostrophia* species lay on the sea bed with their flattish ventral valve downwards and occasionally they could even swim. They evidently moved with their hinge forward, by quickly closing and opening the valves, expelling water from their brachial cavity.

6

 **Brachiopoda**

Dictyoclostus semireticulatus (MARTIN)

Order: Strophomenida
Family: Dictyoclostidae

Strophomenids belonging to the superfamily Productacea occupied a dominant position in late Palaeozoic brachiopod associations. Morphologically they were very diverse and they also included the biggest known brachiopods, such as those of the genera *Titanaria* and *Gigantoproductus,* whose shells measured over 35 cm across. The shells of the members of the superfamily usually have a convex ventral valve and a concave dorsal valve. These brachiopods had no stalk and were mostly unattached; only some – at least in the earlier stages of growth – were cemented. Spines arranged in a specific pattern helped to stabilize the shell in the living biological position and prevented it from sinking into the soft substratum.

The members of the European Lower Carboniferous brachiopod genus *Dictyoclostus* have large shells with a markedly convex ventral valve and a concave dorsal valve. Groups of fine spines grew from the surface of both the valves and along the locking edge of the shell.

1, 2. *Dasyalosia goldfussi,**Upper Permian (Zechstein), Trebnitz, Gera, East Germany. View of a dorsal (1) and a ventral (2) valve; width 21 mm.

3–5, 9. *Horridonia horrida,** Upper Permian (Zechstein), Gera, East Germany. A posterior (3), ventral (4) and dorsal (5) view of a shell. Width of the largest shell 42 mm. 9 – a reconstruction of a living individual.

6. *Muirwoodia* sp., Permian, Salt Range, India. Core of a dorsal valve with various typical characters of the superfamily Productacea – in the centre a median septum and on either side, near the apex, two twin pairs of muscle (adductor) imprints. The lophophore was evidently attached to the large, loop-like structures. The papillose surface is evidence of the presence of short internal spines with an unknown function. Core width 40 mm.

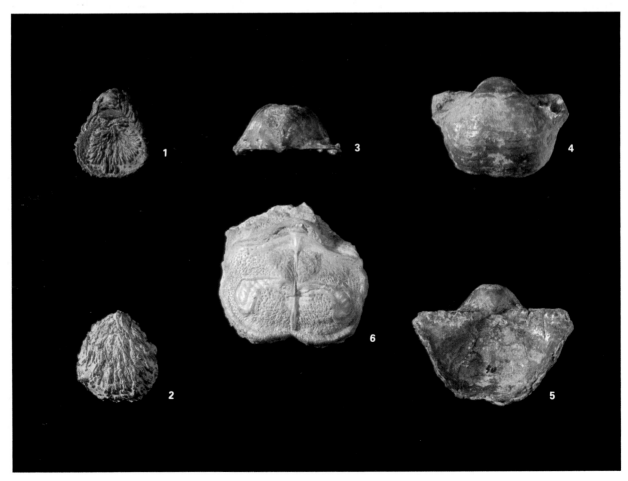

7,* 8. *Dictyoclostus semireticulatus,** Lower Carboniferous (Viséan), Dublin, Ireland, and Clitheroe, England. Ventral valves, width 60 mm, seen from behind (7) and above (8). The fine spines have been broken off.

Horridonia horrida (SOWERBY)

Order: Strophomenida
Family: Dictyoclostidae

The important Permian genus *Horridonia* is known from Europe, the Arctic region, Asia and Australia. The moderately large to large shells have a highly convex ventral valve and a slightly concave dorsal valve. The long spines are concentrated chiefly along the hinge and posterolaterally, on the flattened parts of the shell (fig. 9).

Dasyalosia goldfussi (MÜNSTER)

Order: Strophomenida
Family: Strophalosiidae

The end of the Permian marked the greatest crisis in the entire history (over 580 million years) of the brachiopods, when, among others, the majority of strophomenids died out, together with the last of the pentamerids and orthids.

Dasyolosia shells (Upper Permian, Europe) have an unusual appearance. The ventral valve is slightly convex and the dorsal valve is flat or slightly concave; both are thickly covered with vermiform spines. A certain amount of sediment was evidently retained among the spines on the dorsal valve, so that all that could be seen of the shell were the edges protruding above the substratum.

9

147

Brachiopoda

Punctospirella fragilis (SCHLOTHEIM)

Order: Spiriferida
Family: Spiriferinidae

At the transition from the Palaeozoic to the Mesozoic era, many groups of animals, including brachiopods, died out en masse. In consequence, brachiopods are very rare in Lower Triassic deposits all over the world. During the Middle Triassic they recuperated, however. The very widespread Triassic to Lower Jurassic spiriferinids include the genus *Punctospirella,* whose shells are small to moderately large. The anterior part of the commissure usually formed a pronounced saddle and lobe. The fine sculpturing on the surface of the valves comprises growth lamellae and fine, hollow spines pointing roughly radially from the apex at a very small angle to the surface of the shell.

10

Tetractinella trigonella (SCHLOTHEIM)

Order: Atrypida
Family: Athyrididae

The last known atrypid brachiopods are Triassic species, including those of the widespread European genus *Tetractinella.* At the front of the small shells there are spiky lobes in which sharp ribs leading from the apex terminate.

Tetractinella closely resembles Upper Jurassic terebratulid brachiopods of the genus *Cheirothyris.* The shells of these two genera are cited as an example of adaptive convergence, i.e. of a similar shell morphology adapted to a similar mode of life. The outgrowths on the front of the shell presumably protected the markedly lobate edge of the mantle, which also had a sensory function.

1, 2. *Tetractinella trigonella,** Middle Triassic, Štítník, Czechoslovakia. A shell from the dorsal (1) and ventral (2) aspect. Width of the larger shell 12 mm. This species occurs in both the German and the Alpine Triassic.

3–5. *Halorelloidea rectifrons,** Upper Triassic (Norian), Silická Brezová, Czechoslovakia. A ventral (5), front (4) and dorsal (3) view of the shell. Width of the largest valve 18 mm. Apart from the Western Carpathians, distributed chiefly in the Alps.

Rhaetina gregaria (SUESS)

Order: Terebratulida
Family: Dielasmatidae

The genus *Rhaetina* is a prominent Upper Triassic representative of the terebratulids known from many places in Europe and Asia. The small to moderately large, biconvex shell has a smooth, biplicate surface, i.e. on the dorsal valve there are two ridges separated by a median furrow. The short apex of the ventral valve (which has a relatively large pedicle foramen) points almost dorsally. These brachiopods, anchored by their stalk, held themselves almost vertically, with the umbonal region partly buried in the substratum (fig. 10). They lived both near and on coral reefs, but also sometimes at greater depths.

6–8, 10. *Rhaetina gregaria,** Upper Triassic (Rhaetian), Hindelang, West Germany. A front (6), ventral (7) and dorsal (8) view of the shell. 10 – a reconstruction of a living individual.

9. *Punctospirella fragilis,** Middle Triassic, Würzburg, West Germany. A group of shells in shelly limestone; width of the largest shell 19 mm.

Halorelloidea rectifrons (BITTNER)

Order: Rhynchonellida
Family: Dimerellidae

The members of this European and Asian Upper Triassic genus have transversely oval shells. The dorsal valve is more convex than the ventral valve and is smooth or irregularly ribbed. The commissure is straight and in both the valves there are opposing medial grooves, or else there is a sharp ridge down the centre of the dorsal valve.

Homoeorhynchia acuta (SOWERBY)

Order: Rhynchonellida
Family: Rhynchonellidae

During the Jurassic period spiriferids died out and only two orders of articulate brachiopods remained common; these were Rhynchonellida and Terebratulida. Most rhynchonellids are characterized by a median ridge on their dorsal valve and by a zigzag commissure with a median fold on the anterior margin. The zigzag enabled the animal to take in a large amount of food without having to open the valves very wide. The median fold was the morphological expression of a general tendency among brachiopods to separate suspension inflow and outflow from one another.

The members of the European Lower and Middle Jurassic genus *Homoeorhynchia* have a roughly triangular shell. The dorsal valve tapers off in front to a striking median keel, bordered on either side by a few ribs which fade away towards the apex.

Cirpa fronto (QUENSTEDT)

Order: Rhynchonellida
Family: Wellerellidae

The shells of the members of the genus *Cirpa*, which are found in Lower Jurassic Europe and the Near East, are uniplicate (the ventral valve curves inwards, the dorsal valve has a median ridge and the commissure, in front, forms a dorsally oriented fold). The sculpture consists of sharp ribs extending to the apex.

1, 2. *Torquirhynchia inconstans,* * Upper Jurassic (Kimmeridgian), Nattheim, West Germany. Shells from the ventral (1) and dorsal (2) aspect. Width of the larger specimen 35 mm. The concentric structures in the umbonal region are the outcome of secondary silicification of the shell.

3–5. *Homoeorhynchia acuta,* * Lower Jurassic (Domerian), Kostelec near Považská Teplá, Czechoslovakia. Shells from the dorsal aspect (3), the side (4) and in front (5). Width of the largest valve 18 mm. An important species for the Domerian Stage.

6–8. *Cirpa fronto,* Lower Jurassic, Rudno, Czechoslovakia. Shells from the dorsal (6), frontal (7) and ventral (8) aspect. Width of the largest shell 17 mm. The dorsal valve has only a low ridge in the middle (7).

9. *Rhynchonelloidella varians,* Middle Jurassic (Bathonian), West Germany. Micritic limestone crammed with shells. Width of the largest shell 13 mm.

9

10, 11. *Prionorhynchia quinquipli-cata,* Lower Jurassic (Domerian), Kostelec near Považská Teplá, Czechoslovakia. Shells from the ventral (10) and frontal (11) aspect. Width of the larger shell 30 mm.

10

11

Prionorhynchia quinquiplicata (ZIETEN)

Order: Rhynchonellida
Family: Wellerellidae

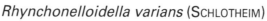

The genus *Prionorhynchia* occurs in Lower Jurassic sediments in Europe and Asia. The roughly pentagonal shells are large, with a uniplicate or straight commissure. The apex of the shell is very small and hooked.

Rhynchonelloidella varians (SCHLOTHEIM)

Order: Rhynchonellida
Family: Wellerellidae

Rhynchonelloidella shells are known from Middle and Upper Jurassic Europe. They are uniplicate, with large numbers of sharp ribs.

Torquirhynchia inconstans (SOWERBY)

Order: Rhynchonellida
Family: Wellerellidae

Brachiopod shells (except for cementing forms) are usually bilaterally symmetrical. The species of the European Upper Jurassic genus *Torquirhynchia* are an exception. Their shells are moderately large, widely triangular and thickly covered with sharp ribs. The right and the left half of the shell are slightly displaced relative to each other.

Zeilleria quadrifida (VALENCIENNES)

Order: Terebratulida
Family: Zeilleriidae

Terebratulids took over from the rhynchonellids as the dominant brachiopods during the Jurassic period and have kept this position ever since. Despite their morphological diversity, it is often impossible to classify them exactly unless we know various details of the internal structure of the shell. The shell of the genus *Zeilleria,* found in Lower Jurassic sediments in Europe, is biconvex, with corresponding furrows on both valves, so that there is a straight commissure. The anterior edge of the smooth shell is divided into two to four lobes.

Loboidothyris subselloides WESTPHAL

Order: Terebratulida
Family: Tchegemithyrididae

The shells of the genus *Loboidothyris* occur in European Middle and Upper Jurassic sediments. Both the valves are convex and smooth, with a uniplicate or sulciplicate commissure (i.e. with a saddle divided by a median sinus). The apex of the ventral valve has a large foramen for the stalk.

Juralina (?) *humeralis* (RÖMER)

Order: Terebratulida
Family: Tchegemithyridae

Juralina is a European Upper Jurassic genus characterized by moderately large shells. The ventral valve is much more convex than the dorsal

1, 2. *Ismenia pectunculoides,** Upper Jurassic (Tithonian), Sontheim, West Germany. A view of the ventral (1) and dorsal (2) aspect; width of the larger shell 15 mm.

3, 4. *Zeilleria quadrifida,* Lower Jurassic (Domerian), Kostelec near Považská Teplá, Czechoslovakia. Shells from the ventral (3) and the dorsal (4) aspect. Width of the larger shell 18 mm. A species characterized by valves with a quadrilobular margin.

5–7. *Juralina* (?) *humeralis,* Upper Jurassic, Petersberg near Goslar, West Germany. A view from the dorsal (5) and ventral (6) aspect and from the side (7); width of the largest shell 15 mm.

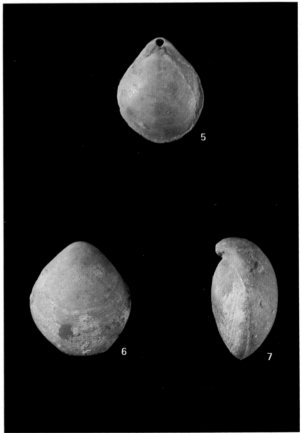

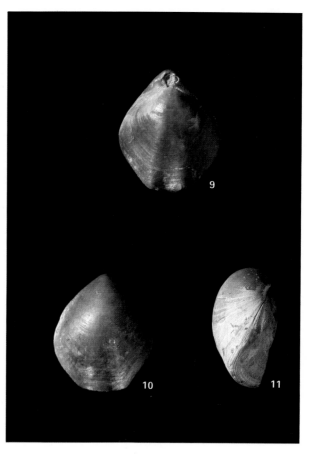

8. *Antinomia* sp., Upper Jurassic, Trento, Italy. Core of a shell from the dorsal aspect; width 43 mm. Mantle canals are clearly discernible on the surface.

9-11. *Loboidothyris subselloides,* Upper Jurassic (Kimmeridgian), France. Shells from the dorsal (9) and ventral (10) aspect and from the side (11). Width of the largest individual 26 mm.

valve, the commissure is straight or uniplicate and the hooked apex has a large pedicle foramen.

Ismenia pectunculoides (Schlotheim)

Order: Terebratulida
Family: Dallinidae

The valves of some terebratulids have a strikingly ribbed surface, e.g. species of the genus *Ismenia* in Upper Jurassic Europe. The shells are small, are wider than they are long and the ventral valve is more convex than the dorsal valve.

Antinomia sp.

Order: Terebratulida
Family: Pygopidae

The morphology of pygopid shells is specifically an expression of the attempt to achieve the greatest possible separation of suspension inflow and outflow. Water (containing food) entered the brachial cavity along the sides of the anterior margin of the shell and (when food and oxygen had been extracted) flowed out and upwards through a deep median notch or opening. *Antinomia* species from Upper Jurassic and Lower Cretaceous strata in Europe and the Arctic region have a triangular shell with a small opening near the apex. The striking ridges found on internal moulds are described as mantle canals or vascular trails and they are branched processes of the coelom. They transported the products of metabolism to the growth margin of the mantle; undoubtedly they also played a role in respiration.

Brachiopoda

Peregrinella peregrina (Buch)

Order: Rhynchonellida
Family: Dimerellidae

In the Cretaceous period, rhynchonellids were still well represented among the brachipods. They primarily inhabited shallow shelf seas. Young individuals were always attached by a stalk to a substrate – often to the shells (or fragments of the shells) of various invertebrates. In many species the stalk subsequently atrophied and the shells lay freely on the sea bed, slightly embedded in the substratum, supported by the highly convex dorsal valve.

Rhynchonellid shells are generally small to moderately large. In the genus *Peregrinella,* from Upper Cretaceous Europe and North America, they are exceptionally large, since they were over 10 cm wide. These brachiopods, in general appearance, are reminiscent of pentamerids. The shell is rounded and has no median ridge or furrow. The ventral valve is substantially more convex than the dorsal valve and has a thick, hooked apex (fig. 9). The commissure is straight. On the surface of the shell there are rough ribs.

9

Orbirhynchia cuvieri (d'Orbigny)

Order: Rhynchonellida
Family: Wellerellidae

A number of brachiopods have been described from the chalk – a typical shallow-water calcareous shelf sediment of the Cretaceous period

Cr

1, 2. *Cretirhynchia plicatilis,* * Upper Cretaceous (Senonian), Brighton, Sussex, England. Shells from the dorsal aspect (1) and the front (2); width 21 mm. The fold in the anterior part of the commissure is clearly asymmetrical.

3–5. *Orbirhynchia cuvieri,* Upper Cretaceous (Turonian), Hitchin, England. Shells from the dorsal aspect (3), from the side (4) and from the front (5); width of the largest shell 17 mm.

6, 9. *Peregrinella peregrina,* * Lower Cretaceous (Neocomian), Châtillon, France. 6 – a shell from the dorsal aspect, width 70 mm. One of the largest rhynchonellids. 9 – a lateral view of the shell.

7, 8. *Cyclothyris difformis,* Upper Cretaceous (Cenomanian), Wilmington, England. A view of the ventral (7) and dorsal (8) valve; width of the larger individual 31 mm. The shells are conspicuous for their width.

6

which, in addition to its whiteness, is often uncemented and has high concentration of foraminiferid and coccolithophorid shells, etc.

The members of the genus *Orbirhynchia* occur in Cretaceous strata in north-western Europe. The shells are small, with a very low ridge on the dorsal valve, and are uniplicate; the commissure has a rounded saddle. The ribs are rounded and towards the apex of the shell they disappear.

Cyclothyris difformis (VALENCIENNES)

Order: Rhynchonellida
Family: Rhynchonellidae

The Cretaceous representatives of the genus *Cyclothyris* have wide shells with a low median ridge on the dorsal valve. The commissure is uniplicate. The apex of the ventral valve curves over dorsally.

7

Cretirhynchia plicatilis (SOWERBY)

Order: Rhynchonellida
Family: Rhynchonellidae

Cretirhynchia, an Upper Cretaceous genus from north-western Europe, has moderately large, biconvex shells with a low ridge on the dorsal valve. The front of the commissure forms a pronounced median fold. The surface of the shell is smooth, or is thickly covered with bar-like ribs.

8

Brachiopoda

Thecidea papillata (SCHLOTHEIM)

Order: Strophomenida
Family: Thecidellinidae

The members of the superfamily Thecideaceae are regarded as the only present-day descendants of the strophomenids, their sole survivors in present-day seas being the species of the genera *Lacazella* and *Thecidellina*. These tiny brachiopods lived cemented to a substrate by their ventral valve, although a few of them were free-living. Their thick-walled shells are somewhat diversely shaped. The ventral valve is deep; the dorsal valve resembles a lid. The structure of the locking device allowed the valves to be opened very wide.

The representatives of the genus *Thecidea*, which occur in Cretaceous formations in western Europe, were a part of the sessile benthos and lived in the shallow sublittoral zone. The ventral valve has high interareas and a closed deltyrium. Conspicuous on the inner surface of the ventral valve are the calcareous supports of the lophophore, whose axis ran in a deep groove.

Terebrirostra lyra (SOWERBY)

Order: Terebratulida
Family: uncertain

The biconvex shells of this west European Cretaceous genus are moderately large and are conspicuous for the unusually long tapering apical part of the ventral valve.

1. *Thecidea papillata,** Upper Cretaceous (Maastrichtian), Maastricht, the Netherlands. Shells and isolated valves; length 6–7 mm.

2–4. *Magas geinitzi,* Upper Cretaceous (Turonian), Malnice near Louny, Czechoslovakia. A dorsal (2), side (3) and ventral (4) view; length of the shells 7–8 mm. The pedicle foramen lies below the curved apex of the shell.

5–7. *Terebrirostra lyra,** Upper Cretaceous (Cenomanian), Le Havre, France. A ventral (5), dorsal (6) and side (7) view of the shell. Length of the largest shell 24 mm.

Cr

Rhynchora costata (NILSSON)

Order: Terebratulida
Family: Terebratellidae

Rhynchora, an Upper Cretaceous European genus, has bulging, biconvex shells. The front part of the commissure is sulcate. The opening left by the stalk is unusually large. The valves were locked together tightly by strong teeth.

Magas geinitzi (SCHLOENBACH)

Order: Terebratulida
Family: Terebratellidae

Magas shells come from Upper Cretaceous formations in Europe. They have a highly convex ventral valve and a less bulging or flat dorsal valve. The ventral valve has a hooked apex pointing obliquely forward. The commissure is straight or sulcate.

Trigonosemus elegans (KÖNIG)

Order: Terebratulida
Family: Terebratellidae

The members of the genus *Trigonosemus* are to be found in Upper Cretaceous layers in Europe and Asia. The thick-walled shells are characterized by a markedly bulging ventral valve whose apical part is much higher than the slightly convex or flat dorsal valve. The front of the commissure is sulcate. The sculpturing consists of dense ribbing.

8, 9. *Rhynchora costata,** Upper Cretaceous, Scania, Sweden. A shell seen from the dorsal aspect (8) and isolated dorsal valves (9). Length 28 mm. The ventral valve was longer and considerably more convex.

10, 11. *Trigonosemus elegans,** Upper Cretaceous (Senonian), Ciply, Belgium. A shell from the dorsal (10) and ventral (11) aspect. Length of the larger shell 30 mm. The very small pedicle foramen is in the apex of the shell and between it and the hinge line there is a large triangular field with interareas and a closed deltyrium.

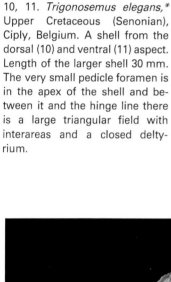

Pygites diphyoides (D'ORBIGNY)

Order: Terebratulida
Family: Pygopidae

Pygites, the Upper Jurassic to Lower Cretaceous representative of the pygopids, is known from different parts of Europe, North Africa and the Arctic region. In young individuals the bizarre, smooth shell tapered off in front into two separate lobes, which moved closer and closer together during growth until they formed a large oval opening in the middle of the shell.

Gibbithyris semiglobosa (SOWERBY)

Order: Terebratulida
Family: Gibbithyrididae

The members of the genus *Gibbithyris* appeared in Europe in the Upper Cretaceous. The shells are biconvex, but the ventral valve bulges more than the dorsal valve. The front of the commissure is straight or sulciplicate. The apex, with the small peduncular foramen, curves obliquely forwards (fig. 8).

1, 2, 8. *Gibbithyris semiglobosa,* Upper Cretaceous (Turonian?), Dover, England. Dorsal (2) and side (1) view of shells; length of the larger shell 31 mm. A typical brachiopod of Upper Chalk. 8 – a reconstruction of a living individual.

3, 4. *Terebratulina chrysalis,* Upper Cretaceous (Senonian), Lüneburg, West Germany. View from the dorsal (3) and ventral (4) aspect; length of the larger shell 19 mm. *Terebratulina* is one of the most widespread brachiopods still extant.

5, 9. *Terebratula ampulla,* Neogene (Pliocene), Italy. 5 – a shell from the dorsal aspect; length 46 mm. The umbonal part of the dorsal valve is overgrown by bryozoans. 9 – a reconstruction of a living individual.

6, 7. *Pygites diphyoides,* * Lower Cretaceous (Neocomian), Štramberk, Czechoslovakia. A ventral (6) and a dorsal (7) view; length of the larger shell 36 mm.

Ng

Cr

8

9

Order: Terebratulida
Family: Cancellothyrididae

Terebratulina chrysalis (SCHLOTHEIM)

The cosmopolitan genus *Terebratulina* has existed since the Upper Jurassic and is still extant. The biconvex shell has a straight or uniplicate commissure. Recent members of the genus live at various depths, in both warm and cold water. Some species tolerate considerable depth and temperature differences. They are anchored to their base by a stalk with a branched, root-like end. Studies of the anatomy of the lophophore and the mantle, which has chitinous sensory bristles (setae) at its periphery, confirmed that the representatives of this genus have a true mesodermal skeleton composed of calcareous crystals joined together in irregular aggregates.

Order: Terebratulida
Family: Terebratulidae

Terebratula ampulla BROCCHI

In the Cainozoic era, brachiopods were only an insignificant component of the benthos, just as they are today. The reason was that they were superseded by molluscs which led a similar existence, but were in many respects much better equipped. Their advantages included greater mobility, the ability of many species to live actually in the substratum and complete separation of suspension inflow and outflow.

The most typical representatives of the terebratulids – the species of the genus *Terebratula* – occur in Miocene and Pliocene sediments in southern Europe. The moderately large to large, oval or round-cornered pentagonal shells are biconvex; the front of the commissure is uniplicate or sulciplicate. The massive, slightly curving, truncated apex is perforated by a large foramen for the stalk (fig. 9).

Mollusca

Helminthochiton priscus MÜNSTER

Order: Neoloricata
Family: Lepidopleuridae

The class Polyplacophora is an ancient, conservative group of molluscs forming an independent evolutionary branch of that phylum. The flat, oval, bilaterally symmetrical body is covered with a mantle. On the head, which is only indistinctly separated from the wide foot, there is just a mouth; eyes and tentacles are absent. The nervous system is simple and the dorsal surface is covered by eight overlapping calcareous plates. The head and the tail plate are semicircular, while the median plates have elongated sides, forward-projecting articular processes (which are also present on the tail plate) and a flat, backward-pointed ridge. Recent chitons (or coat-of-mail shells) live in every sea, chiefly in the littoral zone, attached by their foot to a firm base from which they scrape algae with their radula. As fossils, they make a first, rare appearance in the Upper Cambrian.

Helminthochiton is a Lower Ordovician to Carboniferous genus known from Europe and North America. Its smooth, thick, vaulted plates have a blunt ridge running down the longitudinal axis. The ridged, almost circular tail plate terminates in a protruding process. The median plates are subquadrate, with a recurved beaky ridge (fig. 4).

Archinacella ovata PERNER

Order: Archinacelloidea
Family: Archinacellidae

Monoplacophora are a class comprising primitive, bilaterally symmetrical marine molluscs, some of whose organs still display partial metamerism. The dorsal part of the body is covered with a single, bonnet-like calcareous shell with an anteriorly directed apex. Monoplacophorans are evolutionarily very important and the forebears of most of the molluscan classes are to be found among their Cambrian and Ordovician representatives. Great excitement was caused by the finding, in 1952, of a live monoplacophoran, *Neopilina galatheae,* by the Danish deep sea expedition Galathea. Fossils are at present known only from early Palaeozoic shallow-water deposits.

4

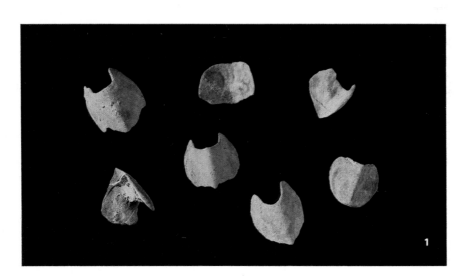

1

1, 4. *Helminthochiton priscus,* Lower Carboniferous (Tournaisian), Tournai, Belgium. Length of the largest plate, complete with processes, 19 mm. Scattered plates. Muscle imprints can be seen on the exposed under side of the head plate (bottom centre). Top left – a tail plate minus the articular processes. The rest are median plates. 4 – a complete shell from above.

2. *Drahomira rugata,* Upper Silurian (Pridoli), Slivenec, Czechoslovakia. A core of a shell with clearly discernible muscle imprints; length 16 mm. The members of this rare genus inhabited the soft bed of shallow Silurian seas.

3, 5. *Archinacella ovata,* Lower Ordovician (Llanvirn), Osek near Rokycany, Czechoslovakia. Length of larger shell 11 mm. *Archinacella* species inhabited relatively shallow (200–300 m) Bohemian Ordovician seas. They are evidently found in larger numbers than any other monoplacophorans. 5 – internal mould with muscle imprints.

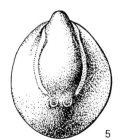

The members of the genus *Archinacella* are rare Lower Ordovician to Lower Silurian monoplacophorans known from Europe and North America. They have small, bulging, circular shells with a blunt, beak-like apex and a few growth wrinkles on their surface. The muscle imprints, except the last (anal) pair, merge to form a horseshoe band bordering the apex (fig. 5).

Drahomira rugata (PERNER)

Order: Tryblidioidea
Family: Tryblidiidae

The Upper Silurian European genus *Drahomira* has spoon-shaped shells with a faintly indicated anterior apex. Concentric undulating ridges mark their outer surface. Seven pairs of usually ovally elongate muscle imprints are a typical feature.

Mollusca

Sinuites sowerbyi PERNER

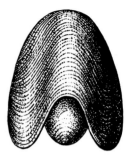

3

Gastropods (snails and slugs) are marine, freshwater or land molluscs with a distinctly separate head and a flat foot for locomotion. Torsion of their internal organs in the early phases of their evolution caused them to lose bilateral body symmetry and their shells began to coil in the three-dimensional spiral characteristic of this group as a whole. Torsion thus differentiates gastropods from the other mollusc classes. Gastropods originated at the beginning of the Cambrian and have survived down to the present.

The single (i.e. unpaired) shell is usually long and conical and coiled in more or less distinct three-dimensional spiral. It is generally dextral, that is to say, if it is placed with the apex pointing upwards and the mouth facing the observer, the mouth lies on the right. The shell begins with a protoconch (larval shell) and has a given number of whorls (turns of 360 degrees). The last — and largest — is known as the body whorl; the rest form the spire. The contact lines between the whorls are called sutures, while the conical depression in the coiling axis on the under side (base) of the shell is the umbilicus. The rimmed opening at the wider end of the shell (the aperture) is distinguished by a free outer lip, an inner parietal lip adjoining the preceding whorl and a columellar lip forming a columella ('little column') encircling the umbilicus. In the aperture of aquatic gastropods there are usually two notches (sinuses), which hold the tube carrying water to the gills (the siphon) and the outlet of the digestive system (the anus). The anal sinus lies in the upper part of the aperture and the siphonal sinus at the division between the outer and the columellar lip, where it often tapers off into a long canal. With progressive growth the sinuses form slit bands or selenizones. The surface of gastropod shells is adorned with spiral and axial (transversal) growth crests, ribs (costae), ridges and spines, etc.

Bellerophontids (suborder Bellerophontina) are a very ancient extinct group of gastropods which lived from the Lower Cambrian to the Upper

1, 3. *Sinuites sowerbyi*, Lower Ordovician (Llanvirn), Prague (Šárka), Czechoslovakia. 1 — internal mould, diameter about 20 mm. Seven specimens preserved in a siliceous nodule (a 'Šárka marble'). Since they are cores, we cannot see the fine growth crests present on the outer surface of these shells. 3 — a posterior view.

1

2. *Tropidodiscus pusillus,* Lower Ordovician (Llanvirn), Prague (Vokovice), Czechoslovakia. Cores, diameter about 5 mm. The incomplete imprint of the large bellerophontid whose surface sculpture has been preserved belongs to the species *Sinuites sowerbyi.*

Triassic period. Their atypical, bilaterally symmetrical shell forms a two-dimensional spiral.

The Ordovician genus *Sinuites,* one of the oldest bellerophontids, is distributed over the whole of the northern hemisphere. Its moderately large, laterally compressed shells taper off on their outer (dorsal) surface into a blunt, rounded ridge. The umbilicus is narrow and the aperture, on its dorsal margin, has a wide, V-shaped sinus (fig. 3).

Tropidodiscus pusillus (Perner)

Order: Archaeogastropoda
Family: Bellerophontidae

The members of the genus *Tropidodiscus* inhabited the northern hemisphere from the Lower Ordovician to the Devonian period. The high whorls of their tiny shells are triangular in cross section and down the back of the shell runs a carinate ridge (keel). There is a wide umbilicus and the narrow, slit-like anal sinus is overgrown by a selenizone with loosely spaced semicircular transverse ridges.

163

Mollusca

Spirina tubicina PERNER

Order: Archaeogastropoda
Family: Craspedostomatidae

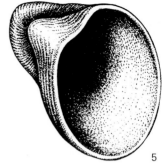

The division of gastropods into subclasses and orders is based chiefly on the anatomy of the soft parts of their body — a fact which is reflected in their scientific names. In the subclass Prosobranchia ('front-gilled' gastropods) the gills lie in the mantle cavity in front of the heart, while in the subclass Opisthobranchia ('back-gilled' gastropods) they lie behind the heart; in the subclass Pulmonata ('pulmonate' gastropods) the surface of the mantle cavity has been transformed to a lung sac. The members of the various subclasses can also be identified from the shape of their shells, but these characters are of merely secondary significance; shell morphology acquires importance only at family, genus and species level.

Spirina shells from European Middle Silurian to Middle Devonian deposits have just a few whorls forming an almost flat spiral. They widen rapidly towards the mouth (fig. 5) and the oval aperture usually spreads out into a wide border. The umbilicus is often filled with a thickening of the inner lip known as an umbilical callus.

Oriostoma dives (PERNER)

Order: Archaeogastropoda
Family: Oriostomatidae

These gastropods are known from Upper Silurian and Lower Devonian strata in Europe and North America. Their low spiral shell, whose few

1, 5. *Spirina tubicina,* Upper Silurian (Ludlow), Prague (Jinonice), Czechoslovakia. Shell diameter 38 mm (1). These abundant Silurian gastropods are characterized by sharply ribbed, abruptly widening shells. 5 – a frontal view.

2, 6. *Oriostoma dives,* Upper Silurian (Pridoli), Prague-Podolí, Czechoslovakia. 2 – a core with a partly preserved shell. Diameter 50 mm. 6 – an operculum.

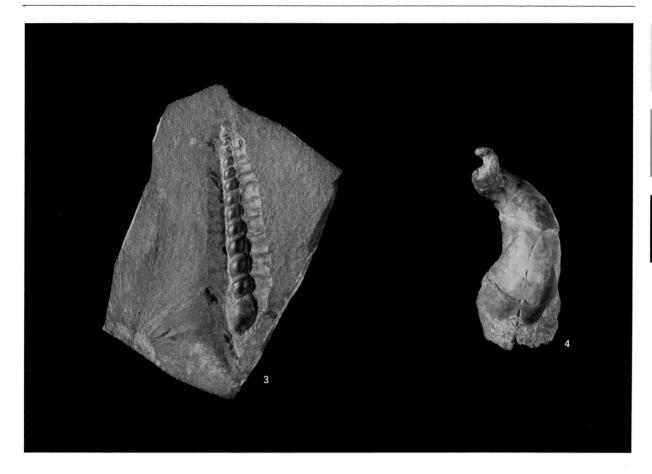

3. *Stylonema solvens,* Lower Devonian (Lochkovian), Kosoř, Czechoslovakia. Shell core, height 55 mm. Owing to their fragility, *Stylonema* (and loxonematid shells in general) are often represented in collections by fragments only.

4. *Orthonychia anguis,* Upper Silurian (Pridoli), Zadní Kopanina, Czechoslovakia. Shell core, height 50 mm. Irregularly undulating growth lines can be seen on the remains of the shell. One of the prettiest members of the genus *Orthonychia,* most of which have only a plain, tall, conical shell.

whorls are circular in cross section, is adorned with spiral ribs structured like densely overlapping scales. The fine axial ribs and scales are less pronounced. The umbilicus is relatively narrow. Very often thick-walled circular opercula are also found (fig. 6).

Orthonychia anguis (RÖMER)

Order: Archaeogastropoda
Family: Platyceratidae

The members of the cosmopolitan genus *Orthonychia* lived from the Silurian to the Lower Permian period. The shells either form strikingly tall, free spirals, or are simply conical, with a high apex. In cross section they are circular or undulatingly circular. The only markings in the smooth surface of the shell are fine and usually irregular wavy growth lines. Many representatives of this order live clinging to the roof of the cup of crinoids and live on the latters' excrements. The undulating edges of the shell, and hence its sculpture also, are the outcome of adaptation to the uneven upper surface of the cup roof of crinoids.

Stylonema solvens (PERNER)

Order: Mesogastropoda
Family: Loxonematidae

The Silurian and Lower Devonian members of the genus *Stylonema* have very slender, turret-like shells composed of a large number of whorls. The oval aperture has a wide, shallow siphonal sinus. The surface of the shell is either smooth or is marked with fine growth ridges.

165

Mollusca

Praenatica gregaria (PERNER)

Order: Archaeogastropoda
Family: Platyceratidae

Representatives of the European and North America genus *Praenatica* are common fossils in Silurian and (especially) Lower Devonian deposits. Their shells are characterized by marked widening of the body whorl, which partly overlaps the older whorls, giving the shell an almost hemispherical form, like a squat cone. *Praenatica* species often occurred in the vicinity of coral reefs and it is possible that, like other platyceratids, they frequented crinoid colonies.

Tubina armata OWEN

Order: Archaeogastropoda
Family: Tubinidae

The decorative shells of the genus *Tubina* abound in Lower Devonian limestone in central Bohemia. They are loosely coiled in an almost flat spiral whose individual whorls are separate from one another. Near the mouth the shell suddenly widens, so that it looks like a tuba. The whorls are oval in cross section; they are adorned with widely spaced, prominent spiral ribs combined with dense, but less pronounced axial ribs. On the outer coil of the whorls, long, hollow spines project from the spiral ribs (fig. 5). *Tubina* inhabited the slopes of coral reefs and biostromas (carpet-like growths of corals, stromatoporids,

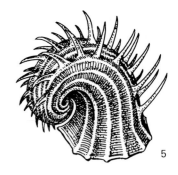

1, 5. *Tubina armata,** Lower Devonian (Pragian), Koněprusy, Czechoslovakia. Shell diameter 23 mm. The long hollow spines which projected from the spiral ribs on the outer perimeter of the whorls have been broken off (1). 5 – a complete shell.

2. *Turbonitella subcostata,* Middle Devonian (Givetian), Paffrath, West Germany. Height of shell 30 mm. Owing to their considerable thickness, the shells are mostly well preserved.

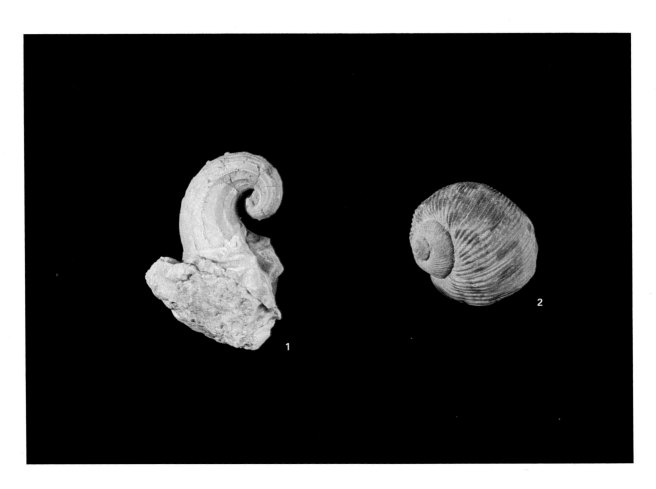

brachiopods, crinoids and other organisms), where they evidently lived on the plentiful supply of algae.

Order: Archaeogastropoda
Turbonitella subcostata (MÜNSTER)
Family: Neritopsidae

The members of the genus *Turbonitella* inhabited Europe from the Middle Devonian to the Lower Carboniferous period. They have thick-walled shells with a flattened base and a moderately tall conical spire. The whorls have a rounded trapezoid cross section, so that their flat outer side is bordered with faint carinate ridges. The shell is adorned with sharp, dense axial ribs, which swell up into elongate protuberances. The aperture is rounded and the dilated inner and columellar lips of the aperture form a strip-like callus.

Order: Mesogastropoda
lanthinopsis arculatus (SCHLOTHEIM)
Family: Subulitidae

3. *Praenatica gregaria,* Lower Devonian (Pragian), Koněprusy, Czechoslovakia. Shell diameter 35 mm. The growth lines are very conspicuous. The dark colouring stems from a carbonaceous substance in the outer organic layer of the shell (the periostracum), which was evidently very vividly coloured during the animal's lifetime.

4. *lanthinopsis arculatus,* Middle Devonian (Givetian), Paffrath, West Germany. Height of shell 57 mm. The well preserved thick-walled shells show that the animals lived in shallow water.

Members of the genus *lanthinopsis* are known from Middle Devonian to Middle Permian strata in America and Eurasia. Their shells can be almost spherical, or elongate and pointed (fusiform). The whorls bulge and the last one is usually very large. The oval aperture is pointed at the top and has a siphonal sinus at the bottom. The surface of the thick-walled shell is covered with prominent growth lines.

Mollusca

Bellerophon cf. *hiulcus* MARTIN
Bellerophon striatus D'ORBIGNY

Order: Archaeogastropoda
Family: Bellerophontidae

Gastropods evolved from monoplacophorans (Monoplacophora). The relatively simple organization of the body organs of monoplacophorans was continuously improved upon and the outcome of the process was torsion, i.e. twisting of the internal organs, which was manifested in the evolutionally more advanced gastropods. Enlargement of the visceral sac required a change in the shape of the shell from flat and conical to tall and conical, and for the shell to be twisted forwards in a flat spiral. For animals with a planktonic or nektonic mode of life, this is not a drawback, but for a benthic existence, which the vast majority of gastropods adopt after the planktonic larval stages have been passed, such a shell is a disadvantage. Together with the visceral sac, it has to be kept vertical and to be held so that it does not get in the way of the head, which is the seat of the nerve centres, the sensory organs and the mouth. By being twisted anti-clockwise, the shell rests on the posterior part of the foot, where it is not in the way and the animal can simply drag it along behind it. Torsion is also responsible for impairment of bilateral symmetry of the body and for the change in the shell from an originally two-dimensional to a three-dimensional spiral. There are only a few species that have symmetrical bilateral conical shells.

In this respect bellerophontids are an interesting group, since they have a bilaterally symmetrical, two-dimensionally spiral (planispiral) shell and thus resemble some monoplacophorans. They died out during the Triassic, so that we do not know what the soft parts of their body looked like. Their key feature is a notch (sinus) in the middle of the outer lip of the aperture, which is absent in monoplacophorans. The notch is

1. *Bellerophon striatus,* Middle Devonian (Givetian), Paffrath, West Germany. Shell diameter 25 mm. View of the outer aspect of a whorl. A conspicuous selenizone and growth ridges can be seen.

2. *Bellerophon* cf. *hiulcus,* Lower Carboniferous, Tournai, Belgium. Shell diameter 20 mm. View of mouth of a shell. The aperture has been damaged, but the narrow sinus is still visible.

3. *Euomphalus pentagulatus,** Lower Carboniferous, St. Doulaghs, Ireland. Shell diameter 48 mm. The shells occur in the sediments of warm, shallow seas, often near biostromes or coral bioherms (reefs).

the anal sinus (as in other archaeogastropods), because members of the bellerophontid genus *Knightites* have paired siphonal notches on either side of it. This shows that the gills and the anus were situated anteriorly, above the head, and is thus evidence of torsion.

The members of the cosmopolitan genus *Bellerophon* lived from the Silurian to the Upper Permian period. Their shells are moderately large and rounded and the aperture has a narrow, convex border. The sinus is a narrow slit, while the selenizone often forms a low carinate ridge; the umbilicus is covered with a callus. *Bellerophon* species lived in shallow seas and were herbivores.

Euomphalus pentagulatus (SOWERBY)

Order: Archaeogastropoda
Family: Euomphalidae

The members of the cosmopolitan genus *Euomphalus* lived from the Silurian to the Permian period, but were commonest in the Carboniferous. Their moderately large to large discoid shells are coiled in a very low spiral. In cross section the whorls have the form of a round-angled pentagon and they are surmounted by a pronounced carinate ridge. The whorls are separated by deep sutures. The umbilicus is very wide and shallow.

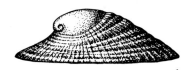

4

Scurriopsis hettangensis (D'ORBIGNY)   Order: Archaeogastropoda
Family: Acmaeidae

The members of the subclass *Patellina* belong to the few gastropods with bilaterally symmetrical shells. The shell has the form of a low to very low cone and is oval in cross section. The reason for this morphological change was that the animal lived in the rocky littoral zone of the sea. The advantages of this environment include an abundance of oxygen and light and a constant supply of food; its disadvantage is the destructive force of the waves, especially the breakers. One way of overcoming the disadvantage is to remain sessile, clinging firmly to some solid base such as a rock or a large boulder. Loss of movement, however, leads to atrophy of various organs and to simplification of body structure in general. Patellids therefore tend to resemble monoplacophorans, the more primitively and simply constructed ancestors of the gastropods, but the similarity is merely superficial, since according to Dollo's law of irreversibility of evolution, once the evolution of an organism has been accomplished, its stages cannot be recapitulated. Torsion in patellids can therefore be observed in the asymmetrical structure of their soft body and in some of them the larval part of the shell is coiled in a three-dimensional spiral.

The representatives of the genus *Scurriopsis* occur in Europe and north Africa; they are among the oldest known patellids. They appeared in the middle of the Triassic and disappeared towards the end of the Jurassic. Their moderately large, thick-walled shells have the form of a low, oval, lop-sided cone with the apex at the front. The only markings on their almost smooth surface are fine concentric and radial lines.

Symmetrocapulus rugosus (SOWERBY)   Order: Archaeogastropoda
Family: Symmetrocapulidae

The members of this further genus of the subclass Patellina, which inhabited Europe during the Jurassic, and possibly the Lower Cretaceous also, have squat, ovally conical and quite large shells whose apex curls asymmetrically forwards (fig. 4).

Purpuroidea morrisea (BUVIGNIER)   Order: Mesogastropoda
Family: Purpurinidae

The large, thick-walled shells of the representatives of the genus *Purpuroidea* are to be found mostly in European Middle and Upper Jurassic deposits, but are also known from Triassic and Cretaceous strata. The last whorl is large and bulging. On the whorls there are a few faint spiral ribs and near the top a number of large, blunt spines. The aperture has a thick outer lip, a low, smooth columellar part and a short, wide siphonal canal.

1. *Scurriopsis hettangensis,* Lower Jurassic (Hettangian), Hettingen, West Germany. Shell length 28 mm. The low, conical, bilaterally symmetrical shell is the outcome of a sessile existence in the littoral zone of the sea.

2, 4. *Symmetrocapulus rugosus,** Middle Jurassic (Bathonian), Minchinhampton, Great Britain. Shell length 32 mm. It is sometimes described under the synonym *S. tessoni.* The shell has been severely abraded, so that the spiral protoconch is not seen (2). 4 – a lateral view.

3 *Purpuroidea morrisea,** Middle Jurassic (Bathonian), Minchinhampton, Great Britain. Shell height 68 mm. The massive shells are characteristic of molluscs living in shallow seas.

Mollusca

Obornella plicopunctata (DESLONGCHAMPS)

Order: Archaeogastropoda
Family: Pleurotomariidae

6

The shells of the members of the ancient Pleurotomariidae family have a flat base, a discoid or conical spire and a typical, long, anal slit in the upper part of the outer lip, which is overgrown by a clearly discernible selenizone. Pleurotomariids are actually 'living fossils'; they have existed since the Triassic period, were abundant in the Jurassic and Cretaceous periods and are now rare inhabitants of the deep parts of the oceans. Like many other ancient molluscs, they originally lived in shallow water and did not move to the less hospitable deeper water until forced to do so by competition from more advanced gastropods. Migration to deep water during their evolution is also known in the case of other organisms, both vertebrate and invertebrate, and bathyal refuges are one of the still discussed problems of palaeontology.

The gastropods of the genus *Obornella*, which lived in Europe during the Jurassic period, have low conical or lenticulate shells with a bulging base and a narrow umbilicus. The short, narrow anal slit is overgrown by a prominent smooth selenizone (fig. 6).

Bathrotomaria reticulata (SOWERBY)

Order: Archaeogastropoda
Family: Pleurotomariidae

The shells of the members of this cosmopolitan Jurassic and Cretaceous genus have a bulging base and a low to moderately tall conical spire. The umbilicus is narrow. The prominent selenizone forms a keel on the outer edge of the flattened whorl, giving it a rounded pentagonal cross section. The anal slit is short.

1, 6. *Obornella plicopunctata,** Middle Jurassic (Bajocian), France. Shell diameter 25 mm. The striking sculpture of the shell is broken near the outer edge of the whorls by a prominent selenizone (1). 6 – a frontal view.

2. *Bathrotomaria reticulata,** Upper Jurassic (Oxfordian), Popilany, Poland. Shell diameter 30 mm. The aperture of the shell has been broken away, so that the short anal slit is not to be seen. At the site of the fracture we can see the beautifully preserved, gleaming nacreous (mother-of-pearl) layer characteristic of the order Archaeogastropoda.

3. *Trochalia pyramidalis,* Upper Jurassic (Kimmeridgian), Hildesheim, West Germany. Shell height 84 mm. The aperture of the shell has been broken off.

4. *Pyrgotrochus conoideus,* Middle Jurassic (Bajocian), Bayeux, France. Shell height 30 mm. The almost regularly conical shell with the knobbly ridge and the inconspicuous selenizone is characteristic of members of the genus *Pyrgotrochus* which live in shallow water.

5. *Eucyclus capitaneus,* Lower Jurassic (Toarcian), La Verpilière, France. Shell height 34 mm. The brownish red colouring is due to the large amount of iron oxide present in the rock.

	Order: Archaeogastropoda
Pyrgotrochus conoideus (DESHAYES)	Family: Pleurotomariidae

Pyrgotrochus lived all over the world from the Jurassic to the middle of the Cretaceous period. The flat-based shells have a moderately tall, conical spire. The outer surface of the whorls is produced to a keel bordered by a row of bosses stemming from the swollen axial ribs.

	Order: Archaeogastropoda
Eucyclus capitaneus (MÜNSTER)	Family: Amberleyidae

The members of the Euro-American genus *Eucyclus* lived from the Triassic period to the Oligocene. Their low-spired shells, with rounded whorls, are adorned with loosely spaced, sharp-edged spiral ribs surmounted, on the upper aspect of the whorl, by bosses or spines.

	Order: Mesogastropoda
Trochalia pyramidalis (MÜNSTER)	Family: Nerineidae

The tall, smooth, conical shells of the representatives of the genus *Trochalia* are known from Middle Jurassic to Lower Cretaceous sedimentary formations in the northern hemisphere.

173

 **Mollusca**

Leptomaria seriogranulata (GOLDFUSS)

Order: Archaeogastropoda
Family: Pleurotomariidae

The members of the cosmopolitan genus *Leptomaria* lived from the middle of the Jurassic period to the Upper Cretaceous. Their low, conical to discoid shells have flattened oval whorls. In the middle of the upper aspect of the outer lip there is a very long sinus. The selenizone is inconspicuous. The characteristic knobbly sculpture is the result of intersection of the fine spiral and axial costae.

Plesioptygmatis buchi (KEFERSTEIN)

Order: Mesogastropoda
Family: Nerineidae

The long, conical, turret-like shells of the many genera of the family Nerineidae closely resemble one another. To be able to identify them exactly it is necessary to cut the shell lengthwise and examine the organization of the folds on the inner walls of the whorls.

The gastropods of the European Upper Cretaceous genus *Plesioptygmatis* have large shells with a narrow umbilicus concealed by a process of the inner edge of the whorls. The cross section of the whorl cavity is rhomboid, with four spiral folds. The suture is sometimes bordered by a row of tubercles.

Torquesia cenomanensis (D'ORBIGNY)

Order: Mesogastropoda
Family: Turritellidae

The European Cretaceous genus *Torquesia* has long, slender, turreted shells with an oval aperture and a large number of whorls. The outer surface of the whorls is so flattened that the sides of the shell are almost straight.

Trochactaeon conicus (MÜNSTER)

Order: Tectibranchia
Family: Actaeonellidae

Gastropods belonging to the subclass Opisthobranchia (back-gilled animals) show a tendency to reduction or complete loss of the shell. In consequence relatively few fossil specimens have been preserved, despite the fact that the earliest known is of Carboniferous age. The shells are mostly spherical, ovoid or oval-fusiform, with only a few whorls. The body whorl often completely overlaps the preceding whorls. The aperture is usually narrow, but widens at the bottom, and is holostomatous (i.e. it has no notches). Planktonic species (order Pteropoda) have tiny, thin, and often non-coiled, conical shells. Opisthobranchs inhabited warm seas.

Members of the genus *Trochactaeon,* which come from Lower and Upper Cretaceous strata in the northern hemisphere, have large, massive, ovoid or squatly fusiform shells. The body whorl almost completely overlaps the older whorls. The narrow aperture widens at the bottom and there are three folds on the columellar lip.

1. *Leptomaria seriogranulata,* Upper Cretaceous (Turonian), Prague-Bílá Hora, Czechoslovakia. Core, diameter 68 mm. A strip of rock beside the mouth hides the long anal sinus.

2. *Plesioptygmatis buchi,* Upper Cretaceous (Turonian), Gosau, Austria. Shell height 102 mm. In the longitudinal section of part of the shell we can see the characteristic organization of the rounded spiral ridges in the cavity of the whorls and hook-like processes of the inner lip covering the umbilicus.

3. *Torquesia cenomanensis,* Upper Cretaceous (Cenomanian), Korycany, Czechoslovakia. Shell height 85 mm. *Tourquesia* species were herbivorous and inhabited the shallow Cretaceous seas of central and western Europe. The shells often occur in groups.

4. *Trochactaeon conicus,* Upper Cretaceous (Turonian), Gosau, Austria. Shell height 102 mm. The section shows progressive dissolution of the columellar folds and the inner walls of the shell. This process took place during the animal's lifetime; it reduced the weight of the shell.

Mollusca

Theodoxus pictus (Férussac)

Order: Archaeogastropoda
Family: Neritidae

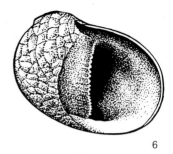

6

Gastropods of the genus *Theodoxus* have inhabited rivers and brackish water in bays and deltas all over the world since the Oligocene. They have tiny shells and the last whorl, which largely overlaps the others (fig. 6), is dorsally hemispherical and ventrally flattened. The semicircular aperture has an anal groove. The inner lip is wide, with a smooth callus and no teeth. The surface of the shell is smooth and glossy, with a coloured pattern which is often also partly preserved on fossil shells. The markings are so variable that it is difficult to find two shells that are alike.

The pigments forming the ornament on mollusc shells are contained in the outer organic layer of the shell, the periostracum, which is composed of many layers of conchiolin. Conchiolin also forms the matrix of the calcareous layers of the shell. When the animal dies, the conchiolin decomposes and the shell turns white and porous. In some mollusc species it is normal for the pigments to infiltrate into the spherolithic-prismatic layer during the animal's lifetime; in that case the pattern is preserved on the fossil shells and with carbonization the original bright colours change to various shades of brown and black.

1. *Theodoxus pictus,* Neogene (Upper Miocene), Třebovice, Czechoslovakia. Height of largest shell 7 mm. These gastropods occurred in thousands in brackish water in the bays of the Miocene sea.

	Order: Archaeogastropoda
Diodora sp.	Family: Fissurellidae

The members of the cosmopolitan genus *Diodora* have uncoiled shells shaped like squat, flat-sided cones. Just below the tip of the shell there is an oval opening lined from within with a thick, truncated callus; the anal canal passed through this opening. The shell has a reticulate sculpture. *Diodora* species lived in shallow water by rocky shores. The oldest finds date back to the Upper Cretaceous.

	Order: Archaeogastropoda
Calliostoma podolica (D'ORBIGNY)	Family: Trochidae

The European genus *Calliostoma* is known from the Miocene down to the present day. The moderately large, conical shells have a flattened base. The aperture is angular, with rounded corners. The columellar lip is straight and smooth. The umbilicus is narrow and slit-like. The thick-walled shell has granular spiral ribs on the outer surface and a nacreous layer on the inner surface.

	Order: Archaeogastropoda
Neritopsis asperata (DUJARDIN)	Family: Neritopsidae

Representatives of the gastropod genus *Neritopsis* have lived all over the world from the Triassic down to the present day. The last whorl on their thick-walled, almost spherical shell is extremely large. Between the whorls there are deep sutures. The aperture is almost circular. The outer lip is thick and is lined with fine ribs, while the columellar lip is hollow and undentated and shows only a trace of a callus.

2, 3. *Diodora sp.,* Neogene (Miocene), France. Length of shells 32 and 33 mm. View of inner (2) and outer (3) surface. Inside the shell we can see a typically shaped callus lining the anal orifice, the dentate edge of the shell and a ribbon-like muscle imprint bordering it.

4. *Calliostoma podolica,* Neogene (Upper Miocene), Mallersdorf, West Germany. Shell height 19 mm. These gastropods inhabit the shallow littoral zone of the sea. They are herbivorous and live on microscopic algae.

5. *Neritopsis asperata,* Neogene (Upper Miocene), Vienna basin, Austria. Shell diameter 22 mm.

6. *Theodoxus concavus* – a frontal view.

177

Mollusca

Tympanotomus margaritaceum
(BRONGNIART)

Order: Mesogastropoda
Family: Potamididae

6

The majority of gastropod species belong to the order Mesogastropoda, whose representatives first appeared in the Ordovician, attained maximum distribution in the Mesozoic era and have persisted, within these limits, down to the present. They have typical tall, spiral shells, in which a siphonal canal appears and grows progressively longer. The shells of some highly specialized genera have a secondarily non-coiled cap-shaped form. The nacreous layer is thin or absent. The operculum is generally corneous (horny), but may even be calcareous (chalky). These gastropods live in the sea, in fresh water and on dry land.

The members of the cosmopolitan genus *Tympanotomus,* known from the Upper Cretaceous onwards, have turreted shells with a flattened base (fig. 6), which are adorned with densely beaded spiral ribs. The uppermost rib is usually more conspicuously developed than the others.

Terebralia bidentata (DEFRANCE)

Order: Mesogastropoda
Family: Potamididae

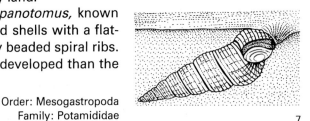

7

The genus *Terebralia* has the same stratigraphic and geographic distribution as the genus *Tympanotonos* and the main features of its shells are also similar. They differ in respect of the structure of the aperture, the more rounded whorls and the much larger, flattened bosses on the spiral ribs which are interrupted by varices. These varices are former thickened apertures, which, as the shell grew, were formed anew periodically.

Turritella terebralis LAMARCK

Order: Mesogastropoda
Family: Turritellidae

Molluscs belonging to the cosmopolitan genus *Turritella* are known from the Cretaceous period down to the present day, but they were most widely distributed in the Tertiary (Cainozoic) era. The turreted shells are of various sizes and have a large number of bulging whorls densely marked with spiral ribs. The clearly discernible growth lines are an important systematic character.

Melanopsis martiniana (FÉRUSSAC)

Order: Mesogastropoda
Family: Melanopsidae

The members of the genus *Melanopsis* have lived all over the world since the Upper Cretaceous down to the present day. The shell has a large final whorl crowned by a rounded ridge. The narrow mouth has a slit-like anal canal and a wide anterior canal. On the parietal and the columellar lip there is a large callus. The smooth-surfaced shell is marked with growth lines.

Tulotoma notha (BRUSINA)

Order: Mesogastropoda
Family: Viviparidae

Gastropods of this genus have inhabited the northern hemisphere since the Palaeocene. They are distinguished from other genera of the same family by their thick-walled shells with roundedly angular whorls and two carinate ridges encircling their periphery.

1. *Tympanotomus margaritaceum,* Palaeogene (Oligocene), Vienna basin, Austria. Shell height 42 mm. A common and very abundant European species, sometimes rock-forming.

2. *Tulotoma notha,* Neogene (Pliocene), Nova Gradiska, Yugoslavia. Shell height 27 mm. The conspicuously fashioned shells of this species occur in the sediments of freshwater basins or in bays with a reduced salinity caused by a large supply of fresh water.

3. *Terebralia bidentata,* Neogene (Upper Miocene), Grussbach, West Germany. Shell height 45 mm. The varices on the whorls are arranged in rows, one above the other.

4,7. *Turritella terebralis,* Neogene (Lower Miocene), Bordeaux, France. Shell height 145 mm (4). Filter-feeding marine gastropods. 7 – a reconstruction of a living individual.

5. *Melanopsis martiniana,* Neogene (Miocene), Bzenec, Czechoslovakia. Shell height 47 mm. This species occurs in large quantities in late Tertiary brackish sediments.

6. *Tympanotomus* sp., a complete shell.

Mollusca

Campanile giganteum (LAMARCK)

Order: Mesogastropoda
Family: Cerithiidae

A comparison with other molluscs shows that gastropods are one of the oldest and most successful groups. They are the only one that has spread to every type of environment. They live in the sea at depths of 5,000 metres, in brackish and in fresh water, on dry land at altitudes of up to 6,000 metres, both in warm and cold regions and in swamps as well as in deserts. They include herbivorous, carnivorous and parasitic species and harmless and venomous types (dangerous even to man). Many of their terrestrial representatives can survive for long periods without food or water. There are more gastropod species than any other type of mollusc; about 105,000 current and almost 20,000 fossil species have so far been described. Among them we find minute, barely visible forms (e.g. *Hydrobia* or *Vertigo*), but also huge species. The shell of the largest extant species, *Syrinx aruanus,* which inhabits tropical seas round Australia, is 55 cm long, while *Campanile giganteum* holds the record among fossil species. The long shells of this genus, which has existed since the Cretaceous period down to the present, measure over 50 cm. They are characterized by a large number of narrow whorls flattened from above and from the side like steps, with a conspicuous suture. The last whorl is large and has a bulging base. The anal sinus is wide. The ridge on the surface of the shell is surmounted by massive, bluntly conical bosses (fig. 7).

Serratocerithium serratum (BRUGUIÈRE)

Order: Mesogastropoda
Family: Cerithiidae

The whorls of the moderately large shells of the Eocene European genus *Serratocerithium* are angular in cross section. They are topped by a conspicuous, sharp carinate ridge with pointed protuberances and below the ridge there are alternating more and less pronounced beaded spiral ribs.

Calyptraea muricata BROCCHI

Order: Mesogastropoda
Family: Calyptraeidae

The existence of the cosmopolitan genus *Calyptraea* dates from the Cretaceous period down to the present. It has thin-walled cap-like shells with only a few whorls; the last whorl is very large and its outer lip forms the entire margin of the shell.

Hipponyx cornucopiae (LAMARCK)

Order: Mesogastropoda
Family: Hipponycidae

The representatives of the cosmopolitan genus *Hipponyx,* which occurred from the Upper Cretaceous to the Miocene, have thick-walled, limpet-like shells whose beak-like apex points backwards. The mouth is oval and inside the shell we can see a muscle imprint shaped like a horseshoe. Various species of this genus were sessile.

1. *Campanile giganteum,** Palaeogene (Middle Eocene), Paris basin, France. Length of shell fragment 190 mm.

2. *Serratocerithium serratum,* Palaeogene (Middle Eocene), Grignon, France. Shell height 67 mm. The picture clearly shows the morphology of the aperture, which, together with the profile of the whorls and the sculpture, is very important for the identification of cerithiids.

3, 4. *Calyptraea muricata,* Neogene (Middle Miocene), Grund, Austria. Shell diameter 27 and 28 mm. Outer (3) and inner (4) view of the shell. In (4) we can see the reduced ventral part of the whorls in the form of a spiral within the aperture.

5, 6. *Hipponyx cornucopiae,** Palaeogene (Middle Eocene), Paris basin, France. Shell height 44 and 57 mm. The outer surface of the shell (6) has been severely abraded; it is overgrown by calcareous algae and is perforated with minute holes made by the boring sponge *Cliona.* On looking inside the shell (5), we can see a striking muscle imprint shaped like a horseshoe.

7. *Campanile* sp., a complete shell.

Rimella fissurella (LAMARCK)

Order: Mesogastropoda
Family: Rostellariidae

The Upper Cretaceous to Recent cosmopolitan gastropods of the genus *Rimella* have small fusiform shells. The oval aperture has a wide siphonal groove and a long, narrow posterior anal canal stretching right to the apex of the shell. The sculpture is formed of transverse ribs (fig. 8).

Mesalia abbreviata DESHAYES

Order: Mesogastropoda
Family: Turritellidae

The many species of the genus *Mesalia* have lived in the seas of the northern hemisphere since the Upper Cretaceous. Their small, turreted shells have rounded whorls and an oval aperture.

Bayania lactea (LAMARCK)

Order: Mesogastropoda
Family: Pseudomelaniidae

The members of the genus *Bayania* are known from the European Eocene. Their tiny, turret-like shells have a pear-shaped mouth. The sculpture is especially clearly discernible on the higher whorls.

Aporrhais pespelecani (LINNAEUS)

Order: Mesogastropoda
Family: Aporrhaidae

From the Upper Cretaceous onwards, the members of the genus *Aporrhais* spread out all over the world. The outer lip of their moderately large, fusiform shells is divided into four long, carinate pointed lobes; the top one is fused with the shell. The top and bottom lobe are actually continuations of the anal and the anterior siphonal canal. On the apertural lobes, the reticulate sculpture is gradually lost.

Drepanocheilus speciosus (SCHLOTHEIM)

Order: Mesogastropoda
Family: Aporrhaidae

The aperture of the shells of the cosmopolitan Upper Cretaceous to Pliocene genus *Drepanocheilus* tapers off into only two lobes – a short siphonal lobe and a long anal lobe, which curves upwards.

Zonaria lanciae (BRUSINA)

Order: Mesogastropoda
Family: Cypraeidae

The shells of the members of the genus *Zonaria* are small and strikingly glossy; in present-day species they are brightly coloured. They look rather like pears, since the last whorl completely conceals the preceding ones. The aperture is slit-like with small teeth. These gastropods occur in warm seas all over the world; they appeared during the Miocene and are still extant.

Trivia dorsolaevigata SACCO

Order: Mesogastropoda
Family: Eratoidae

The cosmopolitan genus *Trivia* has survived from the Eocene down to the present day. The tiny shells resemble those of the genus *Cypraea* in shape, but are cross-ribbed.

8

1. *Rimella fissurella,* * Palaeogene (Middle Eocene), Paris basin, France. Shell height 15 mm.

2. *Mesalia abbreviata*, Palaeogene (Middle Eocene), Grignon, France. Shell height 15 mm.

3. *Bayania lactea,* * Palaeogene (Middle Eocene), Grignon, France. Shell height 15 mm.

4. *Aporrhais pespelecani,* * Neogene (Pliocene), Monte Nuovi, Yugoslavia. Shell height 39 mm. The lobate aperture looks like a pelican's footprint – hence the specific name.

5. *Zonaria lanciae*, Neogene (Miocene), Lapugy, Romania. Shell length 26 mm. All cowry shells are covered with callus; this is secreted by the lobes of the mantle, which cover the shell from outside.

6. *Trivia dorsolaevigata*, Palaeogene (Oligocene), Europe. Shell length 17 mm. View of dorsal aspect of shell.

7. *Drepanocheilus speciosus*, Palaeogene (Middle Oligocene). Gothen, West Germany. Shell height 35 mm. Aporrhaids usually burrow in soft mud and live on organic débris sucked into the mantle cavity by the siphon.

8. *Rimella rimosa* – a complete shell.

Mollusca

Ficus reticulata (LAMARCK)

Order: Mesogastropoda
Family: Ficidae

The members of this genus are distributed all over the world. The last whorl of their large, pear-shaped shell covers the older whorls. The very wide mouth tapers off at the bottom into a long, straight siphonal canal. The thin shell has a reticulate sculpture, in which the spiral ribs sometimes predominate. Stratigraphically, the species of this genus range from the Palaeocene down to the present day.

Natica millepunctata LAMARCK

Order: Mesogastropoda
Family: Naticidae

The genus *Natica,* known from the Cretaceous period to the present day, is characterized by smooth, thick-walled and almost hemispherical shells. The wide umbilicus is often partly or completely covered by a callus. The callus is composed of three bosses — a large medial boss flanked by two almost indistinguishable lateral bosses which are fused with the edge of the aperture. All naticids are predators and feed on other molluscs. They bore through the shell with their radula and secrete an acid which helps to break it down faster. Naticid holes have a wide, concave border. Cannibalism among them is frequent.

Phalium saburon LAMARCK

Order: Mesogastropoda
Family: Cassididae

The members of the genus *Phalium* occur all over the world and have survived from the Eocene down to the present. Their pointedly ovoid

1. *Ficus reticulata,* Neogene (Pliocene), Sicily, Italy. Shell height 54 mm.

2, 3. *Natica millepunctata,* Neogene (Pliocene), Italy. Shell height 26 and 30 mm. Both shells have a coloured design. On the smaller shell (3) we can see the shape of the aperture and the umbilical callus. In the upper part of the whorl there is a hole bored by another naticid.

4. *Tenagodes anguinus,** Neogene (Pliocene), Italy. Shell height 73 mm. The irregularly coiled shell is the outcome of a sessile mode of life and its filter-feeding habit.

5. *Vermetus arenaria,** Neogene (Upper Miocene), Vienna basin, Austria. Shell diameter 60 mm. The similarity to worm tubes is reflected in the generic name.

6. *Phalium saburon,* Neogene (Upper Miocene), Vienna basin, Austria. Shell height 48 mm. The smooth, glossy shell, finely ribbed at the bottom only, in the region of the siphonal canal, is characteristic of the subgenus *Cassidea,* in which this species is usually included.

shell has a large body whorl. The aperture is elongate, wide and pear-shaped, with a deep, curving siphonal canal and a narrow posterior canal. The outer lip of the aperture is bordered by a pronounced rounded ridge. The parietal lip forms an extensive callus. In some species the shell is adorned with flat spiral ribs and bosses.

Tenagodes anguinus (LINNAEUS)

Order: Mesogastropoda
Family: Vermetidae

The members of this genus are distributed all over the world. The tubular shell is first of all coiled in a loose three-dimensional spiral and later irregularly, like a worm. The deep, narrow sinus is overgrown by a conspicuous selenizone. The shell surface may be smooth or ribbed. All vermetids live on plankton, which they snare on sticky threads of slime.

Vermetus arenaria (LINNAEUS)

Order: Mesogastropoda
Family: Vermetidae

This genus is known in Europe from the Miocene to the present. The shell, which becomes attached to solid objects on the bottom, has the form of a thick, irregularly twisted and tightly coiled tube. Its outer surface is covered with more or less pronounced granular longitudinal ribs and growth lines. The shells resemble worm tubes (*Vermes, Serpula*), but generally differ from these by their larger diameter and their sculpture, and by the microscopic structure of their shell.

185

Cancellaria cancellata (LINNAEUS)

Order: Neogastropoda
Family: Cancellariidae

Gastropods belonging to the order Neogastropoda always have a shell with a more or less extended siphonal canal. The horny operculum is non-spiral and in some genera it is missing altogether. This order has existed since the Upper Cretaceous (it is the youngest of all the prosobranchs – hence its name, Neo-) and attained its maximum development in the Cainozoic era.

The stratigraphic range of the genus *Cancellaria* stretches from the Miocene to the Recent and its geographic distribution is worldwide. The thick-walled, moderately large shells have a short, conical spire and a rounded, markedly convex body whorl. The large aperture is pointedly oval, with an anal groove and a narrow siphonal canal. On the surface of the shell, rounded axial ribs and sharp spiral ribs intersect.

Nassarius clathratus (LINNAEUS)

Order: Neogastropoda
Family: Nassidae

The members of the cosmopolitan genus *Nassarius* have survived from the Eocene down to the present day. They have wide, fusiform shells with bulging whorls, the last one of which is large and spherical or cylindrical. The aperture is oval. The aperture has a faintly indicated anal

1. *Cancellaria cancellata*, Neogene (Middle Pliocene), Sicily, Italy. Shell height 31 mm.

2. *Nassarius clathratus*, Neogene (Pliocene), Astigione, Italy. Shell height 32 mm. The outward resemblance to the genus *Cancellaria* is striking; the most pronounced differences are in the structure of the aperture of the shells.

groove and a wide, posteriorly oriented siphonal canal. The thin outer lip has a ribbed inner surface; the columellar lip is straight and short and has no folds. The sculpture, composed of sharp ribs, is very distinctive.

Baryspira glandiformis (LAMARCK)
Order: Neogastropoda
Family: Olividae

3. *Baryspira glandiformis,* Neogene (Upper Miocene), Mikulov, Czechoslovakia. Shell height 43 mm. Striking and abundant species. The shell is covered with a layer of glossy callus so thick that not even the sutures between the whorls can be seen.

The genus *Baryspira* can be found in marine sediments all over the world from the Oligocene onwards. Their pointedly ovoid shells are covered — like those of cypreids — with a deep layer of gleaming callus. The callus is secreted by the lobes of the mantle, which cover the outer surface of the shell. The aperture is an elongate oval, with a deep siphonal notch and a shallow anal groove.

Pterynotus tricarinatus (LAMARCK)
Order: Neogastropoda
Family: Muricidae

4. *Pterynotus tricarinatus,* Palaeogene (Middle Eocene), Grignon, France. Shell height 45 mm. All muricid shells are characterized by varices (former thickened apertures). In the genus *Pterynotus* they recur at intervals of 120 degrees, forming three wing-like borders on the outer surface of the shell.

The genus *Pterynotus* belongs to the large family Muricidae, which is characterized by decorative spinose shells. Muricids are predators and, like naticids, they bore holes in the shells of other molluscs; the holes do not have the typical naticid border, however. The spines on the shells act as a barrier protecting the animal from other drilling molluscs. The genus *Pterynotus* is cosmopolitan and has existed since the Eocene. Their small, thick-walled shells have a triangular, pyramidal spire.

Tudicla rusticula (BASTEROT)

Order: Neogastropoda
Family: Vasidae

Members of the genus *Tudicla* have existed from the Upper Cretaceous period down to the present. They occur all over the world. Their shells have an almost discoid spire, with markedly flattened, angular whorls. The last whorl is large and tapers downwards into a conspicuous siphonal canal. The large aperture forms a wide oval. On the outer surface of the whorls there are two ridges surmounted by bosses which taper off into spines.

Fusinus longirostris (BROCCHI)

Order: Neogastropoda
Family: Fusidae

The members of the cosmopolitan genus *Fusinus,* which has existed from the Upper Cretaceous down to the present, have moderately large, fusiform shells with a large, high body whorl. The aperture is an elongate oval rising to a point. The surface of the shell is covered with intersecting dense small spiral ribs and less pronounced knobbly axial ridges. *Fusinus* shells are mostly to be found in soft argillaceous deposits which formed sedimentary rocks in the deeper parts of the sea.

Volutospina rarispina (LAMARCK)

Order: Neogastropoda
Family: Volutidae

The stratigraphic distribution of these gastropods ranges from the Cretaceous to the Recent and they are to be found all over the world. The last whorl of their widely fusiform, moderately large shells is large and conical. The elongate aperture has an anal groove and a wide siphonal canal.

Lithoconus mercati (BROCCHI)

Order: Neogastropoda
Family: Conidae

At first glance, the conical shells of Conidae species all look practically alike. With their beautifully coloured markings, current species are very popular with collectors.

The genus *Lithoconus,* which dates back to the Eocene and is distributed all over the world, has a very low cone formed of protruding whorls. The body whorl has slightly bulging walls.

Leptoconus diversiformis (DESHAYES)

Order: Neogastropoda
Family: Conidae

The genus *Leptoconus* likewise has worldwide distribution. It is known from the Upper Cretaceous onwards. The moderately large shells have the form of a wide cone, whose upper aspect is characterized by step-like organization of the whorls.

1. *Fusinus longirostris,* Neogene (Upper Miocene), Baden, Austria. Shell height 45 mm. A long siphonal canal is typical of this genus also. In the specimen illustrated here, almost half of it has been broken off.

2. *Tudicla rusticula,* Neogene (Middle Miocene), Grund, Austria. Shell height 83 mm.

3. *Volutospina rarispina,* Neogene (Upper Miocene), Kienberg, Czechoslovakia. Shell height 42 mm. The few poorly developed spines in the upper part of the whorls are a typical feature, after which the species has been named.

4. *Lithoconus mercati,* Neogene (Upper Miocene), Kienberg, Czechoslovakia. Shell height 41 mm. The section shows the internal organization of the shell and the distinctive columella. Many conids reduce the weight of their shells by successively dissolving the thick walls of the inner whorls.

5, 6. *Leptoconus diversiformis,* Palaeogene (Middle Eocene), Grignon, France. Shell height 41 mm (5). All the members of the family Conidae catch small animals by means of a harpoon-like spine formed from the modified radula and connected to a venom gland (6).

Gyraulus trochiformis (Stahl)

Order: Basommatophora
Family: Planorbidae

The subclass Pulmonata (pulmonate gastropods) comprises terrestrial and secondarily aquatic animals with thin holostomatous shells and no operculum. In many species the shell is vestigial or absent. In the cold or dry season some land species form temporary opercula known as epiphragms and seal their shells with them. Pulmonate gastropods are first recorded in the Carboniferous period, but did not become abundant until the Cainozoic era. The order Basommatophora ('base-eyed') mainly comprises aquatic forms whose eyes are situated at the base of the single pair of tentacles.

The tiny shells of the genus *Gyraulus* have only a few whorls and are generally coiled in an almost flat spiral. The profile of the whorls and the shape of the aperture are more or less oval; sometimes there are one or two keels. The members of this genus occur in stagnant fresh water, in particular overgrown lakes and swamps, in the northern hemisphere and date back from the present to the Lower Eocene.

Galba subpalustris (Thomae)

Order: Basommatophora
Family: Lymnaeidae

The first members of the genus *Galba* appeared in the Jurassic period and numerous species still inhabit the whole northern hemisphere. The last whorl of the smooth, thin-walled, fusiform shell is large and ovoid. The suture slants steeply towards the axis of the shell. The various species lived (and still live) in small, overgrown lakes or in swamps.

Helix insignis Schübler

Order: Stylommatophora
Family: Helicidae

The characteristic features of the order Stylommatophora ('stalk-eyed') are two pairs of tentacles and eyes situated at the tip of the second pair. The stratigraphic distribution of these land animals extends from the Upper Cretaceous to the Recent.

The oldest members of the European genus *Helix* are known from the Oligocene. Their almost spherical shells have only a few coils and are often marked with dark spiral stripes. The mouth is roughly semicircular,

1. *Galba subpalustris,* Neogene (Upper Miocene), Velká Lípa, Czechoslovakia. Shell height 25 mm. A common species in freshwater calcareous sediments.

2. *Helix insignis,* Neogene (Upper Miocene), Steinheim, West Germany. Shell height 26 mm. Pre-quaternary finds of land gastropods are relatively rare, because the chances of their being covered and preserved by protective sediment are very small. The shell shown here was one that fell into water.

3. *Gyraulus trochiformis,* Neogene (Upper Miocene), Steinheim, West Germany. Shell diameter about 7 mm. The shells are very variable and range from flat discoid to low conical. The various types have been described as separate species.

4, 5. *Pupilla loessica,* Quaternary (Pleistocene), Prague-Bulovka, Czechoslovakia. Shell height 2–3 mm. An abundant species in central European loess. The very similar *P. muscorum* (5), the type species of the genus, has a tooth on its parietal lip.

with a narrow border along its margin. The slit-like umbilicus is sometimes covered with a callus.

Pupilla loessica LOŽEK

Order: Stylommatophora
Family: Pupillidae

The minute shells of the terrestrial genus *Pupilla,* which has survived from the Pliocene down to the present day and inhabits the northern hemisphere, are cylindrically ovoid and have just a few slightly bulging whorls. The elliptical aperture has a narrow border and the umbilicus is slit-like.

191

Mollusca

Nucula margaritacea LAMARCK

Order: Nuculoida
Family: Nuculidae

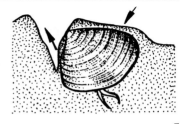

Bivalves (Bivalvia) are aquatic molluscs with a bilaterally symmetrical body consisting of a visceral sac, a retractile foot, paired gills and two dorsally connected mantle lobes which secrete the calcareous shell. They have no head, jaws or radula. The two valves of the shell are joined together by a tightly interlocking hinge, they are opened by an elastic ligament connecting them on the dorsal margin and are closed by powerful adductor muscles on the front and back of the body.

The members of the subclass Palaeotaxodonta are equivalve, have a simple taxodont hinge (with a row of approximately equal teeth), an external amphidetic ligament and two adductor muscles of roughly equal size. The shell has a nacreous inner layer.

The worldwide genus *Nucula,* known from the Upper Cretaceous, has small, round-cornered triangular shells with posteriorly directed umbones. The hinge line is divided into two parts by a resilifer (a fossa for the internal ligament).

1, 2, 7. *Nucula margaritacea,* Neogene, Greece. Height of valves 11 mm. A characteristic taxodont hinge, divided by the ligament pit, can be seen on the inner surface of the left valve (2). *Nucula* inhabit quiet, deep water; they are sessile, burrow a little way into the sediment and live on débris. 7 — a reconstruction; arrows mark the direction of inhalant and exhalant streams.

3. *Nuculana deshayesiana,* Palaeogene (Oligocene), Flörsheim near Mainz, West Germany. Height of left valve 13 mm. An important index fossil for the Middle Oligocene, it abounds in argillaceous sediments.

4. *Synek antiquus,* Upper Ordovician (Ashgillian), Lejškov near Zdice, Czechoslovakia. Length of valves 22 mm. Open valves in shale, seen from above. A species characteristic of deep, still water.

5

Nuculana deshayesiana DUCHASTEL

Order: Nuculoida
Family: Nuculanidae

The valves of the cosmopolitan genus *Nuculana,* known from the Triassic to the present day, are produced posteriorly to a rostrum. The pallial line has a small sinus. Concentric ribs form the sculpture.

Ctenodonta bohemica (BARRANDE)

Order: Nuculoida
Family: Ctenodontidae

The Ordovician genus *Ctenodonta* is known from Europe and North America. The smooth, sharp-pointed oval to elongate valves have anterior umbones. The ligament is amphidetic.

Synek antiquus BARRANDE

Order: Nuculoida
Family: Malletiidae

The members of the European Ordovician genus *Synek* have elongate oval valves with a blunt-tipped anterior umbo. The hinge, with an outer ligament and a curved hinge line, has very small teeth.

Babinka prima BARRANDE

Order: Veneroida
Family: Babinkidae

The species of the European genus *Babinka* from Lower Ordovician deposits have broadly oval valves with a pointed umbo almost in the centre of the upper side. The hinge is heterodont, i.e. with diferent main and side teeth. Between the adductor scars below the umbo we can see eight small muscle imprints. The pallial line has no sinus.

5. *Babinka prima,* * Lower Ordovician (Llanvirn), Osek near Rokycany, Czechoslovakia. Height of core of right valve 15 mm. On the core, which has been well preserved in a siliceous nodule, small muscle imprints can be seen below the umbo; they are considered to be a vestige inherited from monoplacophoran ancestors of the bivalves.

6. *Ctenodonta bohemica,* Lower Ordovician (Llanvirn), Černá Hůrka near Starý Plzenec, Czechoslovakia. Length of left valve 14 mm. Broken off valves seen from above, showing the tiny teeth of the taxodont hinge. The anterior edge of the shell is facing downwards.

4

6

Praecardium primulum BARRANDE

Order: Praecardioida
Family: Praecardiidae

The beginnings and origin of the class Bivalvia are not yet altogether clear. The oldest known bivalve to have been found is the Lower Cambrian *Fordilla troyensis* from New York, which has small, oval, flat-sided shells with a concentric sculpture, a simple ligament and hinge and bivalve type muscle scars. It is assumed that bivalves evolved during the Lower Cambrian from representatives of the class Rostroconchia probably from the genus *Myona,* in which the dorsal margin of the univalve shell became decalcified, resulting in the formation of an elastic ligament and a bivalve shell. The ligament allowed the edges of the shell to be shut tightly, without leaving a chink, and made it easier to forage for food. Consequent on this, bivalves also developed a foot and adductor muscles. It is interesting that, among the few known oldest bivalves (belonging to the Cambrian genera *Fordilla* and *Lamellodonta,* the Lower Ordovician genus *Babinka* and the Middle Ordovician genera *Cycloconcha* and *Lyrodesma*), there are considerable differences in the shape of the shells. This phenomenon is evidently associated with the adaptive radiation of the bivalves. In one respect, however, the finds all concur, i.e. the shells had two valves right from the outset and they were formed from two calcification centres.

The subclass Cryptodonta is the conventional name of a group of heterogeneous, little known and mainly Palaeozoic bivalves with equivalve, thin-walled, dimyarian shells with edentation or a taxodont hinge and an external ligament.

The Silurian and Devonian genus *Praecardium* is known from Europe and North America. The convex shells, with curved and pointed umbones, carry a few flat, radial ribs separated by wide, flat grooves. The taxodont hinge has small teeth.

1. *Praecardium primulum,** Upper Silurian (Pridoli), Prague-Podolí, Czechoslovakia. A right valve, height 25 mm.

2. *Panenka bohemica,* Upper Silurian (Pridoli), Lochkov, Czechoslovakia. A right valve, height 38 mm. *Panenka* is one of several dozen bivalve genera to which Barrande intentionally gave pleasant-sounding Czech names. Since he did so before any rules of nomenclature were published, they are still valid.

3

3. *Cardiolita bohemica,** Upper Silurian (base of Pridoli), Lochkov, Czechoslovakia. Height of the largest valve 21 mm. A group of valves in orthoceratid limestone. On the left, a shell of the cephalopod *Calocyrtoceras cognatum*.

4. *Cardiolita* sp. – valve viewed from the side of the hinge.

4

Order: Praecardioida
Family: Praecardiidae

Panenka bohemica BARRANDE

The members of the genus *Panenka* are European and North American Silurian and Devonian bivalves. They have a large, convex, widely oval shell densely covered with rounded radial ribs. The umbones are prosogyrate.

Order: Arcoida
Family: Cardiolidae

Cardiolita bohemica (BARRANDE)

The representatives of the genus *Cardiolita* (subclass Pteriomorpha) lived in Silurian Europe and North America. They have convex valves, with beak-like prosogyrate umbones. The numerous rounded radial ribs are intersected by wide growth ridges, resulting in a distinctive sculpture (fig. 4).

195

Mollusca

Antipleura bohemica Barrande

Order: Praecardioida
Family: Antipleuridae

In the central European and African Lower Devonian genus *Antipleura,* the valves have large, curved, blunt umbones situated strikingly crookedly in relation to each other, so that the shell looks as though it had been put together artifically out of two left or two right valves. The only other bivalves in which we find this asymmetry are the members of the related genus *Dualina.* The hinge line, which is formed of small teeth, is curved S-wise below the umbones.

Hercynella bohemica Perner

Order: Praecardioida
Family: Antipleuridae

The Upper Silurian and Lower Devonian genus *Hercynella* was distributed over practically the whole of the globe. The large, thin-walled, unequally convex valves have an almost central umbo. Their roughly oval contours are broken by a more or less pronounced ridge leading radially from the umbo to the anterior upper edge, where it forms a pointed 'wing' (fig. 5). These bivalves were originally thought to be patellid gastropods and we still know nothing of their internal structure.

5

Actinopteria migrans (Barrande)

Order: Pterioida
Family: Pterineidae

The subclass Pteriomorphia combines heteromyarian (= anisomyarian) and monomyarian forms of bivalves and, among isomyarian (= homomyarian) bivalves, icludes the order Arcoida. Most of them are sessile types held in place by byssal threads or cemented to their substrate, with a tendency to reduction of the foot and the anterior adductor muscle. Some genera (e.g. the members of the family Pectinidae) may be secondarily free-living and even able to swim. Owing to the convergent and parallel development of many features, a simple morphological characterization is difficult, but fossil finds often confirm the continuity and common origin of individual phylogenetic branches. Representatives of the above subclass are known from the Lower Ordovician to the present.

The cosmopolitan genus *Actinopteria* lived from the Silurian to the Permian, but was abundant only in the Silurian and Devonian. The left valve of the inequivalve shell is convex, while the right one is almost flat, both with the pointed apices situated well forward. The back of the valves is produced on top to a large, pointed wing and the front to a rounded wing, so that the hinge line is long and straight.

1. *Actinopteria migrans,* Lower Devonian (Lochkovian), Kosoř, Czechoslovakia. A left valve, height 25 mm. The highly convex valve has been crushed by rock pressure (the crack running down from the umbo). A characteristic and common genus of Lower Devonian Europe.

2, 3. *Antipleura bohemica,** Lower Devonian (Lochkovian), Lochkov, Czechoslovakia. Height of the larger shell core 37 mm (3); a view from the right side. The core of the smaller shell (2) is presented from above, so as to show the characteristic mutual relationship of the two umbones.

4. *Hercynella bohemica,* Lower Devonian (Lochkovian), Kosoř, Czechoslovakia. A right valve with remains of a shell; height 62 mm. It has been damaged by cracks which were closed by the deposition of calcite. The markedly inequivalve valves (one flat, the other conical) are indicative of a sessile mode of life.

5. *Hercynella nobilis* — right and left valve from above.

196

D

Mollusca

Astarte ovoides BUCH

Shells of bivalves are opened by the ligament which is always on the upper (dorsal) border. On this side we also find the pointed and usually spirally coiled umbones of the valves, which are generally situated well in front. They usually point forwards (i.e. they are prosogyrate) and seldom backwards (opisthogyrate). The ligament which opens the valves is either a strip lying externally over the hinge, or is a small body lying inside the shell on the hinge line (the resilium). The powerful muscles which keep the valves closed usually leave two large scars (anterior and posterior). The posterior scar is generally the larger and if the anterior muscle is not developed it is the only scar. Between the adductor scars occurs the line of little scars, the pallial line, the muscular attachment of the mantle margins. In some burrowing bivalves the pallial line is marked at the back by an indentation — the pallial sinus, the notch in the mantle where the siphons protrude out of the shell.

The subclass Heterodonta comprises marine — and mostly burrow-

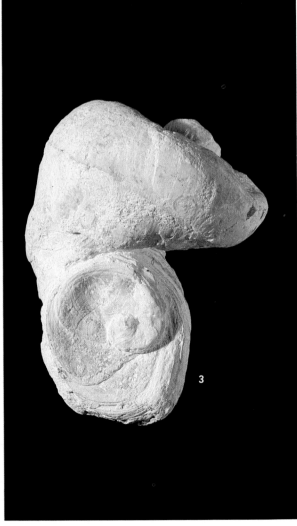

1. *Megalodon cucullatus,* *Middle Devonian (Givetian), Paffrath, West Germany. A left valve, height 51 mm.

2. *Astarte ovoides,* Upper Jurassic (Tithonian), near Moscow, USSR. An internal mould, height 41 mm, seen from the left. The white incrustation is what is left of the weathered shell. Recent representatives of this genus live in cold seas, buried just below the surface of sandy sediment or ooze.

3. *Requienia ammonia,* * Lower Cretaceous (Barremian), Orgon, France. Height of shell 130 mm. A sessile genus, whose members lived cemented to the substrate by their left valve – in the figure the flattened part top right.

4–6. *Diceras arietinum,* * Upper Jurassic (Oxfordian), Coulanges-sur-Yonne, France. A right valve, height 95 mm (4). An anterior muscle scar can be seen below, a posterior scar above (5). 6 – a complete shell.

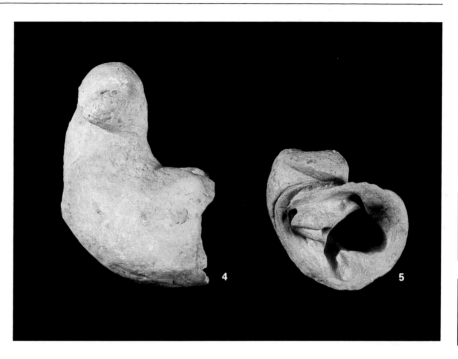

ing – bivalves with a heterodont hinge. The mantle edges are fused, with notches for the siphons. There are usually two muscle scars of roughly the same size (isomyarian). The shell has a porcellaneous (not nacreous) inner surface.

The shells of the cosmopolitan genus *Astarte,* known from the Jurassic down to the present, have prosogyrate umbones in the centre of the dorsum. There are usually two main hinge teeth in each valve, while the lateral teeth are small or absent.

Megalodon cucullatus SOWERBY
Order: Hippuritoida
Family: Megalodontidae

The shells of the genus *Megalodon* are known from Devonian to Triassic deposits. They have smooth, thick, bulging valves with prosogyrate umbones, a massive hinge and an external ligament. The anterior adductor muscle leaves a marked scar. The pallial line has no sinus.

Diceras arietinum LAMARCK
Order: Hippuritoida
Family: Diceratidae

The members of the European and African Upper Jurassic genus *Diceras* have robust shells with valves shaped like spiral horns (fig. 6); they are sometimes attached by the largest right valve to a substrate. On the left valve the hinge has a single large tooth (on the right there are two teeth); deep muscle scars can be seen on either side of the hinge.

Requienia ammonia (GOLDFUSS)
Order: Hippuritoida
Family: Requieniidae

In the Cretaceous period, the members of the genus *Requienia* lived all over the world (except Asia). They have a large, spiral left valve, a flat, lid-like right valve and a hinge similar to that of *Diceras.*

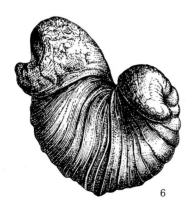

6

Hippurites radiosus DES MOULINS

Order: Hippuritoida
Family: Hippuritidae

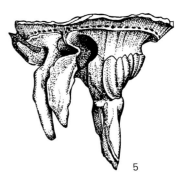

5

Hippuritoids are a distinctive and highly specialized group of bivalves which appeared in the Upper Jurassic, developed very rapidly and died out at the end of the Cretaceous. In association with their sessile mode of life in very shallow water, their fixed valve grew thicker and longer until it formed a cone which resisted the breakers and kept the mouth as high as possible above the bottom. The shell of advanced forms is made lighter by canals or cavities. The free valve was made lighter by reduction to the form of a lid; the long, stake-like hinge teeth prevented it from being torn away. In specialized types the free valve had openings (oscula), so that it did not need to be lifted so often.

Hippuritoida inhabited tropical and subtropical seas, where at first they lived singly in coral reefs. Later, however, they formed groups and thick, spreading carpets. Their environmental requirements were less explicit than those of corals, which they replaced ecologically in less favourable conditions. They are therefore to be found in various types of limestone, calcareous sandstone and marl.

The Upper Cretaceous members of the cosmopolitan genus *Hippurites* have large, massive, conical or cylindrical shells. The right valve is shaped like a hollow cone, while the left one forms a lid with two large peg-like teeth (fig. 5) which fit into sockets in the cavity of the right valve. The outer surface is longitudinally ribbed, with three furrows at the site of the internal shell folds which separate the dental sockets and the muscle insertions from one another.

1. *Hippurites radiosus,* Upper Cretaceous (Maastrichtian), Charente, France. A right valve, height 115 mm. Inside, at the front, we can see the deep dental socket separated by a ligamental ridge and on the left two internal supports, with a socket for the posterior muscle. The animal's body was on the right.

2. *Biradiolites cornupastoris,* Upper Cretaceous (Turonian), Dordogne, France. Height of the shell 135 mm. View from the side.

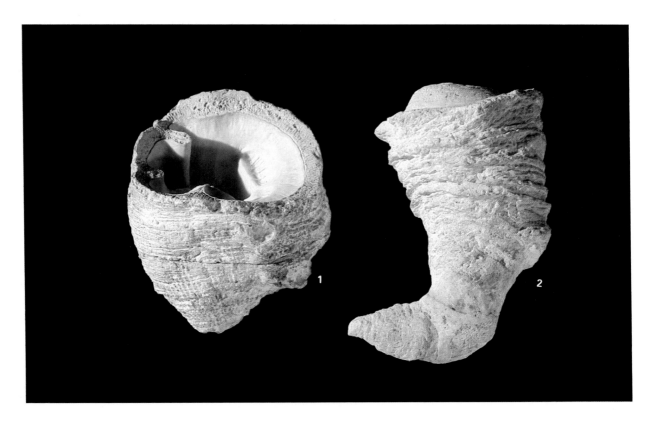

Biradiolites cornupastoris (D'ORBIGNY)

Order: Hippuritoida
Family: Radiolitidae

Cr

The Upper Cretaceous genus *Biradiolites* is distributed over practically the whole of the globe. The large, massive right valve is conical and often curved; the left valve is like a lid. There are cavities in the walls and the ligament is absent. The hinge is the same as in the genus *Hippurites*.

Protocardia hillana (SOWERBY)

Order: Veneroida
Family: Cardiidae

The members of the genus *Protocardia* lived in Europe, Africa and both parts of America from the Upper Triassic to the Cretaceous periods. They have rounded valves with a pronounced umbo. The front and sides of the valves are marked with concentric ribs, the posterior part with a band of radial ribs. The pallial line has a small sinus.

3. *Protocardia hillana,** Upper Cretaceous (Cenomanian), Smrček, Czechoslovakia. A right valve, height 57 mm.

Crassatella macrodonta ZITTEL

Order: Veneroida
Family: Crassatellidae

4. *Crassatella macrodonta,* Upper Cretaceous (Senonian), Sankt Gilden, Austria. Height of shell 37 mm. View of the outer surface of the right valve.

5. *Hippurites* sp., the left valve.

The shells of the European and American genus *Crassatella* have thick, posteriorly truncated valves with an anterior umbo. The hinge is heterodont, with an internal ligament. The adductor scars are pronounced; the pallial line has no sinus. Today *Crassatella* live chiefly in warm climatic belts. The first species date back to the Upper Cretaceous and Miocene.

Lymnocardium vindobonense (PARTSCH)

Order: Veneroida
Family: Lymnocardiidae

Most bivalves are marine animals and tolerate little or no change in the salinity of the water. Only a few species – chiefly in the families Mytilidae, Cardiidae, Veneridae and Mactridae – can also live in brackish water, where they tend to be smaller and to have a thinner and less distinctly sculptured shell. On the other hand, because of the lack of competition, they occur there in vast numbers. These limited associations are supplemented by the members of freshwater genera belonging to the families Corbiculidae and Dreissenidae, which for their part can tolerate raised salinity. The few exclusively freshwater bivalves there are belong to the order Unionida and the family Pisidiidae. Since fresh water dissolves calcareous shells, their shells usually have a thick organic outer layer (periostracum) and the valves characteristically eroded umbones.

The European Neogene genus *Lymnocardium* has convex valves with prosogyrate umbones. The hinge has well developed lateral teeth and small cardinal teeth. The pallial line is generally without a sinus (fig. 8).

Megacardita jouanneti (BASTEROT)

Order: Veneroida
Family: Carditidae

These bivalves have existed since the Oligocene and occur in Europe, Africa and Australia. They have massive valves with anteriorly oriented umbones. The hinge has well developed cardinal teeth and often vestigial lateral teeth. The pallial line has no sinus.

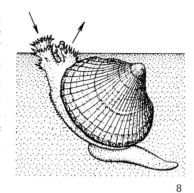

8. A reconstruction of an animal closely related to the genus *Cardium*. Arrows mark the direction of the inhalant and exhalant currents.

9. *Panopea* sp., shell viewed from the side of the hinge.

1, 2. *Lymnocardium vindobonense,* Neogene (Middle Miocene), Velké Bílovice near Břeclav, Czechoslovakia. Height of valves 20 mm. Outer (1) and inner (2) view of a right valve. A common central European Miocene species which often lived in brackish water in river-fed bays.

3. *Panopea menardi,* Neogene (Pliocene), Astigione, Italy. Height of shell 62 mm. These bivalves live in the littoral zone, burrowing deep in the soft sediment. They therefore have long, massive siphons in a fleshy sheath, for which there is a large opening at the back of the shell.

4, 5. *Megacardita jouanneti,** Neogene (Upper Miocene), Gainfahren near Vienna, Austria. Height of the larger valve 48 mm. A left valve seen from without (4) and within (5). A common species of sandy shallow-water marine sediments.

6. *Corbicula semistriata,* Palaeogene (Oligocene), Miesbach, Oberbayern, West Germany. Height of the largest valve 20 mm. An index fossil of Oligocene cyrenian marls (named after *Cyrene,* the old name of the genus) and of the clay layers of German coalfields.

6

Congeria subglobosa PARTSCH

Order: Veneroida
Family: Dreissenidae

The members of this Eurasian Oligocene to Pliocene genus have convex, thick-walled valves with prosogyrate umbones. The pallial line has no sinus. The umbonal part of the valves is divided by a septum for insertion of the muscles of the foot.

Corbicula semistriata (DESHAYES)

Order: Veneroida
Family: Corbiculidae

7. *Congeria subglobosa,* Neogene (Upper Miocene), Brunn near Vienna, Austria. Height of shell 71 mm. A front view of the joined valves, looking like a sheep's hoof. This species inhabited fresh and brackish water.

7

The species of the cosmopolitan genus *Corbicula,* which has survived from the Lower Cretaceous down to the present day, have thick-walled valves with large, rounded umbones. They inhabit fresh or brackish water.

Panopea menardi DESHAYES

Order: Myoida
Family: Hiatellidae

The members of the widespread genus *Panopea* are known from the Cretaceous period down to the present day. They have large, posteriorly truncated, gaping shells with indistinct umbones (fig. 9). Concentric ridges with growth wrinkles form the sculpture. The pallial line has a large, wide sinus.

203

 **Mollusca**

Costacallista papilionacea (LAMARCK)

Order: Veneroida
Family: Veneridae

Bivalve shells are secreted by the edge and the outer surface of the mantle and usually have three layers. The thin outer layer, the periostracum, is organic (formed of conchiolin) and its purpose is to protect the calcareous inner layers. It contains the pigments responsible for the patterns on the shells and is seldom preserved in fossil form. Usually the middle layer, the ostracum, is composed of aragonite or calcite granules organized in perpendicular prisms. The innermost layer, which is usually the thickest, is also the most variable. In more primitive types it is nacreous and composed of many horizontal layers of thin hexagonal aragonite plates. Most often it is porcellaneous, i.e. glossy, opaque, and formed of aragonite lamellae arranged in many alternatingly diagonal rows. Other modifications also exist, however, e.g. with the same structure as porcellaneous layers, but made of calcite (in oysters), or composed of finely granular, homogeneous or laminar aragonite.

The cosmopolitan genus *Costacallista* has inhabited warm, shallow seas since the Palaeocene. The pallial sinus is wide and pointed. The bivalves live embedded in the substratum and obtain food by filtering sea water and utilizing the organic particles left behind.

1, 7. *Tellina interrupta*, Pleistocene, Barbados, France. A left valve, height 37 mm. 7 – a view of the inner side of the right valve.

2. *Costacallista papilionacea*, Neogene (Miocene), Turin, Italy. A right valve, height 33 mm.

3. *Solen vagina,** Neogene (Pliocene), Astigione, Italy. A right valve, length 127 mm. The small umbo can be seen in the top right corner.

Q

Ng

4. *Cordiopsis gigas,* Neogene (Upper Miocene), Italy. A left valve, height 105 mm. One of the largest species of the Veneridae family, it lived embedded in the soft bed of shallow, warm seas.

5,6. *Chama gryphoides,* Neogene (Upper Miocene), Lapugy, Romania. Height of valves 75 and 85 mm. Free valves: right (5), left (6). The outer surface has been worn away by the waves and perforated by boring sponges of the genus *Cliona* and boring bivalves of the genus *Lithophaga* (the two large holes).

Cordiopsis gigas (LAMARCK)	Order: Veneroida Family: Veneridae

This Eocene to Miocene genus is known in Eurasia and Africa. The large, thick valves, with their large prosogyrate umbones, have pronounced growth wrinkles. The pallial sinus is short and rounded.

Tellina interrupta WOODWARD	Order: Veneroida Family: Tellinidae

Species of the cosmopolitan genus *Tellina* have been known since the Oligocene. They chiefly inhabit warm seas, remain embedded deep in the substratum and live on organic débris contained in the sediment; they consequently have a very deep pallial sinus (fig. 7).

Chama gryphoides LINNAEUS	Order: Veneroida Family: Chamidae

Since the Palaeogene to the Recent, members of the genus *Chama* have inhabited the warm seas of Europe and America. Their thick shells have prosogyrate umbones and are cemented to a base by one of the valves, right or left.

Solen vagina LINNAEUS	Order: Veneroida Family: Solenidae

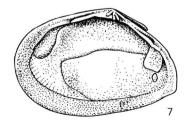

The Eurasian and American genus *Solen* has been known since the Eocene. The long, thin, smooth valves form a tube which is narrow and open in front and behind. The members of this genus live embedded deep in the sea bed and the whole shape of the shell is actually subordinated to the huge siphons.

Mollusca

Hoernesia socialis (SCHLOTHEIM)

Order: Pterioida
Family: Bakewelidae

In bivalves, the plane of bilateral symmetry passes anteroposteriorly through the centre of the body, i.e. between the valves, which are thus usually the same size and shape. In phylogenetically progressive species, however, the valves sometimes differ as regards their shape and sculpture, as well as their degree of convexity. The commonest cause is a sessile mode of life, when one valve is attached by byssal threads or cemented to a substrate when the other acts as a kind of lid. Whether the shell rests on the right or the left valve is not decided at random, but follows a definite law which is usually applied on the genus level. The under valve is generally larger and more bulging. Forms with variously convex valves also exist — though less often — among mobile, burrowing species of bivalves, but here the convexity differences are smaller. Another type of disparity is discordance of the edges of the valves. Cases in which the plane between the valves curves or spirals, so that the valves often do not even match, are more interesting, but this type also tends to occur more in sessile forms of bivalves. Examples of the above irregularities are to be found in every group of bivalves, but the subclass Pteriomorpha is particularly rich in them.

1, 2, 6. *Hoernesia socialis,** Middle Triassic (Ladinian), Weimar, East Germany. Height of shells 26 and 30 mm. (1) right, (2) left valve. An abundant and very often a rock-forming species of the German Triassic. 6 — a reconstruction of a living individual.

3. *Posidonia becheri,** Lower Carboniferous (Viséan), Nassau, West Germany. A disarticulated (disconnected) shell; height of the more complete right valve 38 mm. A common fossil of the Culm. The famous Jurassic *Posidonia* shales contain the species *Posidonia bronni.*

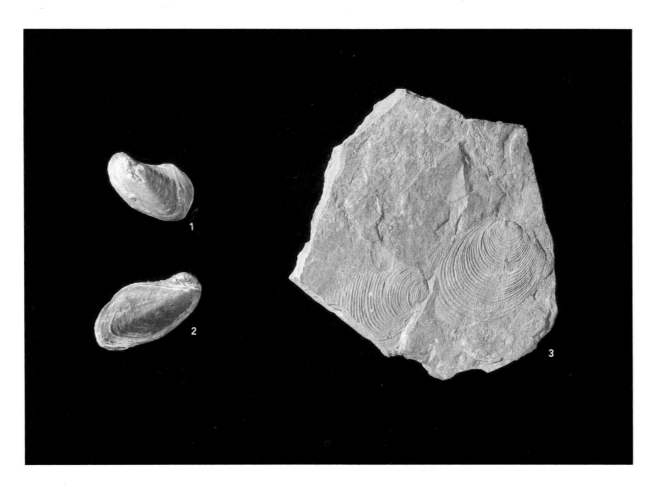

4. *Monotis salinaria,** Upper Triassic (Norian), Hallein, Austria. Height of valve on the left 40 mm.

5. *Rhaetavicula contorta,** Upper Triassic (Rhaetian), Nürtingen, West Germany. Height of the larger valve 17 mm. A Rhaetian index fossil of the German Triassic.

The members of the Eurasian genus *Hoernesia* date from the Triassic to the Middle Jurassic. They have unequally convex, skewed and slightly spiral, winged valves (fig. 6), of which the left one is the larger and tapers off to a large umbo overhanging the straight hinge line, while the right valve is almost flat.

Rhaetavicula contorta (PORTLOCK)

Order: Pterioida
Family: Pteriidae

The representatives of the genus *Rhaetavicula* are to be found in Eurasia and North America in Upper Triassic deposits. They have small, inequivalve, narrow, crescent-shaped valves, twisted like a propeller, with a large, pointed posterior wing and a small anterior wing. The left valve is convex and radially ribbed, while the right valve is almost flat and is smooth.

Posidonia becheri (BRONN)

Order: Pterioida
Family: Posidoniidae

This genus was distributed over virtually the whole globe from the Carboniferous to the Jurassic. The flat valves have no ears and the umbones are situated anteriorly.

Monotis salinaria (SCHLOTHEIM)

Order: Pterioida
Family: Monotidae

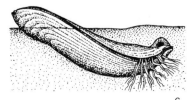

The cosmopolitan Upper Triassic genus *Monotis* has flat, slightly unequally convex valves with anterior umbones. The posterior ear is larger than the anterior ear.

6

Mollusca

Modiolus imbricatus (SOWERBY)

Order: Mytiloida
Family: Mytilidae

Many bivalves belonging to the subclass Pteriomorpha are attached to some object or other by a byssus, a bundle of organic filaments with a similar composition to conchiolin. A byssal gland on the under side of the foot secretes a liquid which, in water, quickly solidifies to threads. The gland communicates with the surface via a byssal fossa, where the liquid collects before being conveyed along the byssal groove to the front of the foot, which can deposit it where it is required. Not all bivalve species possess a byssal gland and in most of those that have one it functions only when the newly sessile planktonic larva is being adapted to a benthic existence. Many forms which are also attached by a byssus in adulthood can shed the byssal threads whenever they need to, move to a different place and form a new byssus. In the mussels of the genus *Mytilus,* which live in the surf zone, this process is particularly interesting. To avoid being swept away by the waves, they loosen only the hind part of the byssus; at the same time they form new threads in front and in this way they progress slowly, but surely. In some permanently attached species (e.g. of the genus *Anomia*), the filaments calcify to a solid column. In the case of bivalves which are cemented in place, either the byssal gland secretes only calcium carbonate or the cement is produced at the mantle edge. Some bivalves (e.g. in the genus *Lima*), build a kind of protective nest of byssal threads round themselves.

The representatives of the cosmopolitan genus *Modiolus* are known from the Devonian to the Recent. Their convex, thin-walled, smooth shell has anteriorly situated umbones. The rounded anterior wing of the valves is hardly distinct. The hinge has no teeth. In the shell, there is a small byssal notch near the umbo (fig 5.) The members of this genus

1. *Modiolus imbricatus,* Middle Jurassic (Bathonian), Great Britain. A left valve, length 47 mm.

2. *Plicatula tubifera,* Upper Jurassic (Oxfordian), Villers-sur-Mer, France. A right valve, height 40 mm. The adhering portion of the valve can be seen near the umbo. The surface is covered with short, hollow spines.

3. *Arcomytilus pectinatus,* Upper Jurassic (Kimmeridgian), Bléville, France. A left valve, length 50 mm. Fine radial ribs and a truncated posterior margin (damaged in the specimen illustrated here) are typical of *Arcomytilus* shells.

208

4. *Plagiostoma giganteum,** Lower Jurassic (Lower Liassic), Degerloch, West Germany. A left valve, height 110 mm. This genus is differentiated from typical members of the family Limidae by its smooth shells. One of the largest Liassic bivalves.

5. *Modiolus* sp., a reconstruction of a living individual.

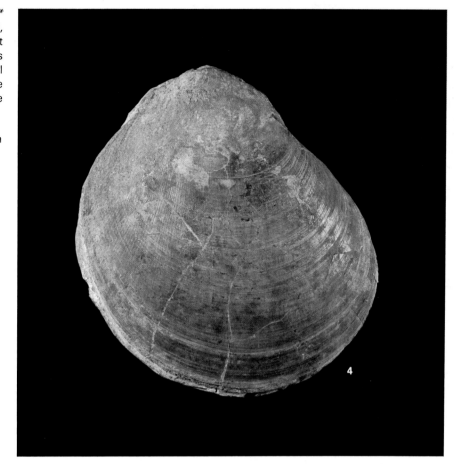

lived singly and in this respect they differ from the related genus *Mytilus,* whose members often collect together in masses.

Arcomytilus pectinatus (SOWERBY)	Order: Mytiloida Family: Mytilidae

The species of the Jurassic to Eocene genus *Arcomytilus* occur in Europe and Africa. Their thin, convex shells are cut off at the back in an almost straight line.

Plicatula tubifera D'ORBIGNY	Order: Pterioida Family: Plicatulidae

Plicatula has existed since the Middle Triassic down to the present day in Eurasia, Africa and North America. The monomyarian shell is irregularly shaped and the unequally convex valves have no ears. They are generally attached to solid objects by the umbo of the right valve.

Plagiostoma giganteum SOWERBY	Order: Pterioida Family: Limidae

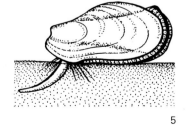

Representatives of the genus *Plagiostoma* are found in Triassic to Cretaceous deposits all over the world. They have large, only slightly convex valves with pointed umbones. The hinge is usually edentulous.

5

Gryphaea arcuata LAMARCK	Order: Pterioida Family: Gryphaeidae

Oysters are a very large and successful group of bivalves. Very little is known of their origin, but they appeared in the Upper Triassic and very soon they had conquered all the seas, except in the polar regions. The oldest known genera – the cold-loving *Gryphaea* and *Liostrea* and the tropical genus *Lopha* – indicate a diphyletic origin for oysters.

All oysters explicitly like shallow water and, except for the family Ostreidae, do not tolerate changes in salinity. They also like warmth and the only genera to have penetrated into cold water are *Ostrea* and *Crassostrea*. Oysters are sessile bivalves and often live with one valve cemented to a firm sandy or rocky substrate with clean, flowing water. They avoid mud where possible, or at least perch on something higher and more solid. Usually they occur in large numbers, some species forming extensive growths and reefs along the coastline.

The genus *Gryphaea* is known from Upper Triassic and Jurassic formations all over the world. The under (left) valve is very thick and markedly convex, with a strikingly coiled umbo. Posteriorly it has a radial fold. The right valve is small and lid-like. The unusual gryphaeid shape of the shell is a manifestation of adaptation to life on a soft substratum. The actual attachment surface is small and rapid upward growth of the valve brought the edge out of reach of the turbid water near the bottom. This gave rise to a characteristic spirally shaped lower valve, which later settled in the soft sediment, embedded there by its own weight (fig. 6). Stability was ensured by the very thick wall of the apical part of the lower valve. A gryphaeid shell form is also to be seen, independently, in other evolutionary lines of oysters, including some which lived on a firmer, sandy substrate, where it enabled them quickly to break free from coherent growths of algae which hindered growth of the young oysters.

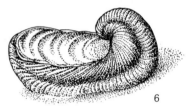

Deltoideum sowerbyanum BRONN	Order: Pterioida Family: Gryphaeidae

The valves of the European Middle and Upper Jurassic genus *Deltoideum* are very flat and are higher than they are wide. The right valve resembles the left one, but is smaller. *Deltoideum* probably evolved from *Gryphaea*.

Lopha marshi (SOWERBY)	Order: Pterioida Family: Ostreidae

The oysters of the cosmopolitan genus *Lopha* have lived in tropical and subtropical waters ever since the Triassic period. The convex valves, which are roughly the same size, have large, sharp radial folds with a profile like an inverted letter V; their number is typical for each species. The folds raise the edges of the shell above the sea bed and increase the area of the opening, while keeping the slit the same width.

1–3, 6. *Gryphaea arcuata,* *Lower Jurassic (Liassic), Göppingen, West Germany. Height of the flat right valve 35 mm. 1 – a left valve from behind, in approximately the natural position; the posterior fold can be seen; 2 – a lid-like right valve, 3 – view of a left valve from above. 6 – shell in a living position.

4. *Deltoideum sowerbyanum,* * Upper Jurassic (Kimmeridgian), Le Havre, France. Two left (lower) valves which have grown across each other; height of the whole specimen 170 mm.

5. *Lopha marshi,* Middle Jurassic (Middle Dogger), Spaichingen, West Germany. A right valve, height 80 mm. A common species of the German Middle Jurassic.

Agerostrea ungulata (SCHLOTHEIM)

Order: Pterioida
Family: Ostreidae

Their sessile mode of life and immobility led, in oysters, to complete reduction of the foot and was also reflected in the shape of the shells. There was no need to tuck the foot away, to adapt form to motion or to be sparing with weight, and a tendency to the formation of shells with rounded contours appeared, since radial symmetry is the best for sessile animals. Oysters only frequent sandy or rocky substrates, which do not make the water turbid, and consequently they did not develop conical and cylindrical forms like Hippuritoida, for instance. Another factor preventing this was the growth of gills responsible for the intake of food and oxygen from the circulating water. The most satisfactory shape for this activity is a shell with triangular valves, with the hinge in the top corner and spaces for the inflow and outflow of water in the other two corners. Lengthening of the gills (often to lobular forms) caused growth of the posterior lower end of the shell — in extreme cases to a crescent-shaped form. Since the bottom valve was fixed and the upper valve was free, the anterior adductor muscle disappeared, the posterior muscle grew larger and the upper valve became lighter (thinner) or smaller. The shape of the valves is also influenced by other factors, e.g. by light (the valves are thinner, more compact and more conspicuously ribbed) and by crowding (the shell is unable to develop its typical shape).

Agerostrea is a worldwide Upper Cretaceous genus. The narrow, curved valves have a convex anterior margin and sharp transversal folds with a V-shaped profile, which grow larger from the centre to the edge of the valves. Posterior to the hinge there is a lobe-like wing.

Arctostrea carinata (LAMARCK)

Order: Pterioida
Family: Ostreidae

In the Cretaceous period the members of the genus *Arctostrea* were distributed throughout all the world seas. They have a narrow, elongate shell with a high longitudinal ridge from which sharp folds run down to the edge of the valves, where they are produced to long triangular spines.

Rhynchostreon suborbiculatum (LAMARCK)

Order: Pterioida
Family: Gryphaeidae

The Upper Cretaceous Eurasian and North American genus *Rhynchostreon* has gryphaeoid valves. The left valve is highly convex, with a rounded ridge, a coiled, beak-like umbo and a radial fold at the back. The right valve is disc-like.

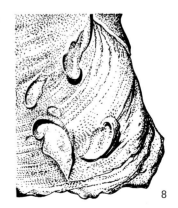

8

1, 2, 8. *Exogyra sigmoidea,* Upper Cretaceous (Cenomanian), Korycany, Czechoslovakia. Height of the right valves 30 and 34 mm. An outer (1) and an inner (2) view. A common species in littoral and sublittoral Cenomanian sediments. Left valves, forming low spiral ridges on the rocks, are less common. 8 – left valves cemented to the shell of another bivalve.

3. *Arctostrea carinata,* Upper Cretaceous (Cenomanian), Korycany, Czechoslovakia. A left valve, height 68 mm.

4, 5. *Agerostrea ungulata,** Upper Cretaceous (Maastrichtian), Hammadah al Hamra Plateau, Libya. Height of the valves 48 and 58 mm. A right valve ground down externally (4) and a left valve internally (5) by sand. Weathered valves of this type cover vast extents of the Sahara.

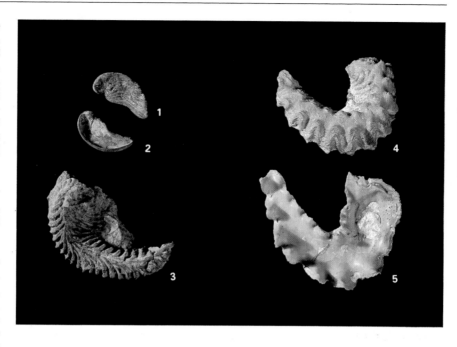

Exogyra sigmoidea (GOLDFUSS)

Order: Pterioida
Family: Gryphaeidae

This small European Cretaceous oyster has flat and narrow right (free) valves with a spirally coiled umbo and a pronounced radial ridge dividing the valve into a steep anterior part and a wide, gently sloping posterior part. The entire surface of the left valve is seated on the substrate (fig. 8). The inner margin of the valves is bordered by a row of small protuberances (chomata).

6, 7. *Rhynchostreon suborbiculatum,** Upper Cretaceous (Turonian), Malnice, Czechoslovakia. Height of valves 100 mm. (6) a left valve with the original coloured stripes, (7) an imprint of the inner surface of a right valve on a shell filling. The species is also known under its old name *Exogyra columba.*

Mollusca

Mytiloides labiatus (Schlotheim)

Order: Pterioida
Family: Inoceramidae

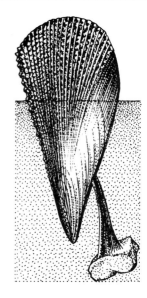

The family Inoceramidae originated in the Lower Jurassic. Its rapid development and great morphological variability allowed its members to settle in the most diverse — but chiefly shallow-water — environments and to spread to all the seas and practically every climatic zone of the Mesozoic era. As a result, in the Upper Cretaceous — the time of their greatest diversity — they became the stratigraphically most important group of bivalves, with all the prerequisites of good index fossils. They evolved quickly and the individual species soon died out, so that they mark short periods of time. Furthermore, owing to their wide geographical distribution, they can be used to correlate very remote geological exposures. They are abundant, well preserved, of reasonable size and relatively easy to determine. The fact that they occur in various sediments, from claystone to coarse-grained sandstone, enhances their usefulness. The rapid elaboration to narrow specialization which made all this possible was also the beginning of the end for them, however, and in the ecological crisis at the end of the Cretaceous they all died out.

The representatives of the cosmopolitan genus *Mytiloides* existed during the Jurassic and the Cretaceous. They have thin, slightly vaulted and only slightly unequal valves with a low posterior wing. The hinge is short and straight and without teeth. These bivalves inhabited warm, shallow seas with a firm sandy floor, to which they were loosely attached by byssal threads. Their flattish, perpendicularly held shells possibly acted as a rudder, which turned with the current so that the intake (inhalant) orifice faced it and the outflow (exhalant) stream followed it.

1, 5. *Pinna quadrangularis,* Upper Cretaceous (Turonian), Hořice, Czechoslovakia. Height of shell 205 mm. 1 — rear view of a slightly deformed shell, showing the commissure. 5 — a reconstruction of a living individual.

2. *Volviceramus involutus,* Upper Cretaceous (Coniacian), Štíty near Šumperk, Czechoslovakia. A spiral left valve, diameter 110 mm. An index fossil for the upper part of the Lower Coniacian.

1

3. *Mytiloides labiatus,** Upper Cretaceous (Lower Turonian), Děčínský Sněžník, Czechoslovakia. Left view of a core, length 130 mm. An index fossil for the European Lower Turonian.

4. *Mytiloides* sp., a reconstruction of a living individual.

4

Volviceramus involutus (SOWERBY)

Order: Pterioida
Family: Inoceramidae

The genus *Volviceramus* is known from Upper Cretaceous Europe and North America. The large, markedly unequal shells resemble gryphaeid oysters. The left (lower) valve is smooth, highly convex and twisted in a spiral, while the right (upper) valve is only moderately convex and is much smaller and more rounded, with concentric ridges. The members of this genus lived in deep, quiet parts of warm seas with a soft clayey substrate, in which the thick spiral valve kept them embedded.

Pinna quadrangularis PHILLIPS

Order: Mytiloida
Family: Pinnidae

The cosmopolitan Carboniferous to present-day representatives of the genus *Pinna* usually have very thin-walled wedge-shaped shells with a long, pointed umbo and a more or less pronounced radial ridge down the longitudinal axis of the valves. These are sculptured with radial ribs which sometimes terminate in scales. The members of this genus live half-buried in the sediment and are supplementarily held in place by byssal threads (fig. 5).

215

Spondylus spinosus (SOWERBY)

Order: Pterioida
Family: Spondylidae

The bivalves of the genus *Spondylus* are to be found in every warm climatic belt from the Jurassic onwards. The sharp-apexed valves differ slightly as regards their convexity; in addition, the right valve (the one by which the animal is usually anchored) is produced to a rostrum with a triangular area. The hinge margin is straight, with small ears; on either side of the resilifer there are always two teeth. The valves have only one pair of muscle imprints. The radial ribs on the outer surface often terminate in spines of varying lengths and shapes, whose function it is to keep the edge of the shell clear of the bottom.

Lima canalifera GOLDFUSS

Order: Pterioida
Family: Limidae

Lima has the same stratigraphy and geographical distribution as the preceding genus. They both have slightly convex valves which are higher than they are long and have small ears. The hinge margin is short and straight, with a small area; teeth are absent or small. The sculpture consists of radial and sometimes squamous ribs. Some species are held fast by a byssus, others lie freely on the sea bed and others again, like pectinids, can swim. Species which construct complicated protective nests for themselves out of byssal threads are something of a rarity.

Chlamys muricatus (GOLDFUSS)

Order: Pterioida
Family: Pectinidae

The stratigraphic range of the worldwide genus *Chlamys* stretches from the Triassic to the Recent. The valves are unequally convex, the left one being usually more vaulted than the right one. The ears are very pronounced and the anterior one is typically larger and longer than the posterior one. The outer surface is thickly covered with rounded radial ribs and concentric crests, which have usually been preserved only in furrows. *Chlamys muricatus*, a sessile species held fast by byssal threads, occurred in protected spots such as cracks and crevices, under overhanging rocks and boulders and in growths of algae, etc. It has a typical long, straight hinge line with a long anterior ear and a pronounced byssal notch below it, and flat, almost equally convex, rough-ribbed valves.

Neithea aequicostata (LAMARCK)

Order: Pterioida
Family: Pectinidae

In the Cretaceous period the members of the genus *Neithea* were spread all over the world. They have a spirally coiled and markedly convex right valve and a flat left valve, both with equal-sized ears. In the hinge, on either side of the resilifer, there are two teeth. This species belonged to the pectinids which live attached to the bottom by a byssus – generally on a firm, sandy and unprotected substrate. Its typical features are a markedly inequivalve shell and a well-developed byssal notch; the ribs are only moderately rough.

1. *Spondylus spinosus,* Upper Cretaceous (Senonian), Kent, England. A left valve with a few spines still preserved; height 50 mm.

2. *Lima canalifera,* Upper Cretaceous (Lower Senonian), Haltern, West Germany. A right valve, height 55 mm; it is seated on a left valve of the species *Chlamys muricatus,* which is 95 mm high and has lost its ear. Both species were sessile and usually lived in quiet, protected spots.

3. *Neithea aequicostata,** Upper Cretaceous (Cenomanian), Hájek near Potštejn, Czechoslovakia. Height of the more convex valve 78 mm. A disarticulated shell clearly showing the differences between the two valves.

Amusium cristatum BRONN

Order: Pterioida
Family: Pectinidae

9

Many representatives of the families *Pectinidae* and *Limidae* secondarily acquired a faculty somewhat unusual among bivalves, i.e. they learnt to swim. Such species evolved from originally sessile, byssate forms, as seen from their inequivalve, monomyarian valves and the byssal notch below the anterior ear. When swimming, a bivalve closes its valves abruptly several times in succession, forcing the water out of the mantle cavity and ejecting it obliquely backwards through slits in the corners of the ears. This periodic opening and closing of the valves produces a fluttering kind of motion, rather like a butterfly in flight. The swimming distance varies with the species and it generally suffices for just a local change of position or for a quick escape from sudden attack. The number of bivalves which can swim for any length of time is very small. They include the members of the genus *Amusium,* Miocene to Recent bivalves inhabiting tropical and subtropical parts of Europe and America, which have thin to transparent valves with small equal ears. They are good swimmers and tend to live more in deep, quiet water.

Flabellipecten beudanti BASTEROT

Order: Pterioida
Family: Pectinidae

The representatives of the Eurasian and North American genus *Flabellipecten* are known from the Miocene down to the Recent. They have unequally vaulted valves with pointed umbones and moderately large ears. The right valve bulges, the left valve is flat or slightly concave (fig. 9).

Anadara diluvii (LAMARCK)

Order: Arcoida
Family: Arcidae

The species of the worldwide genus *Anadara* are to be found from the Upper Cretaceous to the Recent. The valves have spiral umbones and a straight hinge line. Below the umbones there is a triangular area with V-shaped grooves. The hinge is taxodont. The rounded shape of the valves, which distinguishes this genus from the genus *Arca,* is the outcome of a burrowing mode of life (the other members of the family usually live in crevices in the rocks and in other hideouts, held in place by a byssus).

Glycymeris obovatus LAMARCK

Order: Arcoida
Family: Glycymerididae

Glycymeris is likewise a worldwide genus, with a stratigraphic range from the Lower Tertiary to the Recent. The typical thick and convex valves have small, beak-like umbones. The hinge consists of a row of bar-like slanting teeth on either side of the curved hinge plate; in the middle, below the umbo, there are no or only small teeth. The inner edge of the valves is denticulate.

1, 2. *Anadara diluvii,* Neogene (Lower Miocene), Bordeaux, France. Height of valve 33 mm. An outer view of a right valve (1) and an inner view of a left valve (2). The similar genus *Arca* has more elongate valves with anteriorly situated umbones, rough ribs and sharp-pointed ends on the long hinge line.

3, 4. *Glycymeris obovatus,* Palaeogene (Middle Oligocene), Mainz basin, West Germany. Height of the larger valve 55 mm. Views of left valves: from without (3) and within (4).

5, 6. *Amusium cristatum,* Neogene (Pliocene), Astigione, Italy. Height of the larger (left) valve 63 mm. The valves are very thin; on their inner surface they are strengthened by radial ribs (5). The outer surface is smooth, so that it offers less resistance (6).

7, 8. *Flabellipecten beudanti,* Neogene (Lower Miocene), Bordeaux, France. Height of the flat left (upper) valve 51 mm (7). The flattened ribs and only moderately convex right (lower) valve indicate that this was a free-living form capable of swimming for short periods.

9. A reconstruction of a swimming pectinid.

Isognomon sandbergeri (Deshayes)

Order: Pterioida
Family: Isognomonidae

Bivalves do not have a head, radula, jaws or mouth at the anterior end of their body below the anterior adductor muscle and have only adoral lobes or appendages which help in the search for and the intake of food. This, together with their virtual immobility, severely limits the number of ways in which they can obtain sustenance. Most bivalves filter their food out of the water. These are the sessile and sometimes, in part, embedded forms, which take up micro-organisms and small débris from the water sucked in by the gills; in this they are helped by ciliated grooves leading from the mouth aperture to the base of the gills and partly by the gills themselves. The second group comprises bivalves which 'eat' the substratum, i.e. which dig more or less actively in the sediment, from which they collect or imbibe organic particles by means of the processes of the mantle or through the inhalant siphon. This form of obtaining sustenance is particularly widespread among the more ancient and primitive species. 'Predators' (e.g. in the genus *Cuspidaria*) are an interesting, but very small group. They actively suck in small live prey (various molluscs, echinoderm and crustacean larvae) attracted to the ring of sensitive tentacles round the mouth of the inhalant siphon protruding from the sediment; animals caught in this way are crushed

1, 2. *Isognomon sandbergeri*, Palaeogene (Middle Oligocene), Weinheim, West Germany. Height of valves 175 mm. An outer view of a left valve (2) and an inner view of a right valve (1). A large, wide byssal notch can be seen below the umbo.

4. *Isognomon* sp., an individual in a living position.

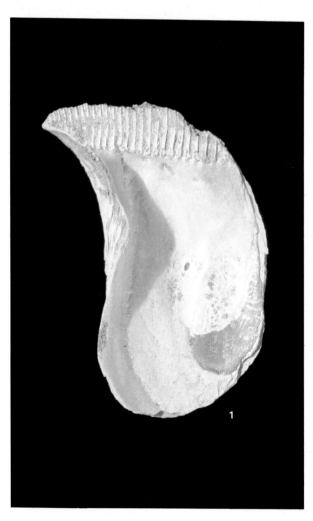

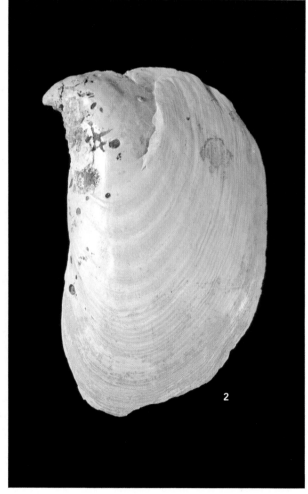

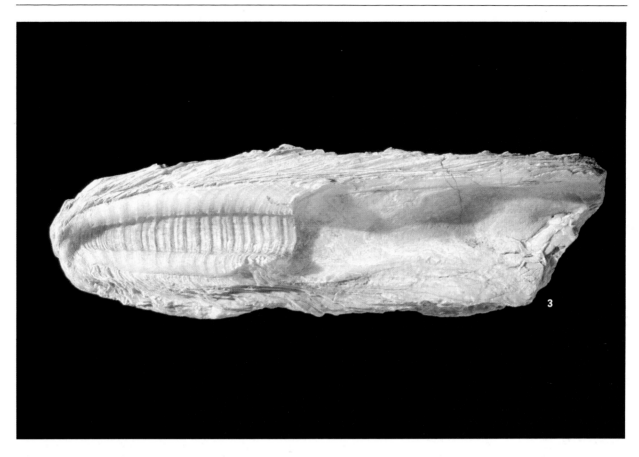

3. *Crassostrea longirostris*, Neogene (Miocene), Dzhabal Rasfah, Algeria. Height of the umbonal part of the right valve 250 mm. On the resilifer (the middle, deeper band in the hinge) we can clearly see the annual growth lines, by which an oyster's age can be determined.

by ridges of muscle in the mantle cavity and are absorbed. The last unusual adaptation is the ability acquired by certain boring bivalves (the genus *Teredo*) to digest cellulose. They bore their way into wood with the rasp-like edge of their greatly reduced valves and live partly or completely on the fillings.

The cosmopolitan genus *Isognomon* dates back to the Upper Triassic. The sharp-pointed umbones of the thick – and usually large and flat – valves project forward; the left valve is only slightly convex. The toothless hinge has a ligamental area in the form of a wide strip with numerous vertical ligamental furrows. The valves of recent species are smaller and thinner than their fossil counterparts. Most *Isognomon* species live in sheltered spots, attached by a thick bundle of byssal threads in a horizontal or vertical position, with the umbo partly embedded in the sediment (fig. 4). They filter their food.

Order: Pterioida
Family: Ostreidae

Crassostrea longirostris LAMARCK

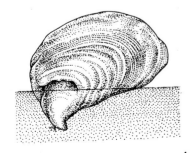

The oysters of the cosmopolitan genus *Crassostrea* have survived from the Lower Cretaceous to the Recent. Their usually large shells are variously shaped, but the majority are tall and slender, with a rough and sometimes ribbed surface with irregular growth laminae. The muscle scar lies right beside the posterior margin of the shell and is closer to the lower edge than it is to the hinge. The genus is geographically widely distributed, because some members also tolerate extremely low temperatures and pronounced changes in salinity.

4

221

Schizodus schlotheimi GOLDFUSS

Order: Trigonioida
Family: Myophoridae

The subclass Palaeoheterodonta comprises both marine and freshwater bivalves with equivalve shells with tightly fitting valves and usually with a nacreous inner layer. The external ligament is amphidetic or opisthodetic. The hinge has two radially arranged main teeth. Lateral teeth are either absent, or are not separated from the main teeth by a space, as in heterodont bivalves. This is an artificially formed subclass and in addition to Trigonioida and the freshwater order Unionoida it also includes Modiomorphoida, which comprises many ancient forms, including the oldest bivalves and the predecessors of the subclasses Pteriomorphia, Heterodonta and possibly other groups as well.

5

The representatives of the worldwide Permo-Carboniferous genus *Schidozus* have smooth valves with anterior umbones and an indistinct, rounded radial ridge at the back (fig. 5). The hinge teeth consist of a large, forked central tooth with one small front tooth in the left valve and of a single front tooth in the right valve.

Myophoria kefersteini MÜNSTER

Order: Trigonioida
Family: Myophoridae

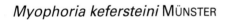

The genus *Myophoria* comes from Eurasian and north African Triassic deposits. The mildly convex valves have anteriorly orientated umbones and, at the back, a sharp radial ridge terminating at the corner edge in a rounded siphonal margin. The hinge resembles the one in the genus *Schizodus,* i.e. it is schizodont.

1, 2. *Myophoria kefersteini,* Upper Triassic (Carnian), Raibl (Cave del Predil), Italy. 1 — a smaller shell from the right side; 2 — a large shell from behind, height 45 mm.

Order: Trigonioida
Scaphotrigonia navis (LAMARCK)
Family: Trigoniidae

3. *Scaphotrigonia navis,** Middle Jurassic (Aalenian), Alsace, France. Height of shell 43 mm. A view of the left side. A common and important index fossil of the Lower Dogger in opalinus zones everywhere.

4. *Schizodus schlotheimi,* Upper Permian (Zechstein), Nieder-Rodenbach, West Germany. A cast of a right valve, height 22 mm. Associated in a limestone fragment with small bivalves of the species *Bakevellia antiqua.*

5. *Schizodus* sp., internal mould with muscle scars.

The now almost extinct family Trigoniidae, which comprises many species, evolved during the Upper Triassic from myophorid ancestors which reached the peak of their development during the Triassic. Trigoniids already abounded during the Jurassic, when they became an important component of the molluscan fauna. Later, owing to their morphological conservatism, they were unable to keep up with other, quickly developing, more advanced groups of bivalves, such as Cardiidae, Pectinidae, Ostreidae and Veneridae, and are slowly dying out. During the Tertiary era, the distribution of this once flourishing family began to be confined to Australia and the surrounding regions. The only species to have survived down to the present day are the members of the genus *Neotrigonia,* which inhabit the eastern coast of Australia and Tasmania.

Scaphotrigonia is a Lower and Middle Jurassic European and North American genus. The thick shells, bluntly truncated at the back, have vertically tapering umbones. The lateral, flattened part of the valves (flank) is strewn with a few tuberculated vertical ribs and has a vertical row of pronounced protuberances on its anterior edge. The wide posterior area or corcelet is smooth, except for the growth folds.

J

T

P

 **Mollusca**

Trigonia interlaevigata QUENSTEDT

Order: Trigonioida
Family: Trigoniidae

Owing to their mode of life, bivalves are mostly tied to the sea floor. If they do not lie or crawl on it, and if they are not cemented to it or attached to it by a byssus, they burrow in soft and bore in hard substrata, which provide them with shelter and food. An oxygen (and, in filtering species, food) supply is assured by gills, which draw water into the mantle cavity via tubular siphons in the hind part of the body. The deeper the bivalve digs, the larger and longer the siphons need to be and the larger must be their opening (marked by the pallial sinus) in the hind part of the mantle. The size of the sinus is thus proportional to the depth to which the animal digs. Very many bivalves dig only a little way down, so that the posterior part of the shell protrudes from the sediment and the sinus is small. These species are generally quite agile and burrow their way through the sediment. The digging rate is important in the wave zone, where the waves are constantly burying the shells or washing them out of the sediment. In such species the shells are mostly thick and moderately convex, with a powerful ligament and strong hinge; the siphons are short and the pallial sinus is small. Species which dig lower down are generally less mobile and the valves are oval and flattened, again with a strong hinge, but with a large pallial sinus; the siphons are long. There are, however, exceptions (e.g. the genus *Lucina*), which can dig an opening above themselves with their foot. Bivalves which burrow really deep down are generally completely immobile. They usually have relatively thin, elongate valves with a weak hinge and, either at the

1, 2. *Trigonia interlaevigata*, Middle Jurassic (Dogger), Bielefeld, West Germany. Height of shells 64 and 71 mm. A side view (2) and a view of the posterior field from behind, showing the different sculpture (1). A common species in European Dogger (Middle Jurassic).

3. *'Unio' inaequiradiatus,* Palaeogene (Oligocene), Miesbach, West Germany. A right valve, length 140 mm. A common species in lake sediments of the German Oligocene, where it often accompanies coal seams. The umbones have usually been eroded by the action of the fresh water.

4. The hinge of a trigoniid.

posterior end, or on both sides, wide gapes for the well-developed foot and huge siphons. Many bivalves also bore holes in limestone rocks and in wood. They do it either mechanically, with the denticulate anterior edge of their valves, which are often severely reduced, or partly chemically, by breaking down the rock with the acid secretions of their mantle glands. The members of most of these species spend the whole of their life in the resultant crypt and are unable to leave it.

The representatives of the cosmopolitan genus *Trigonia* lived from the Middle Triassic to the Upper Cretaceous. The valves have sharp-tipped umbones and a pronounced radial posterior keel. On the flank there are rough concentric ridges which are separated from the keel by a smooth radial fold. The posterior area is narrow, with rows of tubercles formed by the intersections of radial and concentric ribs (fig. 4).

'Unio' inaequiradiatus GÜMBEL

Order: Unionida
Family: Unionidae

Members of the cosmopolitan genus *Unio* have lived in fresh water since the Triassic period. Their shells are very variable and are often strikingly sculptured, especially on the posterior and umbonal part. The shell has a nacreous layer and a thick periostracum. The hinge has two main teeth and two side teeth in the left valve and one main and one lamellar side tooth in the right valve. This once broadly conceived genus is now divided into many independent genera and subgenera.

4

Mollusca

Grammysia hamiltonensis DE VERNEUIL

Order: Pholadomyoida
Family: Grammysiidae

The subclass Anomalodesmata comprises burrowing forms of bivalves with short to elongate equivalve and isomyarian shells with a nacreous inner layer, whose valves do not always close completely at the back. The hinge is weak and teeth are often absent. The siphons are well developed and the mantle is usually ventrally fused. Anomalodesmata have been in existence since the Ordovician.

The representatives of the worldwide Devonian genus *Grammysia* have thick, convex shells with prosogyrate apices. The valves have a smooth surface, with flat concentric ridges and with two oblique furrows leading backwards from the apex. The hinge has two or three small teeth. These bivalves abound in the sandy sediments.

Gresslya gregaria (ZIETEN)

Order: Pholadomyioda
Family: Ceratomyidae

Gresslya is a cosmopolitan Jurassic bivalve genus. The shells have anteriorly situated blunt-tipped umbones, the right one being somewhat higher than the left. The hinge has protuberances and no teeth; the pallial line has a deep sinus. *Gresslya* lived deeply embedded in soft sediment and fed on organic débris.

Pholadomya lirata (SOWERBY)

Order: Pholadomyioda
Family: Pholadomyidae

The stratigraphic range of the worldwide genus *Pholadomya* stretches from the Triassic to the Recent. The large shells have anteriorly situated umbones pointing sharply upwards. The valves are not closed at the back. The sculpture consists of inconspicuous concentric ribs, which, on the front of the valves, intersect similar radial ribs; at the points where they intersect there are tubercles. The hinge has no teeth. The Mesozoic members of this ancient genus lived in shallow water, but later they were ecologically displaced to less favourable conditions in deep water.

Goniomya literata AGASSIZ

Order: Pholadomyoida
Family: Pholadomyidae

The cosmpolitan genus *Goniomya* occurs in the Jurassic and Cretaceous. The thin valves have anteriorly situated inconspicuous umbones. On their surface they have oblique ribs shaped like a wide V. The pallial line has a deep sinus. So far we do not know what the hinge looked like. *Goniomya* burrowed very deeply and the siphons and foot are so strongly developed that permanently open notches were formed for them in the front and back of the shell.

Pleuromya jurassica AGASSIZ

Order: Pholadomyoida
Family: Pleuromyidae

In the Triassic to Cretaceous period the members of the genus *Pleuromya* were distributed all over the world. They burrowed in the floor of warm, shallow seas. The convex valves have anteriorly situated umbones. The surface of the valves is smooth or sculptured with fine concentric lines or ribs. The hinge has protuberances instead of teeth. There is a deep pallial sinus.

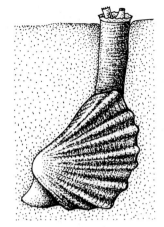

6

1. *Goniomya literata,* Middle Jurassic (Callovian), Popilany, Poland. Height of shell 21 mm.

2. *Pleuromya jurassica,* Middle Jurassic (Bajocian), May, Calvados, France. Height of shell 36 mm.

3. *Pholadomya lirata,* Middle Jurassic (Dogger), Doubs, France. An external mould of a shell, height 71 mm.

4. *Grammysia hamiltonensis,** Middle Devonian (Eifelian), Daleiden, West Germany. Height of shell 33 mm.

5. *Gresslya gregaria,** Middle Jurassic (Bajocian), Elmen, West Germany. Height of shell 44 mm.

6. *Pholadomya* sp. in a living position.

7. *Pleuromya* sp. in a living position.

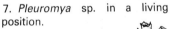
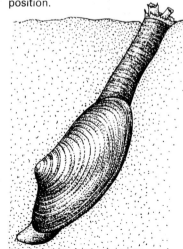

7

Mollusca

Conocardium bohemicum BARRANDE

Order: Rostroconchida
Family: Conocardiidae

A bivalve shell evolved independently in several groups of molluscs, but apart from bivalves the only group in which it normally occurs is the class Rostroconchia, which comprises bilaterally symmetrical molluscs without a separate head, which do not undergo torsion and which have an uncoiled univalved larval shell. During growth the latter breaks up into a bivalved shell with a fixed or fused hinge without teeth and without ligaments. In front, the shell tapers off into a wing-like process with a permanently open gape (often armed with ribs, teeth and lamellae) through which the animal extruded its foot and its filamentous tentacles. Behind there is a tubular rostrum covering the siphons. The muscles leaving large imprints were the ones that extruded the foot and held the visceral sac in place; adductors were absent. The continuous band-like pallial line is supplemented in the dorsal region by a row of small scars.

Rostroconchia are intermediate between bivalves and tusk shells, all of which have common rostroconch ancestors similar to the genus *Ribeiria*. Bivalves developed a ligament between their valves, however, and in tusk shells ventral fusion of the mantle and the shell formed a single narrow tube.

Rostroconchia existed from the Cambrian to the Permian. They lived in the sea, partly buried in the ooze; they were either attached by byssal threads or they moved by means of their foot. Their tentacles were used for catching food.

1–3. *Conocardium bohemicum*, Lower Devonian (Pragian), Koně-prusy, Czechoslovakia. Height of the largest shell 22 mm. 1 – a core with remains of the shell; view of a left valve. 2 – a shell from behind. 3 – a view of the hinge line from above.

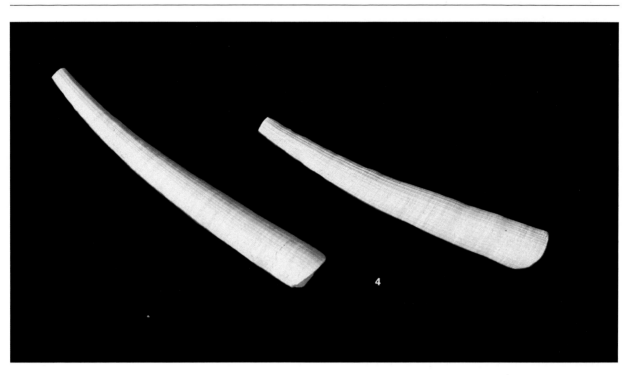

4. *Dentalium elephantinum,**
Neogene (Lower Miocene), Baden
near Vienna, Austria. Length of the
shells 60 and 62 mm.

5. A reconstruction of a living
scaphopod.

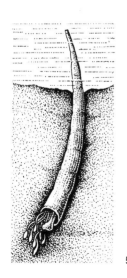
5

Conocardium was a worldwide Ordovician to Permian genus. Its members have a bulging bivalved shell with an oval aperture in the wing-like, widened anterior part. The posterior end of the thick valves is produced to a narrow tubular rostrum. These molluscs abounded at the periphery of coral reefs.

Dentalium elephantinum LINNAEUS

Order: Dentaliida
Family: Dentaliidae

The class Scaphopoda comprises marine molluscs with an elongate, bilaterally symmetrical body, a retractable foot and a rudimentary head without eyes or tentacles. The mantle, fused on the under side, secretes a long, curved, tubular, gradually widening shell open at both ends and resembling an elephant's tusk (hence their vernacular name – tusk or tooth shells). Scaphopods inhabit the deeper parts of all seas, but especially warm seas, where they live, buried obliquely in the soft sediment, with only the narrower tip of the shell protruding (fig. 5), to expel metabolic waste and gametes. Respiration takes place over the whole surface of the body. Food (foraminifera and mollusc larvae) is caught with a ring of filamentous processes (captacula). The oldest scaphopods are known from the Middle Ordovician and a few species still survive.

The still extant cosmopolitan genus *Dentalium* is known from the Lower Cretaceous onwards. The slightly curved shell (concave on the dorsal aspect) is circular or polygonal in cross section. The surface is longitudinally ribbed, but may sometimes be smooth. The aperture at the narrower end is often made wider by a slit or a notch.

229

Maxilites maximus (BARRANDE)

Order: Hyolithida
Family: Hyolithidae

The class Hyolitha comprises bilaterally symmetrical, molluscoid marine animals whose thin, conical, calcareous shell is roundedly triangular or lenticular in cross section and whose apex is sometimes divided internally by septa. The ventral surface of the shell is flattened and terminates in a tongue-like projection. The mouth is covered by an oval, curved operculum with protuberances and teeth on its inner surface. These evidently acted as insertions and supports for the soft parts. Leading from the mouth and along the sides there are sometimes long, tubular, recurved adoral appendages which may have been used to thrust off or to row with (fig. 5). Hyoliths originated in the Lower Cambrian, were abundant up to the Ordovician and died out in the Permian. Their life and habits are veiled in obscurity, but the majority were probably mobile or sessile herbivorous benthos.

The Middle Cambrian European genus *Maxilites* has bulging, conical shells up to 100 mm long, with a semi-elliptical cross section. The ventral 'tongue' protrudes a long way in front of the mouth. The oval operculum has a vertical hinge bar, two shaft-like claviculae (radial ridges) and short hinge processes diverging at an obtuse angle.

Tentaculites raroannulatus BERGER

Order: Tentaculitida
Family: Tentaculitidae

Tentaculitids (class Tentaculita) are extinct marine organisms which were probably molluscs, but may have been annelids. Their minute conical calcareous shells are circular in cross section, can have one layer or more and are sometimes divided by septa. Tentaculitids probably lived as nectobenthos, and in shallow seas probably as plankton. Ordovician and Devonian shales or limestones all the world over often swarm with their shells.

The representatives of the Silurian and Devonian worldwide genus *Tentaculites* have moderately large, narrowly conical, thick-walled shells composed of several layers; the shells have a pointed apex and internal septa (fig. 6).

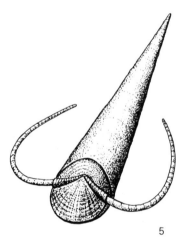

5

Nowakia cancellata (RICHTER)

Order: Dacryoconarida
Family: Nowakiidae

The Upper Silurian to Upper Devonian worldwide genus *Nowakia* has tiny, thin-walled conical shells with a relatively large apical angle and a drop-shaped embryonal chamber. The surface is covered with dense rings and fine longitudinal ribs.

6

1, 2. *Maxilites maximus,* Middle Cambrian, Buchava near Skryje, Czechoslovakia. Length of shell 45 mm; a view of the dorsal aspect (1). On a fragment of rock we can see an internal cast of the operculum of the species *Maxilites robustus,* anterior downwards. The three-pointed groove is the cavity for the bar of the hinge, the processes and the claviculae (2).

3. *Nowakia cancellata,** Lower Devonian (Dalejan), Třebotov, Czechoslovakia. Ribbed shells, length 6 mm. *Stylioline* sp., smooth shells, length 3 mm. These shells occur on the stratal surface of tentaculite shales, together with members of the genus *Nowakia,* but usually in smaller numbers.

4. *Tentaculites raroannulatus,* Lower Devonian (Lochkovian), Bogdanovka, Podolia, USSR. Length of the largest shell 14 mm. A higgledy-piggledy collection of tentaculitid shells and the small shells of brachiopods belonging to the species *Mutationella podolica.*

5. A complete hyolitid shell.

6. *Tentaculites* sp., structure of the shell.

Styliolina sp.

Order: Dacryoconarida
Family: Styliolinidae

The members of the cosmopolitan Upper Silurian to Upper Devonian genus *Styliolina* have minute, slender, thin-walled conical shells without any septa. There is a drop-shaped embryonal chamber and the surface of the shell is smooth.

Mollusca

Bathmoceras complexum (BARRANDE)

Order: Ellesmeroceratida
Family: Bathmoceratidae

Cephalopods are evolutionally the most advanced group of molluscs. Their mouth is surrounded by eight, ten and sometimes even more tentacles. Their organ of locomotion is a muscular, funnel-shaped structure called the hyponome, which is situated on the under (ventral) side of their body. The animal progresses rear end first by periodically squirting water from the hyponome. The oldest representatives of the cephalopods, the nautiloids (subclass Nautiloidea), are to be encountered in Upper Cambrian marine sediments over 500 million years old. Their conical outer shells are straight (orthoceraconic), curved (cyrtoceraconic) or variously coiled. They consist of a posterior phragmocone and an anterior living chamber. The phragmocone is divided by numerous partitions (septa) into a series of partially gas-filled chambers or camerae, one behind the other, and its purpose was to keep the body buoyant. The tiny initial chamber of the phragmocone is known as the protoconch. In every septum there is an opening through which the neurovascular cord (the siphon) passed. The siphon regulated gas pressure and the amount of fluid inside the individual chambers. All the solid structures supporting it are collectively termed the sipho. At the site of the opening the septum usually has a 'neck' drawn out funnel-wise in the direction of the apex of the shell. As a rule, tubular structures known as connecting rings are joined to the septal neck. Together, the septal necks and the connecting rings form the siphuncle, which is a part of the sipho. The living chamber, whose aperture opens at the anterior end of the conical shell, is much larger than the gas chambers and is filled during the animal's lifetime with its body.

The order Ellesmerocerida is the initial group in the evolution of nautiloids. In the Ordovician, when the entire subclass enjoyed the greatest prosperity, the members of this order were distributed all over the world. Their usually minute, straight or slightly curved shells have short gas chambers and a wide sipho, which usually lies on the ventral side, near the periphery. *Bathmoceras* is a very widely distributed Ordovician genus known in central and northern Europe, China and Australia. The thick connecting rings look like cornets fitting into one another and open towards the apex (fig. 3).

Kionoceras doricum (BARRANDE)

Order: Orthocerida
Family: Orthoceratidae

The evolutionally very successful order Orthocerida appeared during the Lower Ordovician. The shell is straight or slightly curved and the siphuncle, which runs close to the axis of the shell, is either narrow and tubular, or is a little inflated inside the gas chambers. In some genera, special calcareous deposits are formed inside the gas chambers and the siphuncle; during the animal's life they helped to keep the shell stable in a more or less horizontal position. The genus *Kionoceras* is known from Ordovician to Carboniferous deposits in Europe, Asia and North America. The shell is roughly circular in cross section and has longitudinal riblets on its surface.

3

1, 3. *Bathmoceras complexum,* * Lower Ordovician (Llanvirn), Prague, Šárka, Czechoslovakia. A core; length 145 mm. In addition to very short float chambers, this genus is characterized by structures like an inverted 'V' inside the sipho. 3 — central part of the shell is removed, with the internal mould well visible.

2. *Kionoceras doricum,* * Upper Silurian (Ludlow), Mořina, Czechoslovakia. Shell length 155 mm.

Mollusca

Dawsonoceras annulatum (SOWERBY)

Order: Orthocerida
Family: Dawsonoceratidae

The scientific classification of nautiloids is based primarily on internal characters of the shells, i.e. on the position and structure of the siphuncle and the nature of the calcareous deposits. A number of genera – and sometimes species – can be determined from their external morphology, however, such as the almost worldwide Silurian genus *Dawsonoceras.* The shells widen very gradually and attain lengths of up to roughly 75 cm. They have pronounced rings and striking undulating growth ridges on the surface.

Michelinoceras michelini (BARRANDE)

Order: Orthocerida
Family: Orthoceratidae

Nautiloids abounded in the warm European Silurian shelf seas. In some places their shells accumulated in such numbers that they formed 'orthoceras limestones'. The currents often caused them all to face the same way, so that even now their long axes are still parallel. *Michelinoceras* is a characteristic and almost worldwide genus whose members lived from the Silurian to the Triassic. The shells are slightly expanding, with long gas chambers, a smooth surface and a narrow siphuncle (fig. 6).

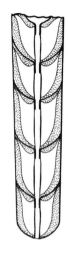

6

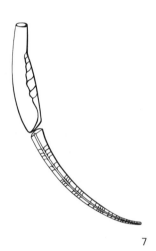

7

1. *Dawsonoceras annulatum,** Upper Silurian (Ludlow), Dudley, Great Britain. Shell length 130 mm. The shell of this common Silurian species is characterized by pronounced rings and by undulating growth lines.

2, 3. *Octamerella callistomoides,** Upper Silurian (Pridoli), Dvorce, Czechoslovakia. Shell length 80 mm. Height of aperture 50 mm. Cores; 2 – the lobulate aperture; two lobes acted as ocular sinuses, and others were used for protrusion of tentacles and the hyponome. 3 – a side view of the core.

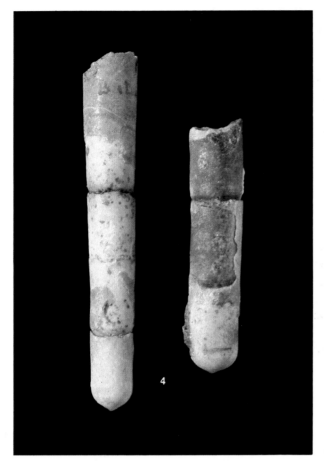

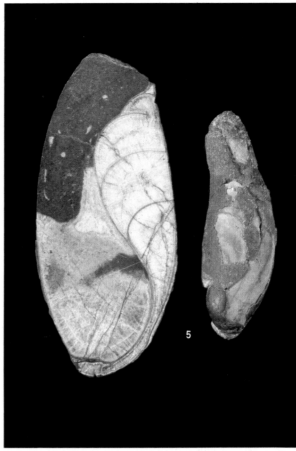

4. *Michelinoceras michelini,** Upper Silurian (Ludlow), Lochkov, Czechoslovakia. Fragments of phragmocone cores from two individuals, lengths 70 and 45 mm. The ratio of the length of the gas chambers to the diameter of the shell is one of the diagnostic characters of nautiloids.

5. *Ascoceras bohemicum,**Upper Silurian (Pridoli), Kosoř, Czechoslovakia. Length of shells 110 and 75 mm (longitudinal polished section). The polished section on the left shows the sigmoidally curved septa inside the shell. After the animal's death the living chamber filled with sediment, while the float chambers remained empty; these later filled with greyish white calcite formed from solution circulating in the rocks.

6. *Michelinoceras* sp., longitudinal section of the phragmocone.

7. *Ascoceras* sp., shell with a longitudinally sectioned phragmocone.

Order: Oncocerida
Octamerella callistomoides (FOERSTE)   Family: Hemiphragmoceratidae

The representatives of the order Oncocerida lived from the Middle Ordovician to the Lower Carboniferous period. Some genera have an extremely narrow and variously modified aperture, from which it is concluded that their owners lived on very small food. The surface of the shell of the members of the Silurian genus *Octamerella* − known in Europe and North America − is ornamented with somewhat indistinct longitudinal ribs and the aperture of full-grown individuals is divided into eight lobes.

Order: Ascocerida
Ascoceras bohemicum BARRANDE   Family: Ascoceratidae

Ascoceratids are rarely found in Ordovician and Silurian deposits in Europe and North America. Juvenile shells are curved. In the adult shell the living chamber was inflated; on the dorsal side it was depressed inwards and a series of gas chambers was formed above it (fig. 7). The original phragmocone was evidently shed during the cephalopod's lifetime. These shells seem to have been suitably adapted for active swimming.

235

 **Mollusca**

Ophioceras rudens BARRANDE

Order: Tarphycerida
Family: Ophidioceratidae

Spiral coiling of shells increases their mechanical strength. If successive whorls do not completely overlap each other, a depression known as an umbilicus is formed round the coiling axis. Incomplete coiling of the first whorl results in the formation of an umbilical perforation of varying sizes in the centre. We find this evolutionarily advanced type of shell in Tarphycerida. The order as a whole attained its peak during the Lower Ordovician and died out at the end of the Silurian. The shells usually have a ribbed surface; the siphuncle has thick connecting rings. Included in this order, with some doubts, is the genus *Ophioceras,* commonly found in Silurian sediments in Europe and North America. The aperture of the shell is divided into lobes. The outer (ventral) side of the whorls is depressed slightly inwards and is bordered by two low ridges (fig. 4).

Peismoceras pulchrum (BARRANDE)

Order: Barrandeocerida
Family: Lechritrochoceratidae

As regards their morphology, and evidently their anatomy also, Barrandeocerida come closest to the only group of nautiloids to have survived to the present day, i.e. to the order Nautilida. Their shells have a thin-walled siphuncle.

In exceptional cases, Palaeozoic molluscs have retained their original markings. In the genus *Peismoceras* – at present known only in central

1. *Peismoceras pulchrum,* Upper Silurian (Ludlow), Prague-Butovice, Czechoslovakia. Shell diameter 68 mm. On the phragmocone, with its very well preserved shell, we can clearly see coloured (brown) narrow longitudinal stripes. The brown colouring is due to fossilization changes in the original pigments.

2. *Ophioceras rudens,* Upper Silurian (Ludlow), Prague-Butovice, Czechoslovakia. A complete core with remains of the shell, whose shape is reminiscent of some Mesozoic ammonites. Shell diameter 40 mm.

3. *Phragmoceras broderipi,* Upper Silurian (Ludlow), Beroun-Dlouhá Hora, Czechoslovakia. Shell diameter 140 mm. An almost complete specimen with remains of the shell. The slit-like mouth on the inner side of the whorl has a lobate process, which protected the soft hyponome.

4. *Ophioceras* sp., frontal view of the aperture.

5. *Phragmoceras* sp., frontal view of the shell.

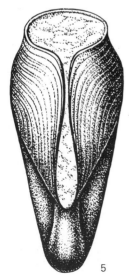

Europe – the surface of the shell is ornamented with narrow longitudinal stripes. In young individuals the shell was coiled in a low three-dimensional spiral; later on the coils loosened and the shell became straight. It has been concluded from the asymmetry of the shell and from other features that these molluscs were not able to swim very fast.

Phragmoceras broderipi BARRANDE

Order: Discosorida
Family: Phragmoceratidae

Morphologically similar nautiloids with a narrow and diversely formed aperture were formerly included in the genus *Phragmoceras.* Today they are described under different generic names and belong to two separate orders – Oncocerida and Discosorida. The latter usually have thick-walled shells with a wide – and inside the gas chambers often highly inflated – siphuncle (frequently with calcareous deposits) and thick connecting rings. They occur chiefly in shallow-water sediments and evidently led a benthic existence. They are an important component of Ordovician and Silurian cephalopod assemblages; at the end of the Devonian they died out. The molluscs of the Silurian genus *Phragmoceras* have highly curved shells which increase rapidly in height. The siphuncle lies near the inner wall of the whorl. In full-grown specimens the shell has a roughly T-shaped aperture (fig. 5). The distribution of this genus is similar to that of *Ophioceras.*

Mollusca

Ptenoceras alatum (BARRANDE)

Order: Oncocerida
Family: Ptenoceratidae

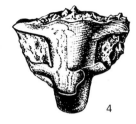
4

During the Devonian, Oncocerida became the commonest group of nautiloids. Alongside cephalopods with an abruptly widening (breviconical) shell and a largely reduced phragmocone, there was a spread of cephalopods with a spirally coiled shell. Despite some reservations, oncocerids are regarded as the ancestors of the nautilids.

Owing to continental drift, Europe lay in the equatorial belt in the Devonian period. The tropical climate favoured the growth of coral and stromatopore reefs and the flourishing of many other groups of animals, including cephalopods. Some of them were closely associated with the reef facies, e.g. *Ptenoceras alatum,* which had loosely coiled shells with a tendency to become uncoiled and whose whorls very quickly increased in width. The aperture of the shells has a markedly undulating edge, with an outer sinus for the hyponome (the organ of locomotion), a pair of lateral ocular sinuses and a shallow sinus on the inner side of the whorl. The lateral sinuses extend at regular intervals to long, winglike processes which made rapid movement impossible (fig. 4). The siphuncle lies on the outer side. *Ptenoceras* is found in Lower Devonian sediments in North America as well as in Europe.

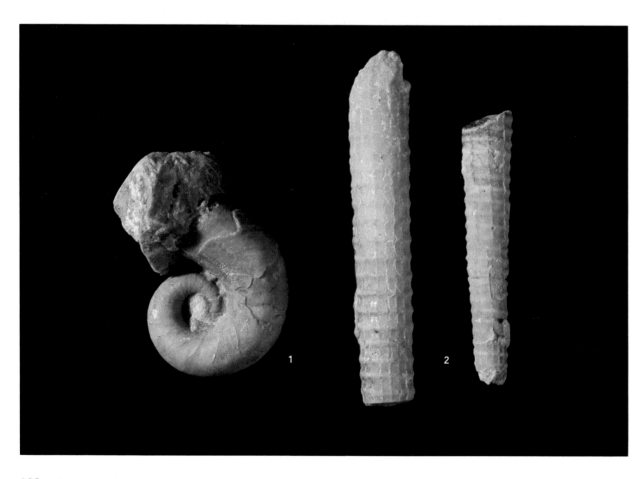

Spyroceras pseudocalamiteum
(BARRANDE)

Order: Orthocerida
Family: Pseudorthoceratidae

D

Apart from nautilids, orthocerids are the only nautiloid order whose stratigraphic range goes beyond the boundary between the Palaeozoic and the Mesozoic eras (their last representatives died out at the end of the Triassic). Their shells have a very diverse inner structure and outer sculpture. The genus *Spyroceras* is abundantly represented in Silurian and Devonian deposits in Europe, Asia and North America. The surface of the gradually widening shells is decorated with strikingly developed rings combined with fine transverse or longitudinal ridges.

Hercoceras mirum BARRANDE

Order: Nautilida
Family: Rutoceratidae

Nautilida are the most advanced, and generically the most diverse, order of the nautiloid subclass. The recent *Nautilus* is the only extant cephalopod genus with an outer shell, four pairs of gills and a still relatively simple nervous system.

Representatives of the order Nautilida appeared in the Lower Devonian and very soon they underwent striking radiation. One of the oldest genera, known in central Europe, is *Hercoceras*. The whorls are markedly compressed dorsoventrally. Another distinctive feature is a series of hollow spinose processes of the aperture, formed ventrolaterally. The sutures are almost straight; the siphuncle lies against the outer wall of the whorls.

1, 4. *Ptenoceras alatum,** Lower Devonian (Pragian), Koněprusy, Czechoslovakia. Shell diameter 40 mm. We can clearly see thickened growth ridges on the shell and a conspicuous sinus for the eyes. The wing-like outgrowths beside the mouth have been broken off (1). 4 – a posterior view of the shell.

2. *Spyroceras pseudocalamiteum,* Early Devonian (Pragian), Koněprusy, Czechoslovakia. Length of shells 55 and 68 mm. The surface sculpture of both fragments is well preserved.

3. *Hercoceras mirum,** Lower Devonian (Dalejian), Prague-Hlubočepy, Czechoslovakia. A core, diameter 120 mm.

 **Mollusca**

Liroceras gavendi PŘIBYL AND BOUČEK

Order: Nautilida
Family: Liroceratidae

The late Palaeozoic was an era of prosperity for the nautilids. Over 100 genera belonging to this period have been described, the majority from Europe, fewer from North America and Asia. Some of them — including the genus *Liroceras* — are very widespread and comprise a large number of species. On the almost spherical shell of this species the whorls markedly overlap one another, forming an involute type of shell. The whorls are kidney-shaped in cross section and the relatively wide siphuncle lies almost in the centre.

Germanonautilus bidorsatus (SCHLOTHEIM)

Order: Nautilida
Family: Tainoceratidae

The change from the Palaeozoic to the Mesozoic era did not make much difference to the evolution of the nautiloids, but only a few orders survived it. *Germanonautilus* is an important Triassic genus known in Europe, Asia, Africa and North America. The members of this genus have moderately involute, smooth shells. The whorls are wide, with a trapezoid cross section (fig. 6). The sutures have a shallow outer (ventral) lobe and a wide deeper (lateral) lobe. The bulging connecting rings are an important feature of the shells, but they can be seen only in polished sections.

1. *Liroceras gavendi,* Upper Carboniferous (Namurian), Ostrava-Poruba, Czechoslovakia. A core, diameter 70 mm.

2. *Germanonautilus bidorsatus,** Middle Triassic (Upper Muschelkalk) West Germany. An incomplete core, slightly deformed by pressure, with strikingly arched sutures on the sides. Diameter 65 mm.

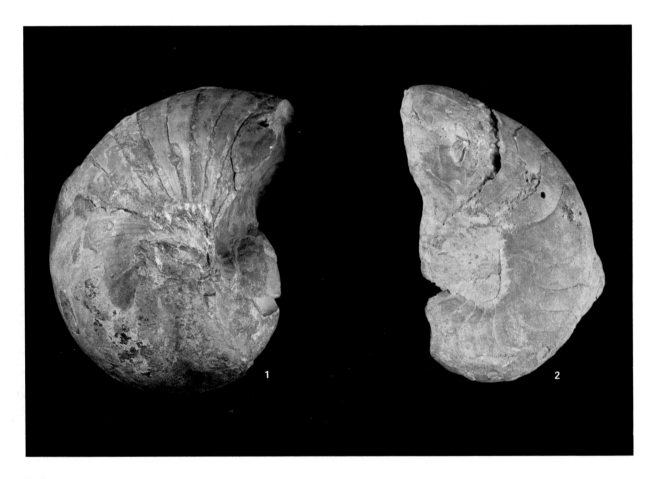

T

C

3

4

5

3. *Conchorhynchus* sp., Middle Triassic (Upper Muschelkalk), West Germany. The massive calcified end of a lower jaw.

4, 5. *Rhyncholithes hirundo,** Middle Triassic (Upper Muschelkalk), West Germany. Lengths 20 and 28 mm. Isolated upper jaws seen from above (4) and from the side (5).

6. *Germanonautilus* sp., a frontal view of the shell.

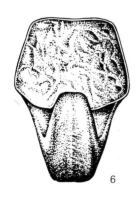

6

Rhyncholithes hirundo (BIGUET)
Conchorhynchus sp.

Rhyncholites

The jaws of recent cephalopods are shaped like a parrot's beak and are formed of chitin. The only exception are the jaws of *Nautilus,* which have calcareous tips. The upper jaw, or rhyncholite, is robust and has a tip shaped like an arrow-head. The lower jaw, or conchorhynch, has a finely toothed anterior edge. Both jaw elements are known from the Triassic to the present. They are assigned to the nautiloids of the superfamily Nautilaceae according to their structure and stratigraphic distribution as rhyncholites and conchorhynchs occur separately from the shells. The gas inside the phragmocone kept cephalopod shells buoyant for some time after the animal died, so that the body fell into the water and the empty shell was carried by the currents far away from where the living individual had been. Parts of jaws are therefore given scientific names of their own.

Finds of jaw elements inside living chambers are very rare. *R. hirundo* – and evidently the accompanying *Conchorhynchus* also – are assumed to have belonged to the cephalopod species *Germanonautilus bidorsatus.* The jaws were a useful adaptation for catching and cutting up prey; for crushing their food, nautiloids, like other groups of molluscs, had a well-developed radula composed of tiny teeth arranged in rows, one behind the other.

241

Order: Nautilida
Family: Nautilidae

Cenoceras lineatum (ZIETEN)

Among recent marine invertebrates it would be hard to find an animal which has received so much attention as the Nautilus (*Nautilus*), a genus which comprises the last living species of the once exceptionally widespread Tetrabranchiata – a group of cephalopods with four gills and an outer shell. Today the Nautilus, as the last genuine living fossil, inhabits circumscribed areas of the Pacific and Indian oceans, in particular the subtropical and tropical zone between south-eastern Asia, Australia and the Fiji Islands. It is a predator, possesses roughly 90 tentacles and lives mainly on crustaceans and dead organisms. It occurs at depths of 400 to 500 metres, in water where the temperature does not exceed 31 °C. The oldest representatives of this genus are known from the Oligocene.

All Jurassic nautilids evolved from the genus *Cenoceras,* which appeared at the end of the Triassic and was the only one to survive the change from the Triassic to the Jurassic. Common to all the shells of this genus are a flattened outer wall, sutures with a shallow outer and lateral lobe and fine longitudinal ridges on the surface of the shell.

Order: Nautilida
Family: Nautilidae

Eutrephoceras sublaevigatum (D'ORBIGNY)

The sharp division between the Mesozoic and the Tertiary eras, which was marked by the mass extinction of numerous groups of organisms,

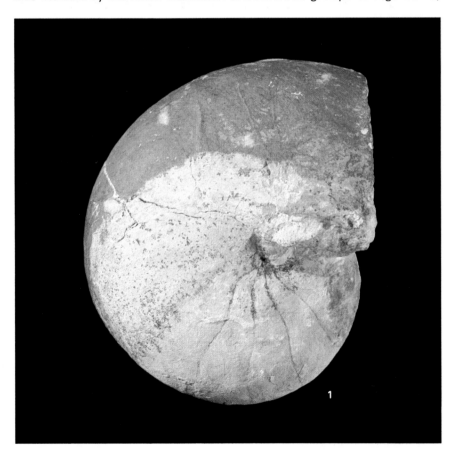

1. *Eutrephoceras sublaevigatum,* Upper Cretaceous (Turonian), Prague-Bílá Hora, Czechoslovakia. A core, diameter 107 mm. These shells can be very large (up to 30 cm).

Ng

Cr

J

3. *Aturia aturi,** Neogene (Miocene), Italy. Shell diameter 23 mm. The pronounced undulation of the sutures typical of this genus is rather an exception in nautiloids.

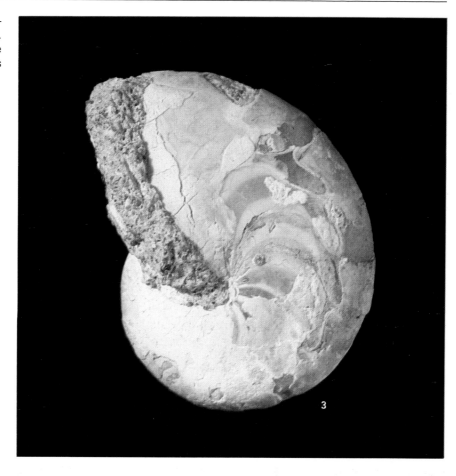

including the ammonites and belemnites, was not reflected basically in any way in the evolution of the nautiloids. The majority of late Cretaceous genera survived into the Palaeogene. Among them was the important cosmopolitan genus *Eutrephoceras,* which did not die out until the beginning of the Neogene. The whorls of its smooth, involute shells are kidney-shaped in cross section; the sutures are slightly undulating and the narrow siphuncle lies, as a rule, near the coiling axis of the shell.

2. *Cenoceras lineatum,* Jurassic (Bathonian), Baden-Württemberg, West Germany. A shell core stained by iron oxides; diameter 64 mm.

Aturia aturi (BASTEROT)

Order: Nautilida
Family: Aturidae

During the Tertiary era the nautiloids gradually declined to one genus. It is interesting that some of the last fossil representatives of the entire group are known from Australia or New Zealand, i.e. from a region very close to the one where the present-day Nautilus lives.

The genus *Aturia* is the most common and widespread Tertiary nautiloid. The whorls of its smooth, discoid shells overlap one another very markedly. One of its most striking features is the course of the sutures, which have a wide saddle (a convexity of the suture pointing towards the aperture) on the outer aspect and a narrow, pointed lobe and a wide, rounded saddle on the flanks. Sutures with a similar pattern, but with simpler individual elements, are to be found in the cosmopolitan genus *Hercoglossa.*

2

 **Mollusca**

Lobocyclendoceras sp.

Order: Endocerida
Family: Endoceratidae

Endoceratids (subclass Endoceratoidea) were an ancient cosmopolitan group of cephalopods confined almost entirely to the Ordovician. In some cases, their usually straight-sided and very gradually widening shells attained gigantic proportions. An Endoceras shell 9.5 metres long has been described in North America; if we also take into account the soft body of the cephalopod, together with the tentacles, we shall not be exaggerating if we put the animal's total length at 15 metres. En-doceratids differ from nautiloids chiefly as regards the structure of the siphuncle. In some genera, the siphuncle was so widened in the early stages of development that it filled almost the whole of the phrag-mocone. It contained not only the neurovascular siphonal cord as in nautiloids, but a substantial part of the animal's body as well. Part of the siphuncle was filled with successive calcareous deposits (endocones), which took the form of cones with a perforated tip fitting one into the other, or of radially organized lamellae.

Endoceratids were evidently not able to swim very well. As a rule they occur in shallow water sediments. In some places their shells have accumulated in vast numbers. In the Baltic region, for instance, we know of 'vaginatum limestones', named after the accumulated shells of *'Endoceras' vaginatum.* The individual illustrated here was thought to be this species, but it actually belongs to the genus *Lobocyclendoceras.* One striking feature, which can be seen on the surface of casts, is a deep sutural lobe on the side where the siphuncle is situated.

Dideroceras sp.

Order: Endocerida
Family: Endoceratidae

Dideroceras is a widely distributed Lower to Middle Ordovician genus known in Scandinavia, the Baltic region and South America. The characteristic generic features can be seen the best in longitudinal polished sections. They are the very long siphonal necks, which stretch over two gas chambers, and, on the ventral edge, the wide sipho with the endocones.

Cameroceras peregrinum (Barrande)

Order: Endocerida
Family: Endoceratidae

The genus *Cameroceras* is distributed over practically the whole world. It occurs in Middle and Upper Ordovician sediments. The elongate shells of this order have almost straight sutures. The wide siphuncle lies against the ventral side of the shell. The septal necks are shorter than in the preceding genus and stretch only as far as the next septum.

1. *Dideroceras* sp., Ordovician, Kinnekulle (Sweden). Length 80 mm; longitudinal polished section. Endocones and very long septal necks can be seen at the edges of the siphuncle.

2. *Lobocyclendoceras* sp., Lower Ordovician (Arenig), Estonia. Length of fragment of the core 95 mm; it features the exposed surface of a siphuncle. In the later growth stages the length of the gas chambers often diminished. Endoceratids are often found in Mecklenburg tills, to which they were transported by the continen-tal ice-sheet during the Quaternary era.

3. *Cameroceras peregrinum,* Middle Ordovician (Llanvirn), Mýto, Czechoslovakia. Length 80 mm; fragment of a core with the siphuncle partly dissected out. Endoceratid siphuncles are rein-forced by endocones; they are therefore better able to withstand destruction and are often found by themselves.

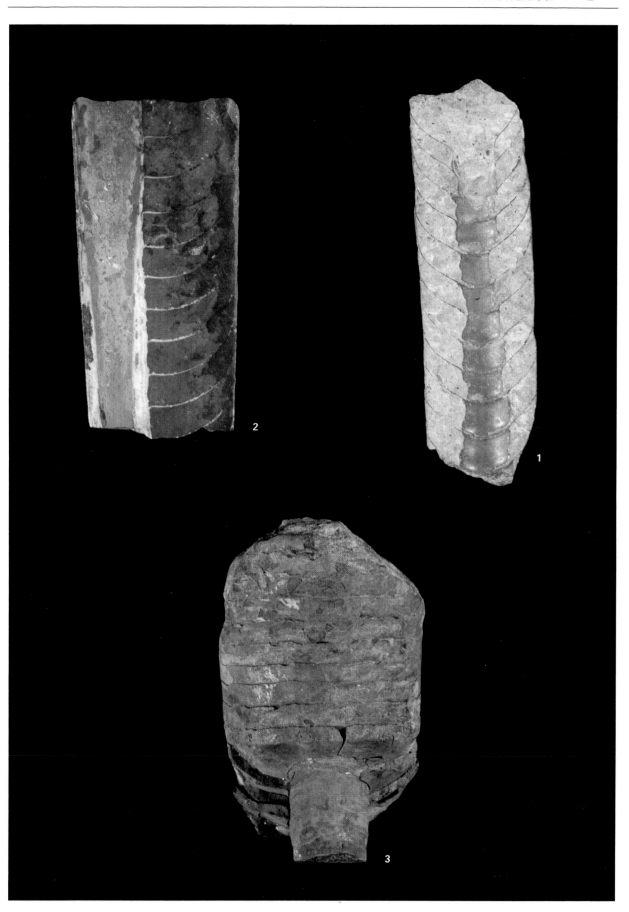

 **Mollusca**

Eushantungoceras pseudoimbricatum (BARRANDE)

Order: Actinocerida
Family: Armenoceratidae

A further specialized group of cephalopods which appeared in the Ordovician were the actinoceratids (subclass Actinoceratoidea). As in the case of orthocerids, their shells were straight or only slightly curved, and usually had a smooth surface. Their characteristic feature is the complicated structure of the siphuncle and the canal system inside it. Actinoceratids were very probably good swimmers and were able, while alive, to maintain a horizontal position of the shell. The complicated structure of the siphuncle also indicates that their way of regulating gas pressure and the amount of fluid in the gas chambers was very highly developed. Some species make good index fossils. The subclass as a whole attained its peak in the late Ordovician and early Silurian; during the Devonian they were progressively pushed into the background and during the Carboniferous they died out altogether.

Species of the genus *Eushantungoceras* have a smooth, straight shell with very low gas chambers and strikingly oblique sutures. The siphuncle, which is very wide and has extremely swollen connecting rings, lies close to the ventral wall of the shell. This genus is known from Silurian strata in central, northern and eastern Europe and in Asia.

Sactoceras pellucidum (BARRANDE)

Order: Actinocerida
Family: Sactoceratidae

The genus *Sactoceras,* which occurs in Silurian deposits in Europe, Asia, Greenland and North America, have a relatively narrow siphuncle. Superficially, without an investigation of its internal structure, the shell looks no different from the similar type of nautiloid shell.

S. pellucidum is one of the few representatives of the entire subclass whose coloured markings are known to us.

Loxoceras breynii MARTIN

Order: Actinocerida
Family: Loxoceratidae

One of the last (Carboniferous) members of the subclass Actinoceratoidea is the genus *Loxoceras,* known in western, central and eastern Europe. Its brevicone shell is dorsoventrally compressed. The moderately large siphuncle lies against the ventral side of the shell. The sutures slant and form a lobe on the side of the siphuncle. The specimen depicted here has weathered favourably, so that the internal structure of the siphuncle can also be seen, including the narrow central canal.

1. *Eushantungoceras pseudoimbricatum,** Lower Silurian (Wenlock), Gotland, Sweden. A longitudinal polished section of part of a phragmocone, length 63 mm. The very wide siphuncle is filled with flat discs composed of calcareous deposits, which have pushed the fleshy part towards the axis of the shell.

2. *Sactoceras pellucidum,* Upper Silurian (Ludlow), Beroun-Kosov, Czechoslovakia. Length of shell 180 mm. The dark longitudinal stripes are remains of the original coloured pattern; such cases are very rare among Palaeozoic fossils.

3. *Loxoceras breynii,** Lower Carboniferous (Viséan), near Moscow, USSR. A core, length 80 mm. The tubular structures in the axis of the siphuncle are the weathered contents of the canals. This type of preservation is not very common.

C

S

Anetoceras hunsrueckianum ERBEN

Order: Anarcestida
Family: Mimosphinctidae

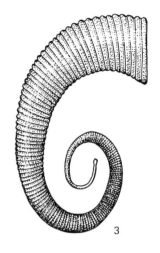

Few groups of invertebrates have enjoyed so much attention from both palaeontologists and lay collectors as ammonoids (subclass Ammonoidea), whose earliest representatives appeared in the Lower Devonian. For about 300 million years they were a dominant component of the marine fauna and right from the beginning they are of primary significance for stratigraphy. In outer shape and structure, ammonoid shells resemble nautiloid shells and it is assumed that ammonoids were descended from bactritid ancestors; bactritids (subclass Bactritoidea) are cephalopods with a straight-sided or curved shell derived from nautiloids belonging to the order Orthocerida. The oldest ammonoids have a number of features in common with bactritids, such as the ovoid initial chamber (the protoconch), the siphuncle lying against the ventral margin (in curved shells against the outer wall), the outer (ventral) lobe of the suture and the laterally compressed cross section of the shell. Morphologically intermediate shells are also known, from straight or gently curved bactritoid shells to loosely coiled ammonoid shells. Ammonoids enjoyed their first period of prosperity during the Devonian, but their true peak unquestionably came during the Mesozoic, when they became very diverse and adapted to most marine environments. At the end of the Cretaceous the whole group died out leaving no

1, 3. *Anetoceras hunsrueckianum,* Lower Devonian (Zlíchovian), West Germany. Shell diameter 75 mm; a deformed specimen (1). A loosely coiled spiral is typical of the shells of the oldest ammonoids (3).

2. *Teicherticeras discordans,** Lower Devonian (Dalejian), Choteč, Czechoslovakia. Shell diameter 30 mm; a deformed specimen.

descendants. Experts have so far identified some 10,000 species of ammonoids.

The first known ammonoids are included in the family Mimosphinctidae. They either have loosely coiled shells (fig. 3), or the whorls touch one another. The sutures are very simple, with an outer, a lateral and (occasionally) an inner lobe. *Anetoceras,* the best known genus, has been found in Lower Devonian deposits, widely distributed in Europe and Asia and also in northern Africa and North America. Its whorls are characterized by a gradual increase in height and have radial or oblique ribs on their surface.

Teicherticeras discordans (ERBEN)

Order: Anarcestida
Family: Mimosphinctidae

Together with shells of the oldest *Anetoceras* species, we also find ammonoids with an evolutionally more advanced type of shell. These shells are evolute, i.e. they are tightly coiled and sometimes have only slightly overlapping whorls. Their sutures already have a distinct inner (dorsal) lobe. In the early phases of growth the shells were very incompletely coiled, however, giving rise to a large umbilical perforation round the coiling axis. These ammonoids belong to the very widespread genus *Teicherticeras.*

In tentaculite shales in the central Bohemian Palaeozoic basin, we find a high incidence of the radially ribbed *T. discordans,* which was recently also found in sediments of the same age in southern China.

249

Mollusca

5

Gyroceratites gracilis Bronn

Order: Anarcestida
Family: Mimoceratidae

The evolution of Lower Devonian ammonoids led to tighter coiling of the shell. The elliptical protoconch was gradually transformed to a spherical form.

The geographically widespread, conservative (evolutionally stagnating) family Mimoceratidae, represented by the single genus *Gyroceratites,* appeared during the late Lower Devonian. It probably evolved from the genus *Teicherticeras.* The shell was thinly discoidal, the whorls were elliptical in cross section, their outer wall was flattened and where it bordered on the lateral walls there were traces of ridges. The sculpture, consisting of somewhat indistinct riblets (fig. 5), bulging towards the apex of the shell, is also characteristic.

G. gracilis is found more frequently than other members of the genus. It occurs in Lower Devonian sediments deposited in the most diverse types of sea bed environments in Europe, Asia and north Africa.

6

Mimagoniatites fecundus (Barrande)

Order: Anarcestida
Family: Agoniatitidae

The ancestors of the evolutionally successful family Agoniatitidae – from which all anarcestids (family Anarcestidae) were evidently originally derived – must also be looked for among the representatives of the genus *Teicherticeras.* The chief characteristic features of agoniatids are their discoid shell with slightly overlapping whorls and a moderately wide or narrow umbilicus. S-shaped growth ridges are present on the surface of the shells. The sutures have only three lobes

1, 2, 5. *Gyroceratites gracilis,** Lower Devonian (Dalejian), Prague-Hlubočepy, Czechoslovakia. 1 – a core of an extremely large individual, 2 – an incomplete specimen with a preserved shell. Shell diameter 56 and 27 mm. 5 – the first two whorls of the shell.

3. *Mimagoniatites fecundus,** Lower Devonian (Dalejian), Bubovice, Czechoslovakia. Shell diameter 47 mm. A very well preserved complete shell with the initial chamber (the protoconch).

4. *Anarcestes plebeius,** Lower Devonian (Dalejian), Prague-Hlubočepy, Czechoslovakia. A phragmocone core formed of yellowish weathered limestone, with clearly discernible sutures on the sides. Diameter 30 mm.

6. *Anarcestes* sp., a cross section of the shell.

— an outer, a lateral and an inner lobe. The genus *Mimagoniatites* is one of the oldest members of the family. It occurs in Lower Devonian deposits in Europe, northern Africa and Asia, in many types of marine sediments. Its main diagnostic characters are the rounded trapezoid cross section of the whorls and the presence of a small umbilical perforation.

Anarcestes plebeius (BARRANDE)

Order: Anarcestida
Family: Anarcestidae

Anarcestids have a characteristic, gradually widening shell with a large number of whorls. The sutures likewise have three main lobes. The oldest members of the group have an incompletely coiled shell, so that there is an umbilical perforation. The first cephalopods of this family appeared before the end of the Lower Devonian, but they were very soon differentiated further, radiated and spread.

The members of the genus *Anarcestes* are characterized by discoid shells of varying widths, with a small umbilical perforation (fig. 6). This type of shell made fast movement impossible. The species of this genus are distributed throughout Lower Devonian deposits in the northern hemisphere.

 **Mollusca**

Agoniatites inconstans (PHILLIPS)

Order: Anarcestida
Family: Agoniatitidae

At the end of the Lower Devonian, ammonoids with an incompletely coiled shell were all replaced by more progressive genera without an umbilical perforation. The older genus *Mimagoniatites* was succeeded by the somewhat conservative *Agoniatites,* which survived without undergoing any pronounced morphological changes up to the end of the Middle Devonian.

The two genera closely resemble each other as regards the outer shape and surface sculpture of the shell and the cross section of the whorls. *Agoniatites* has been described on every continent except Australia and the Antarctic. The wide geographical distribution of some species is interesting; for instance, *A. inconstans* is known from shallow water marine sediments in Europe and in North America.

Pinacites jugleri RÖMER

Order: Anarcestida
Family: Pinacitidae

Pinacitids evidently separated from agoniatids before the end of the Lower Devonian. They have quite diversely shaped shells; the whorls all overlap each other very markedly and are usually laterally flattened. The sutures are more complex than in members of the preceding family.

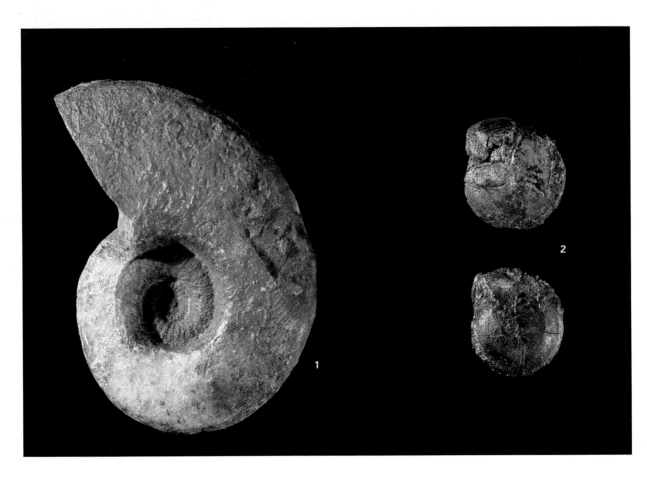

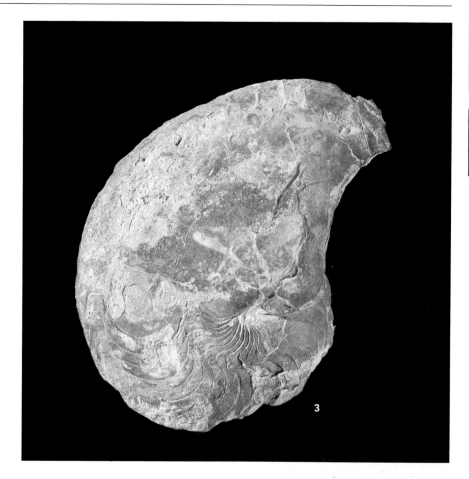

The genus *Pinacites* is easily identified by its lenticular, highly involute shell, the abruptly increasing height of the whorls and the sharp outer wall. They occur in early Middle Devonian deposits in Europe, northern Africa, Asia and North America. The lenticulate shell, with its closed umbilicus and smooth surface, was evidently an expedient adaptation for active swimming.

1. *Agoniatites inconstans,* Middle Devonian (Givetian), Martenberg, West Germany. Shell diameter 45 mm. The specimen comes from sedimentary iron ores deposited in a shallow-water marine environment.

2. *Cheiloceras subpartitum,** Upper Devonian (Famennian), Vápený near Jitrava, Czecho-slovakia. Two pyritized casts, evidently microconches (male shells), diameter 12 and 9 mm. Macroconches (female shells) are roughly double the size.

3. *Pinacites jugleri,** Middle Devonian (Eifelian), Prague-Hlubočepy, Czechoslovakia. An almost complete cast, diameter 112 mm.

Cheiloceras subpartitum (MÜNSTER)

Order: Goniatida
Family: Cheiloceratidae

The goniatites which lived from the Middle Devonian to the end of the Palaeozoic and into the Triassic period were also offshoots of anarces-tids. They are characterized by a spherical to discoid shell with markedly overlapping whorls and (apart from a few exceptions) indistinct sculpture. The sutures are rather complex, the lobes are pointed and the saddles are rounded; the outer lobe is divided by the middle saddle into two part lobes.

The worldwide Upper Devonian genus *Cheiloceras* has lenticulate to almost spherical shells with a concealed umbilicus. Constrictions can be seen on the otherwise smooth shells. This is one of the oldest genera in which sexual dimorphism of the shells has been found; it is manifested in differences in size (macro- and microconches).

Ch. subpartitum is an index goniatid species.

253

Genuclymenia frechi WEDEKIND

Order: Clymeniida
Family: Cyrtoclymeniidae

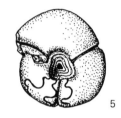

Clymeniida were a distinctive order of Upper Devonian ammonoids which differed from other ammonoids chiefly in respect of their dorsally situated siphuncle (i.e. lying on the inner side of the whorls). They did not appear until the higher Upper Devonian, but very soon they radiated on a large scale and in the short time of their existence they produced more diverse species and altogether outnumbered any of the contemporary groups of ammonoids. Locally they formed '*Clymenia* limestones', which are known on practically every continent. When resolving the problem of the origin of clymeniids, the siphuncle presented the main difficulty. Longitudinal sections of embryonic shells demonstrate that in these early growth stages it lay ventrally, i.e. on the outer wall of the whorls (as in other ammonoids) and that the entire shift to the inner side of the whorl took place in the first three chambers (fig. 4). At present we do not reliably know from what the clymeniids are descended, but they were probably differentiated from anarcestids.

Genuclymenia is an evolutionally primitive genus which is evidently confined to Europe. The sides of the discoid shell are densely ornamented with S-shaped ribs.

Clymenia laevigata MÜNSTER

Order: Clymeniida
Family: Clymeniidae

Species belonging to the family Clymeniidae are characterized by narrowly discoid shells whose whorls increase gradually in height. The whorls are rounded or flattened and sometimes have a 'keel' on their outer surface (i.e. they are carinate). The sutures are simpler than in the preceding species and often have only an inner and a lateral lobe.

The genus *Clymenia,* after which the whole order is named, is not regarded as phylogenetically significant, but as an evolutionally regressive (blind) side branch. The whorls of the shells are oval in cross section and are smooth except for fine and almost straight growth ridges. This genus is known in Europe and has otherwise been described (with some doubts) only in Australia.

Wocklumeria sphaeroides (RH. RICHTER)

Order: Clymeniida
Family: Wocklumeriidae

The shells of ammonoids and nautiloids are coiled in a logarithmic spiral as are most molluscs. The genus *Wocklumeria* is one of the few exceptions. At least the first few whorls of its thickly discoid to spherical involute shells are twisted into the shape of a rounded triangle. The surface of the shell is almost smooth.

Wocklumeria is a stratigraphically important European and North American genus. The shells are low, the whorls have a crescent-shaped cross section and there is a moderately large umbilicus. Triangular coiling with sharp transversal constriction can be seen only on the earliest whorls (fig. 5).

1, 5. *Wocklumeria sphaeroides,* * Upper Devonian (Famennian), Oberrödinghausen, West Germany. A core, diameter 38 mm. A stratigraphically very important species (an index fossil of the uppermost Devonian). 5 – the earliest whorls.

2, 4. *Genuclymenia frechi,* *Upper Devonian (Famennian), Enkeberg near Bredlar, West Germany. Shell diameter 32 mm. The pronounced ribs on the surface of the shell are somewhat unusual in a clymeniid. 4 – the first whorl in a longitudinal section.

3. *Clymenia laevigata,* * Upper Devonian (Famennian), Koestenberg, West Germany. A core, diameter 52 mm. These individuals grew to a relatively large size. They are an important component of some *Clymenia* limestones.

Goniatites crenistria PHILLIPS

Order: Goniatitida
Family: Goniatitidae

Most of the Devonian ammonoids died out at the end of the Lower Paleozoic Era and a whole series of other groups of marine invertebrates met a similar fate. The cause was evidently mountain-forming processes with several phases which led to big palaeogeographical changes. Goniatites again underwent marked radiation in the Lower Carboniferous, however. They developed very rapidly and today goniatites are among the most frequently found and geographically widely distributed fossils. They therefore furnished a basis for detailed elaboration of the stratigraphy of the late Palaeozoic era, since the worldwide distribution of ammonoid genera and even species also continues into the Permian. In general, however, it must be said that ammonoids are only here and there common in Permian sediments and that their incidence in Europe is very limited.

Anarcestids were evidently the starting point not only for clymeniids (which came to a dead end), but also for the orders Goniatitida and Prolecanitida. The generically and specifically smaller order Prolecanitida is the group from which all the Mesozoic ammonoids are derived.

1, 2. *Goniatites crenistria,* Lower Carboniferous (Viséan), Blackburn, Great Britain. Internal mould, diameter 40 and 15 mm. Side (1) and outer (2) view of the whorls. The course of sutures of a goniatite type can be seen very clearly on the cores of both phragmocones.

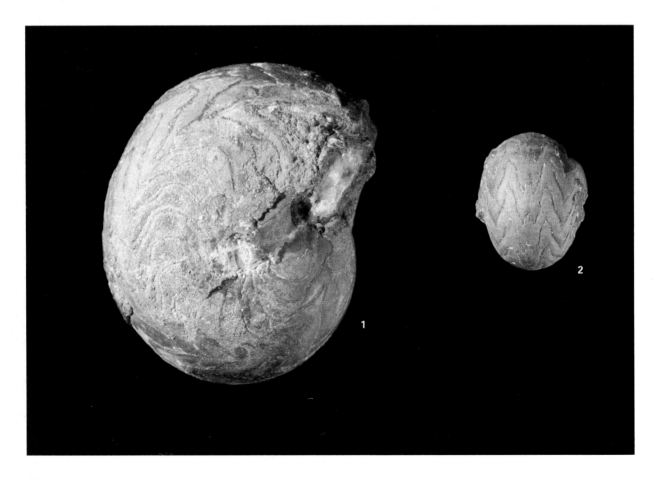

3. *Gastrioceras carbonarium,* Upper Carboniferous (Namurian), Leek, Great Britain. Shell diameter 25 mm. A species with a thick, discoid shell; the relatively wide umbilicus is filled with rock.

The stratigraphic range of the family Goniatitidae is limited to the late Palaeozoic era. The genus *Goniatites* used to be regarded as much larger and species which had little in common with one another were included in it. It is now defined much more strictly. It is characterized by spherical shells with a narrow umbilicus and by somewhat indistinct longitudinal and transverse sculpture which is important for determination of the individual species. This important Lower Carboniferous genus is found in different types of marine sediments all over the world.

Gastrioceras carbonarium (BUCH)   Order: Goniatitida
Family: Gastrioceratidae

Gastrioceratidae are another important family of late Palaeozoic goniatites. They all have a wide umbilicus, reticulate sculpture (at least in the early phases of growth) and conspicuous ribbing; the ribs on the venter usually curve backwards and form a distinct sinus.

The cosmopolitan Carboniferous genus *Gastrioceras* is more diversely shaped than the preceding genus and the shells of its members range from almost discoid to spherical. At the edge of the umbilicus there is conspicuous ribbing. The wide shells of goniatites were not built for fast swimming and their owners probably lived largely on the bed of shallow shelf seas (at depths of up to 200 metres). The ones responsible for their worldwide distribution were evidently the youngest individuals, which floated in the water like plankton and were thus carried long distances by the currents.

 **Mollusca**

Ceratites pulcher RIEDEL

Order: Ceratitida
Family: Ceratitidae

The majority of late Palaeozoic ammonoids died out at the end of the Permian period, but in the early Triassic the whole group entered upon a new period of prosperity. Most of the Triassic genera belong to the ceratitids, whose characteristic feature are their sutures; the typical ceratitic suture has undivided saddles and serrated lobes.

Ceratites s. l., distributed in European Middle Triassic deposits, is the most famous genus of the order. It has laterally and outwardly flattened, evolute shells with a moderately wide umbilicus and rough simple or forked ribs on their surface. Where the ribs fork, there is usually a tubercle (node). There is also a row of nodes along the shoulder of the venter. A not altogether complete evolutionary line of the genus *Ceratites* s. l. is represented in Upper Muschelkalk.

Trachyceras aon MÜNSTER

Order: Ceratitida
Family: Trachyceratidae

The members of the family Trachyceratidae have a ventral groove, bordered on either side by a row of tubercles or a ridge. On the sides of the shell the ribs are curved and are usually surmounted by spirally organized nodes.

1. *Ceratites pulcher,* Middle Triassic (Ladinian), West Germany. A limestone core with sutures of a ceratitic type. Diameter 62 mm.

2. *Trachyceras aon,** Upper Triassic (Carnian), Hallstadt, Austria. Shell diameter 75 mm. The pronounced sculpture, composed of large numbers of small, spirally organized tubercles, is typical of this species.

3. *Monophyllites simonii,* Upper Triassic (Carnian), Hallstadt, Austria. Shell diameter 102 mm. It belongs to a morphologically conservative group of phylloceratids in which the characteristic shape of the shell, with somewhat indistinct sculpture, was retained during the whole time of their existence.

The genus *Trachyceras* is distributed in Middle and Upper Triassic deposits all over the world. The highly involute shells have a narrow umbilicus. The whorls, which are roundedly trapezoid in cross section, have a rounded venter on which tubercles are present. The sutures are of a complex ammonoid type (divided saddles and lobes). *T. aon* is an index ammonoid for the lower part of the Carnian.

Monophyllites simonii (HAUER)

Order: Phylloceratida
Family: Ussuritidae

The first phylloceratids appeared in the early Triassic and survived until the Lower Cretaceous. They were the initial evolutionary branch of all post-Triassic ammonoids. Their shells are largely thin-walled, discoid and slightly involute, are rounded in cross section (sometimes with constrictions) and have rather intricate, characteristically formed sutures. The shells were adapted for depths of 400 to 500 metres, i.e. greater than the depths at which most other ammonoids lived.

The genus *Monophyllites* occurs in Middle to Upper Triassic deposits all over the world. The shells have the typical features of the order. The fine growth lines are S-shaped.

259

 **Mollusca**

Arcestes mojsisovicsi (HAUER)

Order: Ceratitida
Family: Arcestidae

The shells of Triassic ammonoids were far more diverse than those of their Permian predecessors and during the Triassic the number of genera increased very quickly. From the Upper Triassic we know of a whole series of 'heteromorph' ammonoids comprising species with very unusual types of shells.

In appearance, the shells of some members of the family Arcestidae resemble the shells of Palaeozoic goniatites. Their generally smooth surface shows periodic constrictions and the umbilicus is narrow or closed. The sutures are already very complicated and of an ammonoid type, i.e. with richly divided and crenellated lobes and saddles. The family takes its name from the cosmopolitan Middle and Upper Triassic genus *Arcestes,* which is represented by several dozen species grouped in a few subgenera. The genus *Arcestes* bears the features characteristic of the family as a whole.

Flexoptychites gibbus (BENECKE)

Order: Ceratitida
Family: Ptychitidae

Ptychitidae is another important family of Triassic ammonoids. The shell of the youngest specimens is at first almost spherical and highly involute, with a narrow umbilicus. In older individuals it is usually

1. *Arcestes mojsisovicsi,* Upper Triassic (Carnian), Röthelstein, Austria. A cast of a spherical shell from flesh-coloured Alpine Triassic limestone, diameter 49 mm.

2. *Flexoptychites gibbus,* Middle Triassic (Ladinian), Bosnia, Yugoslavia. A core of a flatly discoid shell, diameter 90 mm. Ammonoid type sutures can be clearly seen on the polished part of the phragmocone.

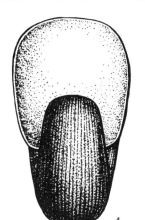

4

discoid and smooth or ribbed. As in the preceding genus, the sutures are already of an ammonoid type.

The shells of the genus *Flexoptychites,* which are distributed in Middle Triassic strata in the Alpine-Himalayan region, have widely spaced ribs on their surface; as distinct from the closely related and likewise very widespread genus *Ptychites,* the ribs are slightly curved.

Cladiscites tornatus (BRONN)

Order: Ceratitida
Family: Cladiscitidae

Some Upper Triassic ammonoids had strikingly large shells. For instance, the thin discoid shells of the well-known species *Pinacoceras metternichi* (family Pinacoceratidae) had a diameter of up to 1.5 metres. The cephalopods of the family Cladiscitidae had robust shells with a uniform appearance. They are highly involute and have flat-sided whorls with a smooth or longitudinally ribbed surface. The sutures have markedly crenellated lobes.

The genus *Cladiscites* is known both in the Alpine-Himalayan region and in the Pacific region, Alaska and north-eastern Siberia. The whorls of the shells are rounded-trapezoid in cross section, with a rounded outer wall. This genus can be identified very easily from the shape of the whorls and their characteristic surface sculpture (dense longitudinal riblets), which is unusual for ammonoids (fig. 4).

3, 4. *Cladiscites tornatus,* * Upper Triassic (Carnian), Hallstadt, Austria. Shell diameter 105 mm (3). 4 — a frontal view.

Mollusca

Psiloceras psilonotum (QUENSTEDT)

Order: Ammonitida
Family: Psiloceratidae

The majority of ceratitid ammonoids which lived during the Triassic died out when that period ended. The only ones to survive the transition to the Jurassic were a few phylloceratids (order Phylloceratida) and members of the order Lytoceratida, which appeared towards the end of the Triassic. The beginning of the Jurassic was marked by explosive radiation of a new order, Ammonitida, the most progressive of all. Their shells have extremely complex sutures and the saddles and lobes are broken up in great detail. This increasing complexity of the sutures can be observed during the ontogeny of the individuals of any species of ammonite, as well as during the phylogeny of the order as a whole. The internal structure of the shells also has many features differentiating Ammonitida from older representatives of the subclass in general and from nautiloids in particular. In the first place, the septa bulge in the opposite direction (i.e. towards the aperture) and the septal necks are likewise oriented in this direction. These characters both developed inside the embryonic shells, whereas in phylogenetically older orders in which this character appers they were formed in the later growth stages. The question of the reason for these changes is still awaiting a satisfactory functional answer.

Psilocerataceae, the oldest superfamily of the order Ammonitida, combine the characters of both phyloceratids and lytoceratids and are regarded as the ancestral group of all other Jurassic and Cretaceous ammonites. They are characterized by smooth evolute shells, or shells

1. *Echioceras raricostatum,** Lower Jurassic (Sinemurian), Baden-Württemberg, West Germany. A cast, diameter 35 mm. A stratigraphically important species. After the animal's death the shell lay on the surface of soft sediment and provided a firm base for a sessile serpulid worm.

2, 4. *Arietites bucklandi,** Lower Jurassic (Sinemurian), Baden-Württemberg, West Germany. 2 – a core, diameter 60 mm. 4 – a frontal view of the shell.

3

3. *Psiloceras psilonotum,** Lower Jurassic (Hetangian), Riedern near Esslingen, West Germany. Shell diameter 50 mm. An almost complete specimen with the shell.

with only faintly marked ribs, by relatively simple sutures and by sexual dimorphism, manifested in differences in the size of the shells (smaller shells being regarded as male and larger shells as female). The whorls of the shells of the cosmopolitan Lower Jurassic genus *Psiloceras* are laterally compressed and have an elliptical cross section. The shells are smooth-surfaced or are marked with only faint radial ribs.

Order: Ammonitida
Family: Echioceratidae

Echioceras raricostatum (ZIETEN)

The Lower Jurassic family Echioceratidae comprises genera characterized by evolute shells with a large number of whorls. On the venter there is usually a sharp keel; the surface is conspicuously ribbed.

Echioceras is a very widespread genus. The whorls are circular in cross section, or are dorsoventrally strongly compressed. The pronounced ribbing on the flanks peters out towards the umbilicus and on the outer side of the whorl.

Order: Ammonitida
Family: Arietitidae

Arietites bucklandi (SOWERBY)

4

The Lower Jurassic genus *Arietites,* a typical representative of the family Arietitidae, has evolute shells with a wide umbilicus. The whorls are almost square in cross section, with a median keel and lateral keels on the venter. The ribs are thick and not branched. On the sides they are almost radial; when they reach the keels they fade away.

263

 **Mollusca**

Schlotheimia angulata (SCHLOTHEIM)

Order: Ammonitida
Family: Schlotheimiidae

The great morphological and sculptural diversity of Jurassic ammonites reflects their unwontedly fast development and adaptation to different environmental conditions. From the geological point of view, the various ammonite species were relatively short-lived. They spread very quickly to different regions and are the most commonly found fossils. The first to make use of these findings was the German scientist A. Oppel, who, in the middle of the last century, elaborated a detailed stratigraphic classification of the Swabian Jura and was thus the founder of modern zonal stratigraphy.

The stratigraphically significant Jurassic ammonites include the members of the family Schlotheimiidae (superfamily Psilocerataceae), which have laterally compressed and strikingly ribbed shells with a smooth venter and sometimes a median groove. The sutures are relatively simple.

Schlotheimia is a worldwide Lower Jurassic genus. Its species have evolute shells with a moderately wide umbilicus. The whorls have an oval cross section. On their surface they have dense, sharp and almost radial ribs, which, near the venter, curve towards the aperture and usually fade away.

Coeloceras pettos (QUENSTEDT)

Order: Ammonitida
Family: Eoderoceratidae

The representatives of the superfamily Eoderocerataceae — also from the Lower Jurassic — are characterized by shells with well-developed ribs, tubercles or spines. Eoderoceratidae have evolute shells with very slightly overlapping whorls and complicated sutures.

1. *Schlotheimia angulata,* * Lower Jurassic (Hetangian), Vorwohle, Braunschwerg, West Germany. Shell diameter 42 mm.

2, 4. *Coeloceras pettos,* * Lower Jurassic (Pliensbachian), Baden-Württemberg, West Germany. 2 — a pyritized cast of a phragmocone with discernible complex sutures, diameter 37 mm. The course of the sutures and changes in them during ontogeny are basic criteria in the determination of ammonites. 4 — a frontal view.

3. *Dactylioceras commune,** Lower Jurassic (Toarkian), Ohmaden near Holzmaden, West Germany. Diameter of the largest shell 72 mm.

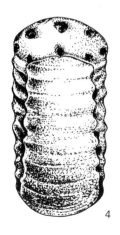

4

The shells of ammonites of the genus *Coeloceras* have dorsoventrally strongly compressed whorls, whose venter is broad and slightly bulging (fig. 4). The dense, pronounced ribs form a typical sculpture.

Dactylioceras commune (SOWERBY)

Order: Ammonitida
Family: Dactylioceratidae

The originally aragonite shell of ammonites, which fossilization processes have usually changed to calcite, is composed (as in nautiloids) of three calcareous layers, with a very thin organic (conchiolin) layer on the surface. They comprise an outer prismatic layer, a middle nacreous layer and an inner prismatic layer. In ammonites, the number of these layers on the inner side of the whorls of involute shells is varyingly reduced. In the family Dactylioceratidae and several other groups there is an extra nacreous layer on the surface of the shells, demonstrating that during the animal's lifetime they were covered with a soft tissue. The species of the worldwide Lower Jurassic genus *Dactylioceras* are characterized by evolute shells with simple or dichotomically branching ribs. In many places, e.g. in Liass deposits near Holzmaden (West Germany), or in limestone concretions near Whitby (Great Britain), they occur en masse.

Mollusca

Androgynoceras maculatum
(Young and Bird)

Order: Ammonitida
Family: Liparoceratidae

Ammonites belonging to the family Liparoceratidae have morphologically very heterogeneous shells. Intermediate forms between various types can also be observed during the ontogeny of individual species. As a rule, the whorls of the shells do not overlap and on their surface they have straight ribs which are usually surmounted by two rows of tubercles. Shells of this shape were definitely not adapted for fast swimming, but are rather indicative of a benthic mode of life.

The whorls of the shells of the Lower Jurassic genus *Androgynoceras* are almost circular in cross section. The thick ribs are separated by wide spaces and always cross the venter. The tubercles are not always adequately pronounced.

Amaltheus margaritatus (De Montfort)

Order: Ammonitida
Family: Amaltheidae

The family Amaltheidae probably evolved from the family Liparoceratidae. Despite its short existence (according to the geological time scale), it managed to spread all over the world. In this blind evolutionary branch we can follow the trend from narrow discoid shells with a sharp keel on the venter to thick-ribbed shells with a roughly

1, 4. *Amaltheus margaritatus,* *
Lower Jurassic (Pliensbachian), Wasseralfingen, West Germany. 1 – a cast with remains of the shell, diameter 50 mm. On the venter there is a striking, cord-like ridge. 4 – a frontal view.

J

2. *Pleuroceras hawskerense,* Lower Jurassic (Pliensbachian), Whitby, Great Britain. A core with remains of the shell, showing the distinct, sharp ribs. Diameter 62 mm.

3. *Androgynoceras maculatum,* Lower Jurassic (Pliensbachian), Whitby, Great Britain. A core, diameter 65 mm.

square profile. Lenticulate (oxyconic) smooth shells seem to have been suitably adapted for fast swimming and tend to occur more in sediments from considerable depths. The roughly contemporary ornamented species were evidently not very good swimmers and their shells are found in shallow-water deposits (they lived at depths of about 40 to 70 metres). A characteristic feature of the shells of the cephalopods of this family is, inter alia, the serrated keel on the venter.

The genus *Amaltheus,* a fair likeness of which is to be found in a book by J. Bauhin at the very beginning of the seventeenth century, has oxyconic shells with a moderately wide umbilicus (fig. 4). The ribs are faint and S-shaped, and the keel on the venter is produced to form a rostrum at the aperture. The best known species, *A. margaritatus,* is an index fossil.

Pleuroceras hawskerense (Sowerby)

Order: Ammonitida
Family: Amaltheidae

The descendants of oxyconic amaltheids have strikingly ribbed shells whose whorls are almost square in cross section. Like the other amaltheids, their domain were the cold seas of the northern hemisphere, although they also infiltrated into the great warm sea known as Tethys.

The genus *Pleuroceras* is distributed in Upper Pliensbachian strata in Europe, northern Africa and Georgia (USSR). When its pronounced, non-branched radial ribs cross over to the venter, they swing suddenly towards the aperture and are lost in the furrows dividing the median keel. Ventrolaterally, the ribs spread out into tubercles (nodes). *Pleuroceras* is one of the few genera of ammonites on which a coloured pattern in the form of radial stripes has been found.

267

 **Mollusca**

Hildoceras bifrons (BRUGUIÈRE)

Order: Ammonitida
Family: Hildoceratidae

The superfamily Hildocerataceae groups together ammonites which, despite the shortness of their existence, attained considerable development and wide geographical distribution. They appeared before the end of the Lower Jurassic and died out during the Middle Jurassic. They are the phylogenetic branch which gave rise, in the Middle Jurassic, to two further superfamilies – Stephanocerataceae and Perisphinctaceae. Sexual dimorphism, expressed in the form of large and small shells (macro- and microconches), appeared in them as a stable character.

The genus *Hildoceras* is a characteristic Lower Jurassic representative of the family and occurs in Europe, northern Africa and Asia. The shells are evolute and the whorls have an almost square cross section. On the sides there is a deep furrow transsecting the ribs bulging towards the apex. The venter is tricarinate, i.e. it has three ridges, separated by grooves (fig. 5). *H. bifrons* is an index ammonite for the Lower Toarcian.

Haugia cf. *illustris* (DENCKMANN)

Order: Ammonitida
Family: Hamatoceratidae

All the members of this family are characterized by a well-developed

5

1, 5. *Hildoceras bifrons,** Lower Jurassic (Toarcian), Cornus, France. 1 – a limonitized core with clearly discernible sutures and a pronounced longitudinal groove on the side. Diameter 33 mm. 5 – a posterior view.

2. *Leioceras opalinum,** Middle Jurassic (Aalenian), Teufelsloch near Göppingen, West Germany. Shell diameter 27 mm. On the venter, the chalky shell tapers off near the mouth into a long rostrum.

keel, striking ribbing and the presence of lateral tubercles. In most cases the ribs are joined together in the tubercles.

The genus *Haugia,* which is confined to the uppermost Lower Jurassic, is known on practically every continent. Its members have a flattened shell and markedly overlapping whorls with a high keel on the venter. The sculpture is not so distinct in full-grown individuals.

Order: Ammonitida
Leioceras opalinum (REINECKE)
Family: Graphoceratidae

The family Graphoceratidae comprises a few genera whose common characters are highly involute, laterally compressed shells with a keel on the venter and with S-shaped ribs.

Leioceras is characterized by oxyconic shells. These shells have a smooth surface or indistinct ribs which disappeared during growth. Full-grown individuals have long processes, lappets, on the sides of the aperture. *L. opalinum* is a very widely distributed species.

Order: Ammonitida
Costileioceras sinon (BAYLE)
Family: Graphoceratidae

Costileioceras is very closely related to the preceding species. The shells are more distinctly ribbed, with a wider umbilicus and specialized sutures. It occurs in European Middle Jurassic deposits.

3. *Haugia illustris,** Lower Jurassic (Toarcian), Hanover, West Germany. A planidiscoid core with a pronounced ridge on the outer aspect of the whorls, diameter 100 mm.

4. *Costileioceras sinon,** Middle Jurassic (Bajocian), Randen near Schaffhausen, Switzerland. A core with excellently preserved sutures, whose saddle and lobes have an extremely intricate pattern. Diameter 85 mm.

Mollusca

Macrocephalites macrocephalus (SCHLOTHEIM)

Order: Ammonitida
Family: Macrocephalitidae

The superfamily Stephanocerataceae, which comprises the families Macrocephalitidae and Sphaeroceratidae, as well as the homonymous family, occupies an important place among Jurassic ammonites. Apart from the characteristic complicated pattern of the sutures, common to all of them, the shells of most of its members are strikingly ribbed and display sexual dimorphism (reflected in their size).

The shells of the members of the family Macrocephalitidae are highly involute and have a narrow umbilicus; the outer surface of the whorls is always rounded.

The Middle Jurassic genus *Macrocephalites* is distributed all over the world. The shells are broadly discoid and the whorls increase rapidly in height; they have a rounded-trapezoid cross section (fig. 5). The surface of the shells is thickly ribbed. The ribs are thin and sharp; just before reaching the middle of the flank they usually fork and continue to the venter directly. The true domain of this genus was the warm seas known as Tethys, but it also extended to colder regions.

Sphaeroceras cf. *brongniarti* (SOWERBY)

Order: Ammonitida
Family: Sphaeroceratidae

Sphaeroceratidae are likewise a Middle Jurassic family. Their charac-

1, 5. *Macrocephalites macrocephalus,** Middle Jurassic (Callovian), Balingen, West Germany. 1 – a core with remains of the shell, diameter 90 mm. A typical species and an index fossil with an involute shell and branching ribs. 5 – a frontal view.

2, 3. *Sphaeroceras* cf. *brongniarti,** Middle Jurassic (Bajocian), France. Cores with remains of the shell, diameter 15 and 26 mm. The smaller microconch (2) belonged to a male, the larger macroconch (3) to a female.

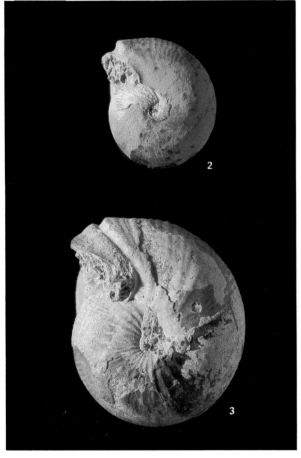

4. *Stephanoceras humphriesianum,** Middle Jurassic (Bajocian), Calvados, France. A core, diameter 130 mm. An evolute type of shell. At the nodal points on the sides, the ribs break up into 3–4 branches.

teristic features are a highly involute shell with a narrow or almost closed umbilicus and an incompletely coiled last whorl. The apertural margin of full-grown shells tapers off on the sides and on the venter into anteriorly orientated lobes.

The genus *Sphaeroceras* occurs in Europe, northern Africa, North America and Asia. The shells are tiny and the whorls are oval in cross section. On their surface they have fine, dense radial ribs, which are the most distinct beside the umbilicus. No ribbing is to be seen on internal moulds.

5

Stephanoceras humphriesianum
(SOWERBY)

Order: Ammonitida
Family: Stephanoceratidae

The shells of ammonites of the family Stephanoceratidae are characterized by slightly overlapping whorls and a wide umbilicus. The ribs beside the umbilicus are simple; at nodal points on the sides they divide into three to four branches.

The Middle Jurassic genus *Stephanoceras* is distributed all over the world. The whorls of young individuals are dorsoventrally compressed; the whorl sides and the venter are rounded. The ribs on the ventral side are straight. Fully developed shells have a thickened, lobate aperture. *S. humphriesianum* is a stratigraphically important species.

Oppelia subradiata (SOWERBY)

Order: Ammonitida
Family: Oppeliidae

The oldest representatives of the superfamily Haplocerataceae are known from the Middle Jurassic and the phylogenetically youngest genera from the end of the Lower Cretaceous. These cephalopods were distributed all over the world, except in boreal regions. Most of them have small, sexually differentiated shells with a high aperture. The shells are laterally compressed to oxyconic in form and there is sometimes a keel on the venter. The aperture, sutures and sculpture of full-grown shells display great diversity. Crescent-shaped ribs are usually present on the surface of the shells.

The shells of the genus *Oppelia* are highly involute. The whorls are almost triangular in cross section and usually have a faint keel. The ribs are rather indistinct. This genus used to include many more species, but according to modern opinion there are only a few which actually belong to it.

1. *Oppelia subradiata,** Middle Jurassic (Bajocian), Bayeux, France. A limonitized core, diameter 40 mm. The genus *Oppelia* was named after the German scientist A. Oppel, who laid the foundations for a detailed stratigraphic classification of the Jurassic formation.

2. *Distichoceras bipartitum,** Middle Jurassic (Callovian), Lautlingen, West Germany. A core, diameter 38 mm. The joining of pairs of ribs on the outer surface of the whorl is a striking character.

3. *Hecticoceras hecticum,** Middle Jurassic (Callovian), Laufen an der Eyach, West Germany. A core with S-shaped ribs and pronounced sutures, diameter 42 mm.

Hecticoceras hecticum (REINECKE)

Order: Ammonitida
Family: Oppeliidae

The Middle Jurassic genus *Hecticoceras* is distributed over almost the whole of the globe. The whorls of its evolute shells (which only slightly overlap one another) are oval or rounded-trapezoid in cross section, with three faint keels on their venter. As with other members of the superfamily Haplocerataceae, sexual dimorphism is manifested in differences in the size of the shells and the shape of the aperture.

Distichoceras bipartitum (ZIETEN)

Order: Ammonitida
Family: Oppeliidae

The genus *Distichoceras* occurs in Middle und Upper Jurassic marine deposits in Europe, Africa and Asia. The shells are moderately involute and the whorls have an almost trapezoid cross section and markedly flattened sides with a low keel. On the inner half of the flanks of the shell the ribs are indistinct; on the outer half they are more pronounced and bulge into protuberances which are sometimes higher than the median keel.

273

Mollusca

Kosmoceras duncani (SOWERBY)

Order: Ammonitida
Family: Kosmoceratidae

The members of the Middle Jurassic family Kosmoceratidae lived chiefly in cold waters in the northern hemisphere. The characteristic features of their shells are a flat ventral side and a row of tubercles on the flanks, at the borderline to the ventral side, or in both places.

Few ammonite genera have been studied in such detail as *Kosmoceras.* An abundance of well preserved material from Middle Jurassic Lower Oxford clays, numbering over three thousand individuals, was used, in the 1920s, by the German scientist Brinkmann, as an example of the progressive development of ammonites as demonstrated from changes in their size and sculpture and in the shape of the aperture. Later, after it was found that sexual dimorphism existed in ammonites, Brinkmann's findings had to be somewhat corrected and his presumed four evolutionary lines reduced by half. Nevertheless, his study is an example of precise stratigraphic palaeontological investigation illustrating the evolution of ammonites at species level. The members of the genus *Kosmoceras* have characteristic evolute shells, whose surface is adorned by large numbers of rather irregular ribs interrupted by a row of tubercles. At the sites of the tubercles the ribs either fork, or new ribs are added between them. On the venter, the rows of tubercles are separated by a smooth strip of shell.

1, 3. *Kosmoceras duncani,* Middle Jurassic (Callovian), Luków, Poland. Shell diameter 70 mm. A macroconch. The shell has been partly dissolved, exposing the nacreous layer, which has kept its original appearance (1). 3 — a microconch.

2. *Quenstedtoceras mariae,* Upper Jurassic (Oxfordian), France. A core with a partly preserved shell, diameter 30 mm. In the case of young or incomplete shells it is hard to tell whether they are macro- or microconches.

The specimen of *K. duncani* illustrated here comes from the world famous locality of Luków in Poland. A large drift block deposited there furnished a tremendous amount of fossil material. Ammonites from this locality (whose nacreous layer was usually preserved) formed the basis of a fundamental study of the sexual dimorphism of ammonite shells by Prof. Makowski. According to Makowski, large shells with an unmodified aperture (macroconches) belong to females and smaller shells with long lobate processes at the sides of the aperture (microconches) belong to males (fig. 3).

Quenstedtoceras mariae (D'ORBIGNY)

Order: Ammonitida
Family: Cardioceratidae

Cardioceratidae are similarly distributed. The species of the Middle to Upper Jurassic genus *Quenstedtoceras* have discoid shells with slightly overlapping whorls and a moderately wide umbilicus. The whorls are flat-sided, oval or triangular in cross section. On their surface they have dense S-shaped ribs; these either branch in the middle of the sides, or new ones are interpolated between them. On the venter the ribs form a V-shape, thicken and produce a suggestion of a keel. Full-grown individuals have no ribbing. In microconches, a rostrum occurs at the aperture as an extension of the keel. *Q. mariae* forms the lowest ammonite zone in Upper Jurassic strata.

Mollusca

Parkinsonia parkinsoni (SOWERBY)

Order: Ammonitida
Family: Parkinsoniidae

A further important ammonite superfamily — Perisphinctaceae — appeared in the Middle Jurassic; their evolution culminated in the Upper Jurassic and they died out at the end of the Lower Cretaceous. Up to now we have no satisfactory explanation of the origin of this superfamily. Its typical characters are a planispirally coiled evolute shell, sharp bifurcate ribs, complicated sutures with a dominant first lateral lobe and sexual dimorphism of the shells, reflected in their size and the shape of the aperture.

The species of the family Parkinsoniidae, which are represented in Middle Jurassic deposits in Europe, Asia and North America, are among the oldest members of the superfamily. Their numerous whorls are roughly trapezoid in cross section. The surface of the shells is ornamented with dense, pronounced ribs, running almost radially on the sides. At the ventral edge they often break up into two branches and curve adorally. On the periphery the ribs are interrupted by a furrow or an area of smooth shell. It is interesting to note the alternation of the ribs, which can be seen in a view of the outer side of the whorl and impairs their otherwise perfect bilateral symmetry. *P. parkinsoni* is an index ammonite for a Bajocian stage.

Perisphinctes plicatilis (SOWERBY)

Order: Ammonitida
Family: Perisphinctidae

The ammonites of the family Perisphinctidae are distributed all over the world, although they preferred warm seas. They died out at the end of the Jurassic. As a rule, their shells are easily distinguishable from those of other ammonite groups, chiefly because of their shape and their bi- or trifurcate ribbing.

The size of the shells of the best known Upper Jurassic genus, *Perisphinctes,* ranges from large to huge. The whorls are almost square in cross section. The inner whorls wear dense ribbing, which, on the last whorl, changes to a short segment with thick, rough ribs. Branching occurs in approximately the middle of the whorl sides or on the ventral lateral shoulder. *P. plicatilis* is a common index fossil for part of the Oxfordian stage.

Ataxioceras polyplocum (REINECKE)

Order: Ammonitida
Family: Perisphinctidae

The Upper Jurassic genus *Ataxioceras,* described in various places in Europe, Asia and Africa, is related to *Perisphinctes.* Its shells usually have laterally compressed whorls and the umbilicus is generally narrower than in the preceding genus. The ribs may actually fork twice in succession — once on the whorl sides and again at the ventrolateral shoulder. One important character for classification are the large irregular constrictions on the shell, which are also pronounced on internal moulds (fig. 4).

1. *Parkinsonia parkinsoni,* * Middle Jurassic (Bajocian), Bobtingen, West Germany. A core, diameter 93 mm. The longitudinal crest on the side of the last preserved whorl is a remnant of the sloping part of the living chamber.

2. *Ataxioceras polyplocum,* Upper Jurassic (Kimmeridgian), locality unknown. A core, diameter 74 mm. Characteristic constrictions can be clearly seen on the last whorl.

3. *Perisphinctes plicatilis,* Upper Jurassic (Oxfordian), Tenczynek near Cracow, Poland. A core, diameter 80 mm. The bifurcately branched ribs are clearly visible.

4. *Ataxioceras* sp., the aperture of the shell.

 **Mollusca**

Peltoceras athleta (PHILLIPS)

Order: Ammonitida
Family: Aspidoceratidae

The complicated pattern of the sutures on ammonite shells has long been a source of speculation as to their functional significance. Most specialists are agreed that the undulating septa and complex sutures were a form of protection against implosion, i.e. they prevented the shells from bursting inwards as a result of hydrostatic pressure. The model for this hypothesis is a mechanical structure capable of withstanding high pressure with the use of a minimum amount of material, while reinforcing the structure (shell) at every point. The undulating edge of the septa provided the best support for the interseptal parts of the walls and reinforced the septum itself. The increase in the complexity of the sutures during ontogeny is a response to relatively slower growth of the shell wall in thickness. The diversity of the course of the sutures was influenced mainly by genetic factors. Numerous mutations in the various evolutionary branches lead to manifold constructional solutions to the problem of strength. The depth at which the various species of ammonites could live thus depended on the shape, internal structure and sculpture of the shells.

The fauna in warm Tethys seas was more diverse than in the seas of colder zones. Among their characteristic elements were the peltoceratids, which also belong to the superfamily Perisphinctaceae. Their

1, 3. *Peltoceras athleta,** Middle Jurassic (Callovian), Villers-sur-Mer, France. 1 – a pyritized core with distinct sutures, diameter 135 mm. A striking difference in sculpture differentiates two successive growth stages. 3 – a posterior view.

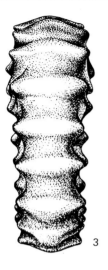

3

evolute shells and prominent sculpture are rather evidence of a benthic mode of life. From the types of sediments in which they are found, it is evident that they lived at various depths, but probably not deeper than 500 metres.

The Middle Jurassic genus *Peltoceras* is distributed over the whole of the globe.The inner whorls of the shells are typically perisphinctoid, with sharp ribbing, while the outer whorls carry rows of tubercles formed on rough, simple ribs. The row of tubercles closer to the outer side of the whorls appeared sooner during ontogeny than the inner row. Over the venter (fig. 3), the tubercles are interconnected by two or three ribs. The macroconches usually carry tubercles and have a simple aperture; the microconches have no tubercles and the aperture tapers off into long lappets. *P. athleta* is an important zonal species.

Euaspidoceras perarmatum (SOWERBY)

Order: Ammonitida
Family: Aspidoceratidae

The stratigraphic range of the almost cosmpolitan genus *Euaspidoceras* goes beyond the limits of the Middle and Upper Jurassic. As distinct from typical perisphinctids, it lacks the 'perisphinctoid' stage with bifurcate ribs. The shells have a ribbed surface, with a row of tubercles beside the umbilicus and along the borderline between the sides and the outer side of the whorl. In young shells, ribs were interpolated between the tubercles, but as the shell grew they were lost.

2. *Euaspidoceras perarmatum,** Upper Jurassic (Oxfordian), Villers-sur-Mer, France. A preserved shell showing the typical sculpture of the species. Shell diameter 60 mm.

Spiroceras bifurcati QUENSTEDT

Order: Ammonitida
Family: Spiroceratidae

A number of Jurassic ammonites, including the members of the family Spiroceratidae, may have lived close to the sea floor. Their shells resemble those of certain Cretaceous ammonites with unusual types of shells, which are now included in the order Ancyloceratida, but the ontogenetic development of the sutures in the two groups was different and shows that they occupy independent positions.

Spiroceras is an important Middle Jurassic genus especially widespread in Europe. A detailed morphological study of the shells, based chiefly on rich material from the species *S. orbignyi,* indicates that they are very variable. In most cases the shell has lost its bilateral symmetry, is very variably sculptured and has asymmetrical sutures. Although the wide geographical distribution of the various species of the genus *Spiroceras* is apparently at variance with their sessile benthic mode of life, it can be attributed to the spread of young by the currents or by active swimming.

Spiroceras has a thickly ribbed shell. The ribs are oriented almost perpendicularly to the axis of the shell and are not branched. On the venter they are interrupted by a strip of smooth shell. Very often there are two rows of tubercles on them — one on the side and the other on the edge of the venter.

Protetragonites quadrisulcatus (D'ORBIGNY)

Order: Lytoceratida
Family: Protetragonitidae

The ammonoids of the order Lytoceratida also belong to the characteristic faunal elements of the Tethys sea. They appeared for the first time in the Upper Triassic. Typical lytoceratids have an evolute shell whose whorls increase relatively in height. On their surface they have straight

1. *Spiroceras bifurcati,** Middle Jurassic (Bajocian), Enningen, West Germany. Shell diameter 35 mm. The way the shells of this genus are coiled is reminiscent of the phylogenetically oldest ammonoids.

2. *Phylloceras bizonatum,* Upper Cretaceous (Coniacian), Lenešice, Czechoslovakia. An almost complete limonitized core, diameter 25 mm.

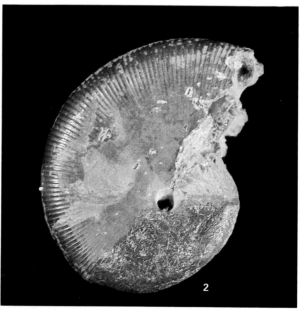

3. *Protetragonites quadrisulca-tus,** Upper Jurassic (Tithonian), Štramberk, Czechoslovakia. The markedly evolute shell is periodically constricted. Shell diameter 66 mm.

or crinkled ridges combined with ribs and constrictions, etc. The sutures are very complex. The family Protetragonitidae have evolute shells with a circular cross section.

Individuals of the genus *Protetragonites* occurring in European Upper Jurassic to Lower Cretaceous sediments have widely spaced straight or slightly undulating constrictions on their shells.

Phylloceras bizonatum FRITSCH

Order: Phylloceratida
Family: Phylloceratidae

The members of the Phylloceratidae family have almost cosmopolitan distribution and boreal regions are the only ones they did not inhabit. Morphologically they do not differ significantly from their Triassic ancestors, but their sutures are very complicated. Like lytoceratids, they were adapted for life at depths of around 600 metres.

The ammonoids of the genus *Phylloceras* s. l. are characterized by highly involute shells with a narrow umbilicus. The fine radial ribs on their surface do not show up on internal moulds.

Laevaptychus

The single or duplicate chitinous or calcareous plates generally termed aptychi are an interesting ammonite structure. As a rule they occur separately from the shells and only on rare occasions have they been found inside the living chamber. In places — usually at great depths — they accumulated in large quantities on the sea bed to form aptychus limestones. From their shape and from the sculpture of their inner and outer surface, several basic morphological types have been differentiated. Since in many cases it is not clear to which ammonite species a given aptychus belongs, they have been named independently of the Linnaean system of nomenclature.

Until quite recently, aptychi were regarded as the opercula of ammonites and hardly anybody doubted the correctness of this interpretation. The latest studies have shown, however, that aptychi are actually part of a special jaw-like apparatus.

The majority of ammonites which lived before the beginning of the Jurassic period had beak-like jaws similar to those of recent dibranchiate cephalopods belonging to the subclass Coleoidea. Simple chitinous plates (anaptychi) representing lower jaws were found for the first time in Upper Devonian goniatites and are also found among psiloceratids,

1, 4. *Laevaptychus,* Upper Jurassic (Tithonian), Solnhofen, West Germany. Width 46 mm. 1 — view of inner surface. Ammonoid aptychi can be very thick. 4 — A reconstruction of the jaws.

2. *Lamellaptychus,* Upper Jurassic (Tithonian), Solnhofen, West Germany. Width 11 mm. The outer aspect of aptychi of this genus have a distinctive lamellar sculpture.

3. *Lamellaptychus* inside the living chamber of an ammonoid of the genus *Neochetoceras* from the same locality. Shell diameter 28 mm.

eoderoceratids and lytoceratids. Two accessory calcareous platelets — aptychi — were sometimes formed on the sides of the anaptychus. They evolved during the Lower Jurassic and can be encountered up to the end of the Cretaceous. Upper jaws (fig. 4) corresponding to most anaptychi and aptychi (which together form the lower jaw), have likewise been found. Some ammonites (such as hoplitids and acanthoceratids) were evidently without aptychi. A further type of jaw, reminiscent of the nautiloid jaw with a calcite tip (a rhynchaptychus), has also been discovered, in Cretaceous lytoceratids. To crush their food more finely, ammonites employed their band-like tongue (radula).

In the individual groups of ammonites we come across different types of aptychi. Aspidoceratids had wide, massive laevaptychi with a bulging, porous surface and with growth lines on the concave surface.

Lamellaptychus   Aptychi

Another important and locally very abundant type of ammonoid lower jaw — *Lamellaptychus* — comes from Middle Jurassic to Lower Cretaceous deposits. These narrow, convex platelets have pronounced and variously curving folds on their internal surface; they belong to haploceratids and phylloceratids. Some of the most famous finds come from Solnhofen in Bavaria, where they more than once lay inside the animal's living chamber.

Neocomites neocomiensis (D'ORBIGNY)

Order: Ammonitida
Family: Berriaselidae

The Cretaceous is the time of the last stage in the evolution of the ammonoids. It is characterized chiefly by the morphologically very diverse ancyloceratids, hoplitids, desmoceratids and acanthoceratids. In the lowest Cretaceous, perisphinctids still abounded. The cosmopolitan family Berriaselidae belong to the same superfamily.

The genus *Neocomites* has involute, flat-sided shells whose whorls have a flattened outer side and a sharp umbilical edge. The S-shaped ribs slant from the edges of the umbilicus towards the aperture; they are branched on the poorly developed umbilical tubercles. On the whorl sides the ribs often branch again, or new ribs are interpolated between them. Elongate, obliquely orientated tubercles are formed on the sides of the flat outer side of the whorls.

Deshayesites forbesi CASEY

Order: Ancyloceratida
Family: Deshayesitidae

Outwardly, the shells of cephalopods of the family Deshayesitidae resemble hoplitids, but a detailed study of the ontogenetic development of the sutures showed that the similar shapes of the two groups of shells were merely a convergent character (i.e. their similarity was determined ecologically and not genetically) and that deshayesitids belonged to

1, 2. *Neocomites neocomiensis,* * Lower Cretaceous (Neocomian), Eyroles, France. Two phragmocones preserved as cores with a limonitized surface, diameter 20 and 22 mm. The typical course of the sutures can be seen on the right (2).

3. *Deshayesites forbesi,* Lower Cretaceous (Aptian), Varfy, France. Shell diameter 25 mm. The course of the sutures is clearly discernible on the limonite phragmocone.

Ancyloceratida. The cephalopods of this family have typical laterally compressed shells with a relatively high aperture and with branched or alternating long and short ribs which completely cross the venter. In later genera whose whorls have a flat venter, the ribs may be interrupted.

The members of the genus *Deshayesites* tend to have evolute shells and beside the edge of the umbilicus the ribs are sometimes higher. Apart from an incidence in Europe and America, this Lower Cretaceous genus is also known in Australia.

Cr

6

Order: Ammonitida
Hysteroceras varicosum (SOWERBY)   Family: Brancoceratidae

Another large ammonite superfamily — Acanthocerataceae — appeared at the end of the Lower Cretaceous. Its very diverse shells are usually surmounted by rough ribs with a tendency to form nodes. Some genera are cosmopolitan, such as *Hysteroceras,* which represents a phylogenetically less advanced ammonite branch.

The members of the genus *Hysteroceras* usually have small evolute shells whose whorls are almost square in cross section. Young whorls have a ridge on their outer surface. The ribs are either forked, or are alternatingly long and short, with umbilical nodes, and in some species there are also tubercles along the borderline to the outer aspect of the whorls.

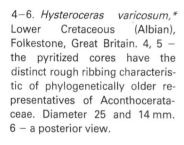

4–6. *Hysteroceras varicosum,** Lower Cretaceous (Albian), Folkestone, Great Britain. 4, 5 — the pyritized cores have the distinct rough ribbing characteristic of phylogenetically older representatives of Aconthocerataceae. Diameter 25 and 14 mm. 6 — a posterior view.

Euhoplites lautus (SOWERBY)

Order: Ammonitida
Family: Hoplitidae

Hoplitids appeared and flourished during the Lower Cretaceous. With the onset of the Cenomanian they rapidly declined, but they did not actually become extinct until the end of the Mesozoic era, along with the other groups of ammonites. The family Hoplitidae is characteristic chiefly of the Middle Albian in the northern hemisphere.

The genus *Euhoplites*, which has been found in Lower Cretaceous deposits in Greenland, as well as in Europe, has evolute shells whose whorls have a flat or concave venter. Above the siphuncle there is a deep groove. S-shaped ribs run between the umbilical nodes and the elongate tubercles on the outer side of the shell.

Anahoplites splendens (SOWERBY)

Order: Ammonitida
Family: Hoplitidae

The Lower Cretaceous genus *Anahoplites* is known in many parts of Europe and Asia. The shells are narrowly discoid and the sides and outer side of the whorls are flattened (fig. 5). The whorls rapidly increase in height; they markedly overlap one another. The densely distributed ribs,

5

1. *Euhoplites lautus*, Lower Cretaceous (Albian), Folkestone, Great Britain. Shell diameter 22 and 17 mm. The chalky surface of the shells shows one of the main diagnostic characters of hoplitids — the umbilical nodes with branching ribs issuing from them.

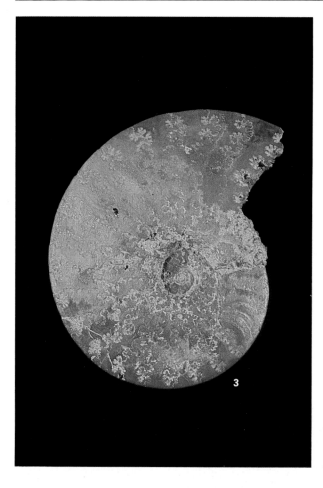

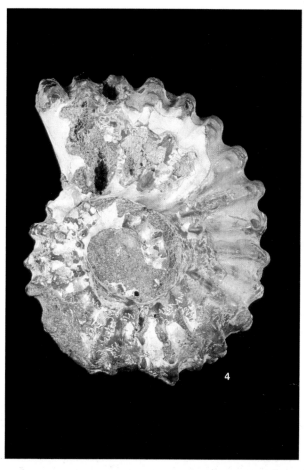

which are slightly S-shaped on the sides, issue in small bunches from indistinct umbilical nodes and are often extremely attenuated. Dense flattish tubercles can also usually be seen on the venter.

Proplacenticeras orbignyanum (GEINITZ)

Order: Ammonitida
Family: Placenticeratidae

The members of the family Placenticeratidae, which is related to the hoplitids, have discoid shells whose whorls have a narrow venter and are usually very poorly sculptured. They appeared at the end of the Lower Cretaceous and died out at the very end of the Cretaceous. They include the Upper Cretaceous genus *Proplacenticeras,* which is known in central and western Europe, Asia and North America.

Douvilleiceras mammilatum (SCHLOTHEIM)

Order: Ancyloceratida
Family: Douvilleiceratidae

The shells of these cephalopods are rounded, dorsoventrally compressed or polygonal in cross section. The ribs at first have pronounced umbilical nodes and ventrolaterally situated tubercles. A row of further tubercles is subsequently formed on the striking rounded ribs on the sides, but with growth of the shell they gradually disappear. *D. mammilatum* is an important zonal species for the Lower Albian.

2, 5. *Anahoplites splendens,** Lower Cretaceous (Albian), Folkestone, Great Britain. The original shell was partly dissolved during fossilization, leaving only remains in the form of the nacreous layer. Shell diameter 37 mm. 5 – a frontal view.

3. *Proplacenticeras orbignyanum,* Upper Cretaceous (Coniacian), Březno, Czechoslovakia. A limonitized core of a phragmocone, clearly showing the fine serration of the sutural saddles and lobes. Diameter 53 mm.

4. *Douvilleiceras mammilatum,** Lower Cretaceous (Albian), Machéromenit, France. A core with remains of the nacreous layer, diameter 63 mm. The wide, rounded ribs with their tubercles are a very striking diagnostic character.

Mollusca

Hamites rotundatus SOWERBY

Order: Ancyloceratida
Family: Hamitidae

The morphological and sculptural diversity of the shells of Mesozoic ammonoids is tremendous. Palaeontologists have always been fascinated by the curious (heteromorphous) forms of some of them (especially Cretaceous species). The unusual, bizarre shapes of these shells are a reflection of ecological adaptation to a given (evidently benthic) mode of life rather than a sign of degeneration of the group. Their stratigraphic range shows that Ancyloceratida, to which most of these ammonoids belong, were a successful order, both ecologically and phylogenetically.

In the initial phases of growth, hamitid shells usually had the form of an open spiral. In older individuals, the spiral was followed by two or three straight or curved segments joined together by a 'knee' bend.

Hamites species are found in Cretaceous deposits over the most of the globe. The whorls are circular or dorsoventrally compressed in cross section. Their surface is ornamented with numerous straight ribs which continue to the venter but are usually interrupted on the dorsal side of the whorls.

1. *Hamites rotundatus,* Lower Cretaceous (Albian), Great Britain. Length of core fragments 70 and 40 mm. Ammonoids with an unwontedly shaped (heteromorphous) shell are typical of the Cretaceous.

2. *Baculites gaudini,* Lower Cretaceous (Albian), Cambridge, Great Britain. Length of core fragments 50 and 60 mm. The spirally coiled parts of baculitid shells were very small, while the straight part attained lengths of up to 2 m.

288

3. *Anahamulina* sp., Lower Cretaceous (Neocomian), Silesia, Czechoslovakia. An incomplete core (the initial parts of the shell are missing) mildly compressed during fossilization in soft marl sediment. Length 105 mm. This genus lacked the coiled young whorls.

Baculites gaudini PICTET AND CAMPICHE

Order: Ancyloceratida
Family: Baculitidae

Baculitids are related to hamitids. Their shells consist of one or two small coils followed by a long, straight or slightly curving part. The whorls may be circular, oval, pear-shaped or even sharp-cornered in cross section. Lower Cretaceous species are small, but shells up to 2 metres long are known from the end of the Upper Cretaceous. Baculitids are often found in vast quantities and it is therefore concluded that they lived in colonies on the sea bed. The shape of their shells indicates that they lived in a more or less vertical position.

Anahamulina sp.

Order: Ancyloceratida
Family: Baculitidae

The genus *Anahamulina* occurs in Lower Cretaceous sediments in Europe and North America. The shell is composed of two parallel arms joined together by a bend. Constrictions can often be seen at the site of the bend. The surface of the shell is densely covered with fine ribs, which are orientated obliquely to the axis of the shell on the first (longer) arm and roughly perpendicularly to it on the shorter arm. At present little is known of the phylogenetic relations of this genus to other genera.

289

 **Mollusca**

Macroscaphites yvani Puzos

Order: Ancyloceratida
Family: Macroscaphitidae

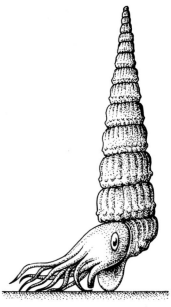

Macroscaphitidae are an evolutionally important group of heteromorph Lower Cretaceous ammonoids. Their shells, at first evolute, subsequently uncoiled. The genus *Macroscaphites* is regarded as the starting point of numerous further groups of Cretaceous ammonoids in which the spiral part of the shell was minimal or had disappeared completely.

The shell of the members of the genus *Macroscaphites,* which is known in different parts of Europe, Africa and Asia, is first of all coiled in a tight spiral. This is followed by a long, slightly curving arm, which recurves again before reaching the aperture. The umbilicus is wide and the whorls are elliptical in cross section. The fine, dense ribs on the coiled part of the shell lead radially to the venter without interruption; those on the non-coiled part of the shell run obliquely to its axis.

Turrilites costatus Meek

Order: Ancyloceratida
Family: Turrilitidae

4

Shells coiled in a three-dimensional (helicoidal) spiral are rather rare among ammonoids. The cosmopolitan family Turrilitidae is one of the exceptions. The shells of the members of this family have a remarkable

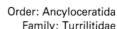

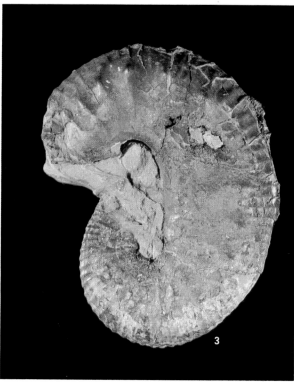

1. *Macroscaphites yvani,** Lower Cretaceous (Neocomian), Great Britain. An almost complete core, diameter of the coiled part of the shell 45 mm. With reference to the position of its centre of gravity, it is highly probable that the shell was held with the coiled part upwards during the animal's lifetime.

2. *Turrilites costatus,** Upper Cretaceous (Cenomanian), Rouen, France. Fragment of a core, height of spiral 57 mm. In shape there is a resemblance to a gastropod. This species was an important component of the benthos of Upper Cretaceous seas.

3. *Scaphites lamberti,* Upper Cretaceous (Senonian), Březno near Louny, Czechoslovakia. A limonite core, length 38 mm.

4. *Turrilites* sp., a reconstruction of a living individual.

internal structure. The siphuncle connecting the individual chambers shifted during growth to the upper margin of the whorls — a position which evidently enabled the animal to keep a larger amount of fluid inside the phragmocone and thus facilitated adaptation to life on the sea bed.

The genus *Turrilites* has tightly coiled shells with a sharply pointed apex (fig. 4). The whorls are almost square in cross section. The surface is ornamented with wide transverse ribs with a rounded profile and three or four rows of tubercles. The sutures are asymmetrical, owing to three-dimensional coiling of the shell. Considering their presumably sessile mode of life, it is surprising that some species spread all over the globe. *T. costatus* is a characteristic Cenomanian fossil.

Scaphites lamberti GROSSOUVRE

Order: Ancyloceratida
Family: Scaphitidae

Scaphitid shells are usually highly involute in the initial phases of growth, but in older individuals they develop a long arm of variable length with a hooked end.

The genus *Scaphites* is distributed over practically the entire globe, in sediments dating from the end of the Lower Cretaceous through most of the Upper Cretaceous. The shells have a relatively short hook-like arm. On the coiled part there are branched or interpolated ribs, umbilical nodes and tubercles situated ventrolaterally. The large living chamber is evidence that the shell was held in a vertical position during the animal's lifetime, with the hooked arm underneath. The animal was probably not capable of much sideways movement.

291

Schloenbachia varians (Sowerby)

Order: Ammonitida
Family: Schloenbachiidae

Some hoplitids still flourished at the beginning of the Upper Cretaceous. One of the oldest families still extant at the end of the Lower Cretaceous were Schloenbachiidae. The members of the genus *Schloenbachia* lived mainly in cold waters of the northern hemisphere, like their ancestors before them.

The genus *Schloenbachia* is a heterogeneous group of ammonites with different types of shells, from involute and flat-sided to evolute with highly swollen whorls. Their characteristic feature is a keel of varying thickness on the venter (fig. 4). Where ribs are discernible, they are curved and at the ends, where they reach the venter, they widen. *Schloenbachia* is the commonest genus of the boreal Cenomanian and in the Anglo-Paris basin it is usually to be found in greater numbers than other ammonites.

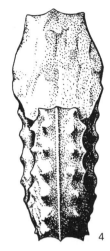

1, 4. *Schloenbachia varians,* * Upper Cretaceous (Cenomanian), Isle of Wight, Great Britain. 1 — a core, diameter 68 mm. 4 — a frontal view.

2. *Mantelliceras mantelli,* * Upper Cretaceous (Cenomanian), Rouen, France. A core, diameter 59 mm. A stratigraphically important Cenomanian species. The spiral line on the side of the shell was left by the following whorl, which was broken off.

3. *Mammites nodosoides,** Upper Cretaceous (Turonian), Prague-Bílá Hora, Czechoslovakia. A core, diameter 160 mm. The shells have a diameter of up to 30 cm.

5. *Mammites* sp., detail of the aperture.

| *Mantelliceras mantelli* (SOWERBY) | Order: Ammonitida
Family: Acanthoceratidae |

The superfamily Acanthocerataceae attained its peak during the Upper Cretaceous. The homonymous family was one of the main components of ammonite assemblages living in Upper Cretaceous seas all over the world; *Mantelliceras* is one of its genera. The shells have only mildly overlapping whorls, wide, slightly curving ribs and usually a flat venter bordered by a row of tubercles. Tubercles are often also formed on the sides and the umbilical shoulders, where they are generally especially distinct. One of the Cenomanian ammonoid zones is named after this species.

| *Mammites nodosoides* (SCHLOTHEIM) | Order: Ammonitida
Family: Acanthoceratidae |

The younger – Turonian – and almost cosmopolitan genus *Mammites* belongs to the same family as the preceding genus. It has evolute shells whose whorls are roughly square or trapezoid in cross section. The venter is usually flattened or concave. The sculpture is striking – blunt umbilical nodes and two rows of prominent tubercles along the venter; in later phases of growth, the paired ventrolateral tubercles joined together to form sharply projecting horns (fig. 5). The broad, widely spaced ribs are only faintly discernible. *M. nodosoides* is a Turonian zonal ammonite.

 **Mollusca**

Acanthoceras rhotomagense (DEFRANCE)

Order: Ammonitida
Family: Acanthoceratidae

The very widespread genus *Acanthoceras* comes from Upper Creta-ceous deposits. The shells have only slightly overlapping whorls with a roughly square cross section. Their dominant feature are seven rows of tubercles round the entire periphery of the whorl (fig. 4). The umbilical row is closest to the coiling axis of the shell; the next two rows are situated ventrolaterally. In old individuals the tubercles on the venter (in the symmetry plane) disappeared and the ventrolateral pair fused to form large horns. As the shell grew, the ribs became less distinct. The relatively wide umbilicus and the conspicuous surface sculpture are unequivocal evidence that acanthoceratids were incapable of fast movement.

Romaniceras ornatissimum (STOLICZKA)

Order: Ammonitida
Family: Acanthoceratidae

The genus *Romaniceras,* which occurs in Cenomanian and Turonian shallow-water sediments in Europe, Africa and Asia, is related to *Acanthoceras.* Its evolute whorls, which are rounded or oval in cross section, are characterized by nine to eleven rows of tubercles, all of the same size, distributed over the periphery of the whorl. The straight, wide ribs are of unequal lengths and are dominated by the tubercles.

1, 4. *Acanthoceras rhotoma-gense,** Upper Cretaceous (Ceno-manian), Saint André, France. A core, diameter 165 mm. This is a prolific, morphologically striking species and one of the strati-graphic zones of the Upper Cenomanian is named after it. 4 – a posterior view.

2. *Romaniceras ornatissimum,* Upper Cretaceous (Turonian), Cítov, Czechoslovakia. A poorly preserved core, diameter 78 mm. The shells have indistinct ribs and are studded with far more tuber-cles than *Acanthoceras* shells.

3. *Lewesiceras sharpei,** Upper Cretaceous (Coniacian), Mladá Boleslav, Czechoslovakia. A core, diameter 210 mm. One of the largest known ammonite species.

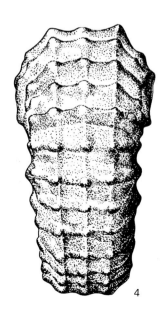

Lewesiceras sharpei (SPATH)

Order: Ammonitida
Family: Pachydiscidae

We cannot leave the Upper Cretaceous ammonites without mentioning the superfamily Desmocerataceae, which comprises the largest known ammonites ever to have existed (the shell of *Parapuzosia seppenradensis* was over 2.5 metres in diameter!).

Pachydiscids, which appeared towards the end of the Lower Cretaceous and reached the peak of their development towards the end of the Upper Cretaceous, were likewise very large. Their shells are moderately involute to evolute, with thick, unbroken ribbing on the outer side of the whorl and often with pronounced tubercles, at least beside the umbilicus.

The Turonian genus *Lewesiceras,* known in Europe, North America, southern Asia and northern Africa, was the ancestor of numerous phylogenetically younger genera. The ribs are slightly S-shaped and on the venter they arch towards the aperture. The inner whorls have shallow constrictions and prominent umbilical nodes, which, in the later whorls, flatten out and merge with the ribs. Interpolated between the main rounded ribs are shorter ribs which do not reach the umbilicus.

295

 **Mollusca**

Collignoniceras woollgari (MANTELL)

Order: Ammonitida
Family: Collignoniceratidae

The question of why a group as ecologically and evolutionally successful as the ammonoids died out at the boundary between the Mesozoic and the Cainozoic eras, without leaving a trace, has never been satisfactorily answered. The tremendous morphological diversity of their shells testified that ammonites lived under the most diverse ecological conditions. The young, which were hatched from tiny eggs, lived like plankton, at least for a time, and subsisted on various micro-organisms. Views on the way ammonites lived in subsequent phases of growth are at variance. According to some specialists, ammonites were mostly benthic animals occurring mainly at depths of 50 to 200 metres and leading a similar existence to gastropods which lived on the substratum. Their jaws were able to collect small and slow aquatic organisms living near the bottom, such as Foraminifera, Ostracoda, small crustaceans (Crustacea), lampshells (Brachiopoda), corals (Anthozoa) and moss animals (Bryozoa), and even dead organisms, as seen from stomach contents which have been preserved. Other scientists demonstrate that the construction of ammonites' shells allowed considerable changes of depth, as in the case of the recent *Nautilus,* for instance. Ammonites are regarded as pelagic animals living in the top 1,000 metres of the oceans, but calculations of the resistance of their shells to hydrostatic pressure

1. *Collignoniceras woollgari,* * Upper Cretaceous (Turonian), Prague-Bílá Hora, Czechoslovakia. A core, diameter 210 mm. The spread of this species is no doubt associated with the biggest floods (transgression) of the Cretaceous period.

2. *Peroniceras tricarinatum,* Upper Cretaceous (Coniacian), Vrbičany, Czechoslovakia. A core, diameter 340 mm. The highly evolute shell has three pronounced, sharp ridges on the outer surface of the whorl.

show that the 1,000 metres' limit is probably exaggerated. There is no doubt that ammonites were incomparably poorer swimmers than recent cuttle-fish or squids, for example. Their main enemies were apparetly marine saurians, fish, crustaceans and other cephalopods.

The family Collignoniceratidae (in the superfamily Acanthocerataceae) is distributed all over the world. The shells of the Turonian genus *Collignoniceras* are involute to evolute and sometimes very bulky. The oblique ribs oriented towards the aperture carry umbilical nodes, tubercles on the edge of the venter and siphonal nodes (in the middle of the venter). As the shell grew, the umbilical nodes migrated to the outer side of the whorl, so that they sometimes united with the ventrolateral tubercles to form massive horns. *C. woollgari* is a zonal fossil for the Upper Turonian.

Peroniceras tricarinatum (D'ORBIGNY)

Order: Ammonitida
Family: Collignoniceratidae

The genera *Peroniceras* and *Collignoniceras* are related. The former is characterized by an evolute shell and whorls with an oval, trapezoid or square cross section. The short, straight ribs with a rounded profile issue from umbilical nodes and terminate on conical tubercles at the edge of the venter; in some species lateral tubercles were also formed. This genus − like the preceding one − occurs in Upper Cretaceous deposits over practically the whole of the globe.

Megateuthis ellipticus (MILLER)

Order: Belemnitida
Family: Belemnitidae

With the exception of the Nautilus, all extant cephalopods (cuttle fish – Sepiida, squids – Teuthida, octopuses – Octopoda) belong to the Dibranchiata (to the subclass Coleoidea). They have more or less reduced internal shells, i.e. covered with soft tissue. The high degree of organization of their body, and especially of their nervous system and the closely associated sensory organs (e.g. the perfection of their eyes), allows cephalopods to be compared with vertebrates. Cephalopods include the biggest invertebrate species ever to have existed. The total length of recent giant squids, including the tentacles, can be as much as 18 to 22 metres. Some cephalopods are extremely mobile. With powerful contractions of their mantle cavity they expel water from the muscular funnel of their hyponome and this natural jet propulsion carries them forward, rear end first, at up to 70 km an hour.

The oldest – and the palaeontologically and stratigraphically most important – dibranchiate order are the belemnitids (order Belemnitida), which probably evolved from bactritids and broke away from them during the later Palaeozoic era. Typical belemnitids are known from the Jurassic and the Cretaceous; the entire group died out in the Eocene. In belemnitids the living chamber is reduced and all that remains is a curved, spoon-like plate (the proostracum) on the dorsal side of the body. The proostracum is followed by the phragmocone, which is more or less embedded in the massive rostrum. The cylindrical, fusiform or digitiform rostra are the most frequently found parts of belemnitid shells. The conical cavity containing the phragmocone is called the alveolus. The tip (apex) of the rostrum is usually pointed. Longitudinal sections of the rostrum show its lamellar structure. In cross section it can be seen to be composed of fibrous calcite (carbonate of lime) crystals which splay out from the longitudinal axial line. Originally the rostra were highly porous and contained a large amount of organic matter.

The rostra of belemnitids of the Jurassic genus *Megateuthis* are 50 to 60 cm long. The posterior (apical) end is grooved, with one ventral and usually two pairs of dorsolateral furrows. The alveolus accounts for one quarter of the length of the rostrum. The animals' reconstructed length is estimated at 3 metres. These belemnitids are known from various parts of Europe and Asia.

Belemnites paxillosus (SCHLOTHEIM)

Order: Belemnitida
Family: Belemnitidae

The cephalopods of this genus are a common component of Lower Jurassic sediments in Europe, Asia and South America. The rostra are more or less cylindrical and taper off to a point. The alveolus takes up roughly two fifths of the length of the rostrum. Dorsolateral grooves are present at the apex.

1, 4, 5. *Megateuthis ellipticus,* Middle Jurassic (Bajocian), Heildesheim, Hanover, West Germany. Length of rostrum about 250 mm (1). Cross section of rostrum (4). A rostrum with a distinctly lamellar structure reminiscent of the annual rings of trees. Rohberg, West Germany. Length 50 mm. Inside the rostrum the phragmocone is divided into chambers (5). Gündershofen, West Germany. Length 80 mm.

2, 3. *Belemnites paxillosus,* Lower Jurassic (Pliensbachian-Toarkian), Moessingen, West Germany. Length 130 and 60 mm; an oyster has settled on the larger rostrum (3). After the animal died, the rostrum lying on the soft sea bed often acted as a firm base for sessile benthic animals.

Mollusca

Salpingoteuthis acuarius (QUENSTEDT)

Order: Belemnitida
Family: Belemnitidae

5

In some belemnitids, the rear end of the rostrum is produced to a cylindrical structure known as an epirostrum. The epirostrum differs from the rostrum mainly as regards its internal structure and the less regular organization of the crystals. In the members of the genus *Salpingoteuthis,* which occur in Lower to Middle Jurassic deposits in Europe and Asia, the epirostrum is many times longer than the rostrum. The rostrum, together with the epirostrum, is very long (20 to 30 cm) and narrow and widens gradually. A ventral furrow and two fine dorsolateral grooves can be seen at the tip. The alveolus is short. At their wider end the rostra sometimes spread out funnel-wise.

Dactyloteuthis irregularis (SCHLOTHEIM)

Order: Belemnitida
Family: Belemnitidae

The scientific classification of belemnitids at genus and species level is based primarily on the general shape of the rostra, the shape of their cross section, the position and size of the furrows often present on their surface, the character of the surface and the depth and position of the alveolus.

Some species of the Lower Jurassic genus *Dactyloteuthis,* whose distribution is similar to that of the preceding species, have a very striking digitiform rostrum.

Hibolites hastatus (BLAINVILLE)

Order: Belemnitida
Family: Belemnopsidae

The tentacles of fossil (and present-day) cephalopods were armed with numerous suckers or hooks. From Solnhofen Upper Jurassic lithographic limestones we possess the remains of arms set with large numbers of hooks, which were described under the generic name *Acanthoteuthis* (fig. 5). It was found out that the arms actually belonged to members of the genus *Hibolites,* which occur in Middle and Upper Jurassic deposits in Europe, Asia, North America and Indonesia. The rostra measure up to 20 cm and taper off to an apex lying in the axis of the rostrum. The short alveolus reaches barely one quarter of the way along the rostrum. A distinct furrow on the ventral aspect leads from the anterior margin to the middle of the rostrum. In cross section the anterior part of the rostrum is dorsoventrally compressed, while near the apex it is circular.

Duvalia dilatata BLAINVILLE

Order: Belemnitida
Family: Duvaliidae

The genus *Duvalia* stretches from the Middle Jurassic to the Lower Cretaceous and is known in Europe, Asia, Africa and Indonesia. Its members have laterally highly flattened rostra; the ventral part of the rostrum is usually very wide and bulges more than the dorsal part. The short, pointed apex lies closer to the dorsal side. The alveolus is short.

1. *Salpingoteuthis acuarius,** Lower Jurassic (Toarkian), Holzmaden, West Germany. Length of rostrum plus epirostrum 190 mm. This species is characterized by very long, thin rostra.

2. *Duvalia dilatata,* Lower Cretaceous (Neocomian), West Germany. Length of rostra 54 and 60 mm. This species differs from other belemnitids in respect of its extremely flat-sided rostrum.

3. *Dactyloteuthis irregularis,** Lower Jurassic (Toarkian), Trimeizel, West Germany. Length of rostrum 72 mm. The digitiform rostrum is unusual among belemnitids.

4. *Hibolites hastatus,** Middle Jurassic (Callovian), Czenstochowa, Poland. Length of rostra 110 and 100 mm.

5. *Hibolites* sp., imprints of hooks on arms, described as *Acanthoteuthis.*

Neohibolites minimus (MILLER)

Order: Belemnitida
Family: Belemnopsidae

The stratigraphic range of the cosmopolitan genus *Neohibolites* stretches from the Lower Cretaceous (Aptian) to the beginning of the Upper Cretaceous (Cenomanian). Neohibolite rostra are small, slightly fusiform and roughly rounded in cross section. The ventral groove is short. The anterior part of the rostrum has seldom been preserved, as the walls are not sufficiently calcareous. The alveolus has sometimes been secondarily destroyed from within, owing to an increase in its original volume and formation of a 'pseudoalveolus'.

Actinocamax plenus (BLAINVILLE)

Order: Belemnitida
Family: Belemnitellidae

The relationships of belemnitids to other dibranchiate cephalopods have not been altogether elucidated, but we know of a series of morphologically intermediate types between belemnitids and cuttlefish in Tertiary deposits. Belemnitids evidently lived on much the same diet as present-day squids, i.e. chiefly on crustaceans, molluscs and fish. On the other hand, belemnitids themselves are known chiefly from the contents of the stomach of marine saurians and certain fishes. Practically the entire order died out at the end of the Cretaceous; the only family to survive the change from the Mesozoic to the Cainozoic era died out at the end of the Eocene. From the Upper Cretaceous, however, we know a series of stratigraphically important genera and species.
The belemnitids of the genus *Actinocamax,* which is widely distributed over the northern hemisphere, have smallish cylindrical or fusiform rostra with a roughly circular cross section. Anteriorly there are indistinct dorsolateral grooves and on the ventral side there is a short alveolar fissure. The alveolus is short and its walls evidently contained too little carbonate of lime. Destruction of the walls of the alveolus gave the end of the anterior part of the rostrum a conical shape.

Gonioteuthis granulata (BLAINVILLE)

Order: Belemnitida
Family: Belemnitellidae

The belemnitids of the European genus *Gonioteuthis* differ from those of the preceding genus in respect of their striking pseudoalveolus and short ventral fissure. The rounded apex tapers off into a short process. One very interesting feature of this and certain other late Cretaceous belemnitids are the vascular imprints on the sides and ventral surface of the rostra.

Belemnitella mucronata (SCHLOTHEIM)

Order: Belemnitida
Family: Belemnitellidae

The important late Cretaceous genus *Belemnitella* is distributed over the northern hemisphere. On the wide anterior end of the rostrum and on the ventral side there is a fissure opening into the alveolus. The alveolus accounts for one quarter to half the length of the rostrum. Vascular imprints can usually be seen ventrally to the dorsolateral grooves (fig. 5).

5

1. *Actinocamax plenus,* Upper Cretaceous (Turonian), Kostelec nad Labem and Nová Ves, Czechoslovakia. Length of rostra 83 and 67 mm. A stratigraphically important species.

2. *Neohibolites minimus,* Lower Cretaceous (Albian), Eilum, West Germany. Length of largest rostrum 30 mm. One of the smallest belemnitid species.

3. *Gonioteuthis granulata,* Upper Cretaceous (Santonian), Braunschweig, West Germany. Length of rostra 60 and 70 mm. Well preserved specimens with pronounced characteristic granulation on their surface.

4, 5. *Belemnitella mucronata,** Upper Cretaceous (Maastrichtian), Kent, Great Britain. Length of rostra 85 and 88 mm (4). An abundant species, whose rostra, washed up by the sea from Cretaceous reefs in north-western and northern Europe, were believed in the Middle Ages to be thunderbolts (Donnerkeile) and to possess magic (healing) powers. 5 – a ventral view.

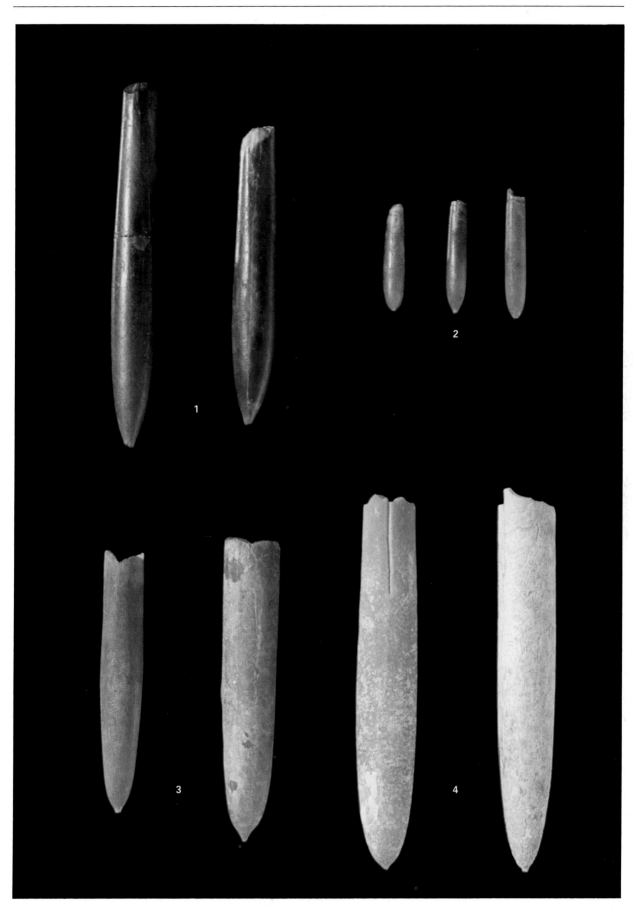

Annelida

Serpula proteus SOWERBY

Order: Sedentarida
Family: Serpulidae

The ancient and evolutionarily extremely important group of the worms (Vermes), whose extant representatives are divided into several independent phyla, left only a few fossil remains behind them. That is a pity, because all the more advanced groups of invertebrates evolved from worms. The majority of finds stem from Polychaeta, phyllum Annelida – 'many-bristled worms' – which formed calcareous tubes (order Sedentaria). Small, toothed chitinous jaws, known as scolecodonts (order Errantida) and commensal growths of polychaetan tubes and tabulate corals (Hicetes, Chaetosalpinx) are frequently found. Various trails, passages and burrows are also fairly common, although the worm that made them cannot always be reliably identified. Tumours made on the stems of crinoids and on tufts of coral by worms belonging to the family Myzostomidae are another relic. Imprints of the worms' soft bodies are exceedingly rare.

The first finds of worm tubes belonging to the cosmopolitan genus *Serpula* come from Silurian sediments, but from the Jurassic onwards they are more abundant. The tubes, which are up to 10 cm long, are irregularly undulating or spiral; they are circular in cross section and are generally attached to the substratum. Small conical opercula are also found occasionally.

1. *Conchicolites confertus,* Middle Ordovician (Caradocian), Trubín, Czechoslovakia. A group of cases, the largest one 13 mm long. These worms overgrew the edge of brachiopod valves and obtained food from the water driven towards the animal's mouth by its whirling ciliated arms.

2. *Serpula proteus,* Upper Cretaceous (Upper Senonian), Kent, England. Diameter of the coiled part of the tube 15 mm.

3. *Glomerula gordialis,* * Upper Cretaceous (Maastrichtian), Maastricht, the Netherlands. Tube diameter 0.5–1 mm, diameter of whole glomerulus 11 mm. The coils of the tube are free, i.e. they do not adhere together.

4. *Spirorbis pusillus*, Upper Carboniferous (Westphalian), the Caroline Mine near Holzwickede, West Germany. Whole tubes on a piece of wood, diameter 1.5–2 mm. *Spirorbis* (fig. 6 – a reconstruction) is today a completely marine genus, but in the past its representatives also lived in fresh water.

5. *Serpula socialis,* Upper Cretaceous (Turonian), Česká Třebová, Czechoslovakia. Length of bundle 60 mm, individual tube diameter 0.7 mm. A fairly common species in finely granular Middle Jurassic to Cretaceous sandstones.

6

Serpula socialis GOLDFUSS

Order: Sedentarida
Family: Serpulidae

The members of this Jurassic and Cretaceous European species form large numbers of almost straight, thin tubes grouped together in thick bundles.

Glomerula gordialis (SCHLOTHEIM)

Order: Sedentarida
Family: Serpulidae

Glomerula is a European Cretaceous genus. The long, thin tubes, which are circular in cross section, are generally twisted into a rounded mass (glomerulus).

Spirorbis pusillus MARTIN

Order: Sedentarida
Family: Serpulidae

Spirorbis species have been abundant everywhere since the late Palaeozoic. Their small, spiral tubes overgrow a variety of objects, including shells and aquatic plants (fig. 6).

Conchicolites confertus (BARRANDE)

Order: Cornulitida
Family: Cornulitidae

The members of the genus *Conchicolites* are known from the Ordovician to the Devonian in Europe and North America. They have small, calcareous, cornet-shaped tubes with thick, transversely furrowed walls and in small groups they overgrow the shells (tests) of other organisms.

305

Arthropoda

Olenellus thompsoni HALL

Arthropods (phylum Arthropoda) are highly organized invertebrates living in water, on dry land and in the air, with the body composed of numerous segments to each of which a pair of articulating segmented limbs was originally attached. The soft parts of the body were protected and supported by a chitin carapace which was shed periodically during growth.

Trilobites (Trilobita, subphylum Trilobitomorpha) are the most well known fossil class of marine arthropods. They appeared at the beginning of the Palaeozoic era and died out right at the end. The carapace is divided transversely into three parts – a head plate (cephalon), a body (thorax) and a caudal plate (pygidium). The front and sides of the roughly semicircular cephalon are folded, making a double edge. The middle of the cephalon (the glabella) is broken up by glabellar furrows or impressions and an occipital furrow, behind which lies an occipital ring. On either side of the glabella are fixed cheeks separated from the free cheeks by a suture. The inner margin of the fixed cheeks is often raised, roughly in the middle, forming a palpebral lobe on which the eyes are seated. Connected to the double front part of the head (often on the under side) there is an unpaired plate of variable width – the rostrum – which is followed on the ventral aspect, directly below the glabella, by another plate, the hypostoma. The thorax is composed of 2 to 44 segments, whose number is constant for adult individuals of each species. In the middle of every segment (tergite) of the carapace there is an axial ring, with a pleuron on either side. The pygidium shows a central (axial) lobe – rhachis, and a lateral (pleural) lobe on either side.

Redlichiids belong to the phylogenetically oldest (Lower to Middle Cambrian) trilobites. Along the sides, their large head tapers off into long genal spines forming part of the free cheeks (an ophistoparian type of genal suture). The thorax is composed of a large number of segments; the pygidium is small.

Trilobites of the genus *Olenellus* occur in Lower Cambrian sediments in North America and Europe. They have a flat carapace and a cylindrical, anteriorly rounded glabella. The pleurae on the sides of the wide thorax are produced to sabre-like points. The last axial ring terminates in a long spine. The pygidium is rudimentary.

Paradoxides gracilis (BOECK)

The species of the genus *Paradoxides* are distributed in Middle Cambrian sediments in Europe, North America, northern Africa and Asia, and apparently in Australia as well. The pear-shaped glabella has two pairs of medially interconnected glabellar furrows and long genal spines. The hypostome and the rostrum are fused (fig. 5). The small, simple pygidium has a segmented axis.

4

1. *Eccaparadoxides pusillus,** Middle Cambrian, Jince, Czechoslovakia. An almost complete core of a carapace; length 34 mm.

2. *Paradoxides gracilis,* Middle Cambrian, Jince, Czechoslovakia. A whole carapace; length 120 mm. Like *Olenellus* in the Lower Cambrian, *Paradoxides* is characteristic of the Middle Cambrian (the paradoxidid level).

3. *Olenellus thompsoni,** Lower Cambrian, Nevada, USA. A thorax with the pygidium; length 50 mm.

4. *Olenellus* sp., the cephalon.

5. *Paradoxides* sp., fused hypostome and rostrum.

306

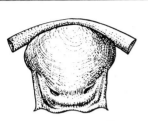

5

Eccaparadoxides pusillus (Barrande)

Order: Redlichiida
Family: Paradoxididae

Cm

The members of the Middle Cambrian genus *Eccaparadoxides* are distributed similarly to the genus *Paradoxides.* The glabella has four pairs of glabellar furrows, the hypostome and the rostrum are free, the thorax is wide and the pygidium has a concave posterior margin or is bordered by spines.

1

3

2

 **Arthropoda**

Hydrocephalus carens Barrande

Order: Redlichiida
Family: Paradoxididae

Trilobites of the genus *Hydrocephalus* occur in Middle Cambrian sediments in Europe, Asia and North America. They have wider carapaces than their relatives in the genus *Paradoxides.* The cephalon has a pear-shaped glabella with four pairs of glabellar furrows, the hypostoma and the rostrum are not fused together, the thorax is composed of 17 or 18 segments and the pygidium is short.

Sao hirsuta Barrande

Order: Ptychopariida
Family: Solenopleuridae

The trilobites' chitin carapace contained calcium salts (in particular calcium carbonate, $CaCO_3$) in varying concentrations. As with other arthropods, the carapace was not capable of continuous growth and had to be shed several times during the animal's lifetime, always with subsequent formation of a new and larger carapace. The earliest phase of growth accessible for study to palaeontologists is the protaspid stage (protaspis) (fig. 5), which is characterized by the appearance of the first solid, simple, discoid carapace measuring 0.25 to 1 mm. In the next, meraspid, stage (meraspis) (fig. 6), loose connections were formed between the parts of the exoskeleton and the number of thoracic

1. *Agraulos ceticephalus,* *Middle Cambrian, Skryje, Czechoslovakia. A cluster of complete carapaces about 20 mm long.

2, 3. *Sao hirsuta,* * Middle Cambrian, Skryje, Czechoslovakia. An exceptionally well preserved complete carapace (2) and a younger holaspid stage (3); lengths 38 and 12 mm.

4. *Hydrocephalus carens,* * Middle Cambrian, Skryje, Czechoslovakia. An almost complete carapace (lacking the free cheeks); length 140 mm. A very abundant species in places, its carapaces grew to as much as 30 cm. The secondary rusty coloration of the carapace is due to a coating of limonite.

5, 6. *Sao* sp., protoaspid and meraspid growth stages.

4

segments rose until there was one fewer than the total characteristic of the given species. All the subsequent stages, in which the animal had a full complement of thoracic segments, are known as the holaspid stage (holaspis).

Sao is one of the trilobite genera whose individual growth stages were described for the first time (in 1852) by J. Barrande. It belongs to the order of ptychopariid trilobites, which attained their peak in the Cambrian. This group is characterized by anterior narrowing of the simple glabella and, as a rule, by an opisthoparian genal suture. The hypostome is attached to the cephalon by a suture or by an uncalcified membrane. There are always more than three segments in the thorax.

Sao is regarded as an endemic central European trilobite genus. The small carapace has a deeply furrowed glabella divided into pronounced lobes, moderately large eyes and short genal spines. The thorax is composed of 17 segments and on each ring (including the occipital ring) there is a long median spine. The pygidial rhachis has only one segment. The entire surface of the carapace is extremely pustulated and it bore hollow and very regularly organized spines which evidently possessed the sensory receptors.

Agraulos ceticephalus (BARRANDE)

Order: Ptychopariida
Family: Agraulidae

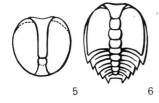

5   6

The genus *Agraulos* occurs in Middle Cambrian deposits in Europe, North America and Asia. Its minute members have a strikingly large cephalon. The glabellar furrows of the short, faint glabella have the form of imprints, the front of the cephalon has a wide border, the thorax is composed of 16 segments and only one segment can be seen in the axial part of the small pygidium.

 **Arthropoda**

Ptychoparia striata (EMMERICH)

Order: Ptychopariida
Family: Ptychopariidae

The members of the genus *Ptychoparia* are common trilobites in Middle Cambrian sediments in central Europe. They are typical representatives of the order Ptychopariida. The morphology of the carapace provides a good basis for a functional explanation of some of the general features of trilobites. It has oval contours, a large cephalon, a huge thorax and a small pygidium. The round-cornered rhomboid glabella has four pairs of glabellar grooves corresponding to outgrowths on the inner surface of the carapace, on which muscles originating from the basal segments of the biramous segmented limbs were inserted. The free cheeks, isolated from the cranidium (i.e. the glabella and the fixed cheeks) by a non-mineralized or only weakly mineralized genal suture, terminate in short genal spines. The sutures were important mainly at moulting time, when the carapace came apart along them, allowing the animal to free itself as from a garment it had grown out of. A striking feature of ptychopariids is the radial pattern on the part of the surface of the free cheeks and cranidium in front of the glabella. It is probably of vascular origin, or is an impression of the surface of the digestive gland, which opened into the stomach just below the glabella. The mouth was evidently situated just behind the hypostoma. The stomach passes into the gut, which led below the median lobe of the carapace, i.e. below the axial rings and the rhachis, and opened on the surface near the posterior end of the pygidium. Ptychopariids have relatively large eyes. The thorax is composed of 14 segments; the pygidium has a pronounced

1. *Ptychoparia striata,** Middle Cambrian, Jince, Czechoslovakia. Two whole carapaces, lengths 70 and 56 mm. Vascular imprints are clearly discernible on part of the surface of the cephalon.

2

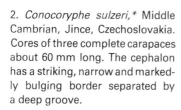

2. *Conocoryphe sulzeri,** Middle Cambrian, Jince, Czechoslovakia. Cores of three complete carapaces about 60 mm long. The cephalon has a striking, narrow and markedly bulging border separated by a deep groove.

rhachial region. The muscles controlling the proximal parts of the thoracic and pygidial limbs were inserted on processes on the inner surface of the carapace, along the sides of the axial rings and the pygidial rhachis.

The trilobites of the genus *Ptychoparia* inhabited muddy or sandy bottoms in relatively shallow seas, where they lived on miscellaneous organic débris.

Conocoryphe sulzeri (SCHLOTHEIM)

Order: Ptychopariida
Family: Conocoryphidae

Conocoryphe species, occurring in sediments of the same age as *Ptychoparia,* are known from Europe, North America and Asia. At first glance the two genera look very much alike, but in *Conocoryphe* the glabella is conical, with three pairs of glabellar furrows. The fixed cheeks are very wide and the narrow free cheeks lack eyes. Vascular scars are also visible on the surface of the cephalon, but they are limited to a narrow strip on the cheeks, near their outer margin.

Conocoryphe was a blind trilobite. It was formerly wrongly assumed that undeveloped eyes belonged to the primitive characters of the oldest arthropods, but the majority of the oldest known Lower Cambrian trilobites generally had compound eyes. Progressive reduction of the eyes in individual lines of trilobites in different periods is a sign of adaptation — usually to a burrowing mode of life. The animal obtained food by swallowing the sediment and digesting its organic parts.

311

Arthropoda

Ellipsocephalus hoffi (SCHLOTHEIM)

Order: Ptychopariida
Family: Ellipsocephalidae

Ellipsocephalus is one of the best known Cambrian trilobite genera and was also one of the first to be described (in 1825). It occurs in Lower and Middle Cambrian strata in Europe, northern Africa and New Brunswick. The semicircular head is much larger than the pygidium. The glabella has a wide border in front of it and is fused as a rule with the occipital ring. The eyes are situated at a considerable distance from the glabella. The thorax has 12 to 14 segments.

Agnostus pisiformis (WAHLENBERG)

Order: Agnostida
Family: Agnostidae

The chief features common to all Agnostida are their small size, the small number of their thoracic segments (only two or three) and their relatively large head and pygidium, which look very much alike. True agnostids have neither a genal suture nor dorsal eyes and it is assumed that they were blind (although the presence of ventral eyes cannot be ruled out). Agnostids are common fossils and are consequently used more and more in stratigraphy. They presumably lived with plankton and, clinging to algae, could have been carried long distances by the ocean currents. Their flattened form could also have been a manifestation of an ectoparasitic existence.

The Upper Cambrian genus *Agnostus* is known in Europe and Asia. The thorax is composed of two segments and in front of it, divided by a longitudinal groove, lies the cephalon. The pygidial axis consists of three lobes, the last one of which, only very slightly widened, does not reach to the narrow marginal border (fig. 5).

1. *Agnostus pisiformis,** Upper Cambrian, southern Sweden. Cephalons and pygidia; length about 2 mm. Mass incidences of parts of Upper Cambrian trilobite carapaces are typical of some southern Scandinavian localities.

2. *Phalagnostus nudus,** Middle Cambrian, Skryje, Czechoslovakia. A complete carapace; length 8 mm. The surface has been secondarily coloured by limonite, which gives the trilobites in Skryje shales a characteristic appearance.

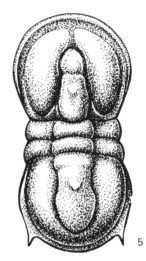

5

4

Phalagnostus nudus (BEYRICH)

Order: Agnostida
Family: Phalacromidae

The representatives of the family Phalacromidae are characterized by a very simply constructed carapace, a smooth cephalon and an undefined (or only faintly indicated) glabella. The pygidium closely resembles the cephalon.

The genus *Phalagnostus* occurs in Middle Cambrian formations in Europe, Asia, North America and Australia. The cephalon is semi-elliptical and the pygidium has a wide border.

Condylopyge rex (BARRANDE)

Order: Agnostida
Family: Condylopygidae

The carapace of the members of this family is strikingly segmented. The frontal lobe of the glabella and the hind part of the pygidial axis are conspicuously expanded. *Condylopyge* species occur in Lower and Middle Cambrian deposits in Europe and North America. The cephalon is approximately square and has a narrow border. The glabella is composed of two lobes, of which the frontal lobe is roughly triangular. The axis of the pygidium is narrower in the middle and is divided into four lobes of unequal length.

3. *Condylopyge rex,** Middle Cambrian, Skryje, Czechoslovakia. A complete carapace; length 8 mm. This is the largest known agnostid: its carapaces attained lengths of up to 20 mm.

4. *Ellipsocephalus hoffi,** Middle Cambrian, Jince, Czechoslovakia. Cores of complete carapaces; lengths 12–15 mm. Mass accumulations of whole carapaces are evidence of mass death of the trilobites – probably owing to a sudden decrease in salinity caused by an increased influx of river water.

5. *Agnostus* sp., a complete carapace.

 **Arthropoda**

Asaphus expansus WAHLENBERG

Order: Ptychopariida
Family: Asaphidae

Trilobites also continued to flourish in the Ordovician, when one of the most widespread groups were asaphids (suborder Asaphina), whose stratigraphic range stretches from the Upper Cambrian to the end of the Ordovician. The usually faintly segmented glabella is often only indistinctly separated from the fixed cheeks. The cephalon has a wide doublure; in many species the rostrum is absent and the hypostome is firmly attached to the margin of the doublure. The thorax is composed of six to nine segments and the pygidium is moderately large to large. True asaphids (members of the family Asaphidae) always have eight thoracic segments. One of the most striking features is progressive obliteration of segmentation of the cephalon and the pygidium. These trilobites were able to roll up into a ball when in danger; in that case the doublure of the cephalon came into close contact with the edge of the pygidium and the distal parts of the pleurae partly overlapped. This position was also naturally adopted by the dying animal. Asaphid trilobites mainly inhabited warm seas.

The genus *Asaphus* comprises very common Lower and Middle Ordovician trilobites of north-western Europe. Neither the cephalon nor

1. *Nobiliasaphus nobilis,* * Middle Ordovician (Caradocian), Zaho-řany, Czechoslovakia. A core of the carapace of a complete individual, length 210 mm. The segmentation of the cephalon is obscured because the hypostoma was forced through the dorsal carapace.

2. *Megistaspis aliena,* Lower Ordovician (Llanvirnian), Praha-Libuš, Czechoslovakia. Core of a carapace (the free cheeks have been broken off); length 32 mm. The carapace of some north European *Megistaspis* species attained lengths of up to 350 mm.

3. *Asaphus expansus,** Lower Ordovician (Arenig), Sweden. A complete carapace; length 67 mm.

2   3

the pygidium has a peripheral border. The long glabella stretches right to the frontal margin of the carapace. The axial rings are wide and the pygidial axis is long and pronounced. The pleural lobes are indistinctly ribbed. *Asaphus* lived on the sea floor, apparently partly buried in it. Its well developed, bulging eyes protruded out of the sediment (in some species the eyes were actually stalked). *Asaphus expansus* was the species in which Pander organs were first discovered. These are outgrowths on the fixed cheeks and the pleural fold and small spaces behind the outgrowths. The function of the protuberances was to regulate overlapping of the pleura when the animal rolled up and the spaces may have been the outlets of metameric excretory organs.

Megistaspis aliena (BARRANDE)

Order: Ptychopariida
Family: Asaphidae

Megistaspis species lived in Lower and Middle Ordovician Europe. The flat carapace has an indistinctly segmented cephalon and pygidium, the eyes are small and spines project from the cheeks.

Nobiliasaphus nobilis (BARRANDE)

Order: Ptychopariida
Family: Asaphidae

The representatives of the genus *Nobiliasaphus* lived in Middle and Upper Ordovician Europe. The flat carapaces grew to lengths of up to 40 cm. The cephalon and pygidium are markedly segmented and are surrounded by a wide border. The cheeks taper off into spines. The terraced sculpturing on the surface of the cephalon, the pygidium and the doublure is very striking. The pygidium is extremely large and V-shaped wrinkles are present on its axis. *Nobiliasaphus* probably lived near the sea floor.

315

Arthropoda

Selenopeltis buchi (BARRANDE)

Order: Odontopleurida
Family: Odontopleuridae

Odontopleurids, with their striking carapace, bristling with spines, lived towards the end of the Middle Cambrian. Their phylogenetically youngest representatives are known from Upper Devonian formations. As a rule, the small carapace has an intricately divided, deeply furrowed glabella. The facial sutures are opisthoparous or proparous (i.e. when the posterior branch of the facial suture intersects the lateral margin of the cephalon in front of the genal angles or spines forming part of the fixed cheeks). The eyes are small; the surface of the cephalon generally carries spines. The hypostome is in contact with the rostrum. The thoracic segments and, as a rule, the tiny pygidium also, are studded with spines.

The genus *Selenopeltis* comprises important Ordovician trilobites distributed in the Mediterranean region and central and western Europe. The oblong cephalon has a wide glabella. The free cheeks are encircled by a pronounced border and long genal spines project from their upper surface. The pleurae on the side of each of the nine thoracic segments terminate in a short, laterally orientated anterior spine and a long spine orientated obliquely backwards. The pygidium has a short axis and on the pleural lobes there is a striking paired bar which is produced to a long spine. The large size and massive construction of the carapace and comparison with extant species of arthropods with spiny carapaces indicate that *Selenopeltis* was a benthic genus. The long spines were evidently a form of adaptation to life on a soft sea floor. Evidence that these trilobites did not burrow in the sediment, even occasionally, is furnished by the discovery of numerous small discoid echinoderms

1. *Selenopeltis buchi,* * Upper Ordovician (Ashgill), Lejškov, Czechoslovakia. A complete carapace, length 41 mm.

2

2. *Dalmanitina socialis,* * Middle Ordovician (Caradoc), Drabov, Czechoslovakia. Length of carapaces 60–70 mm. The accumulation of whole carapaces on bedding planes (lumachelle) is evidence of the mass death of these trilobites owing to a sudden change in the physical or chemical properties of the environment.

belonging to the class Edrioasteroidea, which unquestionably settled on their carapace while the trilobites were still alive.

Dalmanitina socialis (BARRANDE)

Order: Phacopida
Family: Dalmanitidae

The first phacopid trilobites appeared at the outset of the Ordovician and the last died out at the end of the Devonian. The common features of the members of this order include usually proparian facial sutures, a distinct glabella (generally with three pairs of glabellar furrows) and a moderately large to large pygidium. Pronounced articulating facets are often present on the thoracic segments, in association with the animal's ability to roll up.

Dalmanitina species occur in Middle and Upper Ordovician sediments in Europe, northern Africa, North America and eastern Asia. On either side of the cephalon there is a pronounced border. The pear-shaped glabella, which projects beyond the edge of the cephalon, is furrowed by oblique glabellar grooves. Schizochroal eyes are seated on the prominent palpebral lobes; they are formed of a small number of biconvex calcite lenses separated from one another by cuticular tissue. The genal spines are short. The pygidium has six to eight paired ribs and terminates in a long, curving spine. These trilobites were hardly dependent on the character of the sea floor; the construction of their carapace and the perfection of their eyes imply that they belonged to the necton.

317

Arthropoda

Placoparia barrandei PRANTL AND ŠNAJDR

Order: Phacopida
Family: Pliomeridae

Among the phacopid trilobites there are some with completely reduced eyes, e.g. in the genus *Placoparia,* which occurs in Middle Ordovician sediments in Europe and northern Africa. The glabella has three pairs of deep grooves, the fixed cheeks are highly convex and the free cheeks are very narrow. The thorax is composed of 10 to 12 segments; the pygidium is small. *Placoparia* species evidently belonged to the benthos, lived in the temperate and the cold belt and looked for sustenance on and in the sediment.

Bavarilla hofensis (BARRANDE)

Order: Phacopida
Family: Homalonotidae

Bavarilla is the oldest known genus of homalonotid trilobites. Its members lived in the Lower Ordovician of central Europe. They have large eyes, short genal spines project from their free cheeks, their thorax has 13 segments and their small, wide pygidium has three.

Pricyclopyge prisca (BARRANDE)

Order: Ptychopariida
Family: Cyclopygidae

3

Cyclopygids were specialized trilobites with a markedly convex carapace, an exceptionally large, swollen glabella with paired scars and a non-separate occipital ring. The fixed cheeks form a narrow band. The excessively large, hypertrophic eyes, with up to 3,500 biconvex lenses in each eye, occupy practically the whole of the free cheeks and continue to the ventral surface of the carapace, where they either unite or are separated by a narrow strip (fig. 5). The thorax has five to six segments with wide axial rings which, together with the pygidial axis, form a conical median lobe.

1. *Pricyclopyge prisca,** Lower Ordovician (Llanvirn), Osek near Rokycany, Czechoslovakia. Core of a complete carapace, length 45 mm. The dimples on the third axial ring are believed to be light organs.

2. *Ectillaenus parabolinus,* Lower Ordovician (Llanvirn), Prague-Vokovice, Czechoslovakia. Core of a complete carapace, length 60 mm. The degenerate eyes are indicative of a non-predatory habit. These trilobites obtained food either by swallowing sediment or suspended particles, or by devouring dead animals.

3. *Placoparia barrandei,* Lower Ordovician (Llanvirn), Prague-Šárka, Czechoslovakia. A complete carapace, length 40 mm. An individual preserved in a concretion formed by the accretion of sediment round the trilobite's decomposing body.

4. *Bavarilla hofensis,** Lower Ordovician (Tremadoc), Brloh, Czechoslovakia. A group of whole, pressure-deformed carapaces about 30 mm long.

5. *Pricyclopyge* sp., cephalon from the ventral side.

6. *Ectillaenus* sp., an individual in a living position.

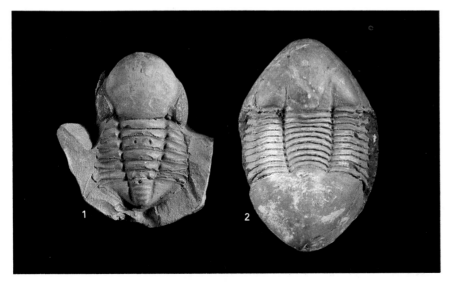

4

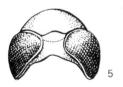

5

The genus *Pricyclopyge* occurs in Ordovician sediments in central and western Europe. The frontally spreading glabella has one pair of muscle scars. In some species, the pleurae of the last (sixth) thoracic segment are produced laterally to spines. These animals, which lived in cold water, probably swam upside down, like recent king crabs (*Limulus*).

Ectillaenus parabolinus (Novák)

Order: Ptychopariida
Family: Illaenidae

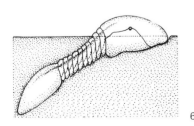

6

Illaenids are characterized by a smooth, domed carapace with terraced ridges. The thorax is composed of eight to ten segments and the large pygidium often resembles the cephalon. Illaenids were adapted for burrowing, chiefly in argillaceous sediments. In complete carapaces – unless they are coiled – the cephalon and the thorax form a given angle, indicating that the head evidently rested on the sea floor and the thorax and pygidium were buried (fig. 6).

Arthropoda

Onnia abducta (PŘIBYL AND VANĚK)

Order: Ptychopariida
Family: Trinucleidae

The representatives of this characteristic Ordovician family have very striking carapaces. The large, semicircular or triangular bulging cephalon has a prominent glabella and a wide perforated border. The cheeks taper off into very long and slender genal spines, the thorax is short, with five to seven segments, and the small pygidium is semicircular or triangular. These trilobites evidently burrowed just below the surface of the sediment. As shown by the discovery of a cavity left by the alimentary tube of a member of the genus *Tretaspis,* the stomach lay inside the glabella and passed posteriorly to the gut. The border apparently acted as a sensory receptor indicating changes in the currents, or was used for digging in the substratum. The digestive glands evidently lay in a cavity inside the border. The long genal spines helped to keep the animal stable on the sea floor (fig. 4).

The representatives of the Middle to Upper Ordovician genus *Onnia* are known from different parts of Europe, northern Africa and South America. The glabella has only one distinct pair of furrows. Eyes are not developed. The occipital ring carries a median spine, which, as a rule, is secondarily snapped off.

Amphytrion radians (BARRANDE)

Order: Ptychopariida
Family: Ramapleuridae

The species of the central and north European Upper Ordovician genus *Amphytrion* show what typical ramapleurids looked like. The semicircular cephalon has an exceptionally wide glabella, produced in front to a short 'tongue', with three pairs of simple glabellar furrows. The large eyes, each of which has up to 15,000 lenses, are in close contact with the

1. *Flexicalymene incerta,* Middle Ordovician (Caradoc), Zahořany, Czechoslovakia. A complete carapace, length 75 mm.

2. *Amphytrion radians,* * Upper Ordovician (Ashgill), Králův Dvůr, Czechoslovakia. A core with remains of the carapace; length 40 mm. The free cheeks have been broken off.

3. *Onnia abducta,* Middle Ordovician (Caradoc), Prague-Velká Chuchle, Czechoslovakia. A complete carapace, length 13 mm.

4. A trinucleid viewed from the side.

3

glabella. Wide genal spines project from the free cheeks. The thorax has 11 segments and on the pygidium there is a short axial region and a long, narrow pleural field terminating in two pairs of marginal spines. The flat, lightly constructed carapace was evidently adapted for life on a soft substratum.

Flexicalymene incerta (BARRANDE)

Order: Phacopida
Family: Calymenidae

Calymenids are common Lower Ordovician to Devonian trilobites with a massive and generally bulging carapace. The round-cornered rhomboid cephalon is split up by three pairs of deep glabellar furrows. The posterior branch of the facial suture intersects the margin of the cephalon in the genal spine. The eyes, as a rule, are small or moderately large. The thorax consists of 12 or 13 segments; the pygidium is moderately large to large. The genus *Flexicalymene* comprises cosmopolitan trilobites whose remains are found today in various types of Middle Ordovician to Silurian clastic sedimentary rocks. The semicircular cephalon has a striking frontal border. The eyes are small. The ribs on the sharply sculptured pygidium extend right to its edges. It is not uncommon to find complete carapaces – exceptionally actually in the original lair. The finds show that these trilobites were burrowers.

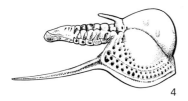

4

Arthropoda

Cromus beaumonti (BARRANDE)

Order: Phacopida
Family: Encrinuridae

The tremendous development of the trilobites during the Cambrian and Ordovician was succeeded, relatively soon (in relation to the more than 350 million years' history of the class as a whole), by a gradual but steady decline, which started in the Upper Ordovician. The generic diversity of Silurian trilobites is far smaller than in preceding formations. *Encrinuridae* are a cosmopolitan family whose stratigraphic range extends from the Ordovician to the Upper Silurian. The cylindrical or anteriorly widened glabella overlaps the frontal edge of the cephalon. The thorax consists of 10 to 12 segments and the pygidium is richly segmented. The pustulated surface of the carapace is a striking feature.

The genus *Cromus* comprises small trilobites living in Silurian Europe, northern Africa and Australia. The glabella has four pairs of glabellar furrows and close beside it lie the eyes. The thorax has 10 segments and there is a large pygidium; the pleurae terminate in short spines. This genus chiefly inhabited shallow water in tropical and subtropical seas. It probably stayed on the sea floor and lived on organic débris on its surface.

Sphaeroxochus mirus BEYRICH

Order: Phacopida
Family: Cheiruridae

Cheiruridae are known from the Lower Ordovician to the Middle Devonian. Many of their genera are cosmopolitan. Their members have small eyes or are blind; they have a rostrum and a free hypostome. The pleurae either terminate in a point or are bluntly rounded; the pygidium

1. *Cromus beaumonti,* Upper Silurian (Ludlow), Zadní Kopanina, Czechoslovakia. An almost complete carapace, length 16 mm. In some places, cephala and pygidia are found very often; finds of whole carapaces are very rare.

2. *Sphaeroxochus mirus,** Lower Silurian (Wenlock), Lištice near Beroun, Czechoslovakia. An isolated cranidium (above) and pygidium (below), measuring 13 and 8 mm respectively.

3. *Bumastus hornyi,* Lower Silurian (Wenlock), Prague-Jinonice, Czechoslovakia. An exceptionally well preserved specimen with an almost completely intact carapace; length 45 mm.

4. *Sphaeroxochus* sp., a complete carapace; lateral view.

has two to four pairs of pleural ribs and spines and a small number of axial rings. The surface is often granular.

The genus *Sphaeroxochus* occurs in Lower Ordovician to Silurian formations practically everywhere except in South America. The cephalon is dominated by a spherical glabella. On both sides, the lower glabellar furrows unite, forming a pair of oval lobes in front of the occipital ring (fig. 4). The pygidium is roughly divided into three pairs of pleurae which terminate in lobate processes. The unwontedly thick, domed carapace constituted suitable adaptation to a benthic existence in the turbulent water round coral reefs and shallows.

Bumastus hornyi Šnajdr

Order: Ptychopariida
Family: Illaenidae

The genus *Bumastus,* a cosmopolitan representative of the illaenids, ranges from the Middle Ordovician to the Upper Silurian. The markedly vaulted carapace is characterized by an almost unsegmented cephalon and pygidium; the thorax has 10 segments. Unlike many Ordovician illaenids, *Bumastus* has strikingly developed eyes. The smooth carapaces testify to a partly burrowing mode of life, but since these trilobites also occur in the vicinity of coral reefs, we assume that they could also have lived in the spaces in these reefs.

4

323

Arthropoda

Prionopeltis striata (Barrande)

Order: Proetida
Family: Proetidae

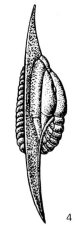

4

Proetids appeared in the Lower Ordovician and attained their prime during the Silurian and Devonian. They are the only trilobite order to have survived into the late Palaeozoic era. Most of them are small, with a rounded cephalon, an anteriorly rounded glabella, opisthoparous facial sutures and large free cheeks (usually with spines). The thorax consists of 17 segments; the pygidium generally has a smooth edge. Proetids attained maximum diversity in shallow, well lit and well aerated water, where they mostly lived on the bottom. The individual species have a restricted stratigraphic and southern geographic range.

Prionopeltis is a Silurian genus known mainly from Bohemia and the Harz Mountains, but has occasionally been found in northern Africa. The carapace is slightly convex, with a wide, lingulate glabella separated from the frontal margin of the cephalon by a wide preglabellar field. The thorax is composed of 10 segments. The pleurae on the pygidium taper off into striking pleural spines. The thin-walled carapace, the shape of the eyes (testifying to a large range of vision) and apparent lack of adaptation to the environment show that prionopeltids were evidently good swimmers.

Aulacopleura konincki (Barrande)

Order: Proetida
Family: Otarionidae

Aulacopleura is one of the commonest otarionid trilobite genera and occurs in Silurian sedimentary rocks in Europe, northern Africa and Greenland. The glabella stretches about half way along the cephalon and the eyes are level with its frontal portion; the thorax has 12 to 22 segments. This genus was among the first proetids to settle in deep water, although it also occurs in shallow-water types of sediments. It probably lived directly on the sea floor or swam just above it.

Bohemoharpes ungula (Sternberg)

Order: Ptychopariida
Family: Harpidae

Harpid trilobites (suborder Harpina) are found in Upper Cambrian to Upper Devonian sediments all over the world. Their large semicircular cephalon, with its wide, double horseshoe border, tapers off into huge genal spines; its surface is strikingly pitted. The eyes are small. As many as 29 thoracic segments have been counted. The pygidium is very small. The function of the cephalic border has not been reliably resolved; it may have been used for raking loose sediment, for swimming or for providing a sure hold on the substratum.

The genus Bohemoharpes, a characteristic representative of the family, lived in Silurian Europe. The glabella is conspicuously cone-like, narrowed in front. The simple eyes are seated on pronounced lobes.

1. Prionopeltis striata, Upper Silurian (Pridoli), Kosov near Beroun, Czechoslovakia. A complete carapace, length 12 mm.

2, 4. Bohemoharpes ungula, Upper Silurian (Ludlow), Kosov near Beroun, Czechoslovakia. A complete carapace (2), length 25 mm. The carapaces are often discoidally coiled (4), i.e. as if bent in the middle of the thorax.

3. Aulacopleura konincki,* Lower Silurian (Wenlock), Loděnice, Czechoslovakia. A cluster of complete and fragmented carapaces covered with limonite; maximum length 20 mm. Mass incidences of these trilobites in this locality are attributed to poisoning by gases released as a result of intensive submarine volcanic activity.

Arthropoda

Leonaspis roemeri (BARRANDE)

Order: Odontopleurida
Family: Odontopleuridae

Spiny carapaces are encountered in various groups of trilobites. They were also formed in the early ontogenetic (protaspid, meraspid) stages of species whose adult carapace was spineless. There is no trilobite order for which spines are as characteristic as they are for odontopleurids. *Leonaspis* is a typical Lower Silurian to Middle Devonian odontopleurid genus distributed in Europe and both Americas. The smallish carapace has a round-cornered oblong cephalon with a wide glabella. Projecting from the sides of the cephalon, the cheeks and the ends of the pleurae there are curved or straight spines. The pygidium is likewise strikingly spiny.

4

1. *Leonaspis roemeri,* Lower Silurian (Wenlock), Loděnice, Czechoslovakia. Length of the largest carapace 9 mm. The environment in which these trilobites lived was often poisoned by escaping gases released by intensive volcanic activity.

Miraspis mira (BARRANDE)

Order: Odontopleurida
Family: Odontopleuridae

The species of the genus *Miraspis* belong to the best known trilobites of European Lower Silurian seas. The cephalon (fig. 4) is wide and semi-elliptical; the glabella has two long, recurved, sabre-like spines and the eyes are seated on long supports. Long, slender genal spines project from the upper surface of the cephalon, whose sides are bordered by fine spines. The thorax is composed of nine segments. The pygidium has 11 pairs of fine marginal spines, of which the third pair is thicker and

2. *Miraspis mira,** Lower Silurian (Wenlock), Loděnice, Czechoslovakia. Length of the smaller carapace 11 mm. Their limited contact with the substratum meant that these trilobites probably fed on small organisms contained in the water.

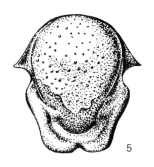

5

longer than the others. The spines pointed upwards and downwards, as well as sideways.

The function of trilobites' spines is a much-discussed subject. By analogy with extant spiny crustaceans, we conclude that they helped to keep very small planktonic individuals and larval stages buoyant. In large individuals they would not have fulfilled this purpose adequately, however; in these they evidently had protective, stabilizing and steering function. The ventrally orientated spines acted as a support on soft sea floors.

3. *Cheirurus insignis,** Lower Silurian (Wenlock), Lištice, Czechoslovakia. An almost complete, pressure-deformed carapace, length 30 mm. This species inhabited warm Upper Wenlock seas and was especially abundant in the vicinity of volcanoes.

4. *Miraspis* sp., a frontal view of the cephalon.

5. *Cheirurus* sp., the hypostome.

Cheirurus insignis BEYRICH

Order: Phacopida
Family: Cheiruridae

Some trilobites in the family Cheiruridae have wide, massive spines. The cosmopolitan *Cheirurus* is an Upper Ordovician and Silurian genus. It is one of the trilobite branches that developed relatively slowly and whose Ordovician and Devonian representatives are very much alike. The glabella, which widens gradually to the front, overlaps the frontal margin of the cephalon. It has three pairs of furrows, of which the basal furrows unite with the occipital furrow. The thorax is composed of 11 segments; the ends of the pleurae are free and terminate in blunt spines. The pygidium has a wide, conical axis and three pairs of short, massive curved spines. The carapace has a pustulated surface.

Arthropoda

Phacops ferdinandi KAYSER
Phacops latifrons (BRONN)

Order: Phacopida
Family: Phacopidae

The Phacopidae were distributed over the whole of the globe and formed a substantial part of the Silurian and Devonian marine fauna. Apart from features which also characterized other representatives of the suborder *Phacopina* (schizochroal eyes, proparian facial sutures, absence of a rostrum, 11 thoracic segments, fully developed articulation of the thoracic segments, etc.), they are particularly notable for their anterior spreading glabella and the rounded end of the pygidium and the thoracic pleurae. Phacopid carapaces are often found partly rolled; when they were completely rolled up, the posterior margin of the pygidium fitted into a furrow on the under side of the cephalon. Rolling up of the carapace is usually regarded as a form of passive defence. The most striking feature, which is common to all the members of the order, but has been studied the most in Phacopidae, are the schizochroal eyes – a peculiar type of highly perfected visual apparatus not encountered in any other group of animals. Phacopids occur in both shallow- and deep-water sediments, but they found the best conditions for their development in shallow seas in the warm climatic belt.

The Lower to Upper Devonian genus *Phacops* comprises trilobites which lived all over the world. Owing to pyritization of the material, X-ray

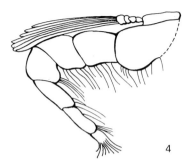

4

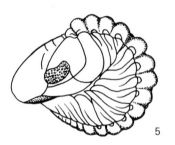

5

1, 4. *Phacops ferdinandi,* Lower Devonian (Lower Emsian), Bundenbach, West Germany. 1 – a complete carapace deformed by pressure; length 61 mm. This trilobite is one of the commonest fossils in Hunsrück Shales, which were formed in a quiet, muddy environment, probably at depths of down to 200 m. 4 – the biramous limb.

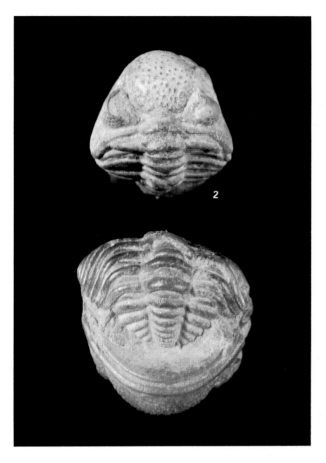

2. *Phacops latifrons,** Middle Devonian (Eifelian), Gerolstein, West Germany. Two complete, tightly rolled-up carapaces with a maximum width of 8 and 10 mm. Rolled-up carapaces were often preserved intact owing to the strong articulation of the thoracic segments of the carapace and the firm attachment of the thoracic skeleton to the cephalon and the pygidium.

3. *Reedops cephalotes,* Lower Devonian (Praguian), Damil near Tetín, Czechoslovakia. A complete carapace, length 26 mm. Whole carapaces are generally found. This species, with its well developed eyes, evidently lived on top of the sediment or swam just above it.

5. *Reedops bronni,* an enrolled specimen; a lateral view.

studies were able to reveal the structure of their body appendages and their alimentary system. Behind the paired, non-branching antennae on the head, three more pairs of appendages were discovered. Similarly constructed biramous limbs were attached to each of the thoracic and pygidial segments. In all trilobites, the segmented limbs were evidently constructed according to a uniform design. The longer main branch (the endopodite) was used for actual walking and the shorter one above it (the exopodite) was used form swimming or breathing (fig. 4). The proximal parts of at least two of the posterior adoral cephalic appendages were toothed and functioned as jaws.

Reedops cephalotes (HAWLE AND CORDA)

Order: Phacopida
Family: Phacopidae

Reedops is closely related to the preceding genus. Stratigraphically it ranges from the Lower Devonian to the early Middle Devonian in Europe, northern Africa, Asia and North America. The carapace is relatively narrow, the glabella is smooth and the frontal lobe markedly overlaps the frontal margin of the cephalon. The segmentation of the pygidium is indistinct.

The members of the genus *Reedops* occur primarily in very fine-grained sediments deposited in deep water.

Arthropoda

Odontochile hausmanni (Brongniart)

Order: Phacopida
Family: Dalmanitidae

The genus *Odontochile* comprises typical Lower Devonian trilobites distributed over most of the world. The elliptical carapace has a wide cephalic border. The glabella is divided by three pairs of deep glabellar furrows. The eyes are large (fig. 7) and the cheeks have long genal spines projecting from them. The large, richly segmented and wide-bordered pygidium is pointed. The pleural lobes have 12 to 15 paired ribs.

Asteropyge punctata (Steininger)

Order: Phacopida
Family: Dalmanitidae

The trilobites of the subfamily Asteropyginae are characteristic of Lower to early Upper Devonian strata of various continents. The spiny pygidium and the long pleural spines were evidently adaptations to life

1, 2. *Asteropyge punctata,* Middle Devonian (Eifelian), 'trilobite fields' ('Trilobitenfelder') near Giess, West Germany. A rolled-up (1) and incomplete (2) carapace; width 17 and 13 mm. Finds from a rich locality whose collecting traditions originated half way through the last century. Some 22 trilobite species (apart from other fauna) are known from the finely granular limestones.

3. *Odontochile hausmanni,* * Lower Devonian (Praguian), Lochkov, Czechoslovakia. A complete carapace, length 30 mm. A species occurring chiefly in very fine-grained limestones which were deposited at depths of more than 200 m.

4

5

D

4. *Digonus gigas,** Lower Devonian (Emsian), Lahnstein, West Germany. An incomplete cranidium, length 40 mm.

5. *Burmeisterella armata,* Lower Devonian (Emsian). Rheinische slate mountains (Rheinisches Schiefergebirge), West Germany. Core of a pygidium, length 38 mm.

6. *Burmeisterella bifurcata,* the cephalon.

7. *Odontochile* sp., detail of an eye.

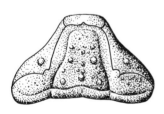

6

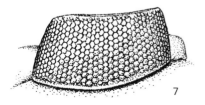

7

on the surface of soft sediment. These features are very well illustrated by the genus *Asteropyge,* known chiefly from Lower and Middle Devonian Europe. X-ray studies of material from Hunsrück shales have contributed interesting findings on the anatomical structure of the body of trilobites and have thus supplemented knowledge based chiefly on unique findings in Burgess Shales (British Columbia, Middle Cambrian) and Utica Slates (eastern USA, Silurian).

Digonus gigas (RÖMER)

Order: Phacopida
Family: Homalonotidae

Typical homalonotid trilobites (subfamily Homalonotinae) are known on every continent from the Silurian to the Middle Devonian. The genus *Digonus,* known in Europe, Africa, South America and New Zealand, is a good illustration of the conspicuous features of the carapace, which is highly convex, strikingly long and narrow. There is no border on the cephalon and no discernible furrows on the glabella. The eyes are small. The thorax has wide, indistinct axial lobes and the pleurae have truncated ends. The pygidium is long and triangular.

Digonus and closely related homalonotid trilobites lived in both warm and cold water, but always in a close relationship to sandy sediment. The smooth, slender carapace and reduced eyes denote adaptation to a burrowing existence. The carapace of some species attained lengths of up to 50 cm.

Burmeisterella armata (BURMEISTER)

Order: Phacopida
Family: Homalonotidae

Burmeisterella is closely related to the genus *Digonus.* It occurs in European Lower Devonian deposits. The spines on the surface of the carapace are a striking feature.

Radioscutellum intermixtum (HAWLE AND CORDA) Order: Ptychopariida Family: Scutelluidae

Scutelluids are known primarily from the warm climatic belts of the Silurian and Devonian periods. They have a wide, oval carapace and the glabella, with three pairs of glabellar furrows, widens noticeably at the front. The free cheeks are very large and the eyes have a kidney-shaped visual surface with up to 4,000 lenses. The thorax is composed of 10 segments. The large pygidium has a very short, triangular axis; the pleural fields have six to eight pairs of radially diverging ribs and a forked median rib, giving the pygidium the appearance of a fan. The carapace is surmounted by striking, regularly organized terraced ridges; in a closely associated pattern there are also large numbers of pores in the carapace, through which sensory 'bristles' (setae) projected. As well as strengthening the carapace, this system evidently had steering and tactile functions, etc.

The genus *Radioscutellum* comprises specialized trilobites known from Lower Devonian Europe. They are characterized by a flat carapace with a rounded pentagonal glabella and small eyes. The semi-elliptical pygidium has a conspicuously developed doublure extending almost to the vestigial axis. These trilobites lived directly on the sea bed in sheltered parts of coral reefs.

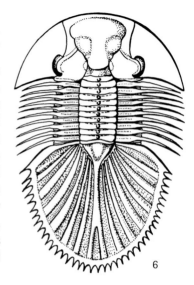

Thysanopeltis speciosa HAWLE AND CORDA Order: Ptychopariida Family: Scutelluidae

Thysanopeltis, one of the phylogenetically most recent genera of the entire family, inhabited the northern hemisphere during the Middle Devonian. Its carapace is morphologically sharply segmented and the eyes are large; the pygidium has a short, trilobate, extremely prominent axis and its posterior edge is bordered by spines of varying lengths (fig. 6).

Acanthopyge haueri (BARRANDE) Order: Lichida Family: Lichidae

Lichids inhabited Lower Ordovician to Upper Devonian seas. The glabellar grooves on the wide glabella are intricately modified. On the large, flat pygidium, which is often lobate and terminates in spines, there are three pairs of ribs. The carapace has a granular (and often spiny) surface. Lichids were primarily shallow-water trilobites and not infrequently they inhabited coral reefs. The order includes the largest known trilobite, the Ordovician *Uralichas*, whose carapace was up to 75 cm long.

The members of the genus *Acanthopyge* are known from Silurian to Middle Devonian sediments all over the world. The cephalon is parabolically shaped, the second and third glabellar lobes are fused and the eyes are set on stalks. The narrow free cheeks taper off into long spines. The thoracic carapace has 11 segments. The pygidial pleurae terminate in long spines. These trilobites lived mainly in shallow, turbulent water in the vicinity of coral biostromes.

1, 2. *Acanthopyge haueri*,* Middle Devonian (Eifelian), Koněprusy, Czechoslovakia. A cranidium (1) and pygidium (2); lengths 22 and 26 mm. The best specimens come from the fillings of fissures inside Devonian coral reefs.

3, 4. *Thysanopeltis speciosa*,* Middle Devonian (Eifelian), Koněprusy, Czechoslovakia. A cranidium (3) and pygidium (4); lengths 22 and 32 mm. This species mainly inhabited shallow water.

5. *Radioscutellum intermixtum*, Lower Devonian (Praguian), Koněprusy, Czechoslovakia. An accumulation (lumachelle) of pygidia measuring up to 50 mm. These lumachelles filled depressions and cavities inside the reef.

6. *Thysanopeltis* sp., a complete carapace.

Arthropoda

Gerastos bohemicus (HAWLE AND CORDA)

Order: Proetida
Family: Proetidae

During the Devonian period, proetids became the dominant trilobites. They flourished particularly in warm shallow seas, near or in coral reefs. The members of the genus *Gerastos* were locally abundant in parts of Lower and Middle Devonian Europe, northern Africa and North America. They are characterized by a high-domed, thick-walled carapace, a wide glabella with indistinct glabellar furrows and large eyes. The thoracic rings and the pygidial axis are very wide. The surface of the carapace is granular or spiny.

Dechenella verneuili (BARRANDE)

Order: Proetida
Family: Proetidae

Dechenella was a widely distributed Middle Devonian genus in the northern hemisphere. The anterior tapering glabella has three or four pairs of deep glabellar furrows. The eyes are large; the cheeks terminate in wide genal spines. The large, elongate pygidium has a conspicuous border and a strikingly ribbed axis with up to 19 rings. *Dechenella* species were most likely benthic trilobites.

1, 6. *Otarion ceratophthalmus*, Middle Devonian (Eifelian), Gees near Gerolstein, West Germany. A complete carapace (1), length including the spine 37 mm, a rolled-up carapace (6).

2, 3. *Dechenella verneuili*,* Middle Devonian (Givetian), Pelm, West Germany. A cranidium (2), length 7 mm, and a pygidium (3), length 8 mm.

4. *Typhloproetus subcarintiacus,* Upper Devonian (Famenian), Dzikowiec, Poland. Two isolated pygidia, length 2.5 mm.

5. *Gerastos bohemicus,* Lower Devonian (Praguian), Koněprusy, Czechoslovakia. A complete carapace, length 30 mm. A species adapted for life in turbulent water in and round coral reefs. Rolled-up carapaces are frequently found.

Typhloproetus subcarintiacus (RICHTER)

Order: Proetida
Family: Proetidae

The blind proetid trilobites of the genus *Typhloproetus* are characteristic of the highest Devonian (Famenian) strata in Europe. The facial suture had evidently lost its functional significance and is therefore indistinct. The free cheeks taper off into short genal spines. The semicircular pygidium has six to ten pairs of ribs on its pleural lobes. *Typhloproetus* species evidently led an at least partly burrowing existence in the floor of deepish seas, as indicated by complete reduction of their eyes, their indistinctly segmented carapace and their incidence in fine-grained types of sedimentary rocks.

Otarion ceratophthalmus (GOLDFUSS)

Order: Proetida
Family: Otarionidae

Otarion is a cosmopolitan genus with a large stratigraphic range (from Middle Ordovician to Upper Devonian). Apart from features characteristic of the family as a whole (e.g. the markedly domed cephalon, the swollen glabella with one pair of glabellar furrows leading to the occipital furrow and pinching off a pair of basal lobes, a small pygidium, etc.), its representatives are particularly conspicuous for their long genal spines and the thickened sixth thoracic segment, which bears a very long, recurved spine. The long genal spines could have played a stabilizing role on the sea bed or during swimming, but as yet we have no satisfactory explanation of the function of the thoracic spine.

335

Arthropoda

Phillipsia truncatula (PHILLIPS)

Order: Proetida
Family: Proetidae

At the end of the Middle Devonian and during the Upper Devonian, most trilobites suddenly died out. The only order to survive from the early into the late Palaeozoic era were Proetida, represented entirely by small forms of not very great diversity. They still existed in the Lower Carboniferous, when they lived in both shallow and relatively deep water (at depths of over 200 metres). We know practically nothing about genuinely abyssal or bathyal species from fossil discovery, however. Deep-water forms died out completely during the Middle Carboniferous; shallow-water representatives survived most frequently in the region of coral reefs. The era of the trilobites, as the Palaeozoic era is sometimes called, ended at the end of the Permian period and the development of the entire subphylum Trilobitomorpha ended with it. The reason for the extinction of this particularly widespread and diverse group of marine arthropods, of which roughly 12,000 species have so far been described and which inhabited the seas for over 350 million years, is not reliably known. The appearance and development of other groups of marine invertebrates and vertebrates, as well as great palaeogeographic changes reflected in the character of sedimentaton and of the climate, undoubtedly played no small role.

Among late Palaeozoic trilobites, the ones encountered most frequently on the territory of present-day Europe are Lower Carboniferous

1. *Phillipsia truncatula,* Lower Carboniferous (Dinantian), Windsor Hill Quarry, Somerset, England. A pygidium length 15 mm. A characteristic trilobite of Carboniferous limestone, a shallow-water sediment of Lower Carboniferous age, with crinoid segments as its main component.

2. *Archegonus laevicauda,* Lower Carboniferous (Viséan), Aprath, West Germany. A slightly deformed thorax and pygidium, length 15 mm. Bottom left: an isolated free cheek with a short genal spine.

3. *Phillipsia gemmulifera,* a complete carapace.

species, some of which occur in fairly large numbers in places and existed for a relatively very short period of time, so that they can be used in stratigraphy. *Phillipsia* is one of a series of important trilobite genera found in shallow-water calcareous sediments in Europe, North America and Australia. Its carapaces are up to 15 mm long. The cephalon and pygidium are roughly the same size. The cylindrical or anteriorly tapering glabella stretches to the rostral border of the cephalon. Moderately long spines project from the free cheeks. The thorax consists of nine segments. The semi-elliptical pygidium has an indistinct border. The surface of the carapace is markedly granular; as in other trilobites, some of the granules probably had the function of sensory papillae (fig. 3).

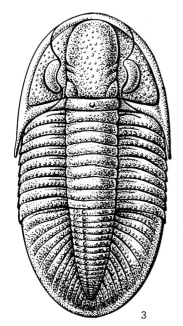

Archegonus laevicauda (SARRES)

Order: Proetida
Family: Proetidae

Just as Lower Carboniferous limestone facies have their characteristic trilobite genera and species, the European trilobites of the genus *Archegonus* occur in Culm facies, i.e. in mainly slaty sedimentary rocks. They have an only slightly domed carapace and a long, anteriorly tapering glabella; the glabellar furrows are indistinct and are oriented obliquely backwards. The pygidium is semi-elliptical and its axis clearly protrudes above the level of the pleural lobes.

 **Arthropoda**

Eurypterus fischeri EICHWALD

Order: Eurypterida
Family: Eurypteridae

Merostomata are evolutionally the oldest and palaeontologically the most attractive class of the subphylum Chelicerata (spiders and allies). Apart from a few exceptions they are among the more rarely found fossils. The oldest Merostomata are known from Lower Cambrian sediments and their most prosperous periods were the Silurian and the Devonian. Only one order survived the transition from the Mesozoic to the Cainozoic and its descendants, numbering a few genera with not many species, still survive in present-day oceans. Their body, like that of all Chelicerata, consists of a cephalothorax (prosoma) and an opisthosoma (abdomen). Of the six pairs of appendages on the prosoma, the first pair, which is situated in front of the mouth, has well developed claws (chelicerae). The second pair, the palps, are followed by four pairs of uniramous limbs with locomotor function. The opisthosoma is composed of 12 segments. The characteristic feature of Merostomata is that the last segment of the opisthosoma (the telson) terminates in a large, tapering spine. Merostomata are all aquatic animals. Their fossil representatives are known from marine sediments and from sediments deposited in brackish and fresh water. Eurypterids are an especially interesting Palaeozoic subclass of Merostomata. In addition to small forms, they include some of the biggest invertebrates of the whole Palaeozoic era, which were over three metres long.

The typical representatives of the genus *Eurypterus* (fig. 2) are known from Ordovician to Carboniferous strata in Europe, Asia and North America. They have a round-cornered, almost square prosoma and a long segmented opisthosoma differentiated to an anterior and a posterior part. On the dorsal surface of the prosoma there are a pair of compound eyes and central ocelli. The chelicerae are small; the first three pairs of legs are relatively short, with spines on every joint, while the next pair has spines at the end of the last (distal) joint. The swimming appendages are very large. The teeth on the adoral side of the coxae of the prosomal appendages acted as jaws. On the ventral side of the prosoma, behind the mouth, there is a striking oval plate (metastoma) covering parts of the wide coxae of the swimming appendages. The first, wider, part of the opisthosoma carries greatly reduced appendages, while the narrower caudal part has none. The telson is shaped like a long, massive spine. The shell contained only small amounts of calcium carbonate and was therefore flexible; it may also have been partly covered by fine bristles. Eurypterids lived in brackish and fresh water. They appear to have been predators and some of them may have had a venom gland. For locomotion they used their enormously enlarged, oar-like last pair of cephalothoracic appendages. Their gills were well protected by their opisthosomal shell and they may thus even have been able to spend short periods on land, or make their way from one pool to another.

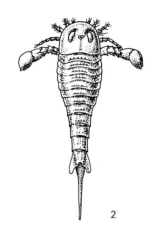

2

1. *Eurypterus fischeri,* Upper Silurian, Buffalo, USA. An almost complete compressed shell; length about 200 mm. An abundant species in places in uppermost Silurian fine-grained dolomites, which were evidently deposited in off-shore lagoons with brackish water.

2. *Eurypterus* sp., a reconstruction.

S

1

 **Arthropoda**

Pterygotus bohemicus (BARRANDE)

Order: Eurypterida
Family: Pterygotidae

Members of the merostome genus *Pterygotus* are found in Upper Ordovician to Devonian deposits in Europe, Asia, both Americas and apparently in Australia as well. Unlike eurypterids, which had small pincers (chelicerae), pterygotids had typical huge toothed pincers, followed by four pairs of appendages of roughly the same size. The last, sixth pair of prosomal appendages had been converted to powerful swimming organs. The opisthosoma terminated in a rounded or oval plate with a central ridge or row of spines on its dorsal surface. The surface of the shell was strikingly sculptured with scales or semicircles known as plicae. Parts of the exoskeleton are among the most frequently found remains. Pterygotids are known chiefly from marine sediments, but they also lived in brackish water. The large pincers, the anteriorly set eyes and the wide, oar-like hind limbs of the cephalothorax are evidence that they were nectonic predators, i.e. animals that actively swim. They grew to a length of up to two metres.

Mesolimulus walchi (DESMAREST)

Order: Limulida
Family: Mesolimulidae

The members of the very ancient and evolutionarily conservative Xiphosura (king crabs), a subclass of Merostomata, are characterized by an oval carapace distinctly divided into three lobes. Palaeozoic xiphosurans had a discernibly segmented opisthosoma, but in Mesozoic forms the segmentation of the opisthosoma was obliterated. Limulids are the

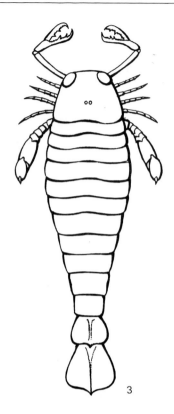

1, 3. *Pterygotus bohemicus,* Upper Silurian (Pridoli), Prague-Velká Chuchle, Czechoslovakia. Chelicerae, length 135 mm. This species (3 — a reconstruction) lived at the bottom of deeper seas covering what is now central Europe.

2. *Mesolimulus walchi,** Upper Jurassic (Tithonian), Solnhofen, West Germany. A core of a complete carapace, length 60 mm.

last xiphosurans still extant and they are akin both to eurypterids and to scorpions. The cephalothorax is slightly vaulted; in the middle there is a glabella, with cheeks on either side. In front, close to the plane of symmetry, there are two simple eyes and behind them, alongside the glabella, are large compound eyes. The prosomal appendages consist of one pair of chelicerae and five pairs of legs; the opisthosoma terminates in a long, sharp spine. Limulids still abound on the floor of the Atlantic shelf off the eastern coast of the USA, in the Indian Ocean and in the mangrove swamps of south-eastern Asia. Bathyal species migrate to the tidal zone to lay their eggs; the larvae pass through a 'trilobite' stage, so called because of its resemblance to a trilobite carapace. Limulids subsist on seaweed, young crustaceans, fish carcases and the like. As well as burrowing, they are able to swim, upside down. Their salt tolerance is high.

The Mesozoic representatives of the genus *Mesolimulus* occur in European Upper Jurassic sediments and are only slightly different from recent limulids. Their exoskeletons are moderately long (15 to 20 cm). The best specimens, including trails on the sea floor, come from Bavarian lithographic limestones. They are unique evidence of life at the bottom of lagoons which were otherwise practically devoid of life.

 **Arthropoda**

Cyclophthalmus senior CORDA

Order: Scorpionida
Family: Cyclophthalmidae

Arachnida (spiders, scorpions and mites), whose fossil representatives are known from the Silurian onwards, are numerically by far the largest class of Chelicerata. In many respects they resemble Merostomata, especially eurypterids, but they are terrestrial animals (perhaps the oldest) and only some of them secondarily returned to the water. That they evolved from Merostomata is more than likely, as seen not only from the outward resemblance of the members of the two groups, but also from the similarity between the leafy structure of the gills on the opisthosomal appendages of Merostomata and the structure of the lung sacs of scorpions and a number of other arachnids. All arachnids have only simple eyes, whose number and localization vary. As a rule, one pair lies in the middle of the cephalothorax and the others (up to five pairs) on the sides. Most arachnids are carnivorous, but some are herbivorous or parasitic. Like other terrestrial arthropods, we seldom find them as fossils and their fossil record is therefore very incomplete. As a rule they occur over limited stretches of territory and consequently there are no cosmopolitan species among them.

Scorpions (Scorpionida) are the evolutionally oldest arachnids. Their segmented abdomen is clearly divided into a large preabdomen (mesosoma) and a narrow postabdomen (metasoma) terminating in a sting. On the carapace there is one pair of median eyes and five pairs of lateral eyes — the largest number among arachnids. Conspicuous among the six pairs of appendages is the second pair — the powerful palps terminating in huge pincers. *Cyclophthalmus senior,* described by the Czech botanist Corda in 1835, is the first fossil scorpion (and the first

1, 2. *Eophrynus prestvicii,** Upper Carboniferous, Great Britain. A cast of a uniquely well preserved individual. The dorsal (1) and the ventral (2) surface of the body; length 25 mm.

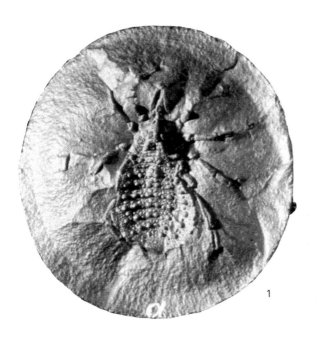

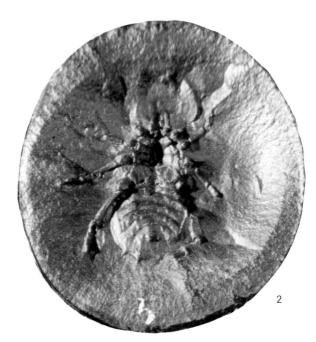

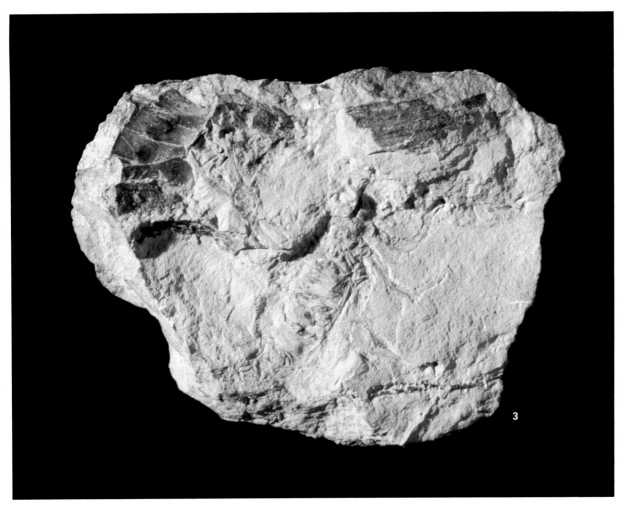

3. *Cyclophthalmus senior,* * Upper Carboniferous (Westphalian), Chomle near Radnice, Czechoslovakia. An almost complete individual, length about 60 mm. The first fossil arachnid ever to be described, preserved in grey shale with large quantities of fossil flora.

arachnid in general) ever to be named. It is known from Upper Carboniferous strata in central Europe. It has a roughly oblong cephalothorax with a slightly inturned anterior edge. The basal parts of the palps are shorter than the pincers.

Eophrynus prestvicii (BUCKLAND)

Order: Trigonotarbida
Family: Eophrynidae

In the late Palaeozoic era arachnids attained their prime and from the Carboniferous period alone we know 12 of all the 16 orders described. Trigonotarbida is an order represented only in the Devonian and the Carboniferous and it includes the second fossil arachnid ever to be discovered; this was *Eophrynus,* found in Upper Carboniferous strata in England, which was described by Buckland in 1836. Its roughly triangular carapace tapers away rostrally to a point. Its abdomen is composed of nine segments; the first tergite is the same width as the posterior end of the cephalothorax. The surface of the carapace is strikingly sculptured and the same applies to the abdomen, which has six pairs of bosses and four spines at the end.

 **Arthropoda**

Leperditia sp.

Order: Leperditicopida
Family: Leperditidae

Ostracoda are small, laterally compressed crustaceans (Crustacea) with a chitinous and more or less calcified bivalved shell enclosing the indistinctly segmented body. The seven pairs of appendages are differentiated to two pairs of feelers and two pairs of jaws on the head and three pairs of legs on the body. The shell consists of å right and a left valve. In some species the valves are conspicuously asymmetrical. Their dorsal margin is joined together by an elastic ligament, which opens and closes them; in addition, many species have a variously modified hinge. Ostracoda date back to the Cambrian. They live in salt, brackish and fresh water, in and on the bottom, or in the plankton. Palaeontologically they are an extremely important group for stratigraphy.

Leperditids are characteristic of the early Palaeozoic era. Their thick-walled, highly calcified shells grew to many times the size of the shells of other ostracods. They have a straight dorsal margin and an almost smooth surface. The right valve is larger than the left, which it overlaps along the free (ventral) margin.

1. *Leperditia* sp., Lower Silurian (Wenlock), Gotland, Sweden. Shells seen from the left and the right side; length 9–12 mm. The muscle fields, formed of a quantity of small imprints, are an important specific character.

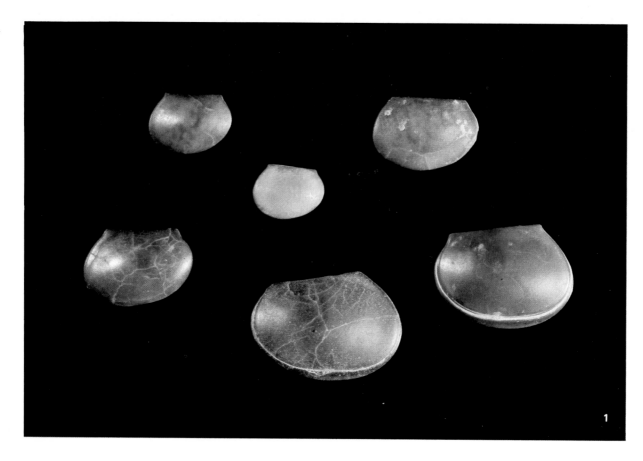

2. *Nodibeyrichia tuberculata,** Upper Silurian (Ludlow), Vidnava, Czechoslovakia. Length of shells about 2.5 mm. A boulder evidently brought by Quaternary glacier drift from the eastern Baltic. The smaller, strikingly sculptured shells belong to *Kloedenia wilckensiana** (length about 1.5–2 mm). Small, unidentified *Cytherellina* shells are also present.

3. *'Cypris' angusta,* Neogene (Upper Miocene), Doubí near Františkovy Lázně, Czechoslovakia. Cypris marl, length of shells about 1.5 mm.

4. *Nodibeyrichia* sp., a female shell.

4

Nodibeyrichia tuberculata (KLÖDEN)

Order: Beyrichicopina
Family: Beyrichiidae

Beyrichiids are one of the most abundant group of early Palaeozoic ostracods. They all have valves of roughly the same size, a straight dorsal margin and a convex free margin, the same internal shell structure and very pronounced sexual dimorphism. *Nodibeyrichia,* a common genus in Silurian Europe, is a typical representative of the order. On its granular surface, prominent lobes and deep grooves are arranged in a characteristic pattern. The front of the shell is flatter than the posterior part. Females have a large spherical sac (fig. 4) on the ventral margin of their shell. These were probably benthic ostracods.

Kloedenia wilckensiana (JONES)

Order: Beyrichicopina
Family: Beyrichiidae

The genus *Kloedenia,* which is related to *Nodibeyrichia,* is a Middle Ordovician to Upper Devonian genus occurring in Europe and North America. The anterior margin of the shells is higher than the posterior margin.

'Cypris' angusta REUSS

Order: Podocopida
Family: Cyprididae

Some ostracods did not become adapted to a freshwater existence until late in the Carboniferous. These forms flourished particularly during the Cainozoic era. Like most recent freshwater ostracods they belong to the cyprids, which are differentiated from marine species by their thin, smooth, oval to triangular shell, which is narrower at the back than at the front.

Arthropoda

Cyzicus blanensis (HOUŠA AND ŠPINAR)

Order: Conchostraca
Family: Cyzicidae

Conchostraca are the only palaeontologically important order of the crustacean class Branchiopoda. They inhabit fresh (and occasionally brackish) water, but fossil representatives are also known from typical marine sediments. Their known stratigraphic range stretches from the Ordovician to the Recent. The bivalved, flat-sided shell almost completely encloses the body and its appendages. It is rather like the shells of some bivalves in form, but it is made of chitin, sometimes with an admixture of calcium salts. Its size varies from 1 to 30 mm. The characteristic anatomical feature of Conchostraca is their second pair of antennae, which have been converted to powerful swimming organs. Conchostraca live planktonically and owing to the high resistance of their eggs, which are spread by wind and water, they are very widely distributed and are consequently of considerable significance for the stratigraphy of freshwater sediments.

Stramentum pulchellum (SOWERBY)

Order: Thoracida
Family: Stramentidae

Barnacles (Cirripedia) are a distinctive class of marine crustaceans, whose only palaeontologically documented order, Thoracida, dates back to the Silurian. A sessile mode of life led to far-reaching changes in the anatomy of these animals. Their originally planktonic larvae settle on a base and acquire a bivalved chitin shell. The front of their body is

1. *Cyzicus blanensis,* Upper Cretaceous (Senonian), Blaná near Zliv, Czechoslovakia. A deformed shell, length 10 mm. Because of their original elasticity, the chitinous shells of Conchostraca are usually deformed in various ways — a feature which often helps to differentiate them from bivalve shells.

Ng

Cr

transformed to a long stalk or a wide pedestal and their antennae and eyes undergo involution, while their biramous thoracic appendages – used for carrying food to their mouth – grow longer; they do not develop an abdomen. Soon after the larva has settled down, five primary non-calcareous plates appear under the bivalved shell; this is then shed and calcified plates are formed under the primary plates. Thoracida attach themselves to rocks, algae, the shells of various invertebrates, fish and cetaceans. They live chiefly in shallow water, but some at depths of down to several thousand metres.

The members of the genus *Stramentum* are known from Cretaceous sediments in Europe, the Near East and North America. They had a well developed stalk protected on either side by five rows of overlapping plates. The upper part, known as the capitulum, was surrounded by nine plates.

2. *Stramentum pulchellum,* Upper Cretaceous (Turonian), Prague-Bílá Hora, Czechoslovakia. Two almost complete skeletons, length 35 mm. A genus related to present-day goose barnacles (*Lepas*), whose stalk is not protected by plates, however.

3. *Balanus* sp., Neogene (Miocene), Italy. A scallop (*Pecten*) shell with acorn barnacles attached; diameter of the skeletons 5–10 mm.

Balanus sp.

Odrer: Thoracida
Family: Balanidae

The genus *Balanus* has been distributed all over the world since the Eocene up to the Recent. Its skeleton is shaped like a truncated cone with six plates, joined together, round its circumference. It is seated directly on its base over a wide surface. Acorn barnacles living on cliffs in the tidal zone are capped by an operculum made of loosely connected plates, which is closed when the tide goes out and prevents the animal from drying up.

Arthropoda

Caryocaris subula CHLUPÁČ

Order: Archaeostraca
Family: Ceratiocaridae

Phyllocarids (subclass Phyllocarida) are an evolutionally important branch of the crustacean class Malacostraca and the palaeontological evidence of their existence goes right back to the beginning of the Palaeozoic era. Apart from the characteristic features common to all Malacostraca (e.g. a carapace more or less completely enclosing the head and body, paired compound eyes on movable stalks, five pairs of cephalic appendages, the first pair of which are biramous feelers or antennules, a distinctly separate body and caudal portion with one pair of appendages on every segment), phyllocarids have a number of specific features of their own. The carapace protects only the front of the body; attached to it, on the dorsal surface, there is an anteriorly loosely attached rostral plate and the abdomen consists of seven segments, the last one of which — the telson — is formed like a spike and often carries a pair of accessory spines. Phyllocarids occur only in marine sediments; in general they are comparatively rare fossils, although locally they may be abundant. Like living species of crustacea, they included active swimmers, drifters and burrowers which lived in mud or under stones in shallow water and at depths of down to 6,000 metres.

1. *Ceratiocaris bohemica,* Upper Silurian (Pridoli), Prague-Velká Chuchle, Czechoslovakia. Part of an abdomen with spines, length 60 mm. One of the largest phyllocarids known (total length up to 75 cm).

2. *Pemphyx sueuri,** Middle Triassic, Kraitsheim, West Germany. A carapace, length about 35 mm. The thick-walled, highly calcified carapace is evidence of a benthic existence.

3. *Caryocaris subula,* Lower Ordovician (Llanvirn), Osek near Rokycany, Czechoslovakia. A cluster of small, compressed carapaces about 10 mm long preserved in a carbonate concretion.

4, 5. *Caryocaris* sp., 4 — the carapace, 5 — the terminal segment.

6. *Ceratiocaris* sp., a reconstruction.

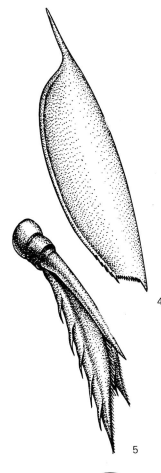

The members of the genus *Caryocaris* lived in the Ordovician period and because of their planktonic mode of life they spread over the greater part of the globe. Their smooth, elongate carapace, which shows signs of a border, tapers off, on the dorsal aspect, into a rostral horn (fig. 4). The terminal segment has a short median spike with two further leaf-like spines on either side (fig. 5).

Ceratiocaris bohemica BARRANDE

Order: Archaeostraca
Family: Ceratiocaridae

Ceratiocaris, another cosmopolitan genus, is known from the Ordovician to the Devonian. Its elongate, more or less oval carapace is longitudinally grooved and in front, on the dorsal aspect, it is pointed. The median spike is longer than the lateral spines (fig. 6).

Pemphyx sueuri (DESMAREST)

Order: Decapoda
Family: Pemphicidae

Eucarids are a class of crustaceans characterized primarily by a carapace covering the whole of the cephalothorax. The most important order, Decapoda, takes its name from its five pairs of legs. As a rule these animals have a large body. The extant Japanese Spider Crab (*Macrocheira kaempferi*) is up to 60 cm long and has a leg span of almost four metres. Decapods date back to the Permian, but they seem to have attained their greatest prosperity in the Recent. Some 8,000 species are known in our present-day seas and oceans, large numbers live in brackish and fresh water and some species have even taken to the dry land.

The genus *Pemphyx* occurs in European Middle Triassic sediments. Its cylindrical, dorsoventrally slightly flattened carapace has two deep cross grooves, with a further groove curving arch-wise behind them.

349

Aeger tipularius (SCHLOTHEIM)

Order: Decapoda
Family: Penaeidae

During the Middle Jurassic decapods flourished and spread in all directions. Since their chitin carapace was not always sufficiently calcified and chitin, after death, is gradually broken down by bacteria, such carapaces were preserved only in places where there were optimum conditions for their fossilization. This was particularly the case in an anaerobic environment in which argillaceous and calcareous sediments rich in liquid and solid hydrocarbons were deposited, or in lagoons where fine chalky matter settled, with important help from unicellular calcareous algae (coccolithophorids). Such lagoons existed where southern Bavaria now lies, for example. In Solnhofen lithographic limestone even the finest details of the carapace are often preserved.

The genus *Aeger* belongs to one of the evolutionally oldest decapod families, whose representatives are characterized particularly by a flat-sided, very thin-walled carapace, a long rostrum and a long abdomen. It is known in Europe from the Upper Triassic to the Upper Jurassic. The first and second pair of feelers (antennae and antennules) are very long. The third of the five pairs of thoracic legs — the long maxillipeds, which helped to handle food — are very striking. The first three pairs have a spiny surface. The surface of the carapace is granular and its light construction shows that it was evidently adapted for swimming.

Pseudastacus pustulosus (MÜNSTER)

Order: Decapoda
Family: Nephropidae

The members of the genus *Pseudastacus*, which are also found in Solnhofen limestone, have a cylindrical cephalothorax with a short triangular rostrum and a deep cervical groove. The surface of the carapace is covered with pustules. The first three pairs of thoracic limbs terminate in claws. The claws on the first pair are the largest; they are long and narrow, with straight rami.

Eryon arctiformis SCHLOTHEIM

Order: Decapoda
Family: Eryonidae

The members of the genus *Eryon,* described in Upper Jurassic strata in Bavaria, Germany, have a wide, dorsoventrally flattened carapace without a rostrum, but with highly developed eyes. The first four pairs of thoracic limbs are armed with claws. The long, flat abdomen has a median ridge. Eryonids are regarded as benthic animals; they evidently lived near the margin of lagoons.

1. *Eryon arctiformis,** Upper Jurassic (Tithonian), Solnhofen, West Germany. An almost complete carapace, length 78 mm. The last four pairs of thoracic limbs are missing.

2. *Pseudastacus pustulosus,** Upper Jurassic (Tithonian), Solnhofen, West Germany. An almost complete carapace, length about 55 mm. The carapace has been obliquely compressed; all that is left of the pairs of feelers are scanty fragments.

3. *Aeger tipularius,** Upper Jurassic (Tithonian), Solnhofen, West Germany. A complete specimen 80 mm long, with both pairs of feelers intact and with clearly discernible thoracic and abdominal appendages.

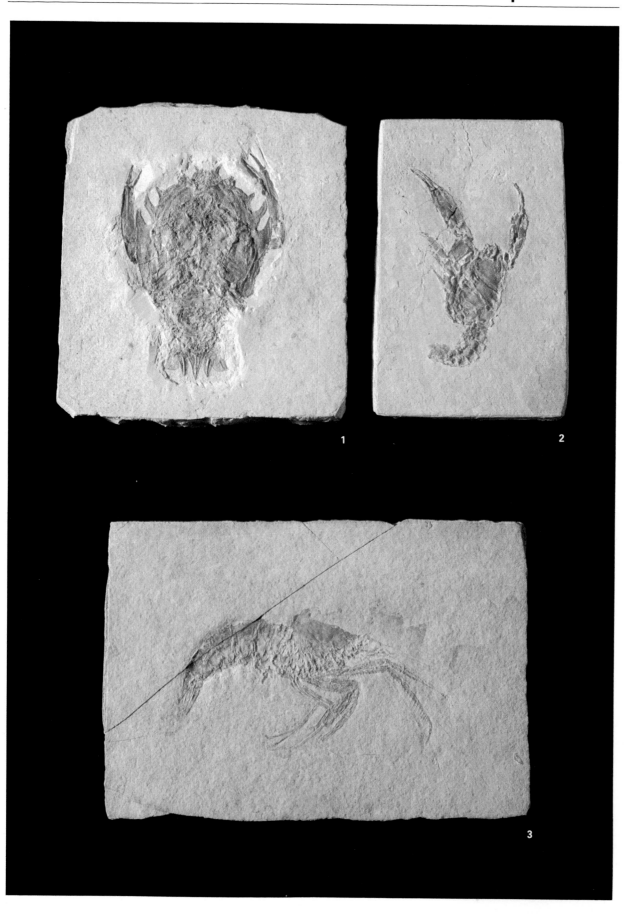

Arthropoda

Enoploclytia leachi (Mantell)

Order: Decapoda
Family: Erymidae

During the Cretaceous period, decapods continued to flourish and develop. *Enoploclytia,* a characteristic and widely distributed genus, is known from Europe, western Africa, Madagascar, North America and Australia. The carapace is carved into pieces by three cross grooves and a median suture. The claws are narrow, with long rami. The surface of the carapace, abdomen and claws is noticeably granular.

Protocallianassa antiqua (Römer)

Order: Decapoda
Family: Callianassidae

The members of this decapod family have a weakly calcified carapace, a well developed median groove or a non-calcified zone and a nuchal groove. The antennules are short and the first pair of thoracic appendages terminates in markedly dissimilar claws. *Protocallianassa* species occur in Upper Cretaceous and Palaeocene sediments in Europe, North America and Australia; they are closely related – and evidently lived in a similar manner – to the present-day genus *Callianassa,* whose members inhabit lairs in the higher part of the tidal zone of warm seas. A high incidence of these decapods is regarded as an ecological indicator of a littoral environment. They are known from brackish water and were among the earliest decapods to become adapted to low salinity. Their highly calcified claws are found quite often.

1. *Polycnemidium pustulosum,* * Upper Cretaceous (Coniacian), Březno, Czechoslovakia. A carapace, length 12 mm. Pronounced small pustules can be seen on the surface of the carapace.

2. *Protocallianassa antiqua,* Upper Cretaceous (Turonian), Morašice near Litomyšl, Czechoslovakia. The difference in the size of the left and right claws is clearly discernible; length of the larger claw 55 mm.

3, 4. *Notopocorystes stokesi,* * Lower Cretaceous (Albian), Cambridge, England. Carapaces, lengths 25 and 30 mm. The ventral view (4) clearly shows the strong claws; 3 – a dorsal view.

5, 6. *Enoploclytia leachi,* * Upper Cretaceous (Turonian), Prague-Bílá Hora, Czechoslovakia. 5 – the anterior part of a carapace complete with claws; total length 115 mm. 6 – a reconstruction.

Notopocorystes stokesi (MANTELL)

Order: Decapoda
Family: Ranninidae

A large number of true crabs whose carapace grew progressively shorter and wider are known from the Cretaceous period. The first (and sometimes also the second) pair of thoracic appendages have claws, but the third pair have none. The short, flattened abdomen is tucked under the ventral part of the cephalothorax; some of its segments are fused together. The abdominal appendages (the swimming limbs) are reduced.

The representatives of the cosmopolitan Cretaceous genus *Notopocorystes* still have an elongate carapace, whose sculpture is characterized by a striking discontinuous median ridge formed of short spines.

Polycnemidium pustulosum (REUSS)

Order: Decapoda
Family: Calappidae

Members of this genus are at present known only from Upper Cretaceous strata in central Europe. They are characterized by a relatively small, wide, short carapace with large eye-sockets, sharp sides and a pustulous surface and by strongly developed claws. The abdomen, which is tucked under the ventral surface of the cephalothorax, has a complete set of abdominal appendages.

6

5

Arthropoda

Zanthopsis dufourii (DESMAREST)

Order: Decapoda
Family: Xanthidae

Decapods continued to flourish in the Cainozoic era also and today they are still a richly represented group of crustaceans, with a wide variety of forms. Crabs and allies are highly specialized for a particular mode of life and are very sensitive to the specific conditions, e.g. the composition of the water, substratum and plankton, etc. Many live on plankton, or collect whatever the ebb tide leaves behind. The littoral zone (i.e. the zone between the limits of the two tides) is especially rich in these animals, but it is not a good environment for their preservation in the fossil state. In particular, practically nothing is known of crustaceans which inhabited rocky shores. Most of the known fossil crabs belong to forms which lived on a sandy or clayey floor or in a coral reef environment. A number of present-day species live in symbiotic or commensal relationships with coelenterates, sponges and molluscs, or use other animals' shells to protect their soft abdomen. The palaeontological record tells us virtually nothing, at present, about such relationships in the past.

The genus *Zanthopsis* comprises the commonest Cainozoic crabs, which in places — especially in warm Palaeocene to Oligocene seas in the northern hemisphere — participated in the formation of 'crab beds'. They have a wide, transversely oval, domed shell with a lobulate or dentate margin and a nodose surface. The large claws are of different sizes, according to the side.

Dromilites lamarcki (DESMAREST)

Order: Decapoda
Family: Dromiidae

The crabs of the Cainozoic genus *Dromilites* inhabited coral reefs in what is now Europe, North America and Australia in large numbers. Their domed cephalothorax is roughly circular and is very strikingly sculptured with structures ranging from nodes to short spines. The carapace has a dentate anterior edge and its posterior third has a rugose surface devoid of nodes.

Harpatocarcinus punctulatus (DESMAREST)

Order: Decapoda
Family: Xanthidae

The genus *Harpatocarcinus* is known from Eocene Europe, North America and eastern Africa. The widely oval, domed carapace does not have a protruding rostrum; it has an almost smooth surface, but a dentate anterior and anterolateral edge. The powerful claws are of unequal sizes.

1,4. *Harpatocarcinus punctulatus,** Palaeogene (Eocene), Marostica (Vincenza), Italy. A common species participating in the construction of 'crab beds'. 1 — the dorsal surface of the carapace, 4 — the ventral surface showing the huge claws and the abdomen tucked under the ventral surface of the cephalothorax. Width of carapace about 90 mm.

2. *Zanthopsis dufourii,* Palaeogene (Eocene), Dép. Landes, France. A carapace, length 35 mm.

3. *Dromilites lamarcki,* Palaeogene (Eocene), Sheppey, Great Britain. A carapace, length 25 mm. A beautifully preserved specimen from the London Clay.

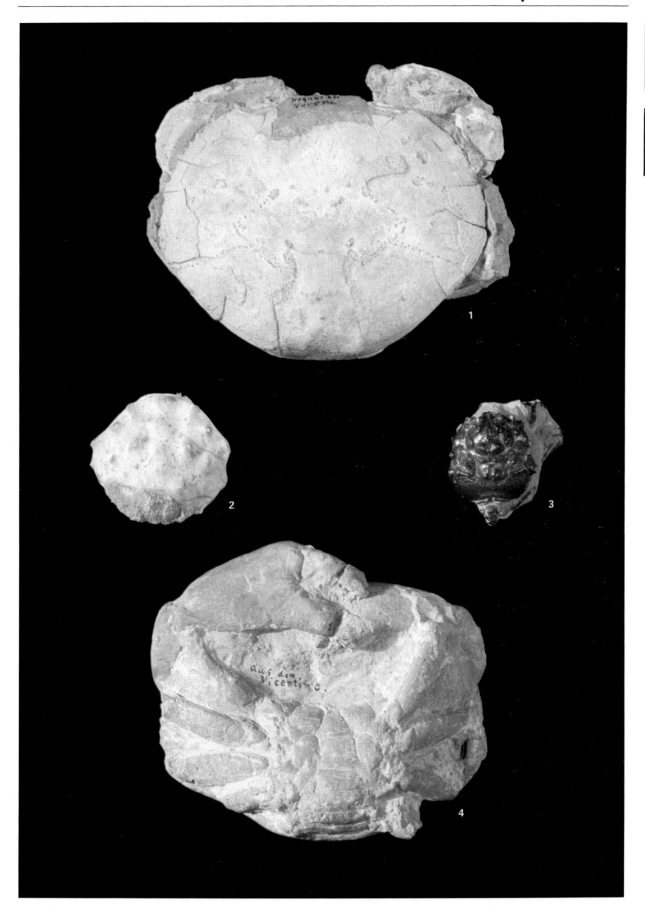

Arthropoda

Euphoberia hystrix FRITSCH

Order: Euphoberiida
Family: Euphoberiidae

Only isolated terrestrial arthropods are found in the fossil state, owing to the much less favourable conditions for their preservation. These rare fossils include millipedes (Diplopoda), which were unusually widespread, especially in Carboniferous forests. They are distinctly divided into a head and a body and sometimes have a clearly separate abdomen. Their body appendages are uniramous. Millipedes breathe by means of tracheae or over the whole of their body surface. They are vegetarians.

Members of the genus *Euphoberia* have been described in Upper Carboniferous layers in Europe and Pennsylvania (USA). They have a wide head, followed by three very short body segments, each with one pair of limbs. The subsequent segments have short paired dorsal spines and forked lateral spines. Ventrally they are divided into two subsegments, each with a pair of appendages.

Bojophlebia prokopi PECK

Order: Ephemeroptera
Family: Protereismatoidea

Insects, the evolutionarily most advanced class of arthropods, made their first appearance in geological history in the Devonian period. They completely adapted themselves to life on dry land and today their species far outnumber those of any other group of animals. An insect's body is divided into a head, a thorax and an abdomen; on the head there

1. *Euphoberia hystrix,* Upper Carboniferous (Westphalian), Nýřany, Czechoslovakia. Part of a body, length 55 mm. Found in cannel, a type of coal rich in bituminous substances and the source of the diverse fauna described by the Czech palaeontologist A. Frič.

2. *Moravamylacris kukalovae,** Lower Permian (Autunian), Jabloňany, Czechoslovakia. A sclerotized front wing (elytron), length 27 mm. The stratigraphically oldest finds of representatives of some groups of insects come from this locality. The dead insects which collected in the shelter of freshwater pools were probably blown there by the wind.

3

3. *Bojophlebia prokopi,** Upper Carboniferous (Westphalian), Kladno, Czechoslovakia. Wing span about 450 mm. A giant nymph of this species, 110 mm long, has also been found.

are one pair of feelers and compound eyes (unless secondarily reduced). On each of the thoracic segments there is one pair of legs; as a rule, there are also two pairs of wings on the thorax.

May-flies (Ephemeroptera) belong to the evolutionally oldest insect orders and date back to the late Carboniferous. Their long, characteristically veined wings can be moved only up and down and cannot be folded on their back − one of the main features of primitive winged insects (Palaeoptera). Another striking feature are the two long cerci and the terminal filament at the end of the abdomen. Some Ephemeroptera grew to considerable proportions, although the one with a wing span of 45 cm found in Upper Carboniferous Bohemian freshwater sediments is an extreme example. Up to now it was considered to be a dragon-fly belonging to the genus *Meganeura,* the biggest insect of all time, with a wing span of up to 65 cm.

Order: Blattaria
Family: Mylacridae

Moravamylacris kukalovae SCHNEIDER

The oldest cockroaches (Blattaria) are also known from the Upper Carboniferous, when they likewise attained the peak of their development. They are the commonest insect fossils of the late Palaeozoic era. Cockroaches have not undergone any important changes during the almost 300 million years for which they have existed.

357

Arthropoda

Tarsophlebia maior HAGEN

Order: Odonata
Family: Tarsophlebiidae

Mesozoic insects are best represented in Jurassic deposits. The best specimens come from Tithonian Solnhofen limestones in Bavaria (West Germany), where 180 species belonging to orders still extant today have been described. Some of the families are different, however, and all the known genera differ from recent genera. Beetles (Coleoptera) and dragon-flies (Odonata) are the best represented, with 45 and 40 species respectively. Dragon-flies, together with may-flies, are the only Palaeoptera still extant. They are striking because of their large size, their long abdomen, their fused mesothorax and metathorax and their long, narrow wings. The members of the genus *Tarsophlebia* are among the most numerous dragon-flies in the lithographic limestone.

Mesochrysopa zitteli MEUNIER

Order: Neuroptera
Family: Mesochrysopidae

'Net-winged' insects (Neuroptera), with 19 known species represented in Solnhofen limestone, are another important insect order. The two pairs of wings resemble each other and are characterized by rich veining. Their thoracic segments are free. *Mesochrysopa* is a relative of present-day lace-wings, but was considerably larger.

1. *Tarsophlebia maior,* Upper Jurassic (Tithonian), Solnhofen, West Germany. An almost complete specimen, wing span 80 mm. Only one pair of limbs has been preserved. The biggest dragon-flies of Upper Jurassic Bavaria had a wing span of up to 190 mm.

2. *Mesochrysopa zitteli,** Upper Jurassic (Tithonian), Solnhofen, West Germany. Body length 25 mm. The unusually large size of Bavarian Upper Jurassic insects is due, inter alia, to the very warm climate at that time.

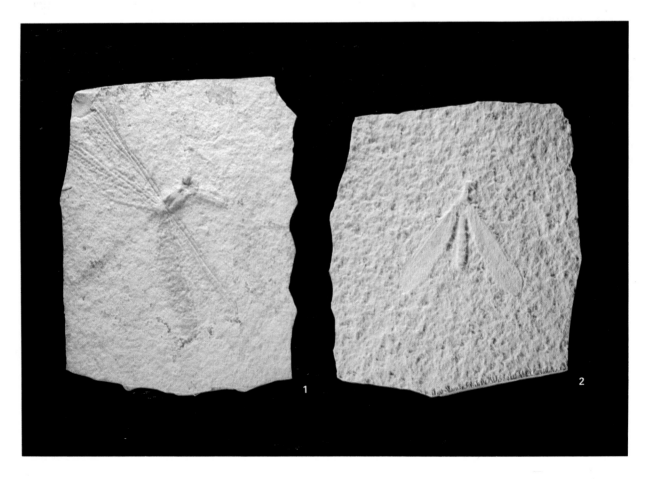

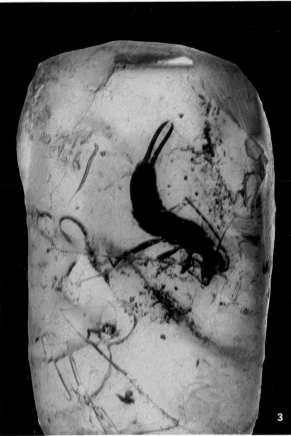

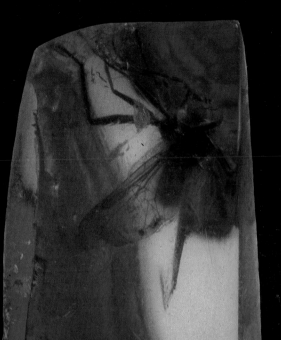

3. *Labia* sp., Palaeogene (Upper Eocene), Baltic region, Poland. Length 10 mm.

4. *Chrysopilus* sp., Palaeogene (Upper Eocene), Baltic region, Poland. Length 7 mm. The richest amber finds come from secondary sites along the Baltic coast. Fragments of amber from the sandy subtratum are often washed up on shore by the waves.

Chrysopilus sp.

Order: Diptera
Family: Rhagonidae

Among the tremendous quantity of insect remains known from the Cainozoic era there are many which have not yet been properly investigated. Amber, a fossil resin from pine trees, is an ideal preserving medium and insect remains preserved in amber were mentioned by Aristotle. As the resin welled forth from injured parts of the trees, it swallowed up tiny organisms, which were unable to free themselves by their own efforts, together with grains of pollen and spores, etc. About 90 per cent of the animal inclusions found in Baltic amber are of insect origin. An evaluation of the plant and animal remains imprisoned in amber gives us a fairly true picture of the environment in which these organisms lived, i.e. of the damp subtropical forests in which organisms of the temperate belt were also represented. The remains of flies (Diptera) are among the commonest.

Labia sp.

Order: Dermaptera
Family: Labiduridae

Earwigs (Dermaptera) formed part of the tremendously rich assemblage of insects in amber forests. They date back to the Jurassic and their fossil representatives are easily distinguished by their elongate body, vestigial first pair of wings and pincer-like cerci.

Echinodermata

Akadocrinus nuntius PROKOP

Order: Atava
Family: Eocrinidae

Echinoderms (Echinodermata) are a very ancient and unusually polymorphous phylum of marine invertebrates whose roots go far back into Precambrian times. Their calcareous, pentamerally symmetrical mesodermal skeleton is composed of a large number of plates and/or spicules. Throughout the body there is a complex water-vascular system − the ambulacral system − formed by transformation of the coelom.

Included among the phylogenetically important classes of sessile echinoderms (subphylum Crinozoa) are the primitive 'stone lilies' (Eocrinoidea), which appeared in the early Cambrian and evidently died out at the end of the Ordovician. Their skeleton, whose pentamerous symmetry was not yet complete, is largely reminiscent of that of extant crinoids. It consists of a theca and arms, which together form the crown, and of a stem. The spherical, cup-shaped or conical theca was composed of plates with a complex system of respiratory pores, and relatively long, fine, unbranched arms (brachioles) composed of two rows of plates grew from its upper surface. The brachioles collected small food particles and conveyed them to the mouth, which, as a rule, was situated in the centre of the thecal roof or tegmen; the anus (periproct) was situated eccentrically. The primitively constructed multisegmented stem kept the animal anchored to the bottom. Phylogenetically older types were attached by the widened base of the theca.

Eocrinoids of the genus *Akadocrinus* occur in Middle Cambrian shallow-water sediments in central Europe. They have an elongate, flat-roofed theca with large numbers of brachioles round the edge. The theca tapers off into a long stem with a wide terminal attachment plate.

Lichenoides priscus BARRANDE

Order: Reducta
Family: Lichenoidae

Lichenoids were highly specialized eocrinoids whose theca was composed of three circlets of five plates each, one above the other (fig. 4). They have been found in Middle Cambrian strata in Bohemia. They are the oldest known sessile echinoderms with complete pentameral symmetry and with a stable number of thecal plates throughout their entire development. The adults probably lived pelagically, since they have neither a stem nor any other means of attachment, while on the other hand they have large cavities, especially in the bottom row of thecal plates.

Macrocystella bohemica (BARRANDE)

Order: Plicata
Family: Macrocystellidae

Macrocystella occurs in Middle Ordovician sediments in western and central Europe. The theca closely resembles the theca of Rhombifera ('cystoids') and there were evidently close phylogenetic relationships between the two classes. The surface of the thin thecal plates is strikingly ribbed, the brachioles are long and the long stem widens below the theca.

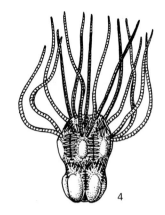

1. *Macrocystella bohemica*, Middle Ordovician (Caradoc), Trubská, Czechoslovakia. A thecal core, height 17 mm. An incomplete specimen, in which the roof, the brachioles and the bottom of the stem are missing.

2. *Lichenoides priscus,** Middle Cambrian, Jince, Czechoslovakia. A core of an almost complete skeleton, together with the long, thin brachioles. Height of theca 13 mm. The serrated edges of the plates correspond to the system of pores and canals running perpendicularly to the sutures between the individual plates.

3. *Akadocrinus nuntius,* Middle Cambrian, Jince, Czechoslovakia. Cores of two almost complete skeletons with the attachment disc broken off. Height of theca 12 mm. This species preferred the sandy bottom of shelf seas.

4. *Lichenoides* sp., a reconstruction.

Echinodermata

Aristocystites bohemicus BARRANDE

Order: Diploporitida
Family: Aristocystitidae

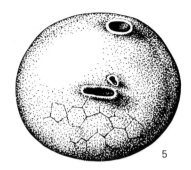

Two other classes of echinoderms, Diploporita and Rhombifera – formerly grouped together under the name Cystoidea –, are also characterized by incomplete pentameral symmetry. The oldest representatives of Diploporita are known from Lower Ordovician strata and the most recent from Middle Devonian. Their spherical or pear-shaped theca is composed of a large number (up to several hundred) of irregularly organized polygonal plates with pairs of pores (diplopores) connected by simple canals which, in the living animal, probably had respiratory function. The mouth is in the centre of the upper surface of the theca; small food particles were transported to it via ambulacral grooves inside the brachioles. The brachioles are composed of a single row of plates. The anus is located eccentrically. In addition, two more openings can be seen on the theca – the opening of the ambulacral system and the genital pore or gonopore. On the under side of the theca there was often a stem. Diploporita were benthic animals inhabiting shallow water.

Aristocystites species are known from Ordovician sediments in Europe, northern Africa, Asia and eastern Australia. The pouch-like or pear-shaped theca is composed of large plates and the under side is usually truncated. The ambulacral system and the gonopore open on to the surface between the mouth and the anus. These species did not have a stem (fig. 5).

Codiacystis bohemica (BARRANDE)

Order: Diploporitida
Family: Sphaeronitidae

Members of the genus *Codiacystis* are known from Bohemian Middle Ordovician strata. The ovoid or bag-like theca is composed of numerous thick-walled plates and has an unwontedly thickened base. The under parts of internal moulds, shaped like the bottom of a wine bottle, are most commonly found.

Homocystites alter BARRANDE

Order: Dichoporita
Family: Cheirocrinidae

Echinoderms of the class Rhombifera appeared in the Lower Ordovician and the last of them died out at the end of the Devonian. Rhombifera have a similarly shaped skeleton to Diploporita, but their pentameral symmetry is more pronounced. The polygonal plates of the theca have a completely different system of pores and internal canals. The pores are arranged in rhomboid fields, each pore opening on to one of two adjacent plates. The brachioles are composed of two rows of plates. These benthic echinoderms were mostly anchored to the bottom by a short stem.

1, 2. *Codiacystis bohemica,** Middle Ordovician (Caradoc), Zahořany, Czechoslovakia. Size 32 and 30 mm. 1 – a core from behind; a cast of the anus can be clearly seen in the theca. 2 – the crater-like depression in a cast of the base was formerly thought to be the mouth.

3. *Homocystites alter,** Middle Ordovician (Caradoc), Zahořany, Czechoslovakia. An almost complete skeleton, height of theca 22 mm.

4. *Aristocystites bohemicus,** Middle Ordovician (Caradoc), Zahořany, Czechoslovakia. Height of theca 70 mm. In places this species formed dense populations on the sandy floor of the Middle Ordovician sea.

5. *Aristocystites* sp., a view of the theca from above.

362

O

Rhombifera of the genus *Homocystites* are known from Ordovician strata in Europe and North America. Their theca, which has an elongate trapezoid outline, is formed of regularly organized plates with striking radial ribs. The arms round the mouth are small and fine. The long stem widens at the base of the theca.

Echinodermata

Echinosphaerites aurantium GILLENHAAL

Order: Fistuliporita
Family: Echinosphaeritidae

Echinosphaerites is the best known genus of the class Rhombifera. Its species are to be found in Lower and Middle Ordovician sediments in almost every part of the world. It was also one of the first 'cystoids' to be described, as early as 1772. The spherical theca is composed of several hundred small polygonal plates. On thecae with a favourably weathered surface we can clearly see the internal canal system, whose organization in rhombs expresses one of the characteristic features of the class as a whole. The canals were covered by a very thin layer, the epitheca, which over the individual plates was marked with concentric grooves evidently associated with progressive growth of the plates. The elevated mouth was surrounded by a few relatively long, branched brachioles. Round the periphery of the eccentrically situated anus there were usually five triangular plates arranged in a low pyramid. When alive, the animals were anchored to the bottom by a very thin stem (fig. 4) or simply by an attachment disc. They lived in shallow water, but below the active wave zone. Their domain was northern Europe, where in some places they occurred in such quantities that they formed limestone banks. They were adapted to life on both a firm and a soft bottom, where they attached themselves to other animals' shells.

Arachnocystites infaustus (BARRANDE)

Order: Fistuliporita
Family: Echinosphaeritidae

The genus Arachnocystites is very closely related to Echinosphaerites. Its members are known from Middle Ordovician sediments in central Europe, northern Africa and southern Asia. Their thecal plates are not so regularly organized and their mouth is not elevated, but they have a thicker stem. The long brachioles are not branched. These echinoderms inhabited the sandy bed of cold shallow seas.

1. Echinosphaerites aurantium,* Middle Ordovician (Llandeilo), Wolkhov-Obukhov, Estonia. The elevated peristome can be seen at the apex of the spherical theca and the anal pyramid at the side. Height of theca 35 mm.

2. Orocystites helmhackeri,* Middle Ordovician (Caradoc), Chrustenice, Czechoslovakia. Height of core 36 mm. This specimen comes from iron ore sediments formed in the shallow shelf sea.

3. *Arachnocystites infaustus,** Middle Ordovician (Caradoc), Zahořany, Czechoslovakia. Height of theca 30 mm. An almost complete skeleton with intact brachioles has been secondarily compressed in a characteristic type of shallow-water sediment – sandy shale.

4. *Echinosphaerites* sp., a reconstruction.

3

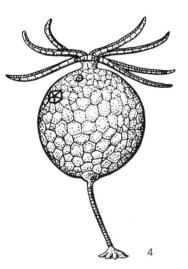

4

Orocystites helmhackeri BARRANDE

Order: Fistuliporita
Family: Caryocystitidae

The species of this genus are known from the European Middle Ordovician. On its upper surface the ovoid theca is produced to two horns – the peristome and the periproct. It is composed of about 50 large hexagonal plates. The brachioles were evidently very small and were therefore not preserved. *Orocystites* lived in shallow water (down to 50 metres deep) and were anchored to the bottom by a stem with a hexagonal cross section (deduced from the shape of the attachment facet at the base of the theca).

Echinodermata

Trochocystites bohemicus BARRANDE

Order: Cincta
Family: Trochocystitidae

One of the palaeontologically most problematic groups of echinoderms is the subphylum Homalozoa, whose representatives lived during the early Palaeozoic. What makes them scientifically attractive is the structure of their skeleton, which in some respects resembles that of Chordata. When classifying biological material, the aim of palaeontologists is to express kinship between organisms in the form of a natural system. In this respect, *Homalozoa* are very troublesome. The chief members of this subphylum are the carpoids (Carpoidea), a heterogeneous group comprising animals with considerable differences in their skeletal structure and anatomy.

Members of the class Homostelea are at present known only from Middle Cambrian strata. Their skeleton consists of a theca and a stalk (stele). The theca is flat and only slightly asymmetrical and is composed of a large number of plates. Large marginal plates encircle the smaller inner plates. Anteriorly there was a small mouth, to which food was transported along the one or two food grooves. The stele corresponds to the stem of sessile echinoderms; it is composed of polygonal plates and is not segmented. The genus *Trochocystites,* known from Middle Cambrian deposits in central and western Europe, is a characteristic representative of the class as a whole. Its members evidently lived on a floor formed of finely granular sediment.

Dendrocystites barrandei JAEKEL

Order: Soluta
Family: Dendrocystitidae

As a class, Homoiostelea are characterized by a greater stratigraphic range (from Upper Cambrian to Lower Devonian) and a greater generic diversity. In addition to a theca and a stele, their skeleton also has an arm-like brachiole for conveying food to the mouth. The theca is slightly asymmetrical or almost bilaterally symmetrical and is composed of a large number of plates of varying sizes. The marginal plates are no different from those in the centre. The posterior end of the dorsoventrally flattened theca is usually concave and near it, on the side, lies the anus. The conical stele, which is differentiated into three parts, arises from the concave posterior part of the theca.

The skeletons of the Middle Ordovician genus *Dendrocystites,* which occurs in central European shallow-water sediments, display the basic characters of the entire family. The rounded-triangular theca terminates in a long brachiole formed by two rows of plates. The anus is surrounded by an anal pyramid; the stele is long and conical. Dendrocystites lived on a sandy bottom and caught small food particles with the raised brachiole.

1. *Trochocystites bohemicus,** Middle Cambrian, Skryje, Czechoslovakia. Length of theca 17 mm. A square peristomal plate is clearly discernible on the small skeleton with its limonite-stained surface.

2. *Dendrocystites barrandei,* Middle Ordovician (Caradoc), Zahořany, Czechoslovakia. Length of theca 35 mm. Beside the complete skeleton of this species there is a core of the 'cystoid' *Arachnocystites.* The thin lines on its surface are the tracks of parasitic worms which lived in the inner wall of the theca.

Echinodermata

Ceratocystis perneri JAEKEL

Order: Cornuta
Family: Ceratocystidae

The greatest number of disputes and conflicting views are associated with the representatives of the class Stylophora. Some scientists regard them as the direct ancestors of the Chordata and as a separate subphylum, Calcichordata; others emphatically reject this view. What is certain, however, is that the members of this group have some features which are common to both echinoderms and chordate animals.

Ceratocystis is a Bohemian Middle Cambrian genus and belongs to the phylogenetically old order Cornuta, whose stratigraphic range stretches into the Middle Devonian. The theca is strikingly asymmetrical, is dorsoventrally flattened and is composed of large polygonal calcite plates. The mouth evidently lay on the narrower anterior side of the theca, between two processes. On what we consider to be the dorsal aspect, on the edge of the theca (close to its posterior end), there are openings comparable to gill slits. Two more openings in this part of the theca are regarded as the outlets of the ambulacral system (the hydropore) and the genital tract (the gonopore); behind them lay the anus. The organ of locomotion (the stele), which was composed of large numbers of small, irregular plates, grew from the posterior end of the theca.

Cothurnocystis elizae BATHER

Order: Cornuta
Family: Cothurnocystidae

This genus, whose members occur in Lower to Middle Ordovician sediments in Scotland and France, has been studied in great detail. On

1. *Lagynocystites pyramidalis,** Middle Ordovician (Llanvirn), Prague-Šárka, Czechoslovakia. Length of thecal core 25 mm.

2. *Mitrocystites mitra,** Middle Ordovician (Llanvirn), Prague-Šárka, Czechoslovakia. A core, length of theca 25 mm. This species occurs together with members of the related genus *Mitrocystella*, which have a narrower, elliptical theca with only three inner plates on the flattened (dorsal) side.

1

2

3. *Cothurnocystis elizae,** Upper Ordovician (Ashgillian), Girvan, Great Britain. Length of theca 12 mm. This mysterious animal lived on the bed of shallow seas; the long stele was evidently used for locomotion over the sandy bottom.

4. *Ceratocystis perneri,** Middle Cambrian, Skryje, Czechoslovakia. Length of theca 28 mm. A complete skeleton of a typical species. The animals lived on sandy sea floor.

5. *Cothurnocystis* sp., a reconstruction.

the bizarre, highly flattened theca, the marginal plates with the respiratory pores are greatly thickened and are clearly differentiated from the numerous small inner plates. The mouth lay in the protruding middle part of the theca, while the anus was near the stele, which bulged like a flask at its anterior end (fig. 5).

Mitrocystites mitra BARRANDE

Order: Mitrata
Family: Mitrocystitidae

Members of the order Mitrata, known from the Lower Ordovician up to the latest Lower Devonian, had a round-cornered trapezoid theca which was flattened on one side (perhaps the dorsal side) and convex on the other. Its only respiratory openings were two pores on the dorsal surface of the theca. The members of the Ordovician genus *Mitrocystites* were evidently adapted to conditions on the sea floor itself or just above it.

Lagynocystites pyramidalis (BARRANDE)

Order: Mitrata
Family: Lagynocystidae

Lagynocystites, a Bohemian Middle Ordovician genus, has a tapering, four-sided pyramidal theca whose under side and upper surface differ markedly as regards their structure. A short process at the tip of the theca covered the mouth. The stele had spines down the sides.

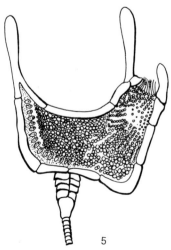

5

369

Cryptoschisma schultzii
(DE VERNEUIL AND D'ARCHIAC)

Order: Fissiculata
Family: Astrocrinidae

Blastoidea are small sessile echinoderms which lived in Palaeozoic seas. The stratigraphically oldest examples date back to the Silurian and the most recent to the Permian. Blastoids have a pentamerally symmetrical theca, usually with relatively short, but non-branching arms (brachioles) and with a stem of varying lengths. The theca is composed, as a rule, of 18 to 21 main plates and a quantity of small plates arranged in rings one above the other. There are three basal plates, followed by a circlet of five radial plates and then by a ring of five deltoid plates. Between the deltoid plates, in deep hollows in the radial plates (i.e. in the main rays of pentameral symmetry), lie the ambulacral fields or ambulacra. A main ambulacral groove runs along the centre of every ambulacral field in a 'lancet' plate and side grooves from either side join it at right angles. Externally, the brachioles continue in the line of the side grooves, bordering the ambulacral field on either side. The brachioles seized small food particles, which the ciliated lining of the ambulacra transported to the mouth. The mouth lies in the centre of the summit of the theca, below a roof composed of small plates. The anus is situated interambulacrally, alongside the mouth. Both main and lateral ambulacral grooves were also covered with small plates. Reaching deep below

1, 2. *Cryptoschisma schultzii*,* Middle Devonian, Leon, Spain. Size 11 and 7 mm. A side (1) and top (2) view of the theca, showing the striking wide petaloid ambulacra.

3, 4. *Cordyloblastus* cf. *eifelensis*, Middle Devonian (Eifelian), Gerolstein, West Germany. Size 6 and 17 mm. The theca from above (3) and from the side (4).

5–7. *Pentremites godoni*,* Lower Carboniferous (Mississippian), Illinois, USA. Size of theca 11 to 16 mm. The view from above (6) shows the spiracles round the mouth; the largest one is associated with the anus. The side view (5) shows the small cover plates of the ambulacra; the view from below (7) shows the basal plates and the base of the stem.

8. *Pentremites* sp., a reconstruction.

the plates of the ambulacral fields there is a complex system of small parallel canals known as hydrospires; these were the specific respiratory organs of blastoids. Blastoids inhabited shallow water with constant slight currents, together with rugose corals, brachiopods, moss animals and crinoids.

Fissiculate blastoids are known from the Silurian to the Permian. The open hydrospires form a row of parallel grooves along the ambulacra. Species of the genus *Cryptoschisma* occur in Devonian strata in Spain. Their tiny conical theca has wide, petaloid ambulacra.

Order: Spiraculata
Family: Pentremitidae

Cordyloblastus cf. *eifelensis* (RÖMER)

In the evolutionally more advanced order Spiraculata, the hydrospires lie below the side plates of the ambulacra and open on to the surface through five single or paired openings (spiracles) arranged symmetrically round the mouth. *Cordyloblastus* occurs in European Middle Devonian deposits.

Order: Spiraculata
Family: Pentremitidae

Pentremites godoni (DEFRANCE)

Blastoids attained their peak in the Carboniferous period. Numerous species of the best known genus, *Pentremites,* occur in North and South America (fig. 8).

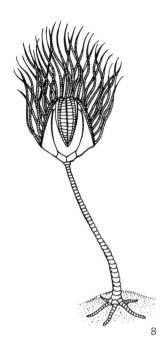

8

5

6

7

Echinodermata

Caleidocrinus multiramus WAAGEN AND JAHN

Order: Disparida
Family: Iocrinidae

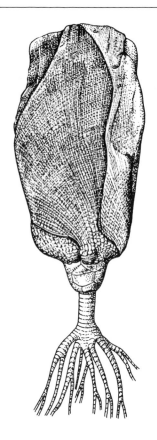

Sea lilies or crinoids (Crinoidea) are sessile for the whole of their life, or at least in the larval stage. Their oldest representatives are known from the Middle Cambrian. Crinoids are the only class of sessile echinoderms (subphylum Crinozoa) to have survived down to the present day. They look more like exotic sea flowers than animals. Their body is characterized by striking pentameral symmetry. In the complicated structure of their endoskeleton it is usually possible to distinguish a stem and a crown. The stem (or column) kept the animal anchored to the bottom and its crown at a given level above the sea floor. It was formed of numerous calcareous plates (columnals) with a central perforation for the neuromuscular cord. In the living animal the stem was to some extent flexible. The crown consisted of a theca and free arms. The theca, composed of a calyx and a roof, enclosed the soft body more or less completely. In the simplest forms, the bowl-like or conical calyx was composed of two or three rings of plates arranged one above the other. Arms of varying lengths, likewise composed of plates (brachials) arose from the top row of calycal plates (the radials). The main function of the arms was to seize food and convey it to the mouth, which lay on the upper surface of the calyx and in many crinoids was covered by a roof. The anus was situated near the mouth.

The subclass Inadunata comprises crinoids whose calyx was formed of firmly connected plates. The free (and usually long) arms branched regularly. The mouth was covered by a roof. Typical species of Inadunata are already known from the early Ordovician; the last representatives of this subclass come from Middle Triassic deposits.

In the species of the Palaeozoic order Disparida, there was only one ring of plates (basals) below the radials; this structure is therefore known

1. *Caleidocrinus multiramus,** Upper Ordovician (Caradoc), Zahořany, Czechoslovakia. A skeleton preserved in micaceous sandstone. Height of crown 15 mm. The root part is missing.

2. *Gisocrinus involutus,* Upper Silurian (Ludlow), Mořina, Czechoslovakia. A crown, height 40 mm. Before dying, the animal coiled the ends of its arms inwards.

3. *Crotalocrinites rugosus,** Upper Silurian (Ludlow), Mořina, Czechoslovakia. A calyx and the adjacent part of the stem. From organodetrital limestones deposited in warm shallow water near coral islands. Height of calyx 35 mm.

4. *Crotalocrinites* sp., a reconstruction.

as monocyclic. Its pentameral symmetry was not yet complete. One of the oldest members of this order, the European genus *Caleidocrinus,* had a finely constructed calyx and long, repeatedly branching arms. The stem was long and thin.

Crotalocrinites rugosus (MILLER)
Order: Cladida
Family: Crotalocrinidae

The members of the order Cladida had a dicyclically constructed calyx, i.e. below the radials there were two rings of plates (basals and infrabasals). The forked arms terminated in numerous processes known as pinnules, whose function it was to seize food. The species of the important Euro-American genus *Crotalocrinites* had a robust, spherical calyx. In the living animal the finely constructed arms (fig. 4) fanned out to form a wide 'basket' for collecting food particles that sank to the bottom.

Gisocrinus involutus BOUŠKA
Order: Cladida
Family: Cyathocrinidae

Gisocrinus species lived from the Upper Silurian to the early Devonian period, in the same region as *Crotalocrinites* species. They had a small conical or bowl-like calyx and massive arms which forked dichotomically several times in succession.

373

Echinodermata

Isolated columnals of crinoids

When crinoids died, their skeletons usually broke up into a large quantity of isolated columnals and plates and these skeletal elements became the main organic component of crinoid limestones – a characteristic shallow-water type of deposit. Even if we glance at such a rock only cursorily, we catch sight of a large quantity of diverse columnals – circular, cylindrical, stellate or square – which in the living crinoids were joined together flexibly by tissue and were covered with a thin epidermis. Down the centre of the stem runs an axial canal. The stem itself is composed of a number of wide columnals (nodals) with a few narrower columnals (internodals) between them. In some evolutionarily more advanced genera, thin segmented processes (cirri) branch from the nodals. In sessile crinoids, the distal columnals (i.e. the furthest removed from the calyx) were transformed to root-like, discoidal and other structures which held the animal in place. The assignment of a given type of columnal to the corresponding genus, based on a study of the morphological features of the crown, is very problematical. Consequently, because of the great stratigraphic importance of crinoids, an independent artificial system has been elaborated for columnals, in which every type of columnal has its own specific name.

Cupressocrinites crassus GOLDFUSS

Order: Cladida
Family: Cupressocrinidae

Cupressocrinites is a specialized Middle to Upper Devonian European genus. A single infrabasal plate, produced by the fusion of five infrabasals, forms the base of the dicyclic calyx. As in other crinoids, the infrabasals lie in the main rays (radii) of pentameral symmetry of the calyx. Above them, in the interradials between the main rays, lie five

1. Different types of isolated stem parts (columnals) (subclasses Inadunata and Camerata), Lower Devonian (Zlíchovian), Prague-Zlíchov, Czechoslovakia. The largest is 12 mm in diameter. The grooves on the contact surfaces made the stem stronger. The large columnal in the centre is a nodal of the important and almost worldwide genus *Diamenocrinus*.

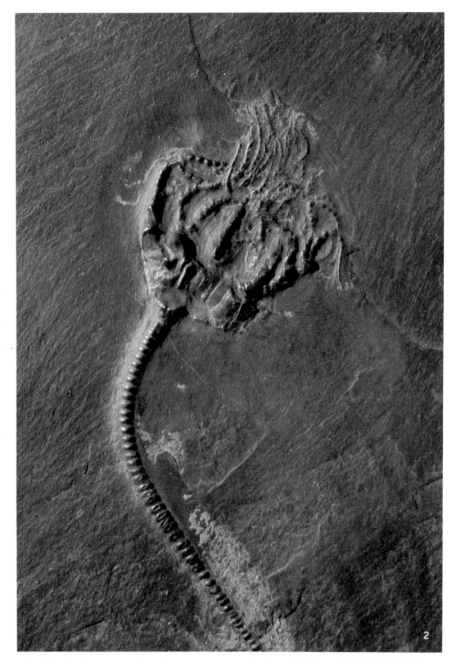

2. *Codiacrinus schulzei,* Middle Devonian (Eifelian), Bundenbach, West Germany. A crown with the adjoining part of the stem. The slender arms lie in the direction of the current. Height of crown 40 mm.

3. *Cupressocrinites crassus,** Middle Devonia (Eifelian), Gerolstein, West Germany. A complete crown with closed arms composed of massive single plates. Height of crown 50 mm.

4, 5. *Cupressocrinites* sp., columnals: 4 – a lateral view; 5 – a view from above.

basals and above these a circlet of five radials, again in line with the main radii. Attached to the radials are five massive arms with fine pinnules along both sides. In the stem, the central (axial) canal is surrounded by three or four peripheral canals (fig. 5).

Order: Cladida
Family: Codiacrinidae

Codiacrinus schulzei SCHMIDT

The Middle Devonian Bundenbach slates from the Rhenish Schiefergebirge contain, inter alia, splendidly preserved crinoid skeletons. One of the commonest genera in European Lower to Middle Devonian sediments in *Codiacrinus,* which has a large, cup-shaped calyx and slender, forked arms composed of a single row of plates (brachials). The stem is circular in cross section.

375

 **Echinodermata**

Encrinus liliiformis LAMARCK

The scientific classification of crinoids is based primarily on the structure of the theca. For a detailed study it is essential to make sure where the front of the crinoid theca is, and where the back. The mouth is usually in the centre and is thus no use as a guide; we therefore employ the anus as our orientation point. The anus is located eccentrically, in the posterior interradius, so that the side opposite it is the anterior side of the theca. In many Inadunata, and in other Palaeozoic crinoids also, pentameral symmetry is impaired by one or a few small plates lying one above the other in the posterior interradius, which are associated anatomically with anal structures. In the skeleton of the calyx the anal plates usually lie between the basals, the radials or the fixed brachials, which also participate in the structure of the calyx.

The family Encrinidae, in which no anal plates are formed, is included, with some doubts, in the subclass Inadunata. It is represented by only one known genus, *Encrinus.* The absence of anal plates, the stratigraphic range of this genus and other features are indicative of certain relationships to the only geologically present-day crinoid subclass, Articulata, which is still represented in present-day seas by an abundance of genera and species.

Encrinus, the best known Triassic crinoid, has been described from the Muschelkalk of West Germany. The generic name *Encrinus,* together with 'Trochites' for columnals, was used for the first time by G. Agricola in the sixteenth century. The low, pan-shaped calyx, with perfect pentameral symmetry, has a concave under side and is composed of three circlets of plates, to which fixed brachials are attached. Growing from the calyx there are ten arms, which are at first composed of one row of plates (the uniserial type) and then of two rows (the biserial type). The ends of the arms are formed of only one row of brachials (i.e. they are uniserial) and are thickly set with pinnules. The biserial type of arm is an evolutionarily advanced character, since it allowed the number of pinnules to be doubled and thus increased food-catching efficiency. The roof of the calyx is only slightly convex. The stem is circular in cross section and carries cirri. Isolated columnals of the stem — *Trochites* — evidently played a decisive role in the structure of the unusually thick *Trochites* limestone (Trochitenkalk) layers formed in the warm, well oxygenated shelf sea.

From the skeletal structure of *Encrinus* and from biological observations of extant crinoids of the subclass Articulata, we conclude that the members of the above genus were rheophilic, i.e. that they lived in flowing water and held their theca with the base of the calyx facing the current. With the ends of their dense, narrow pinnules they caught food particles (chiefly algae, protozoans, small crustaceans and larvae), which the ambulacral grooves inside the arms conveyed to their mouth.

Encrinus liliiformis,* Middle Triassic (Anisian, Ladinian), Crailsheim, West Germany. A crown with the adjoining part of the stem; above the crown an isolated arm with pinnules. Height of crown 65 mm. The structure of the arms clearly shows the change from the uniserial to the biserial type.

Scyphocrinites sp.

Order: Monobathrida
Family: Scyphocrinidae

The stratigraphic range of crinoids belonging to the subclass Camerata stretches from the Lower Ordovician to the Upper Permian. These crinoids were particularly abundant in the Silurian and the Lower Carboniferous. Their structure includes both monocyclic and dicyclic calyces. Firm connection of the thecal plates is characteristic. The roof forms a dome covering the mouth and the adjacent parts of the ambulacral grooves. The anus protruded above the roof. There are striking differences in the number of brachial plates, which, together with other, interpolated plates (interbrachials, etc), participated in the structure of the calyx. Pentameral symmetry of the theca is often impaired by a number of interradially localized anal plates. The free arms of camerate crinoids can be either simple or branched and are set with pinnules. All camerate crinoids had a stem.

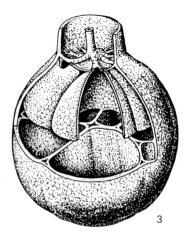

3

The members of the order Monobathrida have a monocyclic calyx. They are represented by the Silurian-Devonian genus *Scyphocrinites,* known in Europe, Africa, Asia and North America, which comprises large specialized crinoids with a crown up to 50 cm high. The pear-shaped calyx is composed of a large number of plates with a radially sculptured surface. The basals and the radials play only a minor role in the structure of the calyx, which, apart from the fused brachials, is formed chiefly of large numbers of interpolated plates. Two equally developed arms grow in every radius and then fork dichotomically several times in succession. Inside the circular stem there is a pentagonal canal. The stem terminates in a curious bulbous float (lobolite) divided into several compartments (fig. 3). The float probably provided the crinoid with some freedom of movement and evidently contributed to its vast geographical distribution. Many specimens show that these crinoids lived in a close and apparently mutually propitious relationship to gastropods of the genus *Platyceras.* The coprophagous gastropods lived on the crinoid's excreta; they perched on the roof of the calyx and often completely covered it. As the crinoid and the gastropods grew, the latter's aperture took on the contours of the roof of the calyx. In some places, *Scyphocrinites* ossicles accumulated in such large quantities that the resultant limestones are named after them. Scyphocrinite limestones were formed in the uppermost Silurian and the Lower Devonian.

Thylacocrinus vannioti OEHLERT

Order: Diplobathrida
Family: Rhodocrinitidae

The order Diplobathrida (whose members have a dicyclic calyx) includes the species of the almost worldwide Lower Devonian genus *Thylacocrinus,* which have a large conical or bowl-like calyx with a low roof. There are 20 to 24 unbranched free arms (usually four to each radius) composed of two rows of plates.

1. *Thylacocrinus vannioti,** Lower Devonian (Emsian), St. German le Guillaume, France. A crown from which the basal part has been broken off and which terminates in four-branched arms. Height of crown 100 mm.

2, 3. *Scyphocrinites* sp., Lower Devonian (Lochkovian), Marouma, Algeria. Crowns uniquely exposed by desert weathering, clearly showing the long, fine pinnules. Height of crown 80 mm. 3 – the lobolite with a partly removed outer wall.

Hexacrinites anaglypticus (GOLDFUSS)

Order: Monobathrida
Family: Hexacrinidae

The genus *Hexacrinites* is known from Upper Silurian to Upper Devonian sediments in Europe, Asia and North America. The simple calyx is formed of three basals and five tall radials, with the first anal plate interpolated between them. The anus lies near the centre or at the margin of the bulging roof. The free parts of the arms are composed of a single row of plates. In every radius there are two arms, simple or branched. When the animal died, the arms were usually detached from the calyx.

Eucalyptocrinites crassus (HALL)

Order: Monobathrida
Family: Eucalyptocrinidae

Members of the specialized cosmopolitan genus *Eucalyptocrinites* are to be found in Upper Silurian to Middle Devonian deposits. The calyx is massive, low and shaped like a flat-bottomed dish and the stem is embedded inside it. The roof is remarkably constructed. On the top there are four large plates; ten elongate vertical plates supported the proboscis-like end of the alimentary tube from inside and outside they formed ten laterally open compartments (chambers) which provided concealment for the arms. The circular stem has a stellate axial canal running down the centre and at its distal end it terminates in thick root-like processes (fig. 5).

Eucalyptocrinites species enlivened coral reefs and shelf seas. They were rheophobic and their arms, spread almost horizontally sideways, caught food particles falling to the bottom. The dense fine pinnules bordering the ambulacral grooves could also have created a little current of their own and in this way have increased the amount of food caught by the arms.

1, 2. *Amphoracrinus gigas,* Lower Carboniferous (Viséan), Clitheroe, Great Britain. Height of calyx 27 mm. A side view of the theca, with the domed roof and outgrowths (1); the base of the calyx with the attachment surface for the stem (2).

3. *Hexacrinites anaglypticus,* Middle Devonian (Eifelian), Gerolstein, West Germany. An isolated calyx with distinctive sculpturing of the plates and the base of the arms. Height of calyx 37 mm.

4. *Eucalyptocrinites crassus,* Upper Silurian (Niagaran), Waldron, Indiana, USA. High interbrachial septa providing concealment for the slender arms and long pinnules project from the tall calyx. Height of crown 70 mm.

5. *Eucalyptocrinites* sp. – a reconstruction.

O

D

S

4

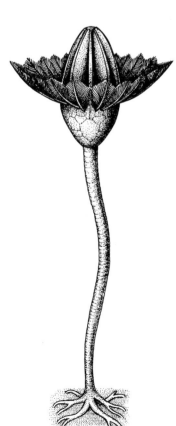

5

Amphoracrinus gigas WRIGHT

Order: Monobathrida
Family: Amphoracrinidae

The peak period of camerate crinoids was the Carboniferous. The interesting members of the genus *Amphoracrinus,* found in Europe, northern Africa, North America and possibly Japan, usually had a low calyx covered by a firm, high domed roof composed of a very large number of plates. The eccentrically situated anal opening protrudes slightly above the roof of the calyx. There are six plates in the basal ring of the calyx (and one interpolated anal plate). The calyx has a granular surface, with numerous small horn-like outgrowths. The arms spring almost horizontally from the calyx.

Echinodermata

Taxocrinus colletti WHITE

Order: Taxocrinida
Family: Taxocrinidae

Flexibilia are a rather small group of Palaeozoic crinoids. The oldest representatives of this subclass appeared in the Middle Ordovician and the last are known from the Upper Permian. Their skeletal structure has a number of characters common to all flexibilian crinoids. The plates forming the calyx were not fixed together in the living animals, but were joined by ligaments which made the whole skeleton far more flexible than the skeletons of the other crinoid subclasses. The bottom of the calyx is usually composed of three infrabasals surmounted by a ring of five basals and then by a ring of five radials. The proximal parts of the arms (closest to the calyx), the plates between them (the fixed brachials and interbrachials) and the anal plates usually participate in the structure of the calyx. The roof consists of a very large number of small plates whose connections were likewise largely flexible. The mouth and the ambulacral grooves leading to it are uncovered. The arms are composed of a single row of plates and have no pinnules; they often fork to form two identical branches. The stem is circular in cross section.

The single order, Taxocrinida, is known from the Ordovician. Its members usually have an elongate crown and a small calyx. The best known genus, *Taxocrinus,* occurs in Middle Devonian to Permian sediments in Europe and North America. The crown has elongate elliptical contours; the arms diverge at the base and branch dichotomically.

Pycnosaccus scrobiculatus ANGELIN

Order: Sagenocrinida
Family: Nipterocrinidae

Representatives of the order Sagenocrinida have a spherical or elongate ovoid crown. The calyx plates were joined together more firmly than in the crinoids of the preceding order, so that the calyx was more likely to be preserved intact. The calyx was generally cup-shaped; the arms were massive.

The Silurian genus *Pycnosaccus* is known in Europe and North America. The spherical crown has a massive calyx distinctly separate from the arms. From the side, all three rings of plates can be seen on the calyx. The radials either have a smooth surface, or have pronounced ridges from the middle of the plate, perpendicularly to the interradial sutures. The wide arms are formed of short brachials. Where the whole crown has been preserved, the distal ends of the arms curve inwards, covering the roof.

Flexible crinoids were adapted to conditions on the sea bed at various depths. Some species lived in deep water, in an environment not very favourable to sessile organisms. If the soft sea floor did not provide suitable anchorage, they attached themselves to mollusc shells.

The species *P. scrobiculatus* lived mainly in turbid shallow water in the neighbourhood of Upper Silurian coral reefs.

1. *Pycnosaccus scrobiculatus,** Upper Silurian (Ludlow), Mořina, Czechoslovakia. A massively built calyx with a distinctively sculptured surface and with short, incurved arms. Height of crown 40 mm.

2. *Taxocrinus colletti,* Lower Carboniferous (Mississippian), Crawfordsville, USA. A crown with a small calyx and powerful, incurved arms. Height of crown 50 mm.

Echinodermata

Seirocrinus subangularis (MILLER)

Order: Isocrinida
Family: Pentacrinidae

Articulata, the most recent crinoid subclass, are known from the Lower Triassic down to the present. Their dicyclic or cryptodicyclic calyx (the infrabasals develop in early ontogenesis and then disappear) has only small basals and is usually much reduced. The arms are always composed of one row of plates, are often richly branched and carry pinnules; they articulate with the radials by means of muscles. The radial and the brachial plates are always perforated. The roof is constructed of thin, flexibly connected plates. Both the mouth and the ambulacral grooves are exposed. Young specimens always had a stem, but most adult individuals lost it, all that was left being its most proximal ossicle, the centrodorsal plate. Recent articulates live in both tropical and arctic waters, at depths ranging from a few metres to 9,000 metres. Up to now, some 650 present-day species have been described. The majority are sessile, but some crawl over the bottom or are even active swimmers.

The order Isocrinida comprises crinoids with a small calyx. The wide contact surfaces (facets) allow articular connection of the arms and radials. The stem, usually long, was partly encircled by cirri.

The important genus *Seirocrinus* is known from the Lower Jurassic. The best specimens come from 'Posidonia' shales near Holzmaden in Bavaria (West Germany). The arms arising from the small calyx branched unequally (heteronomously) several times in succession. The crown was up to 80 cm high and the stem up to 18 metres long. Unique finds tell us that the young animals led a pseudoplanktonic existence, attached to floating pieces of wood. The adults probably belonged to the benthos, i.e. they lived attached to the sea floor. The stem was probably directed obliquely and not vertically.

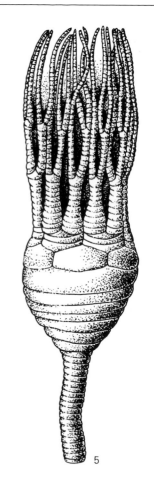

5

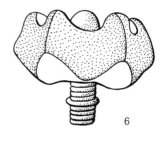

6

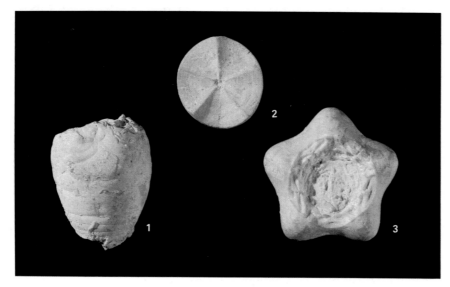

1, 2. *Apiocrinites elegans,* Middle Jurassic (Bathonian), Bradford-on-Avon, Great Britain. Attached to the pear-shaped calyx, which changes over imperceptibly to the widened cylindrical stem, are cheilostomatous bryozoans. Height 40 mm (1). 2 — fusion of a widened stem segment with the calyx, seen from above.

3. *Millericrinus milleri,** Upper Jurassic (Oxfordian), Sontheim, West Germany. Top view of a calyx, showing insertion of the long, massive arms on the wide facets. Width of calyx 45 mm.

4. *Seirocrinus subangularis,** Lower Jurassic (Liassic), Holzmaden, West Germany. A crown and the adjoining part of the stem; height of crown 120 mm. The long, richly branching arms are thickly set with pinnules.

5. *Apiocrinites* sp., the crown with part of the stem.

6. *Millericrinus* sp., the calyx and part of the stem.

Millericrinus milleri (SCHLOTHEIM)

Order: Millericrinida
Family: Millericrinidae

The most striking features of Millericrinida are the large calyx, composed of five basals and five radials, and the stem without nodals and without cirri, which usually had a morphologically modified centro-dorsal plate.

Members of the genus *Millericrinus* are found in European Middle and Upper Jurassic strata. They are characterized by a large, wide and low pentagonal calyx formed of strikingly thick-walled basals and radials separated by distinct sutures (fig. 6). Connected to the base of the calyx is the proximal plate. The calyx of species with a reduced stem was seated directly on the bottom.

Apiocrinites elegans (DEFRANCE)

Order: Millericrinida
Family: Apiocrinidae

The genus *Apiocrinites* occurs in Lower Jurassic to Lower Cretaceous sediments in Europe, northern Africa and North America. The wide, flat proximal ossicles of the stem are firmly fused with the calyx, giving the theca a pear-shaped or ovoid form (fig. 5).

385

 **Echinodermata**

Pterocoma pennata (SCHLOTHEIM)

Order: Comatulida
Family: Pterocomidae

Comatulida are crinoids with a reduced stem, of which all that remained under the base of the calyx was the centrodorsal plate with large numbers of cirri. Like the still extant crinoids, the majority of fossil species inhabited shallow shelf seas (down to 200 metres), often in the vicinity of coral reefs. Under optimal conditions, comatulid crinoids formed dense populations (crinoid meadows). They also included the only active swimmers of the family Antedonidae, which were able to move to sites with better conditions by means of their arms. As in present-day species, the distances they were able to cover were evidently very limited. The members of the present-day genus *Antedon* and of the Jurassic genus *Pterocoma* closely resemble each other.

Pterocoma species are known chiefly from Solnhofen Tithonian limestones; they died out during the Upper Cretaceous (Turonian). A single circlet of cirri arises from the small centrodorsal plate at the base of the calyx. The arms sprouting from the small calyx fork only once, making a total of ten branches; their long pinnules give them a feathery appearance. These crinoids probably floated more or less passively in the water, i.e. they lived pelagically.

Saccocoma pectinata GOLDFUSS

Order: Roveacrinida
Family: Saccocomidae

Adult members of the Mesozoic order Roveacrinida had a small, stemless calyx and a porous skeleton which made them buoyant.

The Upper Jurassic to Lower Cretaceous genus *Saccocoma* is known in Europe, northern Africa and Cuba. The roomy body cavity is closed by the radials and by a small central plate of obscure origin at the base of the calyx. The arms fork almost immediately and from these branches further alternating subsidiary branches (ramuli) are put forth. The best known finds of species of this genus come from Tithonian lithographic limestones near Solnhofen in Bavaria. Calcareous sediment was deposited under specific and unwontedly favourable conditions in a warm lagoon only 30 to 60 metres deep, with markedly salt water, where today it forms layers of platy limestone (Plattenkalk). The bottom of the lagoon was virtually devoid of life, but many species of animals lived above it. Crinoids of the genus *Saccocoma*, which probably lived pelagically, were common among them.

1. *Pterocoma pennata,** Upper Jurassic (Tithonian), Solnhofen, West Germany. A complete skeleton with long feathery arms. Height of crown 120 mm.

2. *Saccocoma pectinata,** Upper Jurassic (Tithonian), Solnhofen, West Germany. A complete skeleton, seen from above. The long arms, which carried pinnules, had spirally-coiled ends. Crown diameter 35 mm.

J

Pseudosaccocoma strambergensis REMEŠ

Order: Roveacrinida
Family: Saccocomidae

The genus *Saccocoma* is related to the genus *Pseudosaccocoma,* whose stratigraphic range stretches from the Upper Jurassic to the Lower Cretaceous. Its members are known in Europe and Asia (Japan). The strongly built calyces are formed of massive plates covered by a compact layer of calcite. The basals, radials and the central plate at the base of the calyx are perforated by canals; the radials have broad articulation surfaces.

P. *strambergensis* is a typical species. It lived in the well aerated water round Upper Jurassic coral reefs in central Europe.

Uintacrinus socialis GRINELL

Order: Uintacrinida
Family: Uintacrinidae

4

The evolution of most articulate crinoids was characterized by structural simplification and general reduction of the calyx, but in the Upper Cretaceous there were some crinoids whose bulky thecae, formed of a large number of plates, were reminiscent of the thecae of certain Palaeozoic camerate crinoids.

The large spherical or oval crowns of the members of the order Uintacrinida have lightly built calyces formed of very thin-walled plates whose base shows no trace of there having been a stem. In addition to the main skeletal elements, the calyx is also composed of varying number of brachials and interbrachials and even of the most proximal platelets forming pinnules. The long arms, which bear numerous free pinnules, branch while still in the wall of the calyx. The roof consists of flexible connected plates and its structure is unusual in that the anus lies in the centre, while the mouth is situated eccentrically.

1. *Pseudosaccocoma strambergensis,** Upper Jurassic (Tithonian), Štramberk, Czechoslovakia. A calyx seen from below, with very small basals and large radials. Calyx diameter 22 mm.

2. *Marsupites testudinarius,** Upper Cretaceous (Senonian), Lüneburg, West Germany. Side view of a calyx, height 33 mm. The calyx is composed of large polygonal plates. At the top on the right is a large brachial plate.

3

3. *Uintacrinus socialis,** Upper Cretaceous (Senonian), Kansas, USA. A complete skeleton with a large pouch-like calyx and long arms with fine pinnules. Width of theca 80 mm.

4. *Marsupites* sp., the calyx and part of one arm.

Crinoids of the genus *Uintacrinus* were distributed over virtually the whole of the globe and led a planktonic existence. It is assumed that their body cavity had special compartments containing a gas or oil particles which reduced the animal's total weight.

Marsupites testudinarius (SCHLOTHEIM)

Order: Uintacrinida
Family: Marsupitidae

The distribution of the crinoids of the Upper Cretaceous genus *Marsupites* is also worldwide. The structural plan of the theca is similar to that of the preceding genus, but the number of plates is smaller. On the surface of the plates there are often pronounced radial ridges. The arms are narrow and biserial and are either completely separate or are joined together by interbrachial plates. *Marsupites* also probably led a planktonic existence and its body cavity may have contained buoyancy-promoting structures similar to those of *Uintacrinus* species.

389

Echinodermata

Urasterella asperula (Stürtz)

Order: Forcipulatida
Family: Urasterellidae

Stelleroids (subphylum Asterozoa, class Stelleroidea) are free-living echinoderms with a radially symmetrical and usually stellate, dorso-ventrally flattened body. The mouth is on the ventral surface and faces downwards. Sea stars (subclass Asteroidea), known from the Middle Ordovician down to the Recent, comprise the most diverse genera and species. Their body is pentagonal, or is shaped like a five-pointed star. The central (body) disc tapers off into arms which contain extensions of all the important viscera. Down the middle of every arm runs an ambulacral groove whose free (distal) end terminates in a calcareous plate with a photosensitive organ; the other end terminates near the mouth. The ambulacral system of asteroids has in general lost its nutritional function and has acquired locomotory function. In every ambulacral groove there are two to four rows of pseudopodia (tube feet) with suction discs connected internally to balloon-like ampullae from which water flows into the tube-feet and back again, thereby altering the tension in the tube-feet and producing suction. The plate at the entrance to the ambulacral system (the madreporite) and the anal vent lie on the dorsal (aboral) surface of the body disc. The skeleton is covered with a thin epidermis whose dorsal surface is strewn with large numbers of thin-walled vesicles acting as external gills. The skeleton itself is composed of numerous loosely connected plates (ossicles). The body's main support is the axial skeleton along the axial grooves, to which a ring of oral plates is attached; the rest of the skeleton is built up on this foundation.

Stelleroids break up soon after death and finds of whole skeletons are consequently rare. Very favourable conditions were needed for their preservation, the chief ones being their quick burial in sediment and the absence of burrowing animals which would have strewn the loose ossicles about. The best specimens of complete asteroid skeletons come from Lower Devonian roofing ('Bundenbach') slates in Hunsrück. The ossicles have usually been pyritized and if they are carefully treated every detail can be seen on them.

The genus *Urasterella* is known from western and eastern Europe and from Canada. The long, narrow arms, which spring from a very small body disc, are rounded in cross section and carry spines, whose main function is to clean the surface in the vicinity of the respiratory vesicles.

1. *Urasterella asperula*, Lower Devonian (Lower Emsian), Bundenbach, West Germany. Size of skeleton 65 mm. The long arms of this common species, lying in line with the current, furnish reliable evidence of the direction of sea floor currents.

2. *Helianthaster rhenanus*,* Lower Devonian (Lower Emsian), Bundenbach, West Germany. Size 110 mm. An almost complete skeleton showing the characteristic features of the genus.

Helianthaster rhenanus RÖMER

Order: Spinulosida
Family: Helianthasteridae

The members of the genus *Helianthaster* occur in European Lower Devonian sediments. The 14 to 16 massive arms spring from a relatively large body disc with a granular dorsal surface. The surface of the asteroid is covered with large numbers of short spines.

Echinodermata

Metopaster hunteri (FORBES)

Order: Valvatida
Family: Goniasteridae

Asteroids are a conservative group of animals, i.e. they evolved very slowly, so that their present-day representatives are hardly any different from their ancient ancestors. A study of the ecology of still extant species can therefore give us a fairly exact picture of the life of fossil species. Like other echinoderms, asteroids are exclusively marine animals occurring in large numbers in both warm and cold water. The largest species have a span of up to 1.2 metres. The sexes are generally separate; another feature is the great capacity of lost parts of the body for regeneration. Most sea stars are predators and live on other sea stars, brittle stars, sea urchins, coral polyps, molluscs and brachiopods, etc. Specially adapted plates bordering the toothless mouth act as jaws. Asteroids either take up bulky fod directly, with their mouth, or convey it to their mouth with their arms, holding it with their tube-feet; they then seize it with the edges of their out-thrust stomach and engulf it. Some asteroids catch their food in a most unusual manner. They settle on the shell of a mollusc or some other animal, force the upper valve open with their muscular ambulacral tube-feet, insinuate the out-thrust edge of their stomach between the two valves, kill and decompose their prey with digestive juices and then suck the soft parts into their stomach and digest it outside their body. Other asteroids, living on small food, catch organic particles with the cilia bordering their ambulacral grooves and convey it in this way to their mouth.

Many species of asteroids lived during the Cretaceous period, but generally only isolated plates are found. The systematics of the subclass as a whole have not been properly elaborated, owing to incompleteness of the data.

The members of the genus *Metopaster* (= *Mitraster*) are known from Upper Cretaceous to Miocene strata in Europe, North America and New Zealand. Their pentagonal skeleton, occasionally with slightly

1. *Metopaster hunteri,* Upper Cretaceous (Turonian), Kent, Great Britain. Diameter 50 mm. Only the large marginal plates have been preserved.

2

lengthened arms, has a body disc with a small number of large, massive marginal plates and densely crowded inner plates.

Order: Granulosina
Calliderma (?) *schulzei* COTTA AND REICH   Family: Goniasteridae

2. *Calliderma* (?) *schulzei,* Upper Cretaceous (Turonian), Hejšina, Czechoslovakia. Diameter 115 mm. A complete skeleton with stout marginal plates. The body disc is formed of small plates. The ambulacra are clearly discernible in the main rays.

The often very lightly built, readily disintegrating skeletons of asteroids have the best chances of preservation in finely granular sediments. The discovery of whole skeletons in coarsely granular sandstones is therefore all the more surprising. The species depicted here has hitherto usually been assigned to the extant genus *Stellaster,* whose skeleton is characterized by a large central disc, short arms and wide marginal plates. These features are also typical of *Calliderma,* whose species are known from the European Upper Cretaceous to Oligocene.

393

Echinodermata

Encrinaster tischbeinianum RÖMER

Order: Eogophiurida
Family: Encrinasteridae

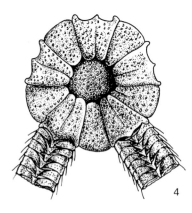

4

Brittle stars (Ophiuroidea), also known from the Ordovician to the present day, are related to sea stars, from which they are easily distinguished, however, by their sharply defined central disc and their long, thin, cylindrical arms. The axial skeleton of their arms resembles a vertebrate spine and endows them with serpentine flexibility. The important viscera are all in the central disc and do not extend into the arms. The mouth, which is on the under side of the body, also acts as the vent. The entrance to the ambulacral system is likewise on the under side of the body. The ambulacral grooves are closed on the under side and the ambulacral tube-feet pass to the exterior only along their lateral margins. Brittle stars occur in different geographical zones and at every possible depth, from littoral water to thousands of metres. They subsist mainly on small organic particles, which they catch with cilia covered with a sticky mucoid fluid. As a rule they lie partly buried in the sediment and catch food with the free ends of their arms; they transport it to their mouth by means of their tube-feet, which are protected by the marginal plates of the arms and by spines. Many brittle stars move over the sea bed actively and quite quickly, while others live as commensals on crinoids, whose feeding habits they share. In other ophiuroids, the oral plates have been converted to jaws and food is conveyed to the mouth by the exceedingly flexible arms. With a few exceptions, ophiuroids are not very common fossils. Recent species locally form large populations (comprising several hundred specimens to a square metre).

The members of the genus *Encrinaster* are known from the Upper Ordovician to the Lower Carboniferous. They have an asteroid-like skeleton. The 'vertebral' halves of the arms do not lie side by side, but alternate. The margin of the central disc has a clearly discernible border.

1. *Furcaster palaeozoicus,** Lower Devonian (Lower Emsian), Bundenbach, West Germany. Two almost complete skeletons, span of the larger one 80 mm.

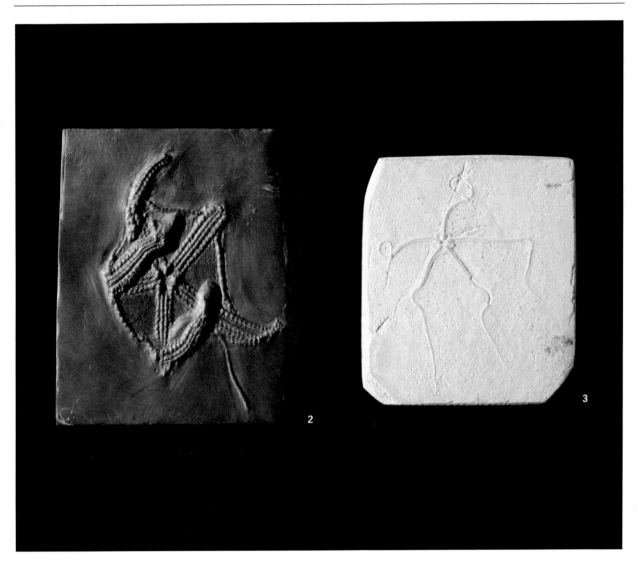

2. *Encrinaster tischbeinianum,* Lower Devonian (Lower Emsian), Bundenbach, West Germany. An almost complete skeleton, diameter 80 mm. The massive arms show that these ophiuroids were not able to travel very fast over the sea floor.

3. *Geocoma carinata,** Upper Jurassic (Tithonian), Solnhofen, West Germany. A complete skeleton, span 80 mm. These are the commonest ophiurids in Solnhofen Upper Jurassic lithographic limestone.

4. *Geocoma* sp., the body disc with two arm bases.

Furcaster palaeozoicus STÜRTZ

Order: Oegophiurida
Family: Furcasteridae

Species of the genus *Furcaster* occur in Upper Ordovician to Lower Carboniferous sediments in Europe, North America and Australia. They are characterized by a relatively large body disc and long arms with needle-like spines of roughly equal size along the sides. The adoral plates form a five-pointed star.

Geocoma carinata (MÜNSTER)

Order: Ophiurida
Family: Ophiuridae

Geocoma is an evolutionally advanced type of brittle star known chiefly from the European Upper Jurassic. The large plates attached to the base of the arms, together with the interradials, form a ring stretching almost to the centre of the body disc (fig. 4). The arm ossicles are cylindrical and the two halves, which are fused, lie side by side.

395

Rhabdocidaris orbignyana (AGASSIZ)

Order: Cidaroida
Family: Cidaridae

Sea urchins (Echinoidea) are the most familiar class in the subphylum Echinozoa. Their oldest known representatives come from Ordovician strata and over 800 species still live in present-day seas. Their internal skeleton, composed of up to several thousand skeletal elements, has movable appendages on its surface, such as spines with protective and/or locomotory function and pincer-like pedicellariae used for protection, grooming and the administration of food. The mouth faces downwards and in many species it has jaws. The skeleton is formed of two main groups of plates. The apical system (on the dorsal aspect) consists of five ocular plates lying in the main rays of pentameral symmetry (i.e. ambulacra). In the interradials (interambulacra) there are five or fewer genital plates with genital duct pores; one such plate, with numerous perforations, acts as a madreporite (the entrance to the ambulacral system). Inside (in 'regular' echinoids) or outside (in 'irregular' echinoids) is the anus vent (the periproct). The other group of plates forms the corona, with five ambulacral and five interambulacral fields. In the ambulacral plates there are perforations for the tube-feet, which had locomotor, respiratory and exploratory function. Both the mouth and the anus were encircled by a leathery membrane, which was often studded with variously organized plates of different sizes.

The subclass Perischoechinoidea comprises the evolutionarily oldest 'regular' echinoids. The only order to have survived to the present day are Cidaria.

Cidarid echinoids have a spherical, orally and aborally flattened skeleton with narrow ambulacra. The wide interambulacra carry striking 'perforated' tubercles (i.e. with a central dimple) surmounted by spines. Fossil species occur chiefly in shallow-water sediments; present-day

1. *Plegiocidaris coronata,** Upper Jurassic (Oxfordian to Tithonian), West Germany. Diameter of skeleton 28 mm. A dorsal view of the skeleton, from which the apical plate system has been broken off.

2. *Rhabdocidaris orbignyana,** Upper Jurassic (Oxfordian-Kimmeridgian), Bléville, France. Length of spines 48 and 58 mm.

Cr

J

3

3. *Tylocidaris clavigera,** Upper Cretaceous (Turonian-Campanian), Charlton, Kent, Great Britain. Diameter of skeleton 26 mm. A few spines are lying round the damaged skeleton.

4. *Plegiocidaris* sp., a lateral view of the skeleton.

4

species live at depths of 4,000 metres. They 'walk' on their long spines. Their massive jaws enable them to live as predators.

The species of the genus *Rhabdocidaris* occur in European Upper Jurassic to Eocene sediments. Their skeletons averaged 10 cm in diameter. The ambulacral pores are joined together by grooves; the spines are long and flattened.

Order: Cidaroida
Family: Cidaridae

Plegiocidaris coronata (SCHLOTHEIM)

The members of the genus *Plegiocidaris* occur in Upper Triassic to Upper Jurassic sediments in Europe. The ambulacral plates have isolated pores, round the tubercles there are marked areolae and the claviform spines have nodose longitudinal ribs.

Order: Cidaroida
Family: Psychocidaridae

Tylocidaris clavigera (KÖNIG)

Tylocidaris is a European Upper Cretaceous echinoid with a squat skeleton composed of large plates. The apical system takes up almost half the diameter of the skeleton. The ambulacral pores are unconnected, the tubercles are smooth and unperforated and the spines are club-shaped.

 **Echinodermata**

Acrosalenia hemicidaroides WRIGHT

Order: Salenioida
Family: Acrosaleniidae

The subclass Euechinoidea comprises evolutionally more advanced echinoids to which the majority of extant species belong. The stratigraphically oldest specimens come from the end of the Triassic. It was evidently the anatomical changes enabling many of the echinoids in this subclass to live at various depths beneath the surface of the sediment that were the cause of their tremendous radiation during the Jurassic. In Euechinoidea, every ambulacrum and every interambulacrum is composed of two columns of plates. The majority of species have a complex masticatory apparatus known as Aristotle's lantern, which is attached by muscles to a circlet of outgrowths on the inner surface of the coronal plates. The echinoid corona grows partly as a result of the deposition of calcareous material over the entire surface of the plates and partly through the formation of new plates on the dorsal surface, along the border of the ocular plates, so that old plates shift towards the oral side during growth. The skeleton either goes on growing for life, or, when the number of plates characteristic of the given species has been attained, it stops growing.

The order Salenioida is known from the Lower Jurassic to the present day. They have an endocyclic skeleton (with the periproct inside the apical plate system). The large ocular and genital plates are joined at the periphery by further (suranal) plates which displace the anus away from the centre. On the interambulacral plates there are large primary (i.e. the ontogenetically earliest) tubercles and a series of small tubercles. The

1, 2. *Acrosalenia hemicidaroides,* Middle Jurassic (Bathonian), Stanton Wiltoh, Great Britain. 1 – a skeleton with spines, diameter of corona 23 mm. 2 – an isolated skeleton, diameter 21 mm. The apical plate system is incomplete.

1

3, 4. *Hemicidaris crenularis,** Upper Jurassic (Oxfordian), France. Diameter of skeletons 35 and 40 mm. The plates of the oculo-genital system encircling the periproct are clearly discernible from above (3). The larger ones are genital plates, the smaller ones ocular plates. 4 — a side view.

5. *Acrocidaris nobilis,** Upper Jurassic (Kimmeridgian), La Rochelle, France. Diameter of skeleton 35 mm. Viewed from above; the opening in the centre is the periproct, with the madreporite beside it.

6. *Acrocidaris* sp., view of the skeleton from below.

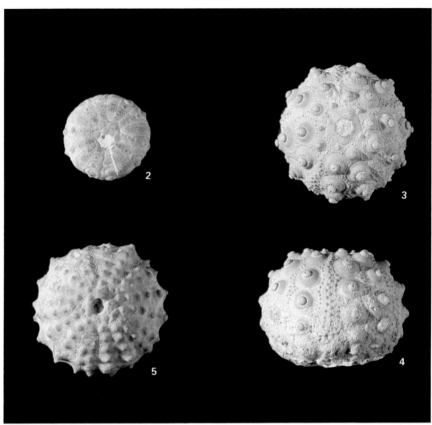

margin of the peristome is usually crenulated to form slits for the external gills.

The genus *Acrosalenia* occurs in Middle Jurassic sediments in Europe and eastern Africa. The skeleton is low-domed and the primary tubercles are perforated.

Hemicidaris crenularis (LAMARCK)

Order: Hemicidaroida
Family: Hemicidaridae

Hemicidarids are known from the Upper Triassic to the Upper Cretaceous. The large suranal plates round the periproct are missing, the primary tubercles are perforated and round the base they are usually crenulated.

Hemicidaris species are known chiefly from Middle Jurassic to Upper Cretaceous shallow-water sediments in most parts of the world. The skeleton is markedly domed and has pronounced gill slits on the flattened oral side. The large tubercles were surmounted by long, slender spines with a finely grooved surface.

Acrocidaris nobilis AGASSIZ

Order: Hemicidaroida
Family: Pseudodiadematidae

Echinoids of the genus *Acrocidaris* are to be found in Middle Jurassic to Upper Cretaceous sediments in Europe and North America (Mexico). They have a low-domed skeleton with relatively wide ambulacral fields. A striking tubercle on each genital plate is a characteristic feature (fig. 6).

6

Echinodermata

6

7

Stomechinus bigranularis (LAMARCK)

Order: Phymosomatoida
Family: Stomechinidae

The skeleton of 'regular' echinoids has a circular outline and the mouth and anus lie opposite to each other: the mouth in the centre of the ventral surface, the anus in the centre of the dorsal surface. We can obtain some idea of how the fossil representatives of this artificial group lived by studying the ecology of present-day echinoids. Most 'regular' echinoids live in warm, shallow seas of normal salinity, with only a few living at depths of several thousand metres. On rocky shorelines they form dense populations and there they defend themselves against the waves by clinging to the rocks with their suctorial ambulacral tube-feet and by excavating holes for themselves by means of their jaws and rotating movements of their spines. Species living on a soft substrate have long, fine, down-turned spines which prevent them from being buried.

Phymosomatoid echinoids, which have existed since the Middle Jurassic, have a regular skeleton with unperforated tubercles. The periproct is encircled by only ocular and genital plates.

Stomechinus occurs in Lower Jurassic to Lower Cretaceous sediments in Europe, Asia and northern Africa. It has a small apical plate system and a large peristome with gill slits.

Glypticus hieroglyphicus (GOLDFUSS)

Order: Arbacioida
Family: Arbaciidae

Arbacioid echinoids have been known since the Middle Jurassic. On their regular skeleton, which has unperforated and somewhat indistinct tubercles, there are numerous nodes formed by the deposition of additional skeletal material on the outer surface.

Glypticus species are found in Middle to Upper Jurassic deposits in Europe, northern Africa and Asia Minor.

Holectypus depressus (LESKE)

Order: Holectypoida
Family: Holectypidae

Echinoids which largely bridged the differences between regular and irregular types also appeared during the Lower Jurassic. They are assigned to the order Holectypoida, of which only two genera have survived to the present day. The mouth of holectypoid echinoids lies in the centre of the ventral surface; the periproct is near the periphery on the dorsal or the ventral side, or beside the mouth. In some species, the ambulacra on the dorsal side are lanceolate or petaloid in form and are known as petaloids.

Holectypus occurs in Lower Jurassic to Upper Cretaceous sediments in Europe and North America. The small, low-domed skeleton has non-petaloid ambulacra and pronounced gill slits round the peristome. The large periproct is on the under (oral) side.

1, 2, 7. Holectypus depressus,* Middle Jurassic (Bajocian), France. Diameter of skeleton cores 23 and 18 mm; dorsal (1), ventral (2) and lateral (7) views. This species lived directly on the sea floor.

3. Glypticus hieroglyphicus,* Upper Jurassic (Oxfordian), Chartraines, Haute-Marne, France. Diameter of skeleton 26 mm. The rough sculpture on the dorsal surface of the corona looks like hieroglyphics and is a characteristic feature of the genus.

4–6. Stomechinus bigranularis,* Middle Jurassic (Bajocian), Dorset, Great Britain. Diameter of skeletons 35 and 30 mm; dorsal (4), ventral (5) and lateral (6) views. The peristome is partly covered with sediment.

Echinodermata

Collyrites analis Desmoulins

Order: Holasteroida
Family: Collyritidae

The order Holasteroida comprises typical 'irregular' echinoids living from the Lower Jurassic down to the present. Their apical plate system is extended or is divided into an anterior and a posterior plate system, giving rise to an ambulacral triad (a 'trivium') in front and a pair of ambulacra (a 'bivium') behind. The foremost ambulacrum has a different size, shape and internal structure from the others. One of the most important features is the development of a 'plastron' on the under side of the corona, behind the mouth. Here the plates of the posterior interambulacrum grow markedly larger and their surface reflects functional specialization. The periproct usually lies on the truncated posterior side of the corona. The peristome is either in the centre of the ventral surface or has migrated anteriorly. Most extant species have a very thin, fragile skeleton and live at depths of 7,000 metres. Fossil species are found mainly in fine-grained sediments (e.g. in chalk and chalky clay).

Collyrites is known from Middle to Upper Jurassic sediments in Europe and North America. The apical plate system is divided. The periproct is situated near the edge of the corona, the rounded peristome anteriorly. The foremost ambulacrum lies in a shallow groove. The tubercles on the surface are very small.

1. *Disaster avellana,* Upper Jurassic, Balingen, West Germany. Length of core 25 mm, dorsal view. The three anterior ambulacra form a trivium, the two posterior ambulacra a bivium.

2, 3. *Collyrites analis,* Middle Jurassic (Bathonian), Decheseul, West Germany. Dorsal (2) and side (3) views of skeletons; length of both 26 mm. When the echinoid died, its large skeleton provided a suitable substrate for an annelid.

4, 5. *Nucleolites scutatus,** Upper Jurassic (Oxfordian), Trouville, France. Length of skeletons 27 and 35 mm; ventral (5) and dorsal (4) views.

6. *Clypeus plotii,** Middle Jurassic (Bajocian), Liesberg, Switzerland. Length of skeleton 67 mm; dorsal view. The petaloid ambulacra, with slit-like pores, are clearly discernible.

Disaster avellana AGASSIZ

Order: Holasteroida
Family: Disasteridae

Echinoids of the genus *Disaster,* from Upper Jurassic to Lower Cretaceous strata in Europe and northern Africa, have an elongate skeleton with the periproct in the truncated posterior part.

Clypeus plotii LESKE

Order: Cassiduloida
Family: Clypeidae

Cassiduloid echinoids (known from the Lower Jurassic to the present) have petaloid ambulacra on the dorsal side of the skeleton. The periproct lies outside the apical plate system. Phyllodia – wider plates in the ambulacral zones surrounding the peristome, which form depressions here – are a characteristic feature. There are no gill slits round the peristome. These echonoids had no jaws in adulthood.

The Middle to Upper Jurassic genus *Clypeus,* known in Europe and Africa, comprises mainly large echinoids with a low skeleton, a pentagonal peristome and shallow phyllodia.

Nucleolites scutatus LAMARCK

Order: Cassiduloida
Family: Nucleolitidae

Nucleolites species occur in Middle Jurassic to Upper Cretaceous deposits in Europe and Africa. The rounded-trapezoid skeleton is high at the edges. The ambulacra on the dorsal side are rather wide, but do not form typical petaloids. The peristome has migrated slightly anteriorly, while the periproct lies in a deep groove on the dorsal surface.

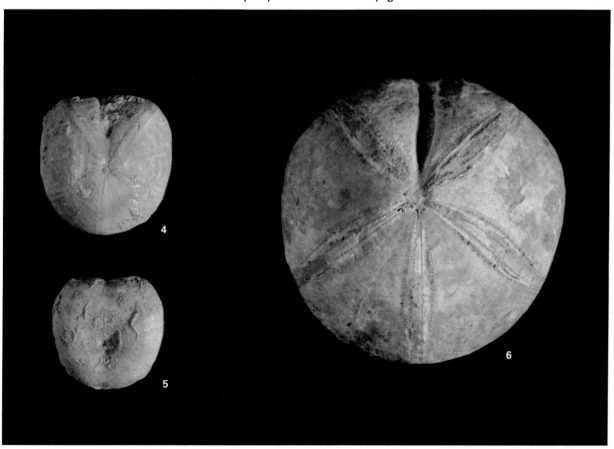

Echinodermata

Catopygus carinatus (GOLDFUSS)	Order: Cassiduloida Family: Nucleolitidae

In some Cretaceous deposits we find a high incidence of tiny cassiduloid echinoids with an almost worldwide distribution. One such genus is *Catopygus,* with a stratigraphic range from the Upper Jurassic to the Lower Cretaceous. The members of this genus have an oval, high-domed and posteriorly wider skeleton. The somewhat indistinct petaloid ambulacra are all in the same plane. The peristome is pentagonal and at the periphery the interambulacra are strikingly widened, like pads.

Oolopygus pyriformis D'ORBIGNY	Order: Cassiduloida Family: Nucleolitidae

If we study the skeletons of cassiduloid echinoids from deposits of various ages, we can see certain interesting evolutionary trends. Apart from changes in a number of special characters (the phyllodia, etc), we find general lengthening of the skeleton and an increase in its height and in the size of the area below the ambulacra. All these characters evidently denote a trend towards more effective and deeper burrowing in the sediment. From a comparison with the morphology of the representatives of other orders which dig deeper and live in burrows in the sea floor, we conclude that the petaloids of cassiduloid echinoids were exposed during the animal's lifetime.

The Upper Cretaceous genus *Oolopygus* is related to *Catopygus,* but its distribution is confined to Europe. The small to moderately large tests of its species are markedly elongate and relatively high. Petaloids are only faintly indicated, but there are pronounced phyllodia round the peristome.

Globator ovulum (LAMARCK)	Order: Holectypoida Family: Conulidae

Holectypoid echinoids likewise underwent marked development during the Cretaceous, when they spread to such an extent that some of them are to be found in suitable types of sediments over practically the whole of the globe.

Globator species are small echinoids from Cretaceous to Eocene deposits in Europe, northern Africa, southern Asia and North America. They have circular or elliptical high-domed skeletons with a flattened or slightly concave oral surface. The ambulacra ray out regularly from the centre of the dorsal side and do not form petaloids. The peristome is rounded or elliptical; the periproct lies on the dorsal side, at the edge of the skeleton.

1–3. *Oolopygus pyriformis**, Upper Cretaceous (Senonian), Aachen, West Germany. Length of skeletons about 20 mm; dorsal view (1) of internal mould and side (2) and ventral (3) views of skeletons.

4–6. *Catopygus carinatus,* Upper Cretaceous (Cenomanian), Le Hâvre, France. Length of skeletons 17–22 mm; dorsal (4), ventral (6) and lateral (5) view. The tubercles on the surface of the skeleton are so minute that they cannot be seen with the naked eye.

7. *Globator ovulum,* Upper Cretaceous (Senonian), Touraine, France. Length of skeleton 17 mm. The view of the ventral sufrace shows the elliptical peristome, which does not follow the symmetry plane, but impairs bilateral symmetry by its oblique position.

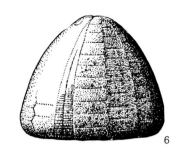

6

Conulus subrotundus MANTELL

Order: Holectypoida
Family: Conulidae

The question of relationships between the various genera of holectypoid echinoids was resolved partly with the aid of one of the less usual palaeontological methods, i. e. by studying the crystallographic orientation of the calcareous plates forming the skeleton. As with all other echinoids — and indeed, with echinoderms in general — each element of the skeleton (each plate, spine, etc) is an independent crystal with a given optic orientation characteristic of the representatives of certain families. One of the genera in which this character was studied is *Conulus*, known from Upper Cretaceous deposits in Europe, northern Africa, Asia and North America. The test is dorsally very high-domed (hemispheroidal or conical), while the oral surface is flat. The ambulacra are non-petaloid, the peristome is only slightly elongate. The elliptical periproct lies on the under side near the margin.

Galerites sp.

Order: Holectypoida
Family: Galeritidae

Galerites is a European Upper Cretaceous genus. Its species have skeletons similar to those of *Conulus* species, but differing in respect of certain special, systematically important characters such as the structure of the ambulacra, the organization of the tubercles on the surface, etc. The peristome is circular or pentagonal; the rounded periproct lies on the under side, near the edge of the skeleton.

Camerogalerus cylindrica (LAMARCK)

Order: Holectypoida
Family: Discoididae

Camerogalerus species occur in European Upper Cretaceous deposits. The skeletons are relatively large and helmet-shaped. The oral (ventral) surface is flat, the peristome is circular and the elliptical periproct lies between the mouth and the edge of the test. The apical plate system is small and inconspicuous. The tubercles on the surface of the skeleton are all roughly the same size.

The ecology of holectypoid echonoids has not been very thoroughly studied as yet. Species of the two extant genera are known from depths of 120 metres. Fossil representatives occur primarily in fine-grained calcareous sediments.

1. *Camerogalerus cylindrica,** Upper Cretaceous (Cenomanian), Kent, Great Britain. Diameter of skeleton about 40 mm; dorsal view.

2, 3. *Galerites* sp., Upper Cretaceous (Senonian), Rügen, East Germany. Diameter of cores about 25 and 35 mm; dorsal (2) and ventral (3) views.

4–6. *Conulus subrotundus,** Upper Cretaceous (Senonian), Kent, Great Britain. Length of skeletons about 30 mm; dorsal (4) and ventral (5) views. 6 — a lateral view of a skeleton of the related species *C. albogalerus.*

Holaster subglobosus AGASSIZ

Order: Holasteroida
Family: Holasteridae

Holasteroida were another evolutionarily successful group of Cretaceous echinoids. The order was named after the genus *Holaster*, whose species occur in Lower Cretaceous to Palaeogene sediments in most parts of the world. The test has a fairly high-domed dorsal surface and a flattened ventral surface. The apical plate system is not divided into an anterior and a posterior group of plates. The anterior ambulacrum is not petaloid, while the other ambulacra are subpetaloid, i.e. they form specialized zones of pores on the dorsal surface of the skeleton, but the pores are not explicitly arranged in a rosette. The semicircular peristome lies at the front of the corona and the periproct in the truncated posterior half. The structure of the posterior ambulacrum on the oral side (plastron) is one of the most important characters for the scientific classification of holasteroid echinoids. Here the plastron forms a labrum ('lip') composed of a plate which circumscribes the peristome posteriorly, of a large episternal plate behind it and of a following column of further plates. The different distribution and size of the tubercles on the surface of the plastron (compared with the surface of the rest of the under side of the skeleton) are no doubt associated with the specialized type of the spines on the plastron.

1. *Holaster subglobosus*, Upper Cretaceous (Senonian), Kent, Great Britain. Length of skeleton 43 mm. This dorsal view of the skeleton clearly shows its heart-shaped form and the course of the ambulacra.

2, 5. *Echinocorys scutatus*,* Upper Cretaceous (Senonian), Kent, Great Britain. Length of skeleton 70 mm; (2) dorsal view, (5) lateral view.

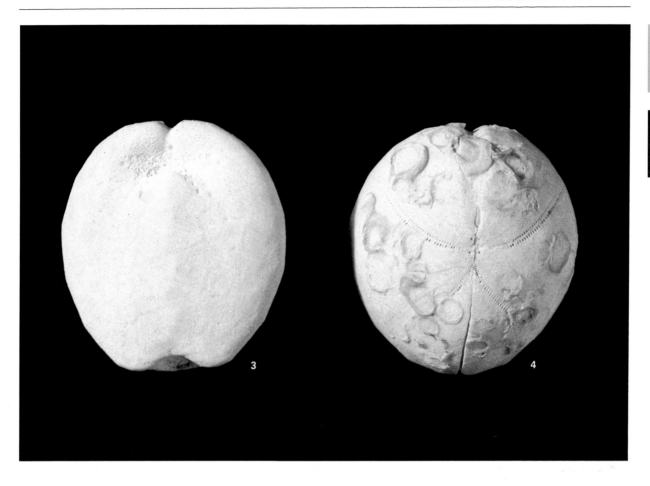

3, 4. *Hemipneustes radiatus,** Upper Cretaceous (Senonian), St. Pietersberg, Maastricht, the Netherlands. Length of both skeletons about 80 mm. On the oral (ventral) side (3) there is a striking zigzag suture between the large plates of the plastron. The dorsal surface of echinoid skeletons often provided a suitable base for other sessile animals, e. g. oysters (4).

Echinocorys scutatus (LESKE)

Order: Holasteroida
Family: Holasteridae

Echinocorys occurs in Upper Cretaceous to Palaeogene sediments in Europe, Asia Minor, Madagascar and North America. It has a high-domed, roughly oval and posteriorly slightly lengthened test, with non-petaloid ambulacra. The peristome is situated far anteriorly and there is no labrum. The plastron is slightly elevated; the periproct lies posteriorly, close to the margin.

Hemipneustes radiatus (LAMARCK)

Order: Holasteroida
Family: Holasteridae

The genus *Hemipneustes*, distributed over Upper Cretaceous Europe, northern Africa, Madagascar and India, comprises the biggest Cretaceous echinoids, whose skeletons measure up to 10 cm. They can be identified best from their high-domed, posteriorly truncated elliptical skeleton and their deeply sunken anterior ambulacrum. The paired ambulacra are subpetaloid. The lunate peristome is situated anteriorly.

Today we know of only one genus of the family Holasteridae; its species inhabit the Indian and the Pacific Oceans, at depths of 250 to 900 metres. Most of the fossil representatives of the family (and of the whole order) occur in fine-grained sediments.

5

409

Echinodermata

Toxaster complanatus (AGASSIZ)

Spatangoid echinoids appeared during the Lower Cretaceous. Since the Upper Cretaceous they have been abundant and some of their species are important index fossils. Their heart-shaped skeleton has two pairs of petaloid or subpetaloid ambulacra and a non-paired, non-petaloid anterior ambulacrum, which often lies in a deep groove. The apical plate system consists of four genital and five ocular plates. The periproct has shifted to the posterior margin of the corona; the peristome is situated anteriorly. The plastron is formed of a single post-oral plate (labrum), with a pair of large sternal plates behind it. The edge of the peristome juts into the corona. These echinoids were adapted to conditions below the surface of the sediment; they had no jaws, but simply swallowed the sediment and digested its organic components. An upward-oriented respiratory canal or funnel of varying lengths brought oxygenated water down into the burrow and some species actually built another, more or less horizontal, waste canal for the removal of excreta and used-up water. Echinoids which lived in a loose substrate reinforced the walls of the two canals with a mucoid fluid, or kept them patent by means of specially modified long spines. Respiration was mediated by ambulacral tube-feet in the petaloids. Depressions in the ambulacra, together with cilia, which may have produced their own current, conducted oxygenated water to the respiratory organs, but the decisive factor were

1–3. *Toxaster complanatus,* Lower Cretaceous (Neocomian), Neuchâtel, Switzerland. Length of skeletons 23 and 32 mm; dorsal (1), ventral (2) and lateral (3) views of skeleton. The absence of fascioles indicates that the echinoids burrowed only a little way into the substratum.

the fascioles — apparently smooth zones on the outer surface of the test, covered during the echinoid's lifetime with dense spines and swirling cilia. The fascioles are characteristically organized in every genus.

Toxaster was one of the initial genera in the evolution of spatangoid echinoids. Its species are known from Lower to Upper Cretaceous sediments in Europe and North and South America. There are no fascioles on the skeletons.

6

4, 5. *Micraster coranguinum,** Upper Cretaceous (Santonian), Kent, Great Britain. Length of skeletons 55 and 60 mm. Excellently preserved skeletons from Upper Chalk. Annelid worms of the genus *Spirorbis* have settled on the dorsal surface. The smooth band across the plastron near the periproct is part of the subanal fasciole (5).

6. *Micraster* sp., a reconstruction of a living individual.

Cr

Order: Spatangoida
Family: Micrasteridae

Micraster coranguinum (LESKE)

Members of the genus *Micraster* are known from Cretaceous to Palaeocene sediments in Europe, northern Africa, Madagascar and Cuba. They belong to the most thoroughly studied fossil echinoids. Wonderfully well preserved Upper Cretaceous material from England has furnished one of the best founded invertebrate evolutionary series there is. It helped to elucidate many associations between structures on the skeleton and the way these echinoids lived. *Micraster* species have a heart-shaped test, in which the closure of the subanal fasciole is a characteristic feature. These echinoids lived in burrows at various depths below the surface of the sea floor (fig. 6). Stratigraphically older species remained close to the surface; more recent species dug farther down.

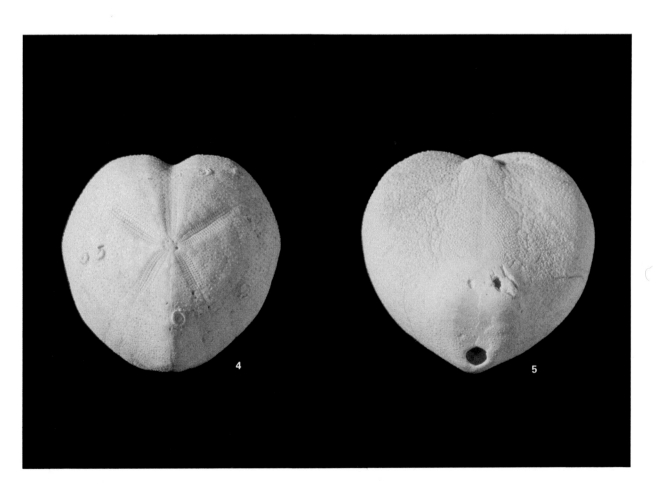

4   5

Echinodermata

Schizaster meslei PERON AND GAUTHIER

Order: Spatangoida
Family: Schizasteridae

Several new orders of echinoids appeared during the Cainozoic era, and several phylogenetically older orders reached the peak of their development. 'Irregular' echinoids continued to dominate. The change from pentameral symmetry to bilateral symmetry was associated with their one-way movement as they burrowed into and through the sediment. Many diverse species of spatangoid echinoids lived during the Eocene, when they occurred mainly in sediments formed in warm, shallow shelf seas; since then they have been gradually dying out. In present-day seas abyssal species are particularly richly represented.

Schizaster species, known from the Eocene to the Recent, are distributed all over the world. The periproct lies on the sheer posterior wall of the high test, which tapers off to a blunt point; the slope to the anterior edge is gentler. The ambulacra are sunken and the anterior one lies in a deep groove. The posterior petaloids are much shorter than the anterior ones. The ends of the petaloids are bordered by a fasciole and further fascioles run along the sides towards the periproct.

Echinolampas cf. *cherichirensis* GAUTIER

Order: Cassiduloida
Family: Echinolampadidae

New radiation of cassiduloid echinoids occurred in the Eocene. Most of them died out quickly at the end of the Miocene, however, and only a few genera are now left. The survivors include representatives of the cosmopolitan genus *Echinolampas*, whose elliptical skeletons have an inflated appearance. The petaloids are open. The peristome is pentagonal or rounded; the adjoining parts of the ambulacra have enlarged, characteristically distributed pores and form phyllodia. Another striking feature is a long zone with a smooth or granulated surface between the

1–3. *Schizaster meslei*, Palaeogene (Upper Eocene), Syrte basin, Libya. Length of largest core 23 mm; 1 and 2 – dorsal views, 3 – ventral view.

4. *Conoclypus subcylindricus*, Palaeogene (Eocene), Kresenberg, West Germany. Diameter of skeleton 37 mm. With its circular outline and ambulacra of equal length, this species, seen from above, looks more like a 'regular' echinoid.

Pg

5. *Echinolampas* cf. *cherichiren-sis*, Palaeogene (Upper Oligo-cene), Darnah, Libya. Length of skeleton 61 mm. Simple spines were inserted on the surface of the tiny tubercles.

peristome and the periproct. *Echinolampas,* with about 300 species — mainly fossil — is one of the largest echinoid genera.

Order: Holectypoida
Conoclypus subcylindricus (MÜNSTER)   Family: Conoclypidae

The majority of holectypoid echinoids died out at the end of the Cretaceous, although a few prominent genera are still known from the Cainozoic era. One of them is *Conoclypus*, whose representatives occur in the Mediterranean region, on Madagascar and in southern Asia and South America. The low-domed skeleton is only slightly lengthened; the ambulacra are petaloid. The periproct lies on the flattened under side, close to the funnel-wise extended peristome.

Echinodermata

4

Echinocyamus luciani LORIOL

Order: Clypeasteroida
Family: Fibulariidae

Clypeasteroids appeared at the end of the Cretaceous, celebrated their peak in the Tertiary (in the Miocene) and still have 24 surviving genera. Their skeletons have a distinct anterior and posterior part and are often strengthened from within by a system of pillars and lamellae. The petaloids on the dorsal side are the same width as the ambulacra, or wider. The peristome lies near the centre of the flat ventral side; the periproct is on the same side. Most species have simple or intricately branched food grooves on their under surface. Clypeasteroid echinoids have a powerful masticatory apparatus. They live primarily in the littoral zone, where they burrow in sand or mud. Cilia in the ambulacral grooves on the under side of the skeleton assure the transport of water and food to the mouth. The echinoids lie in the substratum either horizontally or obliquely, with their anterior part embedded and their posterior part protruding out of the sediment. Apart from man, the main enemies of most echinoids are sea otters (*Enhydra lutris*), specialized species of fish, sea stars and some species of echinoids.

Representatives of the genus *Echinocyamus* have lived all over the world since the Upper Jurassic to the Recent. They have small, slightly flattened and roughly elliptical skeletons with petaloids, whose few simple pores are arranged in pairs. The periproct lies on the under side, some way away from the edge of the skeleton. Some species burrow actively; others living in shelly gravel cover themselves with it by means of accessory ambulacral tube-feet. A similar masking system is also encountered in some 'regular' echinoids.

Sismondia saemanni LORIOL

Order: Clypeasteroida
Family: Laganidae

A flattened test like the one of the members of the cosmopolitan genus *Sismondia* is typical of most clypeasteroid echinoids. *Sismondia* species occur in Eocene to Miocene sediments. The skeleton has elliptical or pentagonal contours and a concave under side. The petaloids are open and the food grooves on the under side are simple.

1. *Sismondia saemanni*, Palaeogene (Middle Eocene), Syrte basin, Libya. Length of largest skeleton 12 mm.

2. *Echinocyamus luciani*, Palaeogene (Upper Eocene), Syrte basin, Libya. Length of largest skeleton 12 mm. The majority of *Echinocyamus* species are confined to the tropical belt.

1

2

3

3. *Clypeaster aegyptiacus*, Neogene (Upper Miocene), Mokattan, Egypt. Diameter of skeleton 145 mm. Striking pores connected by a furrow can be seen on the petaloid ambulacra.

4. *Clypeaster* sp., a transversal section of the skeleton.

Clypeaster aegyptiacus WRIGHT

Order: Clypeasteroida
Family: Clypeasteridae

The worldwide genus *Clypeaster*, with roughly 400 species dating from the Eocene to the Recent, also includes the largest known echinoids. Their rounded-pentagonal skeleton is often very high-domed on the dorsal side and flat or concave on the under side. It is strikingly massive and is strengthened internally by pillars and lamellae (fig. 4). The plates of the apical system have fused to form a conspicuous pentagonal scutum. The peristome usually lies in a deep funnel-shaped depression. The food grooves are simple. The small periproct is on the oral side, near the periphery.

Hemichordata

Dictyonema elongatum BOUČEK

Family: Dendrograptidae

Graptolites (class Graptolitha) are small extinct marine Palaeozoic invertebrates which lived in colonies and whose position in the zoological system remained long unexplained. Their closest extant relatives are hemichordate animals belonging to the class Pterobranchia ('wing-gilled'). Graptolites were sessile animals living in thecae joined together in colonies. They had a lophophore formed of one or several pairs of tentacles, together with feelers, which had the function of catching food and conveying it to the mouth. Like pterobranchids, graptolites lived in double-layered tubular thecae composed of a scleroprotein which was probably allied to chitin. The colonies were formed from a maternal theca (siccula) by budding and their constituent individuals were joined together by a stolon.

Dendroids (Dendroidea) are the evolutionally oldest graptolite class. Stratigraphically they range from the Middle Cambrian to the Upper Carboniferous and during the more than 200 million years of their existence they did not undergo any significant changes. Their dendritic skeletons (rhabdosomes) look like plants and it is not surprising that in the early days of palaeontological research they were thought to be plants. As a rule, the colony was held fast by a basal disc or by root-like outgrowths. Three types of theca – autothecae, bithecae and

1. *Dictyonema elongatum*, Lower Devonian (Lochkovian), Lejškov, Czechoslovakia. Part of a fine-structured rhabdosome, length 75 mm.

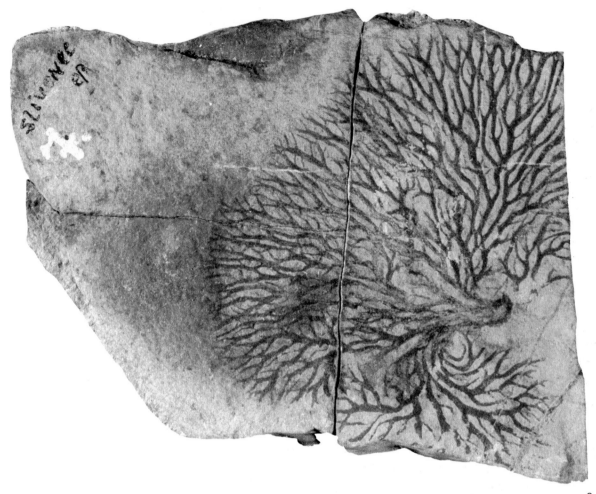

2

stolothecae − alternate in the colony skeleton. The larger autothecae were evidently occupied by female and the smaller bithecae by male individuals, while the stolothecae were autothecae which were not yet fully grown. Dendroids generally led a sessile existence in shallow water, but occasionally they lived epiplanktonically, suspended from algae, for example, by a fibre growing from the base of the colony.

The members of the worldwide genus *Dictyonema* lived from the Upper Cambrian to the Lower Carboniferous. Their funnel-shaped or almost cylindrical colonies are formed of forking (and terminally parallel) branches interconnected by cross-supports (dissepimenta). They were mostly sessile, held in place by the thickened base of the colony, but some of them led an epiplanktonic existence, with a resultant wide geographical distribution.

Order: Dendroidea

Coremagraptus thallograptoides BOUČEK   Family: Acanthograptidae

2. *Coremagraptus thallograp-toides*, Upper Silurian (Pridoli), Prague-Slivenec, Czechoslovakia. An exceptionally well preserved rhabdosome about 55 mm long, with a short stem at its base.

Dendroids of the genus *Coremagraptus* are to be found in Upper Ordovician to Lower Devonian strata in Europe. They are characterized by tuft-like or funnel-shaped rhabdosomes whose relatively thick branches are irregularly interwoven and often meet and unite to form anastomoses.

417

Hemichordata

Didymograptus murchisoni (BOECK)
Order: Graptoloidea
Family: Dichograptidae

True graptolites (Graptoloidea) lived from the Lower Ordovician to the Lower Devonian and reached their peak in the Lower Silurian. Unlike dendroids, their rhabdosomes are simple or only slightly branched, with a relatively small number of thecae of just one type, which are assumed to have held hermaphroditic individuals. The siccula was upside down, i.e. mouth downwards. The thecae were almost always suspended by a fibre (nema) which hardened to an axis (virgula). The stolons by which the individuals in the colony were interconnected were not calcified. Graptolites are stratigraphically extremely important fossils. They evolved unusually quickly and thanks to their planktonic and epiplanktonic mode of life they spread exceptionally far afield; they occur in large quantities and in different types of sediments and as a rule they are relatively easy to identify. They formed the basis of a detailed division of the English Ordovician and Silurian (and later of many other countries) to 'graptolite zones'. Each of these zones, which is characterized by the presence of a given species, represents a length of time averaging 0.7 to 1.5 million years. Since many graptolite species were adapted to life at specific depths, analyses of graptolite associations also furnish certain data on the bathymetric conditions of the environment.

Didymograptus is a prominent cosmopolitan Lower and Middle Ordovician genus. Its rhabdosomes fork into two branches which bud downwards from the siccula, or later diverge sideways.

Petalograptus folium (HISINGER)
Order: Graptoloidea
Family: Diplograptidae

Lower Silurian graptolites are very diverse. The members of the almost worldwide genus *Petalograptus* have a double-rowed rhabdosome (i.e. with thecae on both sides of the axis). The rhabdosome is shaped like a short or a long leaf and the thecae are long, narrow and straight, with a straight mouth. The axis is considerably longer than the lateral parts of the rhabdosome.

Rastrites approximatus (PERNER)
Order: Graptoloidea
Family: Monograptidae

Monograptids are the commonest Silurian graptolites and they also include the evolutionally youngest Lower Devonian species. Their rhabdosomes are arranged in a single row and the thecae, after budding, turned round and grew in the opposite direction to the siccula. The members of the genus *Rastrites*, which occur in Lower Silurian of Europe, North America, Asia and Australia, have thin, straight or curved rhabdosomes with long thecae which project roughly at right angles from the axis of the rhabdosome, at some distance from one another.

1. *Didymograptus murchisoni,** Lower Ordovician (Llanvirn), Prague-Šárka, Czechoslovakia. A rhabdosome composed of two branches; length 25 mm.

2. *Rastrites approximatus,* Lower Silurian (Llandovery), Litohlavy, Czechoslovakia, together with *Monograptus lobiferus* (the straight rhabdosome) and *Petalograptus folium** (the foliate rhabdosome) in weathered shale measuring 100 × 70 mm.

Hemichordata

Spirograptus spiralis (Geinitz)
Spirograptus turriculatus (Barrande)

Order: Graptoloidea
Family: Monograptidae

Graptolite rhabdosomes are often the only fossils found in graptolite shales. This type of sediment, which occurs all over the world and is particularly characteristic of the Lower Silurian, was formed in inadequately oxygenated seas. The reducing environment on the sea floor prevented life from developing both on and in the substratum. The classification of graptolites is based on the shape of the thecae and the general shape of the rhabdosome. The genus *Spirograptus*, so named because of its spiral rhabdosome, occurs in Lower Silurian strata in Europe, North America, Asia and Australia. The ends of the thecae are free and recurved. The mouth is produced to a 'brim' and to narrow, triangular, laterally orientated processes.

Testograptus testis (Barrande)

Order: Graptoloidea
Family: Monograptidae

Testograptus species, which occur in Upper Wenlock layers in Europe, northern Africa and Asia, have a wide rhabdosome in the form of a strongly developed spiral. Every theca has a few long spines beside it on the inner surface of the rhabdosome.

Monograptus flemmingi (Salter)

Order: Graptoloidea
Family: Monograptidae

The members of the genus *Monograptus* – the commonest graptolites – lived all over the world from the Lower Silurian to the Lower Devonian. Their simple, one-rowed rhabdosome is usually straight; less often it is bent or curved. The lower ends of the thecae touch each other; the upper ends are free and recurved (fig. 7).

Retiolites geinitzianus Barrande

Order: Graptoloidea
Family: Retiolitidae

The worldwide Lower Silurian genus *Retiolites* belongs to the double-rowed graptolites. The walls of the rhabdosome are reduced to a mere network, with oblique bars denoting the position of the alternating thecae (fig. 8).

Cyrtograptus lundgrenni Tullberg

Order: Graptoloidea
Family: Cyrtograptidae

Cyrtograptids are characteristic of the Lower Silurian. Their one-rowed rhabdosomes are often branched. At regular intervals, further branches arise from the main spiral branch and these in turn give rise to tertiary branches. In the almost cosmopolitan Lower Silurian genus *Cyrtograptus*, at least the proximal part of the thecae is recurved.

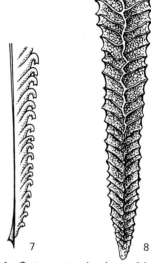

7   8

1. *Cyrtograptus lundgrenni*, in an association with *Testograptus testis*, Lower Silurian (Wenlock), Suchomasty, Czechoslovakia. A piece of shale measuring 90 × 60 mm.

2, 7. *Monograptus flemmingi*, Lower Silurian (Wenlock), Prague-Řeporyje, Czechoslovakia. 2 – plastically preserved parts of rhabdosomes in a calcareous concretion. Length of the larger specimen 40 mm. 7 – a detail of the theca.

3. *Spirograptus spiralis*, Lower Silurian (Llandovery), Grobsdorf, East Germany. A rhabdosome curving in an almost flat spiral; diameter of spiral 27 mm.

4, 8. *Retiolites geinitzianus*,* Lower Silurian (Wenlock). Prague-Motol, Czechoslovakia. A retiform rhabdosome, length 30 mm (4). 8 – a detail of the rhabdosome.

5. *Testograptus testis*,* Lower Silurian (Wenlock), Králův Dvůr, Czechoslovakia. Rhabdosomes with preserved spines. A piece of shale measuring 65 × 70 mm.

6. *Spirograptus turriculatus*,* Lower Silurian (Llandovery), Litohlavy, Czechoslovakia. Rhabdosomes curving in a high three-dimensional spiral. Graptolite shale, 65 × 65 mm.

The 'Dudley plate'

Palaeoecology is the science not of biocoenoses, but of associations of dead organisms and traces of their existence covered by sediment, which are known as taphocoenoses. In these, species which did not fossilize, or which were washed away, are missing, while conversely, they contain species washed in from elsewhere. The science analysing the origin of taphocoenoses is taphonomy and it prepares the basic material for palaeoecology, which in turn investigates interrelationships between fossil organisms and their environment.

'Dudley plates' from English Silurian strata are an example of a taphocoenosis whose composition is not very different from that of the original biocoenosis. They contain an accumulation of twigs from colonies of cryptostomatous and cystoporate bryozoans and alveolitid corals, bulbous algae and trepostomatous bryozoans, rhynchonellid and atrypid brachiopods and fragments of crinoids, whose composition corresponds to that of the organisms carpeting the slopes of coral reefs. The fact that the fragments are simply thrown together, without being crushed, sifted or oriented in a particular direction indicates that they were not carried very far – probably just down the slope of the reef – and that they were deposited in a quiet environment with slow sedimentation.

'Orthoceras' limestones

Being kept buoyant by putrefactive gases and the gases accumulated in their chambers, cephalopod shells were capable of postmortem trans-

1. A 'Dudley plate', Lower Silurian (Wenlock), Dudley, England. Vertical length of plate 90 mm. These accumulations weather out of soft calcareous marls.

2. A polished 'orthoceras' limestone plate, Upper Silurian (Ludlow), Lochkov, Czechoslovakia. Diameter of the larger shell 30 mm. Note the perfect orientation of the shells, the darker limestone, rich in organic matter, in the living chambers and the coarse detrital basic substance of the limestone.

S

O

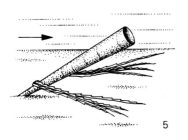

5

3, 5. Graptolites: 3 – *Monograptus flemmingi* (the thick rhabdosome, length 190 mm) and *Cyrtograptus lundgreni* (the thin rhabdosomes) caught and bent by the current over the shell of an orthoconic cephalopod. Lower Silurian (Wenlock), Kosov near Beroun, Czechoslovakia. 5 – a reconstruction; the arrow indicates the direction of the current.

4. *Selenopeltis buchi* overgrown by echinoderms belonging to the genera *Hemicystistes bohemicus* and *Argodiscus hornyi* (centre, right), Middle Ordovician (Llandeilo), Řevnice, Czechoslovakia. Length of trilobite 96 mm. The echinoderms have been preserved as negative imprints, which collectors usually consider to be of inferior value.

port for a long time. Their accumulation in shallows gave rise to orthoceras limestones, known mainly from the Ordovician and the Silurian. The shells in these limestones have been broken by transport and they have often been thoroughly sifted (i. e. there are very few other fossils with them) and oriented by the current or the waves.

Graptolite 'comets'

Palaeoecology
Taphonomy

Graptolites caught by the current and bent over cephalopod shells tell us something about its direction. In this case empty cephalopod shells have sunk obliquely to the bottom, apex downwards, while their mouths followed the current, like the points of a compass (fig. 5).

A trilobite overgrown
by echinoderms

Palaeoecology
Mutual coexistence of organisms

One of the relationships between organisms living together in a common biotope which can be demonstrated in fossil material is commensalism, in which one species benefits from the relationship, while the other neither gains nor loses by it. In Ordovician Europe, edrioasteroid echinoderms grew over the carapaces of large trilobites. The example in the illustration may actually be a case of incipient parasitism, since the large number of echinoderms meant that not only was the trilobite hindered by their weight and by increased resistance when swimming, but also by diminished mobility at places where they had overgrown adjacent ribs.

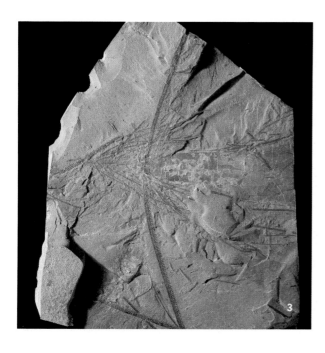

 **Palaeobiology**

Hydrocephalus carens BARRANDE   Palaeopathology

Palaeopathology is the science of the manifestations and healing of diseases and injuries and of congenital or acquired anomalies of the growth and morphology of fossils' bodies.

The pathological adhesion of the right side of the pygidium of a Cambrian trilobite to the last thoracic rib probably occurred during growth, owing to imperfect detachment of the last thoracic segment from the pygidium.

Spiniscutellum umbelliferum (BEYRICH)   Palaeopathology

A radial rib in the left half of a trilobite's pygidium has grown unevenly. Similar crushing and the healing of small injuries to the still soft carapaces are frequent among scutellid trilobites. They are attributable to the wide, tight fold on the under margin of the pygidium, which made it difficult for the trilobite to extricate its hind quarters when moulting.

Ichnospecies *Myzostomites* sp.   Palaeoecology, palaeopathology, trace fossils, Domichnia

On the stems of Ordovician to Jurassic species of crinoids, all over the world, we sometimes come across 'bumps' with one or several round holes in their centre. They were made by parasitic worms akin to the recent genus *Myzostomum*, whose remains were not preserved. The crinoids tried to cope with the damage by mobilizing tissue growth and precisely this pathological, injury-induced growth is evidence of the coexistence of parasite and host.

Teredo sp.   Trace fossils, Domichnia

In addition to actual fossils, we also find traces of their activities (trace fossils) in sediments. These traces are of great palaeoecological, sedimentological and stratigraphic significance and are dealt with by an independent branch of palaeontology – palaeoichnology. Signs of bore holes in hard substrata form an interesting group of traces. The majority of organisms which bored passages for themselves lived in them and subsisted on organic particles filtered out of the water. 'Shipworms' – marine bivalves belonging to the genus *Teredo* – are an exception, since they bore their way into submerged wood with the vestigial valves of their shell and devour the shavings. Their long, circular tunnels grow steadily wider and have a rounded end. They are lined with a thin layer of lime secreted by the mantle.

1. Parts of crinoid (*Crotalocrinites* sp.) stems with *Myzostomites* sp. swellings, Lower Devonian (Pragian), Koněprusy, Czechoslovakia. Length of the longest stem 57 mm.

2. *Hydrocephalus carens*, Middle Cambrian, Skryje, Czechoslovakia. Width of pygidium 25 mm. Probably a congenital deformity, since adhesions resulting from healing processes after injury generally left swellings on the carapace.

3. *Spiniscutellum umbelliferum*, Lower Devonian (Lochkovian), Kosoř, Czechoslovakia. Length of pygidium 38 mm.

4. *Teredo* sp., Palaeogene (Eocene), Isle of Sheppey, Great Britain. Passage diameter about 12 mm. *Teredo* does not like fresh water and wooden vessels can therefore be saved by sailing them into river mouths. For the same reason, the brackish water of the Baltic is a treasure trove of historic wrecks.

5. Ichnospecies *Lumbricaria intestinum*, Upper Jurassic (Lower Tithonian), Solnhofen, West Germany. Coil diameter 35 mm. A common trace fossil in lithographic limestones.

Ichnospecies *Lumbricaria intestinum* MÜNSTER

Trace fossils
Pascichnia

Among the traces of fossil organisms' activities we also find petrified excreta (coprolites). One example is the ichnogenus *Lumbricaria* from European Jurassic formations, which has successively been regarded as everything imaginable, from algae and worms to the viscerae of holothurians and fishes. However, it now seems to be the coprolites of dibranchiate cephalopods, in the form of smooth circular ropes one to four mm in diameter coiled in irregular masses. These calcareous (seldom phosphatic) structures contain fragments of crinoids belonging to the genus *Saccocoma.*

Palaeobiology

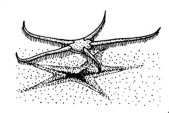

4

Traces of organisms' activities are studied with the aim of determining what produced them and the type of activity used. This is usually neither easy nor conclusive, because one type of trace may be formed by several types of organisms, while the same type of organism generally produces a whole series of different traces. This brings us to the problem of how to classify trace fossils, when the most satisfactory way seems to be to divide them according to the type of activity, i.e. from the ecological aspect. Trace fossils are today generally divided into five groups. Domichnia are dwelling structures (lairs, burrows, tunnels, U-passages, bore-holes and burrowing marks) in the sediment. Fodichnia are feeding traces left by animals which ate their way through the sediment, i. e. various passages which might also have been inhabited for a short time. Pascichnia are grazing traces and gnaw marks – often winding grooves, furrows and strips making maximum use of the surface. Cubichnia are surface resting traces – impressions, depressions and beds which have often kept the shape of the animal that made them. Repichnia are surface traces of creeping and crawling – furrows, grooves, paths and trails.

1. Ichnospecies *Helminthopsis spiralis*, Cretaceous, Marnia, Italy. Trace diameter 4 mm. Probably made by worm-like sediment eaters (quite likely belonging to Enteropneusta). The traces often occur in environments where the water was fairly deep.

1

2. Ichnospecies *Bergaueria* sp., Lower Ordovician (Arenig), Jívina, Czechoslovakia. Diameter of the larger pit 8 mm. Pits probably made by sessile sea anemones or similar coelenterates. They stand out very strikingly in the diversely coloured lamina of tuffite slates.

3. Ichnospecies *Asteriacites lumbricalis,* * Lower Jurassic (Hettangian), Rechberghansen, West Germany. Diameter 30 mm. Made by the body of a brittle star (*Palaeocoma escheri*). The trace has been a trifle obliterated, so that the cast is not very distinct.

4. Reconstruction of the origin of a trace.

European and American sediments from the Ordovician to the Recent often contain a type of trace known as *Asteriacites*, which comprises the imprints left by creeping and burrowing starfish and brittle stars. They are star-shaped, usually five-pointed (fig. 4), often partly obliterated and sometimes have cross furrows made by the pinnules.

Ichnospecies *Bergaueria* sp.

Trace fossils
Cubichnia

This Cambrian and Ordovician type of trace, known from Europe and America, consists of circular, cylindrical or bag-like pits with a hemispherical floor, which often has a wart-like protuberance projecting from its deepest part.

Ichnospecies *Helminthopsis spiralis* (Meneghini)

Trace fossils
Pascichnia

The ichnogenus *Helminthopsis* has been described in Ordovician to Cainozoic deposits. It comprises meandering cylindrical trails (coprolites?) with a circular cross section, a smooth surface and a diameter of about three to four mm.

Ichnospecies *Scolithos vertebralis* FRITSCH

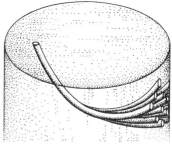

5

It is usually impossible to determine the makers of trace fossils conclusively (and often even approximately) and assign them to a given species; consequently, they cannot be classified under the usual biological nomenclature. On the other hand, because of the large number of types of trace fossils they must be given names for orientative reasons. For technical reasons, a binomial nomenclature is the most satisfactory, since it allows similar types of traces to be placed in groups resembling biological genera and species. 'Ichnospecies' stands for the species and 'ichnogenus' for the genus. At the same time, trace fossil names ought not to be the same as, or reminiscent of, the maker of the trace, since if views on the origin of the trace were to change, such a name could prove misleading. For instance, traces described under the old names *Lumbricaria* and *Chondrites* have nothing to do with either earthworms or algae. We must never forget that the taxonomy of trace fossils is an artificial one and that it applies only to types of traces and not to their makers.

The Cambrian to Ordovician worldwide ichnogenus *Scolithos* covers not very densely distributed, narrow, vertical or slightly slanting circular tunnels made, as a rule, in sandy sediments. The tunnels are unlined and have a smooth or cross-furrowed surface; sometimes they have a funnel-like widened mouth.

Ichnospecies *Monocraterion circinnatum* RICHTER

In sediments all over the world, dating from the Upper Precambrian to the Cainozoic era, we can find a type of trace comprising approximately

1. Ichnospecies *Scolithos vertebralis*, Middle Ordovician (Llandeilo), Prague-Vokovice, Czechoslovakia. Tunnels in quartzite, diameter 2–4 mm. An indicator of a very shallow environment with rapid clastic sedimentation.

2, 5. Ichnospecies *Monocraterion circinnatum*, Lower Ordovician (Tremadoc), Lerchenhügel near Heinersdorf, East Germany. Length 90 mm. The bundle-like tunnels formed by a vermiform organism as it ate its way through the fine-grained sandy sediments have been exposed (2). 5 — a reconstruction.

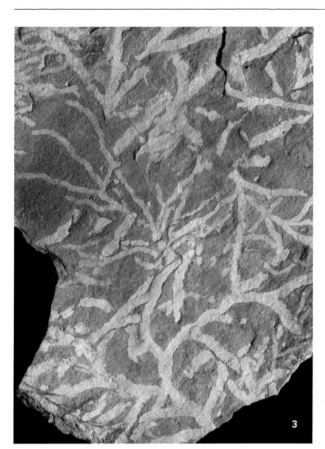

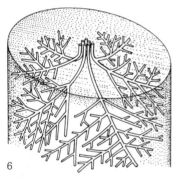

3,6. Ichnospecies *Chondrites* sp., Lower Devonian (Zlíchovian), Radotín, Czechoslovakia. Diameter of tunnels about 3 mm. This type of trace fossil, formed by unknown sediment-eaters, is typical of deep shelf seas. The filling of the tunnels is usually a very different colour from the surrounding sediment (3). 6 — arrangement of the tunnels.

4. Ichnospecies *Zoophycos* sp., Palaeogene (Eocene), Bzová, Czechoslovakia. Fan diameter 210 mm. Characteristic of relatively deep seas near the edge of the continental slope.

horizontal, upturned bundle-like structures which grow wider on one side and branch at acute angles into thin branches. The tunnels are roughly circular in cross section and, under the thin, smooth 'cortex', they are finely cross-furrowed.

Ichnospecies *Chondrites* sp.

Trace fossils
Fodichnia

Chondrites type traces occur in Cambrian to Cainozoic sediments. They comprise dendritic, horizontal passages with the same diameter, which, despite the complexity of their pattern, do not intersect. Their style of branching is reminiscent of a bird's feather. In soft shale sediments they form multi-storey systems in which the main tunnels turn upwards and open on the surface of the sediment (fig. 6).

Ichnospecies *Zoophycos* sp.

Trace fossils
Fodichnia

Zoophycos is a cosmopolitan Cambrian to Tertiary ichnogenus. It comprises large, intricate, fan-like, spirally organized structures formed by animals which ate their way through the sediment, turning their radial passages sideways in a low spiral; the axis of the spiral is a narrow vertical canal open at both ends. Deep down the fan usually spreads out to a width of up to 1.5 metres.

Chordata

Drepanaspis gemuendensis SCHLÜTER

Order: Heterostraci
Family: Drepanaspidae

Vertebrates are another important animal group. Their evolutionary trend was directly associated with the formation of an internal skeleton (endoskeleton), which is the most perfectly developed in vertebrates. The presence of an endoskeleton is accompanied by continuous postnatal development, without any need for larval stages or metamorphosis. The endoskeleton endows vertebrates with considerable mobility, regardless of their size. During their evolution, vertebrates attained the highest degree of physical, physiological and mental perfection and they are the only phylum to have achieved sapientation, i.e. the evolution of a rational being — Man. Except for the very oldest species, vertebrates evolved after the Cambrian period, so that their fossil records are almost complete.

During the Cambrian, several evolutionary lines, grouped together under the designation 'fish-like vertebrates', appeared parallel with each other, i.e. their evolution was not interconnected. It often took place mosaic-wise, however; that is to say, one group (evolutionary branch) overtook the other groups as regards the development of one particular character, but lagged behind them in respect of others. We usually differentiate the branches *Agnatha* (jawless piscine vertebrates), placoderms (armoured fish-like vertebrates), primitive cartilaginous fishes and teleosteans (fishes with a complete bony skeleton).

The members of the class *Agnatha,* which includes the genus *Drepanaspis,* lived from the Upper Cambrian to the Lower Devonian. They were jawless and fed on organic débris lying on the sea bed, which they sucked in through a mouth directly attached to their oesophagus. They also lacked paired fins. Their internal skeleton was cartilaginous, i.e. non-ossified, but many species developed a massive suit of bony armour. In *Drepanaspis gemuendensis* the armour plating was composed of large plates with wide fields of small scales in between (fig. 2). The caudal part of the body was covered with large rhomboid scales and the end of the caudal fin had a truncated appearance. *Drepanaspis* inhabited quiet creeks by the sea, with relatively stagnant water in which organic débris accumulated. Its distribution covers practically the whole of Europe. Finds of complete, well preserved specimens are comparatively rare; fragments of the armour of the front of the body are commoner.

2

1,2. *Drepanaspis gemuendensis,** Lower Devonian, Gemünden, West Germany. 1 — an almost complete individual, total length 36 cm. The golden pyrite crystals on the fossil show that fossilization occurred in a creek with stagnant water and a large quantity of organic material. 2 — a reconstruction.

430

1

 **Chordata**

Pterichthys milleri AGASSIZ

The order Antiarchi belongs to the placoderm class Placodermi, which comprises the oldest known vertebrates with jaws. They are included in the super-class Gnathostomata, a very heterogeneous group stemming from various evolutionary lines. Its first representatives appeared in the Upper Silurian (and possibly even sooner) and the last ones died out at the end of the Devonian. Antiarchi are such strange-looking placoderms that research workers originally considered their remains to be those of crustaceans or testudinates. The common character of the members of the order is a massive carapace covering the anterior part of the body. The anterior fins – or, to put it more accurately, the fore limbs – were covered by plate armour segmented in the same way as in crustaceans. Views on the function of such limbs are many and varied. The most plausible one is that the animals used them to take off from the bottom, since the massive carapace made swimming difficult and they preferred crawling to swimming.

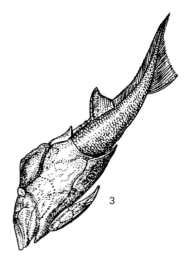

1, 3. *Pterichthys milleri,** Lower Devonian, England. Length of shield 6 cm (1). *Pterichthys* is often cited as the classic example of placoderms and is therefore much sought after by collectors. The number of finds is not very large, however. 3 – reconstruction of a living individual.

432

2,4. *Asterolepis maxima,* Lower Devonian, Nairn, Scotland. Length of shield 9 cm (2). In addition to shields, isolated limbs are also found occasionally. 4 − a reconstruction of a living individual.

D

2

Pterichthys milleri grew to a length of 10 to 20 cm. The massive, domed shield, composed of large plates, tapered off to a pronounced ridge on the dorsal aspect. The armour plating was all in one piece, so that the head was immobile. The eyes were close together on the parietal surface of the head (fig. 3). The posterior part of the body was covered with round scales. *Pterichthys* lived during the Lower Devonian, in what is now western Europe. Parts of the shield or fragments of single plates are generally found.

Order: Antiarchi
Family: Asterolepidae

Asterolepis maxima AGASSIZ

Although similar to the preceding species, this one is larger (20 to 25 cm) and has a more massive shield, whose middle plates overlap the side plates. The limbs are slimmer than in *Pterichthys* and terminate in a sharp process (fig. 4). *Asterolepis* is a typical fossil of Old Red Sandstone, an extensive facies of sandstones and conglomerates, with shale and marl in between, with a characteristic red colouring. This facies is to be found chiefly in northern and north-western Europe.

4

433

Chordata

Carcharodon megalodon AGASSIZ

Order: Selachii—sharks
Family: Isuridae

Chondrichthyes are explicitly marine jawed vertebrates which retain a cartilaginous skeleton for their entire lifetime. The systematic classification of the individual groups is still being investigated.

Sharks are an evolutionally important group of Chondrichthyes. Although their skeleton remains permanently cartilaginous, this is not a primitive character, but, on the contrary, is a sign of marked specialization. It is the cartilaginous skeleton, together with the streamlined body and highly specialized skin, that gives sharks their extreme suppleness and mobility. It does not furnish much material capable of fossilization, however, and so the only part of these animals to have been preserved are their teeth. Sharks usually have a large number of teeth; they are generally triangular, are arranged in several rows, one behind the other, and are used not for biting, but for seizing or tearing prey. The front row of teeth is the one that is used; when it is worn down the teeth bend forward and drop out and their place is taken by the next row.

Sharks are supposed to have originated during the Silurian period, but there is no palaeontological evidence for this hypothesis. The first finds date from the Devonian. Sharks are primarily marine animals; they evolved in the sea and from there they spread to brackish and fresh water. They started to flourish during the Carboniferous and Permian periods, but at the end of the Palaeozoic era many groups died out and in the Jurassic and the Cretaceous periods the survivors underwent tremendous evolutionary modernization. For a long time they competed

1. *Carcharodon megalodon*, Miocene, Kékkoi Kator, Hungary. Width of larger tooth 8.5 cm, of smaller tooth 6.5 cm. Their finely serrated edges make the teeth of large sharks razor-sharp.

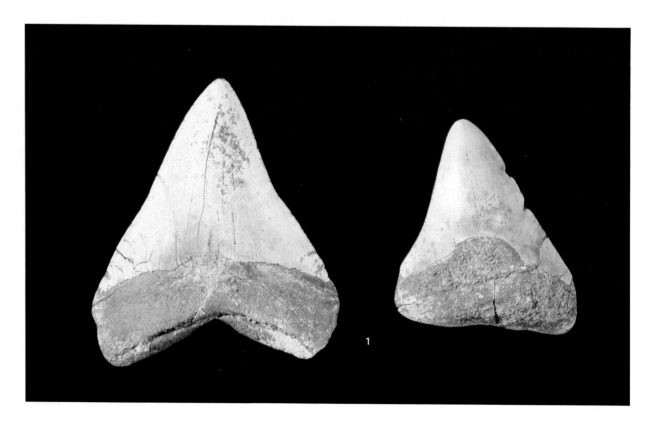

successfully with the fishes (Pisces) and it was not until the end of the Mesozoic era and during the Cainozoic era that they were caught up and overtaken by them.

Sharks of the genus *Carcharodon* (fig. 4) have been known since the Upper Cretaceous onwards. The Man-eater Shark (*Carcharodon carcharias*) still lives in tropical and subtropical seas. Its fossil relative *C. megalodon* likewise inhabited warm seas, but only its teeth have been preserved in the relevant sediments. The main finds come from southern Europe; further north their numbers gradually diminish. The teeth are strikingly large (up to 15 cm high), triangular, flat in front and concave behind. A comparison with *C. carcharias* shows that *C. megalodon* must have measured up to 25 metres!

Order: Selachii – sharks
Scapanorhynchus raphiodon AGASSIZ
Family: Isuridae

This fossil species is related to the Porbeagle or Mackerel-shark, which inhabits the Pacific and Atlantic oceans and measures four to six metres. In groups it accompanies shoals of herring and cod, which are its chief food. It is assumed that *Scapanorhynchus raphiodon* had similar habits, but it was much smaller (only two to three metres). Its thin, needle-like teeth are commonly found in Cretaceous sediments.

Order: Selachii – sharks
Isurus (Oxyrhina) mantelli AGASSIZ
Family: Isuridae

Isurus mantelli, a common inhabitant of Cretaceous seas, has flattened teeth with large points at the sides and a wide one in the middle. A recent relative, the aggressive Mako (*I. oxyrhynchus*), is hunted for sport.

2. *Isurus mantelli,* Cretaceous, Zbyslav, Czechoslovakia. Width of tooth 2.7 cm, height 3.8 cm.

3. *Scapanorhynchus raphiodon,* Cretaceous, Kamajka, Czechoslovakia. Width of tooth 0.8 cm, height 1.9 cm.

4. *Carcharodon* sp., a reconstruction of a living individual.

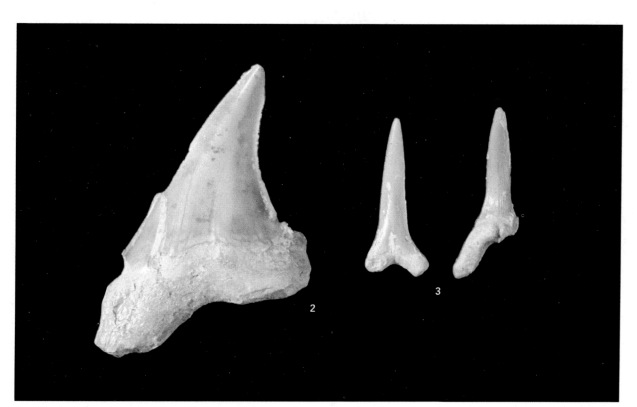

 **Chordata**

Xenacanthus sp.

Order: Pleuracanthodii
Family: Xenacanthidae

In the course of their history, sharks have several times penetrated inland, into fresh water. For example, the present-day species *Carcharhinus nicaraguensis* lives in the fresh water of Lake Nicaragua in Central America.

The genus *Xenacanthus* (fig. 3) originated during radiation of the sharks in the late Palaeozoic era. They were primitive freshwater animals with a cartilaginous skeleton whose cartilages were reinforced with calcium deposits. The vertebral arches were ossified. The snout was armed with numerous characteristically shaped teeth with a large divergent point on either side and a small point in the middle (in most sharks the middle point is larger and thicker than the side points). Behind their head xenacanths had a large dentin — and possibly movable — spine with two rows of tiny, saw-like teeth along its dorsal edge. At present we have no unequivocal explanation of the function of this spine. Perhaps it originally stood in front of the dorsal fin (present-day dog-fishes of the family *Squalidae* have sharp rays in front of both dorsal fins). Xenacanths had a long, slender body without any shortening of the caudal part of the back bone. The dorsal fin commenced behind the head and stretched right to the tail. The structure of the anterior fin is interesting; the mid-axis is segmented and the side rays are arranged round it like the leaves of a palm-tree, forming an 'archipterygial' fin. The only present-day fishes to possess this type of fin are lung fishes (Dipnoi). Like lung fishes, *Xenacanthus* lived in muddy lakes and pools in marshy regions, where it caught smaller fish. If the water level sank too often, or the pool dried up, it was forced to travel over dry land, from one pool to another, in order to survive.

1. *Xenacanthus carinatus* FRITSCH, Carboniferous, Kounov, Czechoslovakia. A complete specimen, length 74 cm. The curved back is due to postmortem rigor of the dorsal muscles; this is a relatively common phenomenon in fossil fishes.

2. *Xenacanthus bohemicus* FRITSCH, Carboniferous, Nýřany, Czechoslovakia. A dentin spine, length 16 cm. The surface of the spine is sometimes variously sculptured.

3. *Xenacanthus* sp., a reconstruction of a living individual.

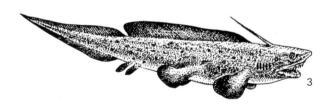

 **Chordata**

Paramblypterus rohani (HECKEL)

Order: Palaeonisciformes
Family: Commentryidae

Fishes (Pisces) originated in the Lower Devonian. They evolved from the same ancestors as Chondrichthyes, but independently. The members of both classes succeeded in changing over to a fully active pelagic existence. They likewise both have paired fins. In the course of their evolution Chondrichthyes became a very conservative group and lost their ability to compete with the fishes. Fishes' skeletons are partly or completely ossified and the fins are reinforced by bony rays supported by a bony base. The evolution of fishes was complicated. It took place in several waves (radiations) and often mosaic-wise; vicariance of forms and species also played a role. The first wave comprised soft-boned fishes (Chondrostei), whose skeleton was not yet completely ossified and which had a lung sac or paired lungs formed by evagination of the alimentary tube, enabling them to breathe atmospheric oxygen. At first the lungs merely supplemented branchial (gill) respiration in muddy water with too little oxygen. Chondrosteans flourished mainly between the Devonian and the Permian (contemporarily with palaeoniscids). Only a few of their representatives have survived down to the Recent (sturgeons and allies – Acipenseriformes).

1. *Paramblypterus rohani,* Lower Permian, Semily, Czechoslovakia. An almost complete specimen, length 20.5 cm. The heterocercous tail and rhomboid scales are clearly discernible; the head is not so well preserved.

1

2

2. *Sceletophorus verrucosus,* Carboniferous, Třemošná, Czechoslovakia. An almost complete specimen, length of body 12.5 cm. The tip of the strikingly long tail is missing. Copper compounds are responsible for the green colouring.

In the older palaeontological literature *Paramblypterus rohani* is named *Amblypterus rohani.* It had a slender, fusiform body covered with relatively large, rhomboid ganoid scales with a gleaming surface layer of ganoin. Structurally the scales resembled those of recent sturgeons (*Acipenser*) or the beluga (*Huso*). Their head was covered with dentin-coated armour plating – a primitive character which no longer appears in the more advanced forms of fishes. The large mouth was armed with numerous small teeth. The paired fins were relatively small and the asymmetrical (heterocercous) caudal fin had a tapering upper lobe. *Paramblypterus rohani* lived in the late Carboniferous and early Permian in the pools and small lakes of central European bituminous coal swamps. Related species colonized the whole of present-day Europe from Great Britain to the west of the European part of the USSR.

Sceletophorus verrucosus FRITSCH

Order: Palaeonisciformes
Family: Carbovelidae

This species was also formerly included in the genus *Amblypterus.* It had a short, high body and a large head with a short snout and strong teeth. The cranial armour is strewn with oval 'warts'. The non-paired fins are large and thick, the paired fins narrower and thinner. The caudal part of the body is strikingly long. Like the preceding species, *S. verrucosus* also lived in pools and small lakes in the bituminous coal swamps of central Europe.

 **Chordata**

Caturus furcatus AGASSIZ

Order: Amiiformes – bowfins and allies
Family: Amiidae – bowfins

Holosteans (bony ganoids) are regarded as the middle stage of the evolution of bony fishes. They still have a partly cartilaginous skeleton; older forms have rhomboid scales, while in more recent forms the scales are almost oval (cycloid). The lungs have generally been converted to an air-bladder. The group flourished during the Triassic and the Cretaceous period, at the end of which the majority died out, when they were displaced by the true bony fishes. The only one to have survived is the Bowfin (*Amia calva*).

Caturus furcatus was a predator with a salmon-like body, a short skull, powerful jaws and strong teeth and an incompletely ossified spine. Its small, almost cycloid scales overlapped one another, thereby making the body armour stronger. The slender caudal fin was forked. *C. furcatus* inhabited central European lagoons during the Jurassic period. In the early Jurassic (Liassic) it was comparatively rare, but in the Upper Jurassic (Malm) it was abundant. The best known finds come from Jurassic limestone in the region of Solnhofen (Bavaria, West Germany).

1. *Caturus furcatus,** Jurassic, Solnhofen, West Germany. A complete specimen, length 42 cm. The forked tail, which gave the species its name (*furcatus*) is clearly visible.

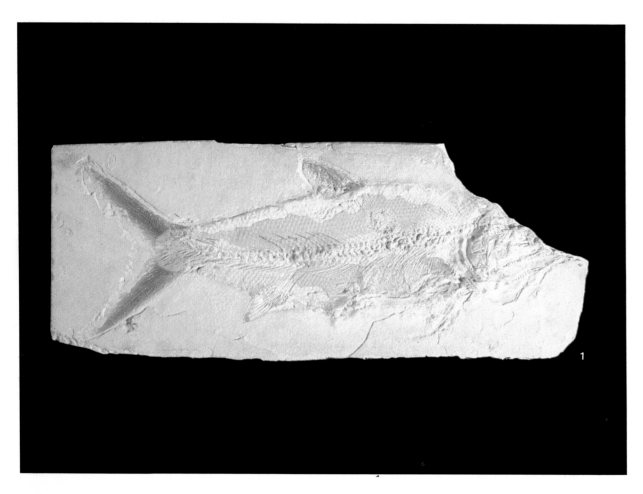

2

2. *Amia kehreri*, Eocene, Wesel, West Germany. A complete specimen, length 27 cm. Note the striking expansion of the caudal part of the body.

3. *Amia* sp., a reconstruction of a living individual.

Numerous well preserved finds are known from Solnhofen, many of them captured in quite curious life situation. Finds of individuals having died while swallowing their prey are well known. These are explicit cases of sudden death, a phenomenon which is much discussed nowadays. In popular literature such finds are often explained as causes of a catastrophe (catastrophic hypothesis). Less attractive but, on the other hand, more probable seems the theory that these animals died from asphyxia while swallowing prey too large for them. Such cases are known from the present times as well (e.g. in pikes). Similar finds have been described from the Upper Jurassic sediments at Karatau, southern Kazakhstan (USSR).

Amia kehreri LAUBE

Order: Amiiformes — bowfins and allies
Family: Amiidae — bowfins

The members of the genus *Amia* (fig. 3) form a kind of transition between the many-boned fishes (Holostei) and the true bony fishes (Teleostei). Their long, cylindrical body ends in an outwardly symmetrical, but internally asymmetrical (internally heterocercous) caudal fin. The caudal part of the body merges with the upper half of the caudal fin, but is cut short, as in the case of symmetrical (homocercous) fins; this gives rise to the curious widening of the tail characteristic of the genus *Amia*. The thin cycloid scales, which are not coated with ganoid, overlap one another like tiles. The still extant Bowfin lives in lakes in the southern part of the USA (Florida, Texas) and in the Mississippi and its tributaries. Its functioning lungs allow it to breathe atmospheric oxygen. Fossil forms, which likewise lived in fresh water, have been found from western Europe (France) to central Europe (Czechoslovakia).

3

 **Chordata**

Leptolepis sprattiformis AGASSIZ

Order: Leptolepiformes
Family: Leptolepidae

The bony fishes (Teleostei) are the most advanced group of fishes. They have a completely ossified skeleton and the dermal bones of the head are joined to the brain-case (endocranium). The gill slits are covered with an operculum which has its own skeleton. The lungs — with a few rare exceptions — have been transformed to a hydrostatic organ (the air-bladder). The cycloid scales overlap tile-wise. Bony fishes were already successful in the Cretaceous period, when they not only displaced chondrosteans and holosteans, but also invaded the sea on a large scale and supplanted the more primitive selachians. They flourished in the Cainozoic and Quaternary eras and most of these families and genera are still extant.

1. *Leptolepis sprattiformis,* Jurassic, Solnhofen, West Germany. A complete specimen, length 6.5 cm. The backward curvature of the skeleton is the outcome of postmortem rigor of the dorsal muscles.

J

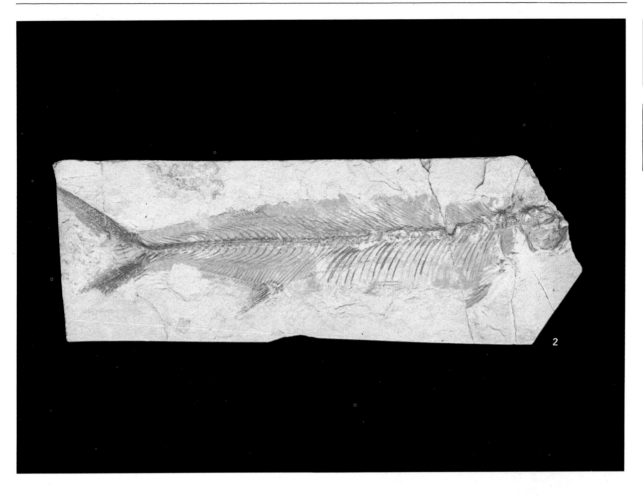

2. *Thrissops formosus,** Upper Jurassic (Malm), Kehlheim, West Germany. A complete specimen, length 45 cm. The skull is somewhat damaged, so that the type of dentition cannot be seen.

The genus *Leptolepis* comprised many species which inhabited Europe, the two Americas, western Asia and north Africa from the Lower Jurassic to the Lower Cretaceous. *Leptolepis sprattiformis* was hardly any longer than a finger and because it looked a little like a sprat (*Sprattus sprattus*), it was named after it. It inhabited central European lagoons, evidently in shoals, as large numbers of individuals are often found together.

Thrissops formosus AGASSIZ

Order: Elopiformes
Family: Elopidae

Thrissops is related to the genus *Leptolepis,* but it was much larger. It was probably a nimble predator, since it had strong teeth and a strikingly thick caudal fin. It inhabited central Europe from the Lower Jurassic to the Lower Cretaceous.

Chordata

Leuciscus papyraceus BRONN

Order: Cypriniformes – carps and allies
Family: Cyprinidae – carps and minnows

From the Cainozoic era onwards, among the fossil remains of bony fishes we find representatives of families, and even of genera, known today. Among them are the cyprinid fishes, which have a geographically extremely wide area of distribution. Cyprinids have protrusible, tooth-

1. *Leuciscus papyraceus,* Lower Miocene, Lužice near Most, Czechoslovakia. A complete specimen, length 6 cm. It occurs in finely layered sediments (hence its specific name), which have often not hardened very much, however, making these fossils difficult to recover and conserve.

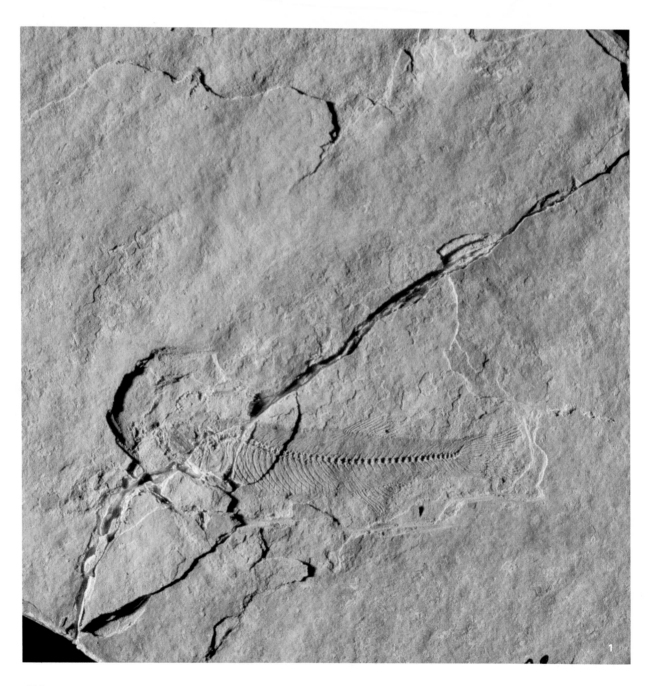

less jaws, but their fifth branchial arch has been transformed to oesophageal teeth. They include the genus *Leuciscus,* which is distributed over Europe, North America, Asia and Africa.

Leuciscus papyraceus had a flat-sided body covered with relatively large scales. The fins were relatively small compared with the body. This genus lived in fresh water and its remains are found fairly frequently in lake sediments in soft coal (lignite) basins.

Order: Clupeiformes – herrings and allies
Family: Salmonidae – salmonids

Thaumaturus furcatus REUSS

Salmonids are relatively very widely distributed today and in the geological past, particularly in the Tertiary. They are characterized by large numbers of sharp teeth at the edge of their mouth.

Thaumaturus is related to salmon and trout (genus *Salmo*). It lived in fresh water and was a common inhabitant of the basins of lakes in the coal-bearing Miocene.

2. *Thaumaturus furcatus,* Lower Miocene, Kučlín, Czechoslovakia. A complete specimen, length 5.5 cm. Found in diatomites, showing that this fish preferred lake basins with clean water.

445

 **Chordata**

Serranus ventralis AGASSIZ

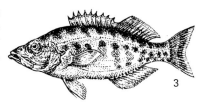

The bass family has an abundance of species; recent ones alone number over 600. The majority live in the sea and prefer warm water. They tend to remain near the shore and seldom venture into deep water. Some species grow to a huge size, while others are brilliantly coloured, like *Serranus scriba.*

  S. ventralis (fig. 3) lived in the early Cainozoic, in the south of Europe, which at that time was covered by the sea. It presumably lived in the same way as recent sea bass, i.e. it frequented rocky shores and the sides of coral reefs, where it caught small fish and crustaceans. The question of its colour must unfortunately be left to our imagination.

1, 3. *Serranus ventralis,* Eocene, Monte Bolca, Italy. 1 – a complete specimen, length 24 cm. The second dorsal fin of bass is immediately behind the firs, so that they almost unite. In perch (Percidae) they are always separate. 3 – a reconstruction of a living individual.

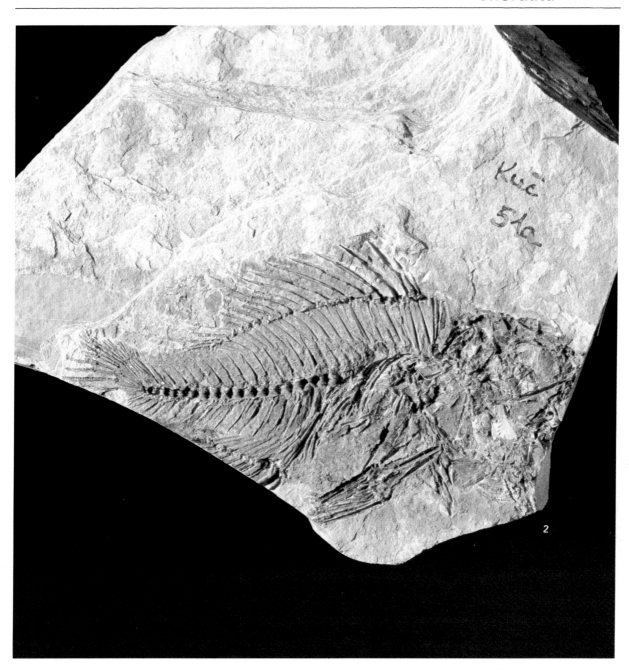

2. *Bilinia uraschista,** Middle Oligocene, Kučlín, Czechoslovakia. A complete specimen, length 9 cm. As with most fishes, far oftener than whole skeletons one is more likely to find single skeletal elements, which the layman has difficulty in identifying.

Order: Perciformes − perch and allies
Family: Serranidae − bass

Bilinia uraschista (REUSS)

Unlike the bass *Serranus ventralis, Bilinia uraschista* did not live in the sea, but in fresh water in Tertiary central Europe. It belongs to the bass family, but in addition to characters typical of bass it has many others reminiscent of the skeletal structure of perch, so that it is intermediate between the two families, as it were. Similarity of the members of two different families is attributed to convergence of species living in the same environment and leading the same type of life.

447

Chordata

Ceratodus kaupi AGASSIZ

Order: Ceratodiformes – lung-fish
Family: Ceratodidae

Lung-fish are a relatively primitive, but at the same time highly specialized, group of freshwater bony fish. They have a cartilaginous or only partly ossified skeleton; they retain the notochord (*chorda dorsalis*) for the whole of their life and vertebrae are never formed. The paired fins are of the archipterygian type. The air bladder opens into the oesophagus and fulfils the function of lungs. Special organization of the limbs and the ability to breathe atmospheric oxygen allows lung-fish to survive temporary droughts. Lung-fish evolved from primitive cartilaginous fish during the Middle Devonian, at the same time as crossopterygians, but unlike the latter they had no special evolutionary significance and are now no more than a peculiar disappearing line. Three genera have survived down to the present and all of them live in shallow fresh water in tropical swamps. They are able to survive the dry season in a state resembling anabiosis, usually buried deep in the mud. They can be either carnivorous or herbivorous. It is assumed that fossil lung-fish lived in the same manner.

1. *Ceratodus kaupi,* Triassic, Hoheneck, West Germany. A dental plate, width 5 cm. In the fish's mouth, the processes of the plate were directed outwards, while the rounded base was directed towards the middle of the palate.

2

2. *Macropoma speciosa,* Cretaceous, Prague, Czechoslovakia. A complete specimen, length 45 cm. It is rare to find such a well preserved individual.

The members of the genus *Ceratodus* inhabited Europe during the Triassic and Jurassic. We find particularly large, flat dental plates covered with lumpy enamel, which were formed by fusion of rows of teeth. Other parts of the skeleton are seldom found.

Order: Coelacanthiformes
Family: Coelacanthidae

Macropoma speciosa REUSS

The members of the order Coelacanthiformes belong to the crossopterygians (Crossopterygii), another specialized evolutionary branch of the fish. Their spine is not completely ossified and the central axis of their paired limbs, or achipterygia, has the form of a muscular shaft. Such limbs were useful not only for swimming, but also (and mainly) for crawling on the land. The lungs were well developed and pulmonary respiration was improved by nostrils opening into the oesophagus. Crossopterygians evolved during the Devonian from cartilaginous fish or similar forms and became adapted to life in shallow, muddy lakes and swamps. Pulmonary respiration and the structure of their limbs allowed them to survive droughts, to travel over land from one pool to another and to look for food on the boundary between water and land — an abundant source of nourishment which had not previously been utilized. We look upon crossopterygians as the ancestors of the amphibian order *Osteolepiformes.*

The members of the order *Coelacanthiformes* not only took to the land; on the contrary, during the Mesozoic era most of them took to the deep sea. One of these — and the only species still extant — is *Latimeria chalumnae,* which has survived in its present form for some 70 million years. *Macropoma speciosa* lived in shallow central European seas during the Cretaceous.

449

 **Chordata**

Letoverpeton austriacum (FRITSCH)

Order: Seymouriamorpha
Family: Discosauricidae

Amphibians (*Amphibia*) were the first vertebrates which began to make themselves independent of an aquatic environment. Their embryos, however, still develop in the water and the adult animals also return to it. The first group of amphibians, following on from the crossopterygians, were the stegocephalians (*Stegocephala*), to which *Letoverpeton* belongs.

Letoverpeton was a lizard- or salamander-like amphibian. At the back of its wide skull there were deep otic notches for the ears. The trunk was covered with armour plating composed of tiny scales. In the early stages of its development the animal breathed with gills and its skeleton was not yet ossified; during later development the skeleton progressively ossified and the gills disappeared. Scientists therefore regarded the various growth stages as separate species. *Letoverpeton* inhabited shallow swamp water overgrown with luxuriant vegetation in which it sought both shelter and food (insects and their larvae, small fish and young stegocephalians).

Palaeobatrachus grandipes (GIEBEL)

Order: Anura (Salientia) – tail-less amphibians
Family: Palaeobatrachidae

Tail-less amphibians are an evolutionary line which broke away from stegocephalians at the end of the Permian. In association with adaptation to a very specific form of locomotion (leaping and swimming by

3

1,3. *Letoverpeton austriacum*, Permian, Bačov, Czechoslovakia. 1 – a complete specimen, length of skeleton 17 cm. The localization of the otic notches on the skull corresponds to the place where fishes have their branchial skeleton. The notches caused the rear of the skull to be produced to conspicuous processes. 3 – a reconstruction of a living individual.

2, 4. *Palaeobatrachus grandipes,* Miocene, Veselíčko, Czechoslovakia. 2 – a complete specimen, length of skeleton 8.5 cm. Anuran skeletons from lignite keep very badly and need to be conserved by a special technique. The carbonaceous sediment in the photograph is prevented from crumbling away by a plaster bed. 4 – a swimming individual.

2

4

means of their hind legs), their skeleton became lighter (in particular their ribs grew shorter and their skull bones were reduced) and their pelvic girdle, together with the sacral bones, was characteristically modified to provide flexible attachment for their hind limbs.

Palaeobatrachus grandipes is a Mesozoic anuran reminiscent of recent clawed toads (*Xenopodidae*), which today live only in tropical Africa. Their skeletal remains abound in freshwater sediments in western Bohemia and in both parts of Germany. Sometimes, in addition to skeletal elements, we also find very well preserved imprints of the internal organs and the skin, even with traces of colouring; tadpoles and eggs are also found. Palaeobatrachids spent the whole of their life in water, where their well developed lungs enabled them to remain submerged for a very long time. Like clawed toads, they probably subsisted on small crustaceans, insect larvae and small fish, while in turn they provided nourishment for many other animals (crocodiles, snakes and aquatic birds, etc).

Chordata

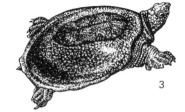
3

Trionyx bohemicus LIEBUS

Order: Chelonia — testudinates
Family: Trionychidae — soft-shelled
freshwater turtles

Reptiles, which evolved from stegocephalians, were the first typically terrestrial animals. An extra-aquatic existence necessitated a series of morphological adaptations and especially changes in embryogenesis. To enable the reptile embryo to develop on land, an egg wrapped in membranes and a leathery or chalky shell was formed. As well as containing nutrients, the egg was a substitute for an aquatic environment; it protected the embryo from mechanical injury and from drying up and it also helped to control its metabolism. Further essential changes included the formation of a tegument which would prevent the body from drying up, perfection of pulmonary respiration and modification of the circulatory and excretory systems, etc. And last but not least, the skeleton had to be reconstructed, in particular the limbs, which were used for locomotion and had to carry the body.

Reptiles — especially big ones — are very attractive material, but for collectors they are not so easily available, since they are to be found mostly in Asia and North America. They are also very hard to get at and their recovery requires a whole scientific expedition. In Europe there are relatively few fossil land reptiles, since in the Mesozoic era, the 'Golden Age' of reptiles, the greater part of Europe was covered by sea. In the

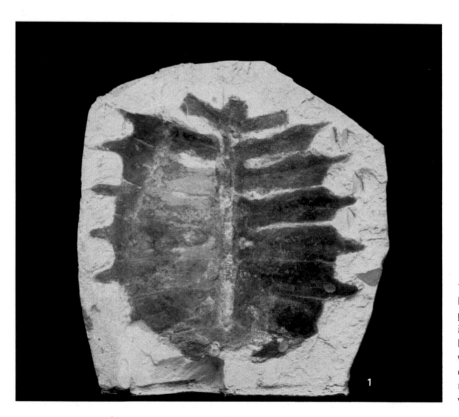

1, 3. *Trionyx bohemicus,* Miocene, Břešťany, Czechoslovakia. A carapace, length 24 cm. The carapace is not fused with the plastron, but is merely kept in contact with it by means of characteristic digitiform processes (1). 3 — a reconstruction of a living individual.

2, 4. *Emys orbicularis,** Pleistocene (Eem), Gánovce, Czechoslovakia. 2 – a carapace, length 17 cm. The fossil is a negative impression of the carapace in travertin; the indentation in the centre is a negative imprint of the spine. 4 – a reconstruction of a living individual.

Tertiary and Quaternary eras, testudinates were one of the few groups of reptiles that occurred in Europe.

Unlike the other groups of testudinates, soft-shelled freshwater turtles do not have horny plates on their shell, which is usually small and flat and is covered with a thin skin; their feet are webbed. Recent species inhabit the large rivers of the more temperate parts of Africa, Asia and North America. Soft-shelled freshwater turtles live on fish, molluscs, crustaceans and insects. *Trionyx bohemicus* inhabited freshwater basins of central Europe and evidently had the same habits as its present-day relatives.

European Pond Turtle
Emys orbicularis LINNAEUS

Order: Chelonia – testudinates
Family: Testudinidae

The still extant genus *Emys* dates back to the Upper Eocene. It has a relatively large, slightly domed and almost oval shell. The plastron is joined to the carapace by ligaments. The European Pond Turtle was typical of periods of warm climatic changes (interglacials) during the Pleistocene, when its distribution extended to central Europe and quite a long way north in western Europe. When a cold period (glacial) started it always migrated southwards. Contemporary populations inhabit southern Europe, where they frequent stagnant or slow-flowing water. They live on roundworms, aquatic arthropods, frogs and fish.

453

Cave Bear
Ursus spelaeus ROSENMÜLLER

Order: Carnivora – beasts of prey
Family: Ursidae – bears

3

Together with the mammoth and the hairy rhinoceros, the Cave Bear is one of the most typical animals of the late Pleistocene, when it was common all over Europe; the only place where it was less frequent was in regions of an explicitly steppe character. It lived in caves and thus fully merits its name. Cave bears of all ages frequented caves; they hibernated in them, gave birth to their young in them and, when they were old, they died in them. As a result we know of many European caves with 'bone layers' composed almost entirely of the bones of cave bears. The Cave Bear was about one third bigger than the Brown Bear. Apart from its size, the skull is notable for its high forehead, which is much higher and more domed than that of the Brown Bear. Despite its menacing appearance, the Cave Bear was largely a vegetarian and in the summer lived almost entirely on plant food. We can tell this from its flat and often worn-down molars. Cave bears were much hunted by early palaeolithic hunters, but their existence was never seriously jeopardized by them. Far more severe was the negative effect of the decrease in forest area during the last of the glacial periods. The cold steppe, with nothing but grass, deprived the Cave Bear of its sources of nourishment, with the result that it died out in the first half of the Würm glacial.

1, 3. *Ursus spelaeus,* Pleistocene (Würm), Sloup, Czechoslovakia. 1 – a skull, total length 47 cm. The skull comes from a 'bone layer' in a cave which was used for hibernation. 3 – a reconstruction.

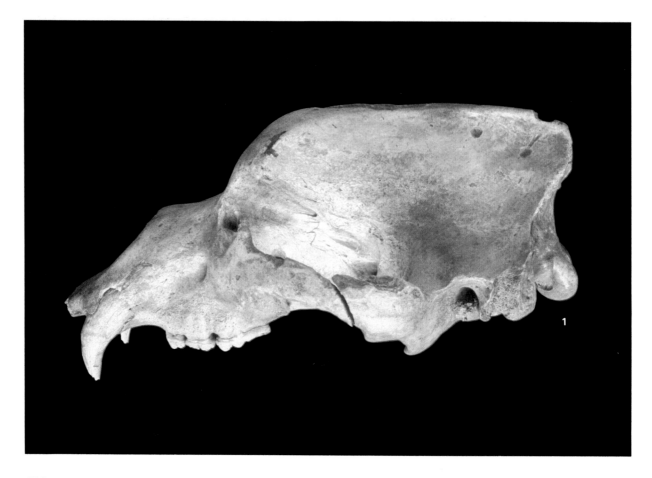

Brown Bear
Ursus arctos LINNAEUS

Order: Carnivora — beasts of prey
Family: Ursidae — bears

Q

Today the Brown Bear is one of the commonest and most abundant members of the bear family. It probably evolved during the Mindel glacial in eastern Asia and migrated to Europe during the Holstein interglacial. It spread still further during the Eem interglacial and at the end of the Würm glacial, when it took the place of the now extinct Cave Bear among the European fauna. The Brown Bear was — and is — a forest animal, but it has also penetrated into the tundra and other regions adjoining forests. Its large, cusped molars show that it is omnivorous and, in fact, it will eat anything edible within sight. It hunts the young of large mammals (reindeer, deer and horses) rather than the sturdier adult animals and it does not even despise carrion, although its teeth are not made for crushing large bones. The wide geographic distribution of the Brown Bear is due to its tremendous plasticity. Both in the past and in the present it has formed a number of geographic races (subspecies) and local forms differing in respect of their size and colouring. Many such forms used to be described as separate species (e.g. the recent American Grizzly or the Pleistocene Taubach Bear). Today the number of brown bears is declining, partly owing to hunters, but chiefly as a result of projects which interfere with the forests in which they live.

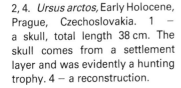

4

2, 4. *Ursus arctos,* Early Holocene, Prague, Czechoslovakia. 1 — a skull, total length 38 cm. The skull comes from a settlement layer and was evidently a hunting trophy. 4 — a reconstruction.

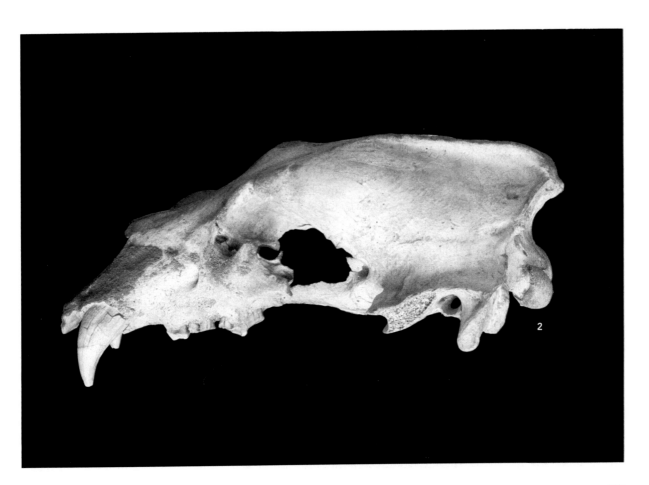

2

Wolverine (Glutton)
Gulo gulo (LINNAEUS)

Order: Carnivora – beasts of prey
Family: Mustelidae – mustelids

The Wolverine is the biggest mustelid beast of prey; present-day gluttons can grow to a length of 1 metre (including the tail). Today gluttons live mainly in the taigas and wooded tundras of northern Europe, Asia and America. In the late Pleistocene they settled mainly in the tundra and the adjoining cold (loess) steppes. Wolverines spread in central Europe at the end of the Riss glacial; during the Würm glacial they were common over all parts of Europe that were free from ice and they even infiltrated into Italy and the Balkans. They are characteristic mainly of very cold fluctuations in the climate (stadials). At the end of the Würm glacial the Wolverines retreated north, together with the spreading forests, but were still present in northern Germany and Denmark in the early Holocene. The Wolverine moves in a series of high, bounding leaps; this may look rather comical, but it is certainly less fatiguing than if the animal had to plough its way through the deep snow. It lives chiefly on large rodents (lemmings, hares), small beasts of prey (e.g. foxes), birds and fish. It may also attack young reindeer and deer. Its powerful teeth enable it to crush small bones. Oecologically it was a late Pleistocene rival of the wolf, but it never formed packs. Wolverine remains have been found mostly in loess and in caves.

Cave Hyena
Crocuta spelaea (GOLDFUSS)

Order: Carnivora – beasts of prey
Family: Hyaenidae – hyenas

Together with the Cave Lion and the Cave Bear, the Cave Hyena completes a well-known triad of late Pleistocene beasts of prey. It came from Asia and spread across China as far as western Europe. In appearance it was not very different from the Spotted Hyena (*Crocuta crocuta*) and is sometimes actually regarded as a subspecies (*C. c. spelaea*). Perhaps it was bigger and more robust, but that is normal in species or subspecies living in places with a cold climate. In Europe, the Cave Hyena spread together with the older mammoth fauna during the Riss glacial. It was a nomadic animal and wandered from place to place and from one type of country to another, although it seems to have preferred open country with herds of large ungulates. It lived on carrion and its powerful teeth (more highly specialized than those of any other hyena) were able to crush the most massive bones, such as the limb bones of rhinoceroses. Bones with the marks of hyenas' teeth on them are found quite often. The Cave Hyena died out during the last part of the Würm glacial, when the cold (loess) steppe disappeared. Bones, teeth, skulls and whole hyena skeletons are frequently found in caves and in other Pleistocene sediments (loess, river sand, travertin, etc).

1, 3. *Gulo gulo,** Pleistocene (Würm), Srbsko, Czechoslovakia. 1 – a lower jaw, total length 10.5 cm. The jaw came from a karst chimney in which the careless animal met its death from a fall (Sturzfauna). 3 – a reconstruction.

2, 4. *Crocuta spelaea*, Pleistocene (Würm), Srbsko, Czechoslovakia. 2 – a lower jaw, total length 17.5 cm. The jaw came from the same locality as the jaw of the Wolverine and its owner met the same fate. 4 – a reconstruction.

Q

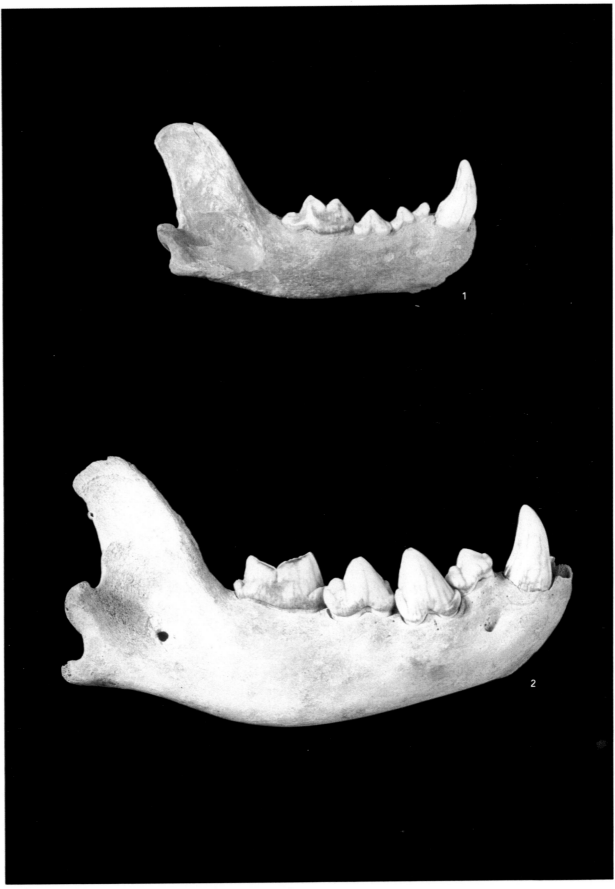

Chordata

Wolf
Canis lupus LINNAEUS

Order: Carnivora — beasts of prey
Family: Canidae — canine beasts of prey

The Wolf is probably descended from a canine carnivore inhabiting Europe between the Pliocene and the Pleistocene. A small form described as the Mosbach Wolf (*Canis lupus mosbachensis*) lived in the early Pleistocene. True wolves did not appear until the Riss glacial and from the Eem interglacial onwards they were abundant all over Europe. Recent wolves can tolerate a wide variety of climates and they can live in the tundra, in forests, in steppes and in semi-desert country. Palaeontological finds indicate that the distribution of Pleistocene wolves was the same as that of present-day wolves and that they had identical habits. In the summer wolves live in couples and subsist on small vertebrates (chiefly rodents), while in the winter they form packs and hunt large mammals; in the Pleistocene these were mainly reindeer, red deer, Irish elks (*Megaloceros*) and horses. In the postglacial period the number of wolves has steadily decreased, mainly as a result of man's activities.

Cave Lion
Panthera spelaea (GOLDFUSS)

Order: Carnivora — beasts of prey
Family: Felidae — feline beasts of prey

The Cave Lion is the biggest and best known feline beast of prey of the European glacials. It was often bigger than present-day African lions, and judging from paintings in caves the males did not have either a mane or the tufted tail typical of African lions. Instead, cave lions had a long, thick coat similar to the coat of the Siberian (Ussuri) Tiger. They inhabited cold steppe country and in the interglacial periods they also lived in bushy steppes and wooded regions. They mainly hunted horses and in cave drawings the two are always depicted together (cf. the association of recent African lions with zebras). Unlike African lions, which live in families, the Cave Lion was a solitary animal. This is borne out by the isolated finds of bones and skeletons and by the fact that cave paintings never show lions in groups. Cave Lions received their name from finds of bones in caves, but actually they spent very little time in caves (perhaps in the winter, although there is no evidence that they hibernated) and lived most of the year in the open. The bones found in caves belonged either to animals which went there to die, or to lions which happened to fall into the cave and were unable to get out again. Cave Lions appeared in Europe at the end of the Cromerian interglacial, but did not become abundant until after the Riss glacial. They were distributed over the whole of Europe and mainly inhabited open steppes, although they did not actively avoid forests. They died out at the end of the Würm glacial.

1. *Canis lupus,* Pleistocene (Würm), Prague, Czechoslovakia. A lower jaw, length 15.5. cm. The jaw came from loess layers formed in the cold steppe in the late Pleistocene.

2, 3. *Panthera spelaea,* Pleistocene (Würm), Srbsko, Czechoslovakia. 2 — a lower jaw, length of fragment 20 cm. The jaw belonged to a young cave lion which (perhaps while chasing prey) fell into a karst chimney. 3 — reconstruction.

Q

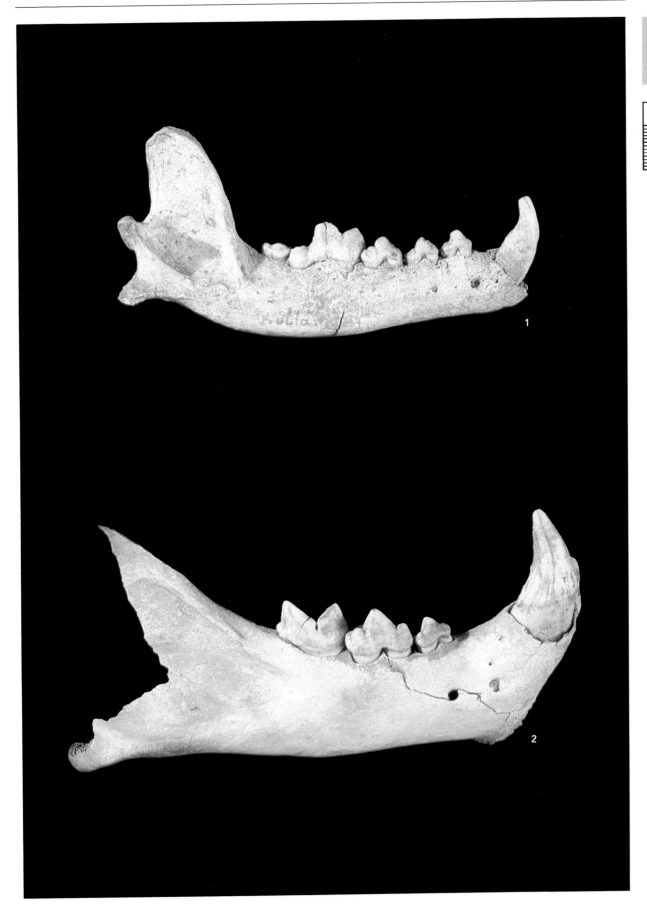

Palaeotherium magnum
CUVIER

Order: Perissodactyla – odd-toed ungulates
Family: Palaeotheriidae

Ungulates are a highly heterogeneous group composed of several completely independent evolutionary lines. In modern zoological systems scientists therefore divide them into several orders. One feature characteristic of all ungulates is that the digits do not terminate in a claw, but in a variously formed hoof which strengthens the limb on impact with the ground and in the rebound. The formation of a hoof is a manifestation of adaptation to rapid locomotion; practically all ungulates are good runners. Being explicitly herbivorous, they often collected together in large herds and their remains are consequently found more often than those of the largely solitary beasts of prey. Species which lived solitarily or only in small 'family' groups were all very big, so that again their remains were more likely to be fossilized. Despite this, finds of whole skeletons are exceptional and only isolated bones are mostly found. The most interesting ungulate groups for collectors are horses, rhinoceroses, proboscideans and large even-toed ungulates.

The equine evolutionary line is a classic example of the phylogenetic development of vertebrates, but it is also an illustration of distorted views on phylogenesis. Without being aware of it, we involuntarily tend to regard evolutionary series from the point of view of extant species, making them, in our mind, the be-all and end-all of the whole of preceding evolution, as it were. In actual fact, the phylogenesis of all forms and groups is far more complex and more diverse. Apart from the equine evolutionary line *'Eohippus – Equus'*, there are further, parallel evolutionary lines of equids comprising both light and heavy forms. *Palaeotherium* was one of the heavy forms. In size and appearance it was remarkably like a tapir. It had a thick neck, three-toed limbs and small splayed hooves like a tapir's. Earlier reconstructions also depict it with a tapir's proboscis, but according to recent research it did not have a proboscis. Palaeotheres were descended from North American 'eohippi' (*Hyracotherium*) which found their way to Europe during the early Eocene. They did not become specialized for a life in the steppe, but took to swampy forests. They died out during the early Oligocene, when they were evidently supplanted by the tapirs. Finds of large skeletal units are rare, but bone fragments and teeth are found in lignite basins.

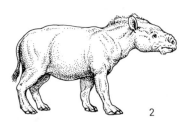

1, 2. *Palaeotherium magnum,** Eocene, Débruge, France. 1 – a fragment of an upper jaw, length 23 cm. The jaw was found during work in a lignite basin; the organic matter has been largely carbonized. 2 – a reconstruction.

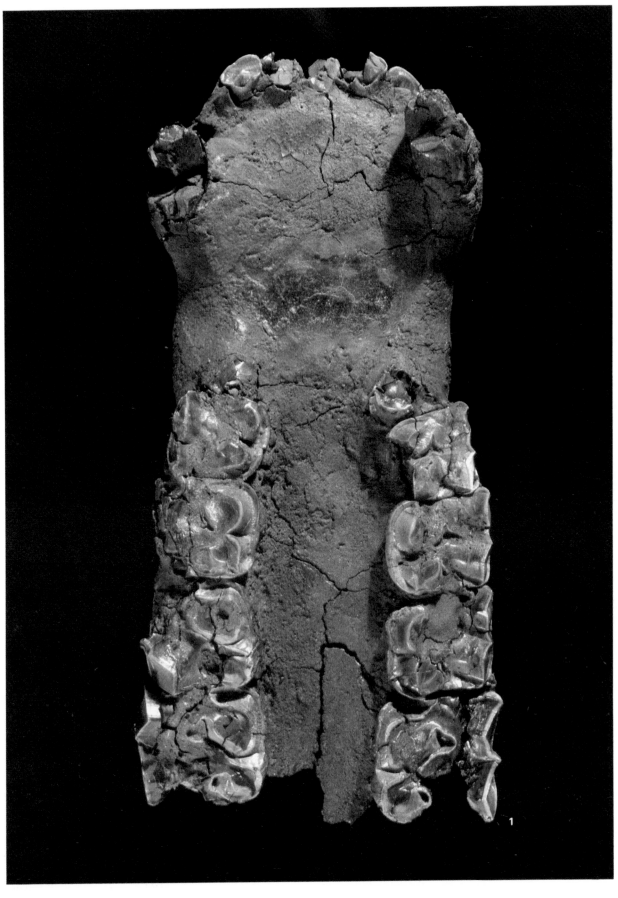

 **Chordata**

German Loess Horse
Equus germanicus NEHRING

Order: Perissodactyla — odd-toed ungulates
Family: Equidae — horses

During the Pleistocene, Europe was inhabited by many species of the genus *Equus* whose evolutionary relationships (and sometimes systematic position) are by no means clear. Convergence of individual species was frequent, i.e. a new invading species would adopt the mode of life and outer appearance of its supplanted predecessor (predecessor in time, but not in evolution). As a result of climatic changes, various species formed numerous races and forms adapted to the new geographical and climatic conditions.

Roughly from the time of the Riss glacial, the German Loess Horse, which took its name from the many finds made in loess (brick-clay), began to spread over the whole of Europe. It was a lightly built, moderately large horse with a round head and a bulbous nose, somewhat like the Przewalsky Horse in appearance, since we know its colour from cave paintings. Loess horses lived in large herds, rather after the manner of present-day zebras. They mainly inhabited cold steppes in which loess layers were deposited, but during the Eem interglacial they also lived in deciduous woods. The huge herds of loess horses provided food not only for the big Pleistocene beasts of prey (cave lions and hyenas), but also for palaeolithic man. Loess horses died out at the end of the Würm glacial. It is not clear what significance they had for domestication of the horse in Europe.

1. *Equus germanicus,* Pleistocene (Würm), Prague, Czechoslovakia. Teeth of an upper jaw, length of row 18 cm. Found in loess dug up in a brick-field for the purpose of making bricks.

2. *Equus germanicus,* Pleistocene (Würm), Srbsko, Czechoslovakia. A fore foot (autopodium), length of first phalanx 8.5 cm. The fore limb came from a karst chimney into which the animal evidently fell while running away from a predator.

3, 4. *Equus hemionus,* Pleistocene (Würm), Korno, Czechoslovakia. 3 — a fore foot (autopodium), length of first phalanx 7.5 cm. The bones came from cave sediments dated as early Würm (the end of stadial 'W$_1$' and the beginning of interstadial 'W$_{1/2}$'). 4 — a reconstruction.

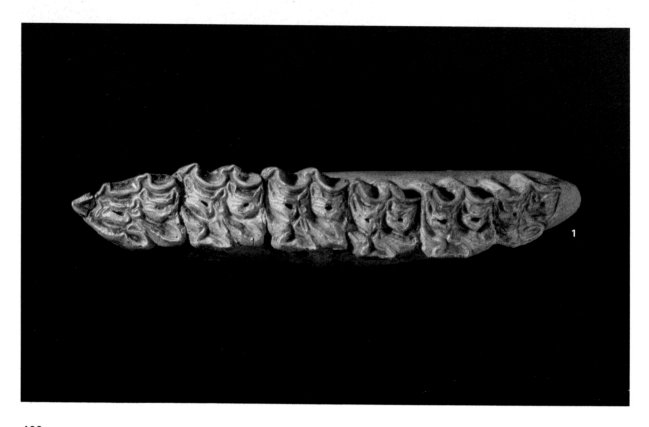

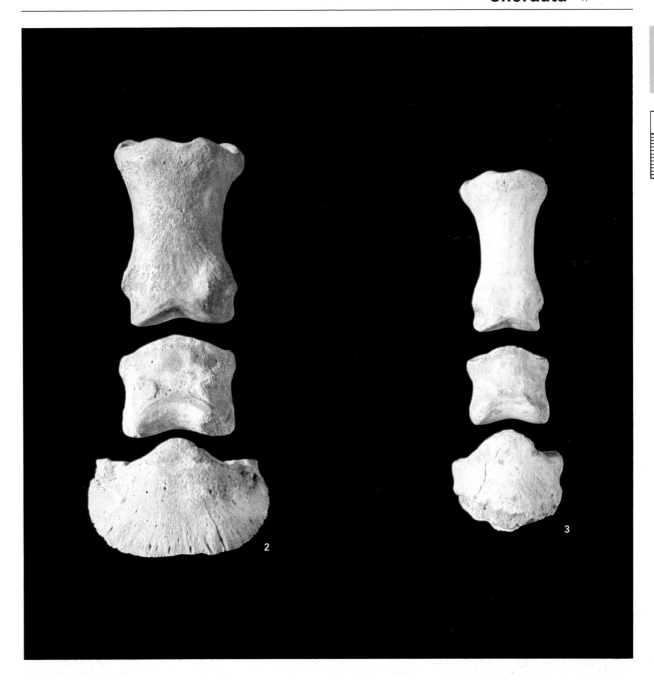

2

3

Mongolian Wild Ass (Kulan)
Equus hemionus PALLAS

Order: Perissodactyla − odd-toed ungulates
Family: Equidae − horses

In present-day Asia asses inhabit dry steppes and semi-deserts from the Black Sea region to Mongolia. They are characterized by a small build and long, slender limbs. During the Pleistocene they only occasionally visited Europe. They lived there at the outset of the most recent glacials (Riss and Würm), when the weather became drier, but was not yet cold, and when dry, but still relatively warm, steppe (not loess steppe) spread over Europe. After a short time they evidently always withdrew to Asia again. It is interesting to note that their bones are found mainly in caves, to which they were dragged by beasts of prey.

4

463

 **Chordata**

Merck's Rhinoceros
Dicerorhinus kirchbergensis
(JÄGER)

Order: Perissodactyla — odd-toed ungulates
Family: Rhinocerotidae — rhinoceroses

3

Rhinoceroses were an important component of the European mammalian fauna during the Pleistocene, but in the Holocene fauna they were notable for their complete absence. Their robust, heavy bones have been preserved relatively well in various Pleistocene sediments and they are quite good index fossils for the relevant period of time. The various species of rhinoceroses were specialized for life in different types of environments, from warm forests to cold steppes and tundras, so that they also bear witness to conditions in nature at that time.

Merck's Rhinoceros (also known as the Kirchberg Rhinoceros) was a typical animal of the later European interglacials. Some research workers consider it to have been descended from the Etruscan Rhinoceros (*Dicerorhinus etruscus*), while others regard it as merely the ecological successor of that species, without any phylogenetic associations (i.e. as a case of convergence). Unfortunately, no complete skeleton of Merck's Rhinoceros has so far been found and many controversial questions are therefore still unresolved. Merck's Rhinoceros inhabited deciduous woods, park-land and savannahs. Its main area of distribution was western Europe and the western part of central Europe. Further east (in drier regions with a continental climate) it became increasingly rarer. It was one of the animals hunted by early

1, 3. *Dicerorhinus kirchbergensis,** Pleistocene (Eem), Prague, Czechoslovakia. 1 — upper molars, length of complete row 16 cm. As distinct from the Woolly Rhinoceros, the ridges (lophodes) on the molars run almost perpendicular to the oral cavity. 3 — a reconstruction.

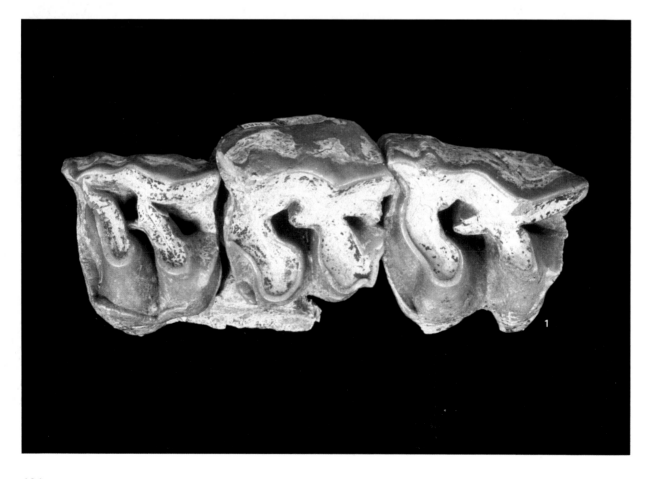

2

2, 4. *Coelodonta antiquitatis,* * Pleistocene (Würm), Letky, Czechoslovakia. 2 – upper molars, length of complete row 23 cm. The ridges on the molars run markedly obliquely backward. 4 – a reconstruction.

palaeolithic man. It died out in central Europe at the end of the Eem interglacial and the only place where it survived to the beginning of the Würm glacial was Spain.

Woolly Rhinoceros

Coelodonta antiquitatis
(BLUMENBACH)

Order: Perissodactyla – odd-toed ungulates
Family: Rhinocerotidae – rhinoceroses

People always think of the Woolly Rhinoceros as the faithful companion of the Mammoth. Although characteristic of the later European glacials, it is not of European origin and we must look for its forebears among the early Pleistocene rhinoceroses of Nihovan in China. These Asian rhinoceroses infiltrated into Siberia and probably became adapted to a cold climate there, so that by the time they arrived in Europe they were explicitly fond of the cold. They settled in cold steppes over practically the whole of Europe and at the peak of the later glacials they actually spread to the Mediterranean region. The Woolly Rhinoceros was a typical grazer and lived mainly in the cold steppes of the later glacials (Riss and Würm). It did not consort in herds, but roamed about alone or in small family groups, like present-day African rhinoceroses. At the end of the Würm glacial it either died out in Europe, or migrated north-east in the wake of the receding ice-sheet. It is possible that small herds of Woolly Rhinoceroses lived somewhat longer in Siberia than in Europe. Bones and teeth are found fairly frequently, especially in loess, river deposits and caves.

4

Deinotherium giganteum KAUP

Order: Proboscidea — proboscideans
Family: Deinotheriidae

3

Deinotheres were an independent branch of proboscideans with no descendants. In appearance they were not very different from true elephants, except that they had a lower and flatter skull. Their most outstanding feature, however, was that the symphysis of their lower jaw turned down almost at right angles and bore a pair of short, thick, recurved tusks. The molars were of a tapir or primitive mastodon type and show that this evolutionary branch became independent very early on. Deinotheres occurred mainly in western and central Europe, where they inhabited damp forests with luxuriant vegetation and lived on foliage and tree shoots. This conclusion is based on the shape of their teeth, their characteristically formed lower tusks (adapted for holding foliage in place), their short trunk and long limbs and, indirectly, their steady tendency to increasing height. Perhaps it is not exaggerating too much to describe deinotheres as 'giraffe-like proboscideans'. Deinothere remains (usually teeth or fragments of tusks) date from the late Tertiary; finds of intact bones or large skeletal units are very rare.

Trilophodon angustidens CUVIER

Order: Proboscidea — proboscideans
Family: Trilophodontidae

Proboscideans are a group of mammals with a rich and interesting history. During the late Mesozoic and early Quaternary they successfully colonized all the continents (except Australia) from the tropics to very cold latitudes and from the plains to the mountains. To look for their origin we must go to Egypt and right from the outset we can follow a series of different evolutionary trends. For instance, the members of the genus *Moeritherium* lived in water, like hippopotamuses do today. The 'classic' group of proboscideans are the mastodons. Their incisors were progressively transformed to short tusks, while the number of cusps on their molars (originally four) steadily increased. They had a short neck and developed a trunk.

Trilophodon angustidens was a rather primitive mastodon. Its tusks — present in both jaws — were relatively short. The symphysis of the lower jaw was produced to a shovel-like structure which supported the short trunk (a little in the same way as in tapirs), instead of letting it hang down as in true elephants. Trilophodons occurred mainly in western Europe, where they lived near lakes in rather dry forested regions, but some related species inhabited swamps like tapirs. A complete trilophodon skeleton, found near Sansan in France, can be seen in the Musée d'Histoire naturelle in Paris, but one is more likely to find isolated teeth or fragments of tusks.

4

1, 4. *Deinotherium giganteum,** Upper Pliocene, Eppelsheim, West Germany. 1 — an upper molar (M^2), crown 85 × 85 mm. The cusps of deinothere teeth have fused to form ridges — three on the first lower molar (M_1) and two on the other teeth. 4 — a reconstruction.

2, 3. *Trilophodon angustidens,** Upper Miocene, Sansan, France. 2 — a lower molar, crown 135 × 60 mm. Mastodon molars often have an increased number of cusps, which do not unite to form either ridges or lamellae and are relatively free. 3 — a reconstruction.

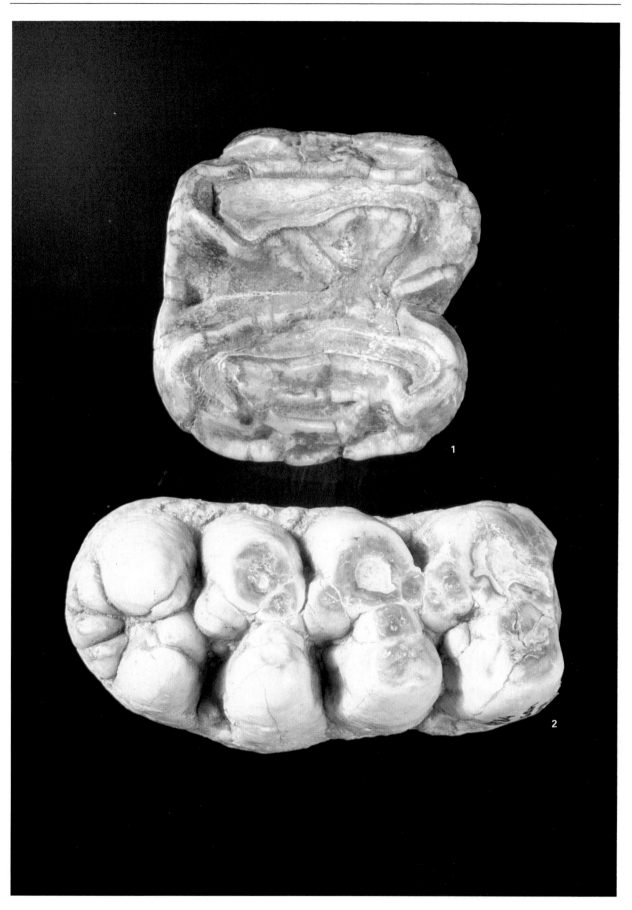

Forest Elephant
Palaeoloxodon antiquus (FALCONER)

Order: Proboscidea – proboscideans
Family: Elephantidae – elephants

The true elephants represent the highest point in the evolution of proboscideans. They appeared in Europe at the beginning of the Pleistocene and formed a series of interesting and stratigraphically important types. They had relatively long tusks, which grew only in their upper jaw. Their dental cusps were converted to narrow, flat lamellae and the number sharply increased.

The Forest Elephant lived in Europe in the warm periods of the Pleistocene. It is generally held to have evolved in the earliest part of the Pleistocene from the Southern Elephant (*Archidiskodon meridionalis*), as a phylogenetic branch adapted to a warm climate. It was bigger than the Mammoth, its head was small in relation to its body, its straight, massive tusks were curved only at the tips and it had long limbs. It inhabited grassland and deciduous forests, but also penetrated into the conifer forests of the temperate belt. It is typical of the later European interglacials (starting with the Cromerian); when the climate turned cold, it retreated from central Europe southwards and its place was taken by the mammoths. At the end of the Eem interglacial it withdrew to the Mediterranean region and its last representatives died out in Spain in the last phase of the Würm glacial. During the Eem interglacial it was often hunted by man. Hunters usually lay in wait for it near travertin waterfalls, to which the animals came to drink. Many finds thus come from central European travertin strata. Finds of isolated bones and teeth are numerous; only a few complete skeletons have been found.

Woolly Mammoth
Mammuthus primigenius (BLUMENBACH)

Order: Proboscidea – proboscideans
Family: Elephantidae – elephants

Mammoths are undoubtedly the most familiar animals of the European Pleistocene. As their smallish ears, thick hairy coat and fat hump tell us, they were adapted to life in the cold steppe. They were often hunted by palaeolithic hunters, who made paintings, engravings and statuettes of them. These artefacts, together with mammoth finds in Siberia, provided scientists with exact information on what mammoths really looked like.

Mammoths inhabited the whole of Europe (except the parts covered by the continental ice-sheet). At the peak of the glacials they migrated to southern Europe and in the interglacials and interstadials they moved north again. At the end of the Würm glacial the mammoths retreated north-eastwards in the wake of the shrinking ice-sheets and the last of them disappeared in Siberia in the earliest part of the Holocene. Palaeolithic hunters were not responsible for their extinction. Mammoths were adapted to life in the cold steppe and when, at the end of the Würm glacial, this formation was progressively replaced by forests until it finally disappeared, the mammoths vanished too, since they were unable to adapt to a different environment. Finds of mammoth bones, teeth and tusks are frequent, especially in loess and in river sediments, but their recovery is technically exacting, because they often disintegrate.

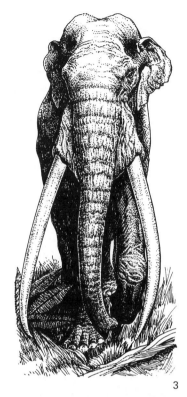

3

1, 3. *Palaeoloxodon antiquus,* Middle Pleistocene, northern Italy. 1 – a lower molar (M$_1$), length of occlusal surface 16 cm. The dental lamellae are much further apart than on the corresponding molar in the mammoth. 3 – a reconstruction.

2, 4. *Mammuthus primigenius,** late Pleistocene (Würm), Věstonice, Czechoslovakia. 2 – a lower molar (M$_1$), length of occlusal surface 14 cm. The dental lamellae are crowded close together. 4 – a reconstruction.

4

Q

Palaeomeryx kaupi V. MEYER

Order: Artiodactyla – even-toed ungulates
Family: Cervidae – cervids (deer)

2, 4. *Palaeomeryx kaupi,* Miocene, Tuchořice, Czechoslovakia. 2 – an upper molar (M^1), crown 14 × 18 mm. A palaeomeryx fold can be seen on the lower edge of the tooth, between the anterior and posterior ridge. 4 – a reconstruction.

Geographically, cervids are confined to Europe, Asia and north Africa. The only exception is the wapiti, which infiltrated into North America from Asia during the Pleistocene and still lives there. The centre of origin of the cervids is probably Asia, where they were differentiated during the early Oligocene from the same ancestors as primitive giraffes. Their characteristic feature are their antlers which (except in the case of reindeer) are worn only by the males.

Palaeomeryx kaupi is one of the oldest cervids. It is related to the Muntjac (*Muntiacus*) and comes from the same evolutionary line as the roe deer (*Capreolus*). Neither the female nor the male had antlers, but the male had long, curved canines which protruded from its mouth. The teeth of all the members of the genus *Palaeomeryx* were characterized by a 'palaeomeryx fold' – a small crease on the inner (lingual) aspect of the molars between the anterior and posterior ridge (lophos) of the crown, which does not occur in later cervids. *Palaeomeryx* inhabited

4

1, 3, 5. *Dicrocerus furcatus*, Miocene, Steinheim, West Germany. 1 — a fragment of a left upper jaw with teeth ($P^4 - M^2$), length of middle tooth (M^1) 12×12 mm. 3 — an antler, total length 14 cm. Note the high pedicle, which has grown with the animal's age, while the number of points has remained the same. 5 — a reconstruction.

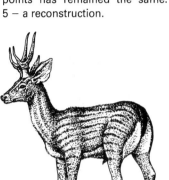

5

early Tertiary forests (mainly damp and marshy ones) in central and western Europe. Its hooves were spread out fanwise to prevent it from sinking into the soft, boggy soil. These cervids died out at the end of the Miocene. Their remains can be found in lake sediments in lignite basins, in tuff or in travertin strata.

Dicrocerus furcatus HENSEL

Order: Artiodactyla — even-toed ungulates
Family: Cervidae — cervids (deer)

Dicrocerus furcatus was a small deer related to the Muntjac and was the first cervid to possess antlers. The antlers were still primitive, were forked and had no tines. In appearance, *Dicrocerus* closely resembled *Palaeomeryx*, or (because of the small antlers) roe deer. It probably came to Europe from Asia and inhabited forests in the more temperate climatic zones. A typical Miocene animal, it died out at the beginning of the Pliocene without leaving any descendants. Its bones and teeth are to be found in similar sediments to those containing *Palaeomeryx* remains.

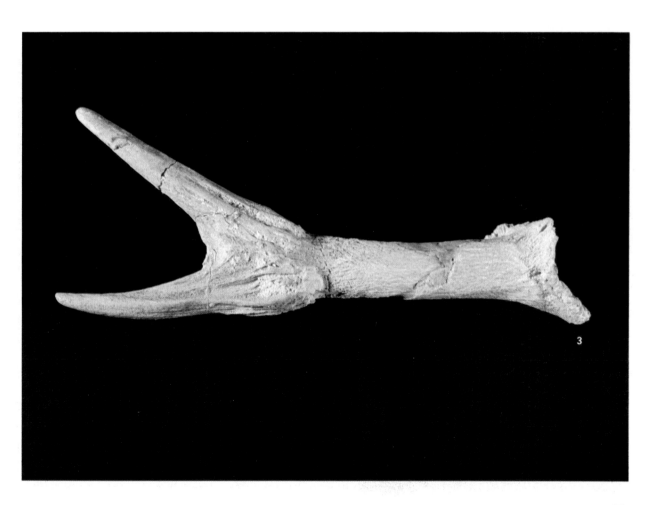

3

 **Chordata**

Red Deer
Cervus elaphus LINNAEUS

Order: Artiodactyla – even-toed ungulates
Family: Cervidae – cervids (deer)

The Red Deer is the geologically most recent deer. It is assumed that it evolved at the end of the early Pleistocene from the 'crown-less' *Cervus acoronatus,* which lived in Europe during the Cromerian interglacial. The development of the Red Deer's antlers culminates in the formation, at the tip of the pedicle, of a 'crown' of three tines issuing, as it were, from a single point. The oldest deer with a 'crown' are known from the Mindel glacial and the Holstein interglacial; they inhabited park-like country and relatively warm forests in Europe and Asia. Their variability was enormous. On the basis of their size, but mainly of the structure of their antlers, a whole series of local or period races, subspecies and even species has been described, although their validity is often questionable. On islands, deer very often produced local pygmy forms. The Red Deer abounded in central and western Europe during the Eem interglacial and the interstadials of the Würm glacial, and in the Holocene it became a permanent component of the European forest fauna. Its remains are to be found in various types of sediments formed during the warmer phases of the late Pleistocene and on the sites of human encampments.

Reindeer or Caribou
Rangifer tarandus (LINNAEUS)

Order: Artiodactyla – even-toed ungulates
Family: Cervidae – cervids (deer)

The Reindeer is a very typical animal of the cold steppe and tundra of the later glacials. It appeared in Europe at the end of the Günz glacial, but did not become abundant until the Würm glacial. Its phylogenetic origin is obscure. The Reindeer came to Europe as a fully adapted element of the arctic fauna, but so far nobody knows when and where its adaptation took place. The systematic classification of reindeer is also very complex and chaotic. Many subspecies and local forms of present-day reindeer are recognized, the main differential characters being the colouring of their coat and the structure of their antlers. No such criteria can be applied to the determination of fossil reindeer, of course, when generally all we have at our disposal are single bones or fragments of antlers. Consequently, after many discussions it is now generally accepted that Pleistocene European reindeer belong to the north European species *R. tarandus.* Reindeer were distributed over the whole of Europe except the parts covered by the continental ice-sheet, but they generally steered clear of forests. With the spread of the forests of the temperate belt at the beginning of the Holocene, the reindeer were pushed further and further north until all that is left today of this once abundant and prosperous species are a few scanty residues living in Scandinavia. Reindeer remains are found in large quantities in all sediments, but especially those of the late Pleistocene.

1. *Cervus elaphus,** early Holocene, Prague, Czechoslovakia. An antler, length of fragment 53 cm. Red deer antlers are characterized by longitudinal grooving and a well-developed rose at the base; the fragment here lacks the 'crown'.

2. *Rangifer tarandus,** late Pleistocene (Würm), Prague, Czechoslovakia. An antler, length of fragment 66 cm. Reindeer antlers are characterized by a smooth surface, an elliptical cross section and a poorly developed rose. The palmated end – corresponding to the Red Deer's 'crown' – was not preserved on this fragment.

Q

 **Chordata**

Giant Red Deer or Irish Elk
Megaloceros giganteus
(BLUMENBACH)

Order: Artiodactyla — even-toed ungulates
Family: Cervidae — cervids (deer)

The Giant Red Deer is neither a true deer nor an elk, but a special form of steppe cervid which evolved from big early Pleistocene steppe deer with specifically constructed antlers. During evolution the Giant Red Deer grew bigger and bigger, and so, in particular, did its antlers. The largest measurable set found to date had a span of 3.7 metres. With such a 'head' these animals obviously could not live in the forest, so they mainly inhabited cold steppes and tundra throughout Europe. They held their head and neck horizontally like reindeer; they did not form herds, but lived solitarily like elks. With the end of the Würm glacial they gradually died out and Ireland was the only place where they persisted to the beginning of the Holocene. The presence of the Giant Red Deer in Europe in prehistoric times and its identity with the 'Schelch' in the Niebelungenlied have not been altogether proved. Finds of more or less complete skeletons are known from Irish peat-bogs; otherwise only isolated bones or fragments of antlers are found (especially in loess).

1, 3. *Megaloceros giganteus,** Pleistocene, Dolja, Yugoslavia. 1 — a left antler, length of fragment 80 cm. The antler is indistinctly grooved like a deer's antler (the grooving may have been obliterated by fossilization) and has an elliptical cross section like a reindeer's antler. 3 — a reconstruction.

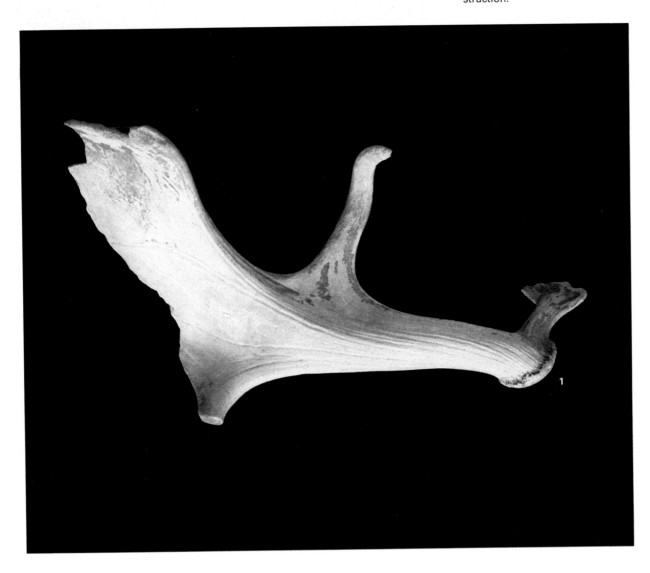

2. *Capra ibex,* Pleistocene (Würm), Radotín, Czechoslovakia. A skull, length of horn shaft 23 cm. Ibexes have more massive horn shafts than goats and sheep; their postcranial skeleton is also more robust.

Ibex
Capra ibex LINNAEUS

Order: Artiodactyla − even-toed ungulates
Family: Bovidae − bovids (hollow-horned ruminants)

Some skeletal finds from the early Pleistocene are classified as ibex remains, but the demonstrated history of the ibexes does not start until the time of the Riss glacial. We know of skull fragments from this period with slightly divergent horn shafts, which were recovered from gravel and sand in the river Saale near Camburg, East Germany. The find was described as *Capra camburgensis* and is considered to be the initial form of late Pleistocene ibexes. Ibexes were mountain-dwellers, but also lived partly in wooded steppe. During cold stadials they came down from their upland plateaus into river gorges and when it grew warmer again they returned to higher altitudes. This gave rise to dissociated populations with a quantity of isolated local forms (in the Pyrenees, the Alps and the Carpathians, etc). During the late Pleistocene ibexes colonized all the young mountain ranges of central and southern Europe and crossed Transylvania to invade the Crimea and Palestine. They were common (and often the favourite) game of palaeolithic man. Ibex bones are often found in river deposits, in hunters' encampments or in cave sediments (after being devoured by beasts of prey).

 **Chordata**

Bison priscus BOJANUS

Order: Artiodactyla — even-toed ungulates
Family: Bovidae — bovids (hollow-horned ruminants)

True horned cattle (subfamily Bovinae) are a phylogeneticall very young group. Although the beginning of their evolution goes back to the late Tertiary, it was not until the Pleistocene period that genera extant today were formed. All recent species date from the Holocene. Two genera in particular played an important role in mammalian assemblages of the European Quaternary — the bison (*Bison*) and the ox (*Bos*).

Bison priscus appeared in western and central Europe during the Mindel glacial. It was a big, robustly built animal standing up to two metres high at the shoulder. Its strikingly large semicircular horns had a span of up to 120 cm. *Bison priscus* attained its prime in the Riss glacial, when it produced a series of local forms which are sometimes described as separate subspecies. In the Eem interglacial and the Würm glacial it attained its greatest geographical distribution and spread from the grasslands to the adjoining wooded steppe. It was commonly hunted by late palaeolithic man and is therefore also known to us from cave paintings (e.g. in Altamira, Spain), engravings and figurines, etc. With the end of the Würm glacial, when the area covered by forests of a present-day type increased at the expense of the steppe, *Bison priscus* began to die out and to be replaced, in forest assemblages, by the European Bison or Wisent (*Bison bonasus*). Bison remains are found

1, 3. *Bison priscus*, Pleistocene (Würm), Prague, Czechoslovakia. Length of skull (without horns) 60 cm. The skull is much wider than that of the Aurochs, with prominent eye sockets and slightly curved, but not twisted horn shafts (1). 3 — a reconstruction.

3

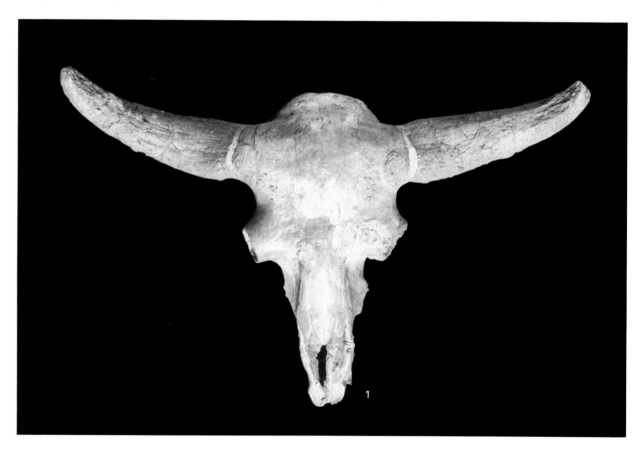

1

2, 4. *Bos primigenius,* Holocene, Dašice, Czechoslovakia. 2 — a skull, total length 66 cm. Together with it is a horn shaft, early Holocene, Drevenik, Czechoslovakia. The skull is much narrower than the bison's and the eye sockets are not very prominent, while the horn shafts display pronounced torsion. 4 — a reconstruction.

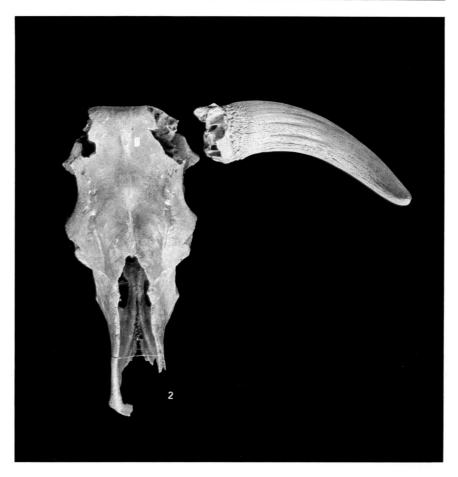

fairly frequently in loess, river sediments, caves and human settlements, but in most cases they are only single bones or mere fragments.

Aurochs
Bos primigenius
BOJANUS

Order: Artiodactyla — even-toed ungulates
Family: Bovidae — bovids (hollow-horned ruminants)

The Aurochs is related to south-east Asian bovids from the Siwalik region in India and it began to infiltrate into Europe during the Holstein interglacial. It was more massively built than present-day domestic cattle and in some cases was more robust than bison. The characteristic feature of the Aurochs is that its horns curved sideways, upwards and forwards. The Aurochs originally inhabited damp forests and riparian woods, but from the Eem interglacial onwards it also lived in grass-land. During the Würm glacial, in western and central Europe it even became adapted to life in forests in the cold belt and actually penetrated into the tundra. Holocene finds come mainly from peatbogs and the sediments of old river arms originally overgrown by riparian woods, showing that the Aurochs returned time and time again to its initial type of habitat. The Aurochs survived in Europe up to the seventeenth century and it was man who was mainly responsible for its extinction. The cause was not hunting, however, since hunting the Aurochs was both expensive and dangerous, but rather the destruction of the Aurochs's natural environment to make way for agriculture.

Injury and deformation of bones

In addition to studying actual organic remains, palaeontologists also investigate various manifestations of fossil organisms' previous activities and submit authentic information on their life. In the case of animals with very few parts capable of fossilization, traces of their activities are often the only evidence of their existence.

One of the branches of palaeobiology of interest to collectors is palaeopathology, which is concerned with pathological changes in bones, in particular following fracture or disease. Fractures already occurred in the oldest fishes and in amphibians, reptiles (especially big species), birds and mammals, they were common. We know of the most diverse types, from a simple clean fracture to complicated fractures with displacement of the fracture surfaces. If a fracture was not a direct cause of death, it healed and, according to the degree of injury, the bone either simply grew together again, or various types of callus were formed at the site of the fracture.

Traces of disease are just as interesting to the collector as fractures. The disease may have involved the bone itself, or the soft tissues round the bone. Some lesions originated in connection with functional stress, or were related to ageing. Animals suffered from spondylosis (outgrowths on vertebral bodies) or arthrosis (outgrowths on the large joints). Pathological changes in shape (deformation), especially of the limbs or spine, made the animal less mobile and very often, indirectly or directly, led to its death.

Very often we can observe tooth marks on the bones of fossil vertebrates. If they are the marks of predators, they were usually made in association with the hunting of prey. Marks of scavengers' (e.g. hyenas') teeth could have been made after death. Rodents — for which bones were a source of calcium — left very characteristic tooth marks on bones. Bones gnawed down by rodents were very often thought to be man-made artefacts.

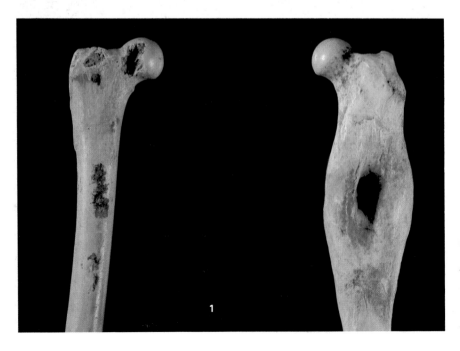

1. *Vulpes vulpes* (Fox), Holocene, Řeporyje, Czechoslovakia. On the right a healed complicated fracture of a femur in which torsion and displacement of the fractured parts occurred. On the left, for comparison, an intact femur from the same locality.

2. *Ursus spelaeus* (Cave Bear), Pleistocene (Würm), Sloup, Czechoslovakia. Metacarpals, length 8.4 cm. Both bones show traces of inflammatory processes which led to pathological deformation of the surface of the bone.

3. *Equus germanicus* (Loess Horse), Pleistocene (Würm), Srbsko, Czechoslovakia. A phalanx, length 8.7 cm. The same pathological deformation as in fig. 2.

4. *Equus germanicus,* Pleistocene (Würm), Srbsko, Czechoslovakia. Head of a tibia gnawed by a beast of prey (a hyena?). Dimensions of head 7.5 × 5 cm.

5. *Cervus elaphus* (Red Deer), Holocene, Beroun, Czechoslovakia. Base of an antler nibbled by a small rodent. Diameter of antler 4.5 × 3.6 cm.

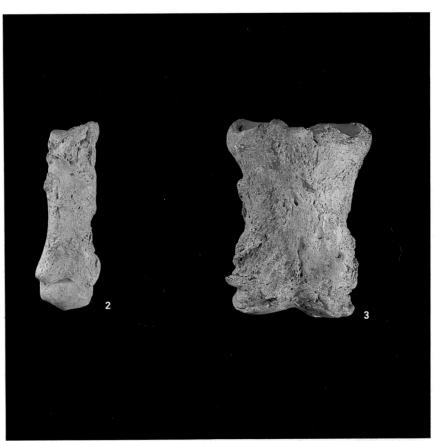

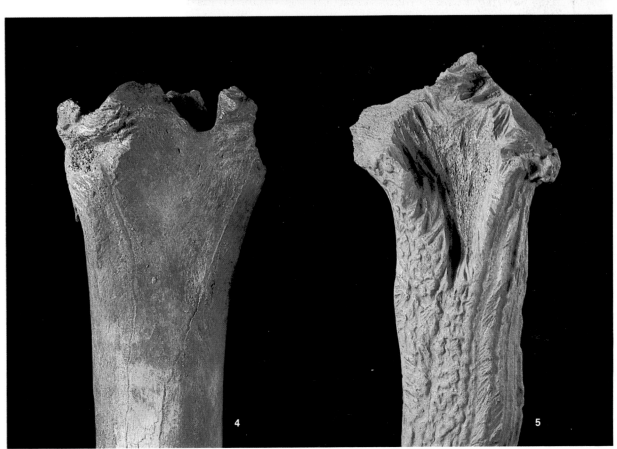

Traces of vertebrates' movements

The geologically oldest finds of this type date back to the Devonian of Pennsylvania and Australia. Their abundance everywhere from the Carboniferous onwards gave rise to a special branch of palaeontology — ichnology or palaeoichnology. We know the tracks of amphibians, reptiles (the tracks of big saurians are especially attractive), birds and mammals.

It is generally difficult to determine the species of vertebrate to which a given footprint belongs. Research workers consequently describe the marks themselves as genera or species and classify them in artificial taxonomic groups (taxa) which naturally do not have the validity of the natural zoological system. In a few cases scientists have already succeeded in determining at least the zoological (palaeontological) genus of the animal which made the tracks.

Footprints are the commonest finds, but occasionally an animal will leave the mark of its tail and belly behind it when walking, running or crawling on soft ground. Movement traces were preserved only if they were quickly covered over with soft sediment or first of all dried very quickly. In rare cases traces of swimming are preserved. Swimming tracks left by Permian amphibians and reptiles are rare; traces left by Mesozoic and Tertiary fishes and turtles are more numerous.

On very rare occasions we may find the lairs of small mammals (mainly in loess) or birds' nests (in Quaternary travertins).

1. *Saurichnites salamandroides* FRITSCH, Lower Permian, Kalná, Czechoslovakia. Dimensions of tracks about 1 × 1 cm. The tracks of a hardly identifiable Permian stegocephalian.

2. *Saurichnites calcaratus* FRITSCH, Lower Permian, Lomnice nad Popelkou, Czechoslovakia. Length of imprint 6 cm. The tracks of a large Permian amphibian.

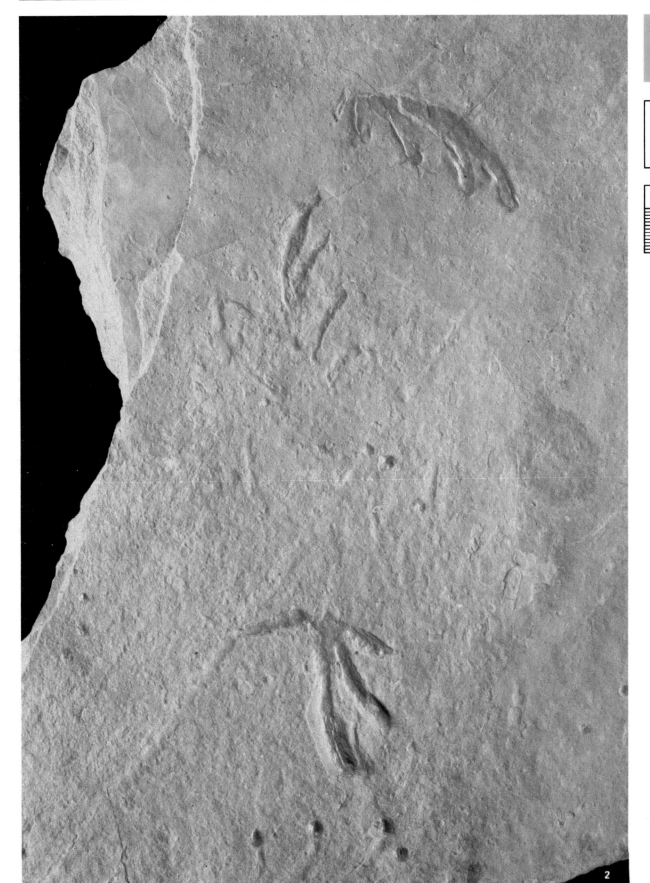

 **Palaeobiology**

Coprolites are the petrified faeces of fossil animals. Like their tracks, they are often one of the few proofs of the existence or local incidence of organisms which did not possess many tissues capable of fossilization. By analysing coprolites we can sometimes determine the diet of the animal which produced them; we may find in them insect or crustacean shells, small fish-bones or other vertebrate bones, etc.

Fish coprolites are the best known and the most thoroughly investigated. They have a characteristic spirally coiled surface corresponding to the spiral fold in the small intestine of many present-day bony and cartilaginous fishes (e.g. sharks, sturgeons, etc). They abound in Permo-Carboniferous and Jurassic sediments and very often they actually lie in the fish's abdominal cavity or in its immediate vicinity. Like tracks, fish coprolites are classified in an artificial system of 'genera' and 'species'.

Mammals' faeces are also found relatively often, especially in Permian strata. By analysing the coprolites of North American edentates (Gravigrada), scientists actually determined the types of plants on which these animals lived. Large numbers of coprolites stem from beasts of prey, especially Pleistocene species. Cave Bear and Hyena coprolites are frequently found in the caves in which the animals lived or hibernated; less often they are found in loess. These coprolites are not classified artificially, since they can be compared with the coprolites (faeces) of present-day species, although frequent deformation sometimes makes their identification difficult.

Q

C

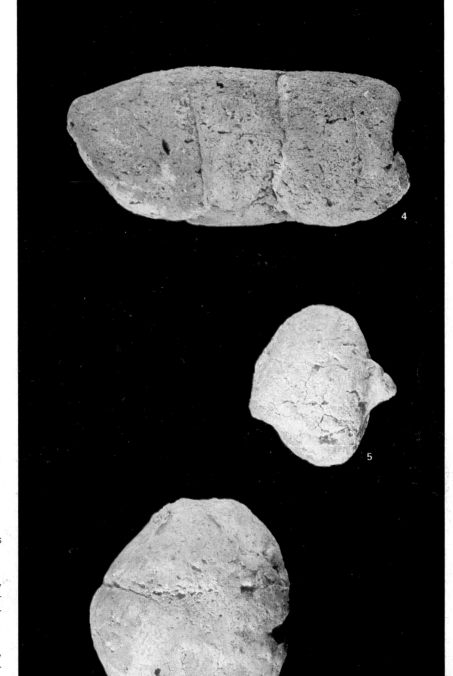

1–3. Coprolites of Carboniferous fishes:

1. *Coprolithes magnus* FRITSCH, Carboniferous, Hrabačov, Czechoslovakia. Two coprolites, dimensions of larger one 8 × 3.5 cm.

2. *Coprolithes olivoides* FRITSCH, Carboniferous, Kounová, Czechoslovakia. Dimensions 3 × 1.5 cm.

3. *Coprolithes pupoides* FRITSCH, Carboniferous, Kounová, Czechoslovakia. Dimensions 1.8 × 0.7 cm.

4–6. Coprolites of beasts of prey (probably of the Cave Hyena and perhaps of the Cave Lion), Pleistocene (Würm), Srbsko, Czechoslovakia. Dimensions: 4–6.0 × 2.5 cm, 5–2.5 × 2.5 cm, 6–4.5 × 3.5 cm.

The collection, preparation and conservation of fossils

When a collector is just starting, the first question he asks himself is where he should go to look for fossils and how he should set about it. Although palaeontology is a biological science, it is specific in that it deals with extinct organisms preserved in a layer of the Earth's crust. Palaeontology as a hobby therefore requires not only some knowledge of biology, but also a knowledge of geology, of how to distinguish the main rock types, and a grasp of the nature of the commonest geological structures and phenomena.

Fossils occur primarily in sedimentary rocks formed as a result of the deposition of mineral particles or rock fragments transported by wind and water, etc. Plants and animals, together with chemical processes, coparticipate in their genesis, often to an important or even decisive degree. Not all sedimentary rocks were equally conducive to the formation of fossils. For example, coarsely clastic sediments (composed of coarse fragments) do not, as a rule, contain fossils. Many permeable rocks were secondarily decalcified as a result of weathering processes and thus did not offer favourable conditions for the preservation of fossils. Poorly preserved fossils also occur in rocks slightly metamorphosed by heat or pressure, through contact with igneous rocks or by the action of geological (tectonic) processes displacing them to deeper levels of the Earth's crust, where their structure and their mineral and/or chemical composition changed. It is most exceptional for fossils to be found in igneous rocks, except tuffs (rocks formed of volcanic ash). The commonest fossiliferous rocks are limestone, slate (shale), claystones, marls, sandstones, loesses and cave earths. In general, fossils are far more numerous in sediments of marine origin than in continental deposits.

If a collector is able to distinguish between the basic types of rocks, a detailed geological map will be an adequate aid for further orientation. Such a map will give him a definite picture of the geological structure of the chosen terrain and show which are the most promising parts for fossil collecting and which are constructed of metamorphosed rocks, or of intrusive or effusive igneous rocks, and are consequently 'sterile' for the collector. Further necessary information concerning at least the best known localities will be found in a number of geological publications. In a terrain made up of sedimentary rocks, there are all kinds of suitable places — a quarry, a natural rock face, the bottom of a stream, a railway cutting or a sunken road, the newly excavated foundations of a house or a well, or a ploughed field, etc.

The most handsome fossils are often found in rubble, if the rocks have weathered favourably. Such fossils are not always of scientific value, however, because we do not know their exact place in the geological section. Rocks should be chipped away parallel with their stratification, i.e. with what was once the surface of the bed. It is rare for fossils to lie counter to their bedding, although it is possible — mainly in sediments formed as a result of submarine slides or in land suddenly washed into the sea, or if the animal was one which originally lived in the sediment.

Armed with some theoretical knowledge, a suitable prospecting hammer (or, better still, two hammers of different sizes), a chisel, a pair of pincers (for collecting in shales), a magnifying glass (giving 8- to 10-fold magnification), packing material (bags, newspaper sheets, gauze, cotton-wool), a geological map, a writing pad, a pencil and possibly a camera, the collector sallies forth into the terrain. Of course, it is only natural that a palaeontologist, who is interested in a specific problem, behaves differently in the terrain from an ordinary collector whose aim is to find the greatest possible number of nice fossils. At the same time, we would remind the reader that amateur collectors often work in close cooperation with specialists and that amateurs have more than once become celebrated palaeontologists.

An experienced collector is further guided by the following principles:

a) he does not limit his collection to the representatives of just one group of organisms, but sees in every fossil he finds potentially important palaeontological evidence;

b) he collects both cores and imprints ('positives' and 'negatives'), because the two are often complementary. Cores are casts of the inner wall of the shell, while imprints are a reproduction of the outer wall;

c) he tries to acquire the largest possible number of specimens of every species he finds;

d) he does not dissect the fossils out on the spot. It is often better not to isolate them, but to collect them together with a piece of rock of an appropriate size, which can supplementarily furnish basic information on the fossil's age. This is particularly important in cases in which the collector is unable to identify reliably the stratigraphic level of the find himself;

e) he notes the way the fossils are oriented in the sediment, associations of organisms and the relationships of fossils to the type of sediment, etc., since like that he also accumulates important palaeoecological information.

Every fossil we take away must be carefully wrapped up (to prevent it from being damaged during transport) and the site of the find must be noted immediately as accurately as possible. Fossils from different localities are wrapped up separately to avoid confusion over their provenance.

Severely damaged specimens should be glued together − at least partly − on the spot, or the position of the individual parts of the find should be noted. Fossils lying in loose or highly weathered sediments can be removed by hand or with soft (entomological) forceps, or they can be washed out by means of sieves with different sized meshes, according to what size fraction we require. Skeletal and palaeobotanical material sometimes needs to be partly conserved on the spot (e.g. by impregnating it with suitable conserving agents).

Many of the fossils we find cannot be put in a collection without first preparing and/or conserving them. The vast literature on these questions is cited in practically every palaeontology manual. The extent to which the amateur collector does his own preparing and conserving depends on the purpose for which his collection is intended and on the collector's technical equipment and experience. As a rule, he confines himself to

mechanical preparation for which he uses prospecting hammers, chisels and needles of various sizes. An electrical vibrator tool with exchangeable bits is very useful, but fine dissection with a vibrating needle must be done under a stereoscopic microscope. Fossils often need to be washed and for this we use a fine brush and water with detergent. Fossils in argillaceous rocks are not washed, but we take care that these rocks do not dry too quickly, since in that case they might disintegrate, together with the fossils. Pincers are often satisfactory for making rock samples smaller. Sometimes the collector will try to make a polished section, e.g. of a silicified trunk or the shell of a cephalopod, but if he does not do it properly he may spoil the fossil. Large or silicified fossils must often first of all be cut apart in a laboratory and polished afterwards. In palaeontological laboratories, specimens are ground with electrical grinders with a horizontal cast-iron wheel edged with self-adhesive abrasive paper, or with moistened powdered carborundum of a given grainage, using first coarse and then increasingly finer powders, taking care that the finer powder is not contaminated by the coarser one. Special powders are used for polishing; they include (for example) chromic oxide and opal detritus and others and they are sprinkled on to damp velvet or some similar fabric. An amateur can grind fossils by hand if he takes a number of moistened mirror glasses, on each of which he places abrasive powder of a different particle size, or if he uses special abrasive papers.

It very often happens that while we are trying to loosen a fossil, it snaps or is damaged in some other way. Luckily, a fossil is not a postage stamp and does not lose its scientific value if it is glued together. For sticking fossils together we use adhesives which, if necessary, can be dissolved after they have dried.

Fossils are conserved only if it is necessary for their preservation. For this purpose we employ highly diluted acetone-soluble adhesives or artificial resins. The choice of the conserving agent depends on the nature of the fossil material. It is therefore best to consult an expert on these questions beforehand, or at least to study the technical literature. On principle, we never lacquer fossils to 'improve' their aesthetic appearance.

The palaeontological collection

Cleaned, prepared and conserved fossils should be placed in small boxes. Oblong boxes of several standard sizes are the most satisfactory. It is best if every larger box has double the area of the next smallest box (e.g. 4×6 mm, 8×6 mm, 8×12 mm etc.). Glass or plastic tubes are suitable for small specimens. In every box or tube we place a small label giving the basic data on the specimen or group of specimens concerned, with the name of the owner at the top and the accession number below it. Like scientific institutions, a careful collector keeps an 'accession catalogue' giving a survey of the material in his collection. He numbers the various finds as they come and enters these numbers, together with further basic information, in the catalogue. There must also be room on the label for the fossil's scientific name. The most important datum of this 'birth certificate' of every fossil is the most detailed possible identification of the site (the locality) and the stratigraphic age of the find. Lastly comes the name of the finder and the year in which the fossil was found. When handling palaeontological material it is very easy for the label to come unstuck, or for confusion to arise over the locality. A painstaking collector never relies on his own memory. Fossils wrongly labelled (or worse still, unlabelled) as regards their locality lose much of their scientific value; it is therefore a good thing (if the nature of the material allows it) to mark the name of the locality in black or white Indian ink on the rock itself, preferably on the under side or in such a manner that it does not damage the fossil or spoil its appearance. The material can now be put in the collection, for which sets of drawers, cases or boxes – if possible of the same size – are the best place. A collection can naturally be arranged in various ways – systematically, stratigraphically or geographically, or by combining all three aspects. Some collectors want their collections to contain as many groups of organisms of different stratigraphic ages and from as many places as possible; such collections are primarily of educative value. Collectors who concentrate on a given region or locality which is easily accessible to them and to which they can pay undivided attention acquire scientifically more valuable collections.

The determination of fossils

Obviously, no serious collector will be satisfied merely with placing fossil material in his collection without knowing what it actually is. Exact determination of the species a find belongs to is often very complicated even for an expert, let alone a beginner. In palaeontology there is no determination key for any of the big groups (e.g. invertebrates, vertebrates, higher plants) allowing any fossil finds to be placed in the right species. Mineralogists and botanists, for instance, possess such a key, but in palaeontology it is impossible because fossils are so often incomplete. There are, however, keys allowing fossil plants and animals to be placed in certain higher categories such as phyla, classes and subclasses (that is the type of key given in this book), or confining them to an extremely narrow choice of genera. In the case of vertebrates the situation is still more complicated, because similar aids can be drawn up for given separate groups of bones (e.g. the long bones). Scientific accuracy of the determination of fossil finds depends not only on the expert knowledge of whoever is identifying them, but also on his possibilities of studying the vast and constantly growing palaeontological literature. In some cases it is actually necessary to compare fossil animal or plant remains with the type material, on the basis of which the relevant taxon was originally determined. Often it is not even possible to assign a well preserved specimen to a genus or species with certainty, because we lack important details of its internal morphological and/or anatomical structure. A collector just beginning must therefore, at first, turn to somebody from the staff of a museum, a geological institute or a university for help with the identification of his finds. Relatively soon, a good collector will learn to find his way about in his material and be able to place it in a particular higher systematic category. A study of the basic literature and a comparison of his finds with material exhibited in palaeontological collections open to the public will enable him to identify a large number of fossils satisfactorily. The determination of finds is also much easier if they come from a locality or from strata whose contents have been described and discussed in a monograph.

Stratigraphic tables (the geological time scale)

Era	Period	Epoch		Age and lower stratigraphic units		Folding	Time scale (millions of years)
				Northern Europe[4]	Alps[4]		
QUATERNARY	Holocene	Late Middle Early					
QUATERNARY	Pleistocene	Late		Vistulan	Würm		
QUATERNARY	Pleistocene	Late		Eemian	Riss-Würm		
QUATERNARY	Pleistocene	Middle		Warthian	Riss II		
QUATERNARY	Pleistocene	Middle					
QUATERNARY	Pleistocene	Middle		Saalian	Riss I		
QUATERNARY	Pleistocene	Middle		Holsteinian	Mindel-Riss		
QUATERNARY	Pleistocene	Early		Elsterian	Mindel		
QUATERNARY	Pleistocene	Early		Cromerian	Günz-Mindel		
QUATERNARY	Pleistocene	Early		Menapian	Günz		
QUATERNARY	Pleistocene	Early		Waalian			
QUATERNARY	Pleistocene	Early		Eburonian	Danubian		1.8
TERTIARY*	Neogene	Pliocene	U. L.			Alpine	
TERTIARY*	Neogene	Miocene	U. M. L.			Alpine	
TERTIARY*	Palaeogene	Oligocene	U. M. L.			Alpine	
TERTIARY*	Palaeogene	Eocene	U. M. L.			Alpine	
TERTIARY*	Palaeogene	Palaeocene	U. L.			Alpine	65
MESOZOIC	Cretaceous	U.		Maastrichtian Campanian Santonian Coniacian Turonian Cenomanian	} Senonian		
MESOZOIC	Cretaceous	L.		Albian Aptian Barremian Hauterivian Valanginian Berriasian	} Neocomian		130
MESOZOIC	Jurassic	U. (= Malmian)		Portlandian (Tithonian) Kimmeridgian Oxfordian			
MESOZOIC	Jurassic	M. (= Dogger)		Callovian Bathonian Bajocian Aalenian			

Era	Period	Epoch	Age and lower stratigraphic units	Folding	Time scale (millions of years)
MESOZOIC	Jurassic	L. (= Liassic)	Toarkian Pliensbachian Sinemurian Hettangian	Variscian (Hercynian)	
	Triassic	U.	Rhaetian Norian Carnian } (Keuper)		204
		M.	Ladinian Anisian } Muschelkalk		
		L.	Scythian (Buntsandstein)		245
PALAEOZOIC	Upper — Permian	U.[3]	Thüringian[3] (Zechstein)		
		L.[3]	Saxonian[3] Autunian[3] (Rotliegendes)		290
	Upper — Carboniferous	U.	Stephanian[3] Westphalian[3] Namurian[3]		
		L.	Visean Tournaisian		350
	Lower — Devonian	U.	Famennian Frasnian		
		M.	Givetian Eifelian		
		L.	Emsian Dalejan[2] Zlíchovian[2] Pragian Siegenian[1] Lochkovian Gedinnian[1]	Late Caledonian	400
	Lower — Silurian	U.	Pridolian Ludlovian		
		L.	Wenlockian Llandoverian	Early Caledonian	425
	Lower — Ordovician	U.	Ashgillian		
		M.	Caradocian Llandeilian		
		L.	Llanvirnian Arenigian Tremadocian		500
	Lower — Cambrian	U. M. L.			
PRECAMBRIAN			PROTEROZOIC	Cadomian (Assyntian)	570
			ARCHAIC		2,500

The Tertiary is not divided up in detail owing to differences in the staging of the various sedimentary basins. In the Quaternary, the dotted areas denote the cool climatic intervals.

1,2 — local terms for Rhenish and Bohemian Devonian development stages;
3 — central European and west European division.
4 — north European and Alpine scales are applied as regional stages, exclusively in the Quaternary of Europe.

U. = Upper, M. = Middle, L. = Lower
* The term Tertiary is applied here as a synonym of the Cainozoic.

Bibliography

Beurlen K. (1978): Welche Versteinerung ist das?. – 224 pp. (10. ed.), Kosmos Naturführer, Kosmos, Franckh'sche Verlagshandlung, Stuttgart.

Boucot A. J. (1981): Principles of benthic marine paleoecology. – 447 pp. N. York.

British Cainozoic Fossils. – 130 pp. (5.ed.), British Museum (Nat. Hist.), London. 1975.

British Mesozoic Fossils. – 205 pp. (5.ed.), British Museum (Nat. Hist.)., London 1975.

British Palaeozoic Fossils. – 208 pp. (4.ed.), British Museum (Nat. Hist.)., London 1975.

Clarkson E. N. K. (1983): Invertebrate Palaeontology and Evolution. – 323 pp., London, Boston, Sydney.

Drushchits V. V. (1974): Palaeontology of Invertebrates (in Russian). – 528 pp., Izdatelstvo Moskovskoho Universiteta, Moscow.

Frey R. W. (ed.) (1975): The study of trace fossils. – 562 pp., Springer Verlag, Berlin, Heidelberg, N. York.

Gothan W., Weyland H. (1973): Lehrbuch der Paläobotanik. – 677 pp. (3.ed.), Akademie-Verlag, Berlin.

Krumbiegel G., Walter H. (1979): Fossilien sammeln, präparieren, bestimmen, auswerten. – 336 pp. (2.ed.), VEB Dtsch. Verl. Grundstoffind., Leipzig.

Kummel B., Raup D. (1965): Handbook of paleontological techniques. – 852 pp., W. H. Freeman and Comp., S. Francisco, London.

Lichter G. (1980): Fossilien bergen, präparieren und ausstellen. – 144 pp., Kosmos, Franckh'sche Verlagshandlung, Stuttgart.

McKerrow W. S. (1981): Palökologie. – 248 pp., Kosmos, Franckh'sche Verlagshandlung, Stuttgart.

Moore R. C., Teichert C. (ed.) (1953 – onwards): Treatise on invertebrate paleontology, Pt. A – X, 29 vols. up to now, Univ. of Kansas Press, Lawrence.

Müller A. H. (1976 – onwards): Lehrbuch der Paläozoologie, Band I–III, 7 vols., (3.ed.), Gustav Fischer, Jena.

Murawski H. (1983): Geologisches Wörterbuch. – 281 pp., F. Enke, Stuttgart.

Němejc F. (1959–1975): Palaeobotany I–IV (in Czech). – Academia, Prague.

Orlov Y. A. (ed.) (1958–1964): Principles of Palaeontology (in Russian). – 15 vols, Izdatelstvo Akademii Nauk SSSR, Moscow.

Piveteau J. (ed.) (1952–1969): Traité de paléontologie. – 7 vols, Masson et Cie., Paris.

Pokorný V. (1958): Grundzüge der zoologischen Mikropaläontologie. – 2 vols, VEB Deutsch. Verl. Wiss., Berlin.

Richter A. E. (1981): Handbuch des Fossiliensammlers. – 464 pp., Kosmos, Franckh'sche Verlagshandlung, Stuttgart.

Rixon A. (1976): Fossil animal remains – their preparation and conservation. – 304 pp. The Athlone Press of University of London, London.

Roemer A. S. (1966): Vertebrate palaeontology. – 468 pp., Univ. Chicago Press, Chicago, London.

Stanley S. M., Raup D. M. (1971): Principles of Paleontology. – 390 pp., V. H. Freeman and Comp., S. Francisco, London.

Špinar Z. (1960): Fundamentals of the Palaeontology of Invertebrates (in Czech). – 836 pp., Nakladatelství ČSAV, Prague.

Špinar Z. et al. (1965): Systematic Palaeontology of Invertebrates (in Czech). – 1052 pp., Academia, Prague.

Wegner H. (1976): Die Fossiliensammler. (4.ed.), Thun et München.

Ziegler B. (1975): Einführung in die Paläobiologie, Teil 1, Allgemeine Paläontologie. – 245 pp. (2.ed.), E. Schweizerbart, Stuttgart.

Index

(Numbers in *italics* refer to illustrations)

Index

Index